Society and Law

Karen E. Hayden
Merrimack College

ROWMAN & LITTLEFIELD
Lanham • Boulder • New York • London

Executive Editor: Nancy Roberts
Assistant Editor: Megan Manzano
Executive Channel Manager – Higher Education: Amy Whitaker
Interior Designer: Rosanne Schloss

Credits and acknowledgments for material borrowed from other sources, and reproduced with permission, appear on the appropriate page within the text.

Published by Rowman & Littlefield
An imprint of The Rowman & Littlefield Publishing Group, Inc.
4501 Forbes Boulevard, Suite 200, Lanham, Maryland 20706
www.rowman.com

6 Tinworth Street, London SE11 5AL, United Kingdom

Copyright © 2020 by The Rowman & Littlefield Publishing Group, Inc.

All rights reserved. No part of this book may be reproduced in any form or by any electronic or mechanical means, including information storage and retrieval systems, without written permission from the publisher, except by a reviewer who may quote passages in a review.

British Library Cataloguing in Publication Information Available

Library of Congress Cataloging-in-Publication Data
Names: Hayden, Karen, author.
Title: Society and law / Karen E. Hayden.
Description: Lanham : Rowman & Littlefield, [2019] | Includes bibliographical
    references.
Identifiers: LCCN 2019013704| ISBN 9781538101919 (cloth : alk. paper) |
    ISBN 9781538101926 (pbk. : alk. paper) | ISBN 9781538101933 (electronic)
Subjects: LCSH: Law—Social aspects. | Sociological jurisprudence. | Rule of
    law. | Lawyers.
Classification: LCC K376 .H39 2019 | DDC 340/.115—dc23 LC record available
    at https://lccn.loc.gov/2019013704

∞™ The paper used in this publication meets the minimum requirements of American National Standard for Information Sciences—Permanence of Paper for Printed Library Materials, ANSI/NISO Z39.48-1992.

Brief Contents

Contents

List of Figures

Preface

I TAUGHT SOCIETY AND LAW CLASSES for about 18 years before I decided to write a textbook on the topic. One of my primary goals was to write a book that looks first and foremost at society and then secondly at how laws emerge to address societal needs, wants, and expectations. Most similar books are titled "Law and Society." I called this book *Society and Law* on purpose because, without society there would be no need for laws. Societies call upon laws to perform a multitude of tasks: to keep citizens safe from harm, to socially control and punish some members of society, to settle disagreements between and among individuals, groups, and institutions, to establish marriages and families, to protect property, to regulate industries, to grant rights and freedoms, and to protect those rights and freedoms. This book examines why individuals, groups, and institutions rely on laws and the legal system to perform all of these tasks, how it does this, and how effective the legal system is in completing the various tasks that are required by society.

The book addresses the social context of law, the legal structure, and the relationship between law and society in such a way that will interest and engage undergraduate students studying sociology, criminology, criminal justice, and social justice. Law and society texts typically present legal topics as opaque and dry. Students view the material as too theoretical and, frankly, boring. I wanted to write a book on society and law that students would read and see their own lives, interests, concerns, and career aspirations reflected in it's pages. I use examples that my students have brought up in my classes, or examples that I have brought to class that resonated with students. College aged students have grown up with technology, and this is integral to the world around them. I have found that using examples of how law interacts and intersects with new technologies keeps students interested and keeps me on my toes. My students tend to know more than I do about new technologies and new forms of social media, therefore

I keep my examples and understanding of technology, law, and social change up-to-date.

Whenever possible, I also attempt to inject humor into my classroom and my writing. *Society and Law* addresses heavy topics: cyberstalking and revenge pornography, deaths due to unsafe products or unsafe workplaces, laws that upheld slavery and segregation, the internment of Japanese immigrants and Japanese Americans during World War II, disproportionate minority sentencing and the death penalty. By bringing humor into the classroom and into this book, I do not attempt to make light of these very serious topics. However, I do hope to break up the gravity of these topics with some comic relief. One of the complaints about other law and society texts that I have heard from students is that they present topics in ways that students see as monotonous. There is too much black text on white pages, and not enough visual interest. I hope that my text addresses this valid complaint and makes the topic presented in society and law less dense, more understandable, and even enjoyable to undergraduates. I summarize the material as succinctly as possible and incorporate examples of new laws, changes in laws, and legal cases that connect the material to students lives.

I would like thank all of the people who have supported my efforts in writing this book. First and foremost are my students; past, present, and future. Their feedback and suggestions enrich my teaching and this book. Secondly, I want to thank my teachers and professors. I learned from many extraordinary educators, but two stand out for their kindness, intellect, and humor, Professor Bud Khleif of the University of New Hampshire and Professor Michael Brown of Northeastern University.

Colleagues and friends have supported my efforts along the way and hopefully I have thanked them all. I will do so now just in case I forgot: Kerry Johnson, Deb Margolis, Jackie Gillette, Alex Thomas, Greg Fulkerson. Thanks to the members of my writing group, Nicole Frisch and Alyssa Yetter. Thanks especially to Alicia Malone for reading and commenting on Chapter 6, and finally thank you to members of my book club for sharing their love of the written word: Marilyn Randall, Maryellen Rancourt, Elizabeth Pell, Cheryl Leone, Patricia Herman, Decia Goodwin, Connie Nucci, Miki Yanagihara, Joanna Sanferrare, Nancy Klein, and Annette Krawietz.

Thank you also to reviewers, their feedback on the chapters helped me enormously:

Avi Brisman, Eastern Kentucky University
Marshall DeRosa, Florida Atlantic University
Laura Fidelie, Midwestern State University
Shane Gleason, Idaho State University

Cyntoria Johnson, Georgia State University
Mahgoub Mahmoud, Tennessee State University
Rita Shah, Eastern Michigan University
Alex Thomas, State University of New York- Oneota
Anthony Vander Horst, Kent State University

Special thanks go to Nancy Roberts from Rowman & Littlefield for sticking with me and this project. Thanks also to Megan Manzano for her help. I would like to extend my gratitude to Rajeswari Azayecoche and Sreejith Govindan at Integra as well.

My family has been a constant source of patience, reassurance, and humor throughout this process. Thank you, thank you to Mark and Evelyn. Thanks always to my mom and dad. Many, many thanks to Kath, my mirror, my (other) editor, my sounding board, my sister. Thanks also to Anthony and John, I have great brothers-in-law. Thanks also to my brothers, Mike and Pete, and my sisters-in-law, Linda and Deb. And thank you to my nieces and nephews, Ellie, Cal, Ben, Emily.

About the Author

KAREN E. HAYDEN is professor and chair of the Department of Criminology and Criminal Justice at Merrimack College in North Andover, Massachusetts. She teaches and writes about society and law; girls, women, and crime; images of rural people and places in popular culture; and rural crime.

1

Introduction

◆ ◆ ◆

NO PART OF OUR LIVES IS UNTOUCHED BY LAW. Legal terms and legal language saturates our consciousness. Law is complex and contradictory. It provides the grounds for our personal security, equality, and the freedoms that we should take for granted. But law can also distort and complicate our lives. In his book *Democracy in America* ([1835] 1961), Alexis de Tocqueville (1805–1859), a French aristocrat who traveled through the United States to study a developing democracy said, "scarcely any question arises which does not become, sooner or later, a subject for judicial debate" ([1835] 1961:223). De Tocqueville observed as far back as the 1800s that U.S. society was more focused on legal debate than it's European counterparts. Even de Tocqueville could not have predicted the extent to which law now occupies the American public's consciousness; it is the subject of countless movies, television shows, and books. Today there are approximately 1,300,705 licensed lawyers working in the U.S. legal system (American Bar Association 2015). Television personalities including Nancy Grace, Greta Van Susteren, and Dan Abrams make their careers by talking endlessly about current legal cases on 24-hour television news stations. The law is an occupation and a preoccupation in our lives.

In American society it is not uncommon to hear people say, "There ought to be a law!" in response to social problems, or any event that negatively affects people. In fact, "There Ought to be a Law!" now has its own acronym, TOBAL, making it almost as recognizable as NIMBY or "Not in My Back Yard." For example, Senior *Huffington Post* writer Radley Balko has a website, *The Agitator*, which features a "There Oughtta Be a Law" column covering controversial legal issues including: drug, alcohol, and tobacco policies; civil liberties; and policing controversies. The U.S. is, for better or worse, a **litigious** society. This means its citizens are prone

1

to engaging in lawsuits to settle even minor disputes. In response to particularly horrific events we often call on our legislators to enact new laws. However, as they rush to enact them, we tend to forget that these laws can have long-term, unforeseen effects. Sometimes, the reality is that a new law can create new problems, or aggravate the problem it was intended to solve.

American sociologist Robert K. Merton (1910–2003) examined the latent and manifest functions of all social phenomena. **Manifest functions** are the intended, obvious functions of individual actions, social structures, and social policies. **Latent functions** are the unclear and unforeseen functions of these social phenomena. Merton also used the term **dysfunction** to refer to the unanticipated, negative consequences (or outcomes) that run counter to the intended purpose of individual actions, social structures, or social policies (Merton [1949] 1957:60–69). Using Merton's analysis of the types of social functions, Sociologists and legal scholars can study the outcomes of legal changes on individuals, groups, and society.

MANIFEST FUNCTIONS OF LAW

Merton's distinction between the manifest and latent functions has been used to analyze a range of social structures and social issues including interracial marriage, social stratification, religious and social rituals, fashion, bureaucracy, and propaganda. Merton defined **manifest functions** as the needs, interests, conscious, and explicit purposes of social activity. Specifically, manifest functions are "those objective consequences contributing to the adjustment of the [social] system which are intended and recognized by participants in the system" (Merton [1949] 1968:51). A manifest function is what is *supposed* to happen when a law is enacted. Ideally, the public recognizes a social problem and calls on lawmakers to solve it by making it illegal, or by placing restrictions on the problem, and the problem is solved. In reality, legal solutions to social problems are not often so straightforward.

Manifest Functions of Law

CASE IN POINT

Legal Restrictions on Young Drivers

In the past decade, many states have enacted tougher laws for young drivers, sometimes called Junior Operator Laws or Graduated Driver Licensing Laws. In fact, all states now have some form of driving restrictions for people under the age of 18. Restrictions can include bans on using cell phone, curfews, and limits on the number of passengers in vehicles being driven by young people. New Jersey even requires young drivers to attach a "Novice Driver Decal" notice to their license plates so that police officers can easily identify young drivers who are breaking the graduated driving laws (Governors Highway Safety Association 2012). New Jersey's provisions, known as Kyleigh's Law, emerged in response to a fatal car accident in 2006 that involved a 17-year-old driver who crashed his car into a tree, killing himself and his 16-year-old passenger Kyleigh D'Alessio. Kyleigh's law requires all drivers under the age of 21 to attach a red decal to the upper left-hand corner of their license plate. The law also imposes a curfew, places restricts the number of passengers allowed in a vehicle, prohibits use of electronic devices while driving, and requires seatbelts to be used (Curry et al. 2013).

Istock/tommaso79

New drivers are subject to junior operator laws.

In Massachusetts, concerned citizens and state legislators called for young operator driving restrictions to be enacted in response to several tragic car accidents involving drivers, who were under the age of 18 in 2005 and 2006. In one accident two teenage sisters, Shauna and Meghan Murphy, died when the car they were passengers in crashed into a telephone pole. The car was driven by a 17-year-old friend; both speed and alcohol were cited as factors in the accident (Kocian and Phillips 2006). The girls' family established the Murphy Sisters Foundation to teach young drivers safe driving habits (see http://www.murphysisters.org).

In another horrific crash a 17-year-old girl, Andrea Goncalves, and her 10-year-old brother Joshua, were killed when the car she was driving struck a tree. This accident came on the heels of another crash in Massachusetts that killed two 16-year-olds. Amanda Nadeau and Scott Connolly were killed when the vehicle driven by Connolly, according to police at very high speeds, crossed several lanes of traffic and struck a tree (Helman 2006). Connolly, who police said was traveling at very high speeds, had only obtained his junior operator's permit less than six months prior to the accident. Amanda Nadeau's mother, Julia Rodriguez, became a vocal proponent of stricter driving laws for young drivers, and even fought to increase the driving age in Massachusetts to 17½ (Misha and Levenson 2006). While the increased age requirement did not ultimately become law in the state, several restrictions were placed on young drivers.

By 2007 new junior operator laws took effect in the state of Massachusetts. These laws limit the number of non-family passengers allowed in vehicles driven by those under 18 years old, and place curfews on young drivers. In addition to imposing extra restrictions, the Massachusetts Junior Operator Laws also set stiffer penalties for young driver infractions. The state's penalties are far-reaching; they increase driver's education requirements and ramp up penalties for all driving infractions by 16- and 17-year-old drivers (Moskowitz 2010). For example, a junior operator caught on a first-time speeding offense is subject to a fine, a license suspension of up to 90 days, and a $500 license reinstatement fee. He, or she, must also attend a four-hour driver training class and retake and pass the driving exam to restore their driving privileges (Moskowitz 2010:A1). As state senator Steven A. Baddour, co-chairperson of the Joint Committee on Transportation, said, "We intentionally made the penalties aggressive because we wanted to send a message to young drivers that when they get behind the wheel, their priority should be getting from point A to point B safely" (Moskowitz 2010:A19).

The manifest, intended function of young operator driving restrictions was to make people safer on the road, to decrease traffic accidents, injuries, and deaths involving young drivers. It appears that the underage driving restrictions in the state of Massachusetts have achieved this intended effect (Carroll 2009). In the three years directly before the new law, 16- and 17-year old drivers were involved in 79 fatal crashes. The law took effect in 2007 and, as *The Boston Globe* reported:

> There were 20 [fatal accidents] the next year [2008], 15 the year after that [2009], and six over the last year—the first full year in which all junior operators on the road had started driver's ed after the requirements changed .... Reported accidents of all kinds—from

minor dings to fatal crashes—among junior operators as well as 18-year-old drivers have diminished steadily as well: 21,310 in calendar year 2006; 20,129 in 2007; 17,238 in 2008; and 13,214 last year, 2009. (Moskowitz 2010:A19).

The Massachusetts State Registry of Motor Vehicles touted the new restrictions stating, "This clearly has had its desired effect" (Moskowitz 2010:A1). The Governor of Massachusetts at the time Deval Patrick agreed stating, "Our number one priority is protecting the safety of the travelling public, and our successful implementation of the Junior Operator License Law is clearly reducing teen driver crashes and saving lives" (Moskowitz 2010:A1). For all intents and purposes, legal restrictions on young drivers are an example of the law serving its intended function. This example also illustrates the potency of laws in protecting citizens: laws can, and should, provide grounds for the safety and security of the citizenry.

According to a preliminary study, New Jersey's Graduated Driver Licensing Decal laws also proved effective in meeting its intended purposes. In a recent study conducted by Curry et al. (2013), the authors found a 14% increase in young driver citations, and a 9% decrease in police-reported crashes among drivers under the age of 21.

The rest of the country experienced a similar trend. The Governors Highway Safety Association (GHSA) reported that between 2007 and 2010, when many states enacted stiffer driving laws for teens, driver deaths of 16- and 17-year-olds decreased by almost half. However, nationally there appeared to be a slight change in this trend in the first six months of 2012. Traffic deaths of 16-year-olds actually increased from 86 to 107 (24%) compared to the same six-month period in 2011, when deaths of 17-year-olds increased from 116 to 133 (15% [GHSA, "Spotlight on Highway Safety" 2012]). The state of Massachusetts saw one driver death of a 16- or 17-year-old in the first six months in 2011 and two deaths in the first six months of 2012. However, while this was a 100% increase, and any preventable death of a young person is too many, these numbers are still very low when compared to the years prior to the enactment of junior operator laws. New Jersey maintained its downward trend in this period with two deaths in the first six months of 2011 and one in the first six months of 2012 (GHSA "Spotlight on Highway Safety" 2012). Despite the recent uptick in young driver deaths nationally, the good news is that deaths of young people on the roads remains much lower than they were in the very early years of the twenty-first century (GHSA 2012).

LATENT FUNCTIONS OF LAW

Laws can also have unintended consequences, which Merton called **latent functions**. Latent functions are initially unrecognized and may only become evident after the law has been in effect for months, or even years. Even in the case of young driver restrictions, which as discussed above appear to be quite successful in meeting their intended purposes, there are unintended consequences. When the New Jersey decal law was passed critics suggested that it would make young drivers more vulnerable to predators. Others argued that the decal amounted to an invasion of privacy and challenged the law in the state's Supreme Court. New Jersey's Supreme Court decided that these potential, unintended consequences were not persuasive enough to outweigh the benefits of the law. The court upheld Kyleigh's Law with a 6–0 decision (Spoto 2012).

We need to consider the unintended functions of junior operator laws more generally. Some teenagers need to drive to get to their jobs, and their jobs contribute to the family economy. Therefore, poor and working-class teens with after-school jobs would be more negatively affected by a 90-day suspension of their driving privileges. This is just one of countless examples of laws, or legal changes, affecting people of lower socioeconomic class more directly and more negatively than people of the middle or upper classes. We will return to the topic of law and inequalities of race, class, gender, and power in Chapter 6: Law and Social Control, Chapter 10: Gender, Inequality, and Law, and Chapter 11: Race, Inequality, and Law.

The latent, collateral functions are often unforeseen, yet Merton argued that the sociological study of latent functions is crucial for making new discoveries about the social world. He said, "There is some evidence that it is precisely at the point where the research attention of sociologists has shifted from the plane of manifest to the plane of latent functions that they have made their distinctive and major contributions" (Merton [1949] 1957:64). When recognizing and analyzing the unexpected outcomes of new laws, sociologists have contributed to our socio-legal knowledge about both the good and the harm that legal changes can bring about. Let us, in Merton's words, shift to the plane of latent functions to examine a legal and political hot potato: Residency restrictions for sex offenders.

Latent Functions of Law

CASE IN POINT

Residency Restrictions for Sex Offenders

No one relishes the idea of living next door to a sex offender. We have all heard the horrific stories of serial child molesters who abduct, sexually assault, and kill children. These are exactly the types of cases that prompt citizens to say, "There ought to be a law (TOBAL)!" along with "not in my backyard (NIMBY)!" The cries of TOBAL and NIMBY have been heard by state policy-makers. Many states across the country have imposed some form of residency restrictions on sex offenders in an attempt to create buffer zones around schools, parks, day-care centers, and bus stops. In some cases, places of worship are also included in the protected zones because they offer classes and other activities for children. The manifest or obvious intention of residency restrictions is to keep sexual predators away from children: To keep children safe in the places predators are likely to be.

Istock/joshuaraineyphotography

Homeless encampment: Due to residency restrictions, many sex offenders end up homeless.

However, an unforeseen or latent function of such proximity ordinances is to make it nearly impossible for sex offenders to find legitimate housing. In some cases these restrictions even render them homeless. In Georgia, where sex offenders are not allowed to live within 1,000 feet of schools, places of worship, parks, and other areas where children gather, a group of homeless sex offenders set up an encampment in a wooded area behind a suburban office park (Bluestein 2009). In some cases probation officers directed sex offenders to the encampment, knowing there was no other place they could find to live that meets the state's proximity requirement (Bluestein 2009).

In Florida, with its strict 2,500 foot sex offender residency restriction, a large, loose collection of homeless sex offenders live under a causeway overpass that has become known as the Julia Tuttle Causeway camp. Approximately 70 people live under the overpass in tents and makeshift shacks with no running water or sewerage system. Another Florida settlement emerged in a park in

Broward County where more than 100 sex offenders congregate nightly (Skipp and Campo-Flores 2009). Not only are residency restriction laws, which were enacted to address a social problem, *causing* another social problem—homelessness—they are also working *against* their initial intent. When sex offenders are pushed to the margins of society, and onto the streets or under bridges, they can become more dangerous and more difficult to track by their probation and/or parole officers. Transient populations are notoriously hard to keep track of and therefore the primary objective of the law is made difficult, if not impossible, to achieve. Two leading scholars of residency restrictions, Jill S. Levenson and Leo P. Cotter, further state, "sex offender statutes inadvertently may increase risk by aggravating the stressors (e.g., isolation, disempowerment, shame, depression, anxiety, and lack of social supports) that can trigger offenders to relapse" (2005:169). The outcome here is that if a homeless child molester living under a bridge does not garner a lot of public sympathy, people should be concerned that sex offender homelessness is working at cross purposes to the law's manifest function. The public is not any safer and there is no guarantee that children are protected using these buffer zones.

Legalese: Vagrancy

Vagrancy is the condition of wandering from place to place without a job or occupation (Chambliss 1964). While the term has fallen out of favor, homelessness is the more common term in modern language, many states still had vagrancy laws on the books until the 1970s when the Supreme Court overturned them. The court found the laws unconstitutional because they assumed future criminality, not actual behavior (*Papachristou v. City of Jacksonville*, 1972).

As criminologist William J. Chambliss illustrated in his influential study on the topic, the first laws against vagrancy in Great Britain were drafted in the Fourteenth Century. Feudal landowners wanted to ensure that they had a readily available labor force in need of work. The early vagrancy laws required that any and all able-bodied, persons under the age of 60 had to work for anyone who offered them employment. Refusal to work could and often did result in imprisonment. The laws gradually fell out of favor for several centuries. In the U.S. during the late Nineteenth to early Twentieth Centuries new vagrancy laws were enacted to create a labor force after the Civil War when freed African slaves were forced into a new form of servitude. This threatened them with imprisonment if they did not work for plantation owners, mining companies, or other owners of industries (Chambliss and Hass 2012; Chambliss 1964).

DYSFUNCTIONS OF LAW

Along with latent and manifest functions, Merton also recognized social dysfunctions. As with the case of residency restrictions, some of the latent or unintended consequences of laws can also prove dysfunctional. Merton defined **dysfunctions** as "any process that undermines the stability or survival of a social system" (Merton [1976] 1996:96). He further explains that "A social dysfunction is a specific inadequacy of a particular part of the system for meeting a particular functional requirement. Social disorganization can be thought of as resultant of various social dysfunctions" (Merton [1976] 1996:96). The transience and social disorganization that results from sex offender residency restrictions are both unintended and dysfunctional to the larger social order.

When considering other dysfunctions of law, laws can become outdated and used for purposes beyond their initial intention. For instance, blue laws dating back to the colonial period still exist in many New England states. Blue laws typically prohibit activities on moral or religious grounds (Sheldon 2016). These archaic laws most often prohibit activities on Sundays, such as the purchase of alcoholic beverages because Sundays were Sabbaths—holy days—and thus set aside for worship in the Puritan faith practiced by the colonists. Puritans in Virginia and the New England colonies imported some of their Sabbatarian traditions to America. In fact, some historians suspect that the term "blue laws" is derived from the religious laws that were bound in blue books dating back to the 1600s (Roberts 2016). However, in Massachusetts blue laws reached well beyond Sunday prohibitions and restricted all manner of behavior including; spitting on the sidewalk, committing adultery, checking into a hotel under an assumed name, and frightening a pigeon away from someone's front lawn. While these laws are clearly outdated, and in some cases unconstitutional, they have remained on the law books for over 300 years (LeBlanc 2008).

Similarly, but perhaps more insidious, are laws on the books that were enacted for one purpose and then fall out of usage only to be resurrected for another function. Sociologist William J. Chambliss studied how laws that have fallen into a period of dormancy, or inactivity, can be resurrected for new forms of social control (Chambliss 1964). For example, in Massachusetts in 1913, the state Senate passed a law prohibiting the marriage of two people in the state whose union would not be legal in the state in which they resided. At the time, the manifest function of the law was to prohibit people traveling to the state to enter into mixed-race marriages. These marriages had been legal in the Commonwealth of Massachusetts since 1843, but controversy surrounding people entering the state for the purpose of mixed-race marriages spurred the 1913 prohibition. The law remained on the books even after the 1967 Supreme Court case of *Loving v. Virginia* overturned anti-miscegenation laws—laws against mixed-race marriages—throughout the United States.

In 2003, when Massachusetts became the first state in the nation to allow same-sex couples to marry, the then Attorney General Thomas Reilly revived the 1913 law in an attempt to block out-of-state same-sex partners from traveling to Massachusetts to marry and then returning to their home states. The then Governor, Mitt Romney, agreed with Attorney General Reilly and said the law must apply to same-sex unions. After several challenges by same-sex couples, the 1913 law was repealed in 2008. As we will discuss in more detail in Chapter 8: Law and Social Change, same-sex marriages are now the law of the land in the U.S., overturning any legal prohibitions against same-sex couples from entering into a legal marriage contract. A closer examination of anti-miscegenation laws is presented in Chapter 11: Race, Inequality, and Law.

Another major dysfunction of law was identified by American legal scholar Donald Black (1989). Black argues that many kinds of discrimination and disadvantage are built into the legal structure and can be dysfunctional. Black quotes Anatole France (1844–1924) who said, "The law, in its majestic equality, forbids the rich as well as the poor to sleep under bridges, to beg in the streets, and to steal bread" (1894). But to whom are these laws most often applied? By and large, laws are constructed by those who already hold power in society. Therefore, the law has many dysfunctions, not least of which is the inequality built into its very construction and execution.

Laws have also supported some of the worst evils in our society—slavery, wars, and treaties that nearly eliminated the Native American population of North America, the internment of Japanese citizens and Japanese-Americans during World War II, and the disenfranchisement of 50 percent of the American population (women) until 1920. In this book, we examine both the positive and negative consequences of current laws, legal changes, and legal issues. We will look at same-sex marriage laws, laws that attempt to determine racial and ethnic identity, and the state of law and gender discrimination in the U.S.

Laws can both help and hinder. De Tocqueville and other scholars of the American legal structure have acknowledged both the positive and negative aspects of law on our lives. On the positive side, there is the **social contract**—laws keep tyranny at bay and grant us individual rights and freedoms. The social contract is a cornerstone of an organized society; it is the idea that individuals willingly enter into a state of governance in return for protection of their individual freedoms, their rights, and their general social welfare. The earlier discussion of junior operator laws provides an example of the social contract. The law was put in place to protect junior operators, and all drivers on the roads, from dangerous mistakes. If young people want to drive they willingly submit to the state's requirements.

Critics of the law argue that these and other driving laws, such as seatbelt requirements, represent the government as so-called "nanny state"—the notion of an overly protective government that wants to control all aspects of it citizens' lives. But the laws are increasing the safety of people on the roads. Being a member of society presents a trade off between the loss of some individual choices and freedoms and the increased welfare and safety of citizens of the nation-state.

De Tocqueville and countless other legal scholars also note the negative aspects of law. In fact, de Tocqueville worried about the tyranny of the majority, as did James Madison the fourth president of the United States, "father" of the Constitution, and author along with Alexander Hamilton and John Jay, of the Federalist Papers. Just because a lot of people vote for something, or call on their legislators to enact a new law, does not make it right or beneficial. Madison's system of checks and balances was intended to ensure that no one branch of the government gained too much power and that the tyranny of the masses will not threaten the liberty of individuals. Madison believed, "Justice was the end of government. It is the end of civil society" (https://www.billofrightsinstitute.org/founding-documents/primary-source-documents/the-federalist-papers/federalist-papers-no-51/).

The apparatus of law gives vast power to judges, lawyers, and legislators. Judges can exercise their power arbitrarily; they are human beings who may harbor personal biases or conflicts with other human beings for instance, the lawyers trying cases before them. They are also given an enormous amount of institutionalized power and protection, which can lead to abuses of power. A horrifying example of judicial abuse of power played out in northeastern Pennsylvania, in what came to be known as the "kids for cash" scandal. In 2009 two judges in the Luzerne County Juvenile Justice System, Judge Mark Ciavarella and Judge Michael Conahan, were sentenced to lengthy prison terms for misdeeds involving their treatment of juvenile offenders. Throughout the first decade of the 2000s, the two judges sentenced over 2,000 juveniles to detention centers for minor infractions. Since the judges had financial stakes in the construction of the private detention center, Pennsylvania Child Care, and in keeping the building filled with juvenile offenders, these cases involved the blatant abuse of the power and trust that the people of Luzerne County had granted these judges (Ecenbarger 2012).

Judge Conahan pled guilty to taking kickbacks for placing children in the privately owned Pennsylvania Child Care facility. He also pled guilty to money laundering and other federal offenses (Ecenbarger 2012). Conahan is serving 17 years in a federal prison. Judge Ciavarella, who the court determined played a larger role in the scandal, was found guilty of twelve federal felonies including racketeering (running an illegal business), bribery (taking or giving money, goods, or services to influence a person to act dishonestly), extortion (obtaining money, goods, or services through threats or intimidation), money laundering (making money that was obtained illegally look legal), and conspiracy (planning to commit a crime) (Ecenbarger 2012). Ciavarella is serving 28 years in federal prison.

This scandal exemplifies the individual and institutionalized abuses of power and law. The judges involved were embedded in a culture of silence that protected them and allowed their abuses to go unchecked. They grew emboldened by the "zero tolerance" and "get tough on juvenile offenders" wave that swept the country after the Columbine and other school shootings in the late 1990s and early 2000s. While these two individuals were clearly in the wrong, larger cultural forces also shared some of the blame.

LAW AS A SOCIAL CONSTRUCTION

Karl Marx said that people make their own history, "but [they] do not make it out of the whole cloth; [they] do not make it out of conditions chosen by [themselves] but out of such as [they] find close at hand" (1852:9).

What do we mean when we say that law is a social construction? Anything that emerges through human interactions that take place within

"Around here his word is law."

Source: Edward Koren, New Yorker/CartoonStock.com

linguistic, economic, political, and legal contexts is a social construction. Laws are human constructs; we create laws to address social problems, settle disputes, and to exert power over others.

What do we mean by **law**? Among scholars there is no universally agreed definition of *law*. If you want a definition of law, ask a legal scholar then, if you want another definition of the law, ask another legal scholar, and so on. One legal scholar, Max Radin, warned, "Those of us who have learned humility have given over the attempt to define law" (1938:1045). Another legal scholar, Oliver Wendell Holmes, preferred a simple, pragmatic definition of law as "the prophecies of what the courts will do, in fact and nothing more pretentious" (1897:460). Even poets have grappled with the question, "What is law?" In W. H. Auden's Poem, "Law, Like Love," the writer illustrates the difficulty of defining both concepts. Auden wrote:

> Law, say the gardeners, is the sun,
> Law is the one
> All gardeners obey
> Tomorrow, yesterday, today.
> Law is the wisdom of the old,
> The impotent grandfathers feebly scold;
> Law is the senses of the young.
> Law, says the priest with a priestly look,
> Expounding to an unpriestly people,
> Law is the words in my priestly book,
> Law is my pulpit and my steeple.
> Law, says the judge as he looks down his nose,
> Speaking clearly and severely,
> Law is as I've told you before,
> Law is as you know I suppose,
> Law is but let me explain it once more,
> Law is The Law (1983:1101–1102).

Perhaps the perfect definition of law does not exist, but this is a book about society and laws, therefore, working definitions of both terms are required. The term *society* is often used but rarely defined. A **working definition of society** is the largest form of a human group. Members of a society typically share a common territory and governance, as well as a common culture and social institutions, including the family, the economy, and law. A **working definition of law** for the purposes of this book is a body of norms or rules that regulate the actions and interactions of individuals, groups, institutions, and societies. Laws are the codified social norms of society. **Norms** are established rules of conduct. To **codify** a norm means to write it into legal code and classify it among other legal codes to make it official.

MAX WEBER'S SOCIOLOGICAL APPROACH
TO THE STUDY OF LAW

One of the most influential conceptualizations of law within the sociological tradition is the one proposed by Max Weber (1864–1920). In his book *Economy and Society* ([1905] 1978), Weber defined law as a body of rules maintained through **consensus** and **coercion**. According to Weber, consensus is agreement about how and why laws are made and what their purposes are. **Consensus** is the notion that there are deeply held standards of behavior upon which people agree and to which they willingly consent. **Coercion** is the enforcement of norms through the use of organized governmental power. As Weber states, "an order will be called a law if it is externally guaranteed by the probability that coercion, physical or psychological, to bring about conformity or avenge violation, [and] will be applied by a staff of people holding themselves especially ready for that purpose" (1947:127). Coercion includes all forms of **negative sanctions**, or punishments, for the violation of norms. Negative sanctions can include fines, community service, probation, and time in jail or prison.

To illustrate Weber's concept of law, let's look at the setting of a college classroom. A college classroom contains elements of both consensus and coercion. Typically, there is consensus about the roles of student and professor, and there is agreement on the terms set forth in the syllabus. People enter the class because they have agreed to be there and to act in accordance with the roles and the expected behaviors attached to those roles.

However, coercion could come into play if a student violates the norms of the class, if he or she is late every day, interrupts class, plagiarizes a paper, hands in someone else's work, or cheats on an exam. If a student breaks any of the rules set forth in the syllabus or the college's or university's honor code, there will be sanctions including a failing grade on the assignment or in the class, and depending on the extent of the infraction expulsion from the school. These are negative sanctions.

Professors can also be the subjects of coercion if they act improperly—if they discriminate against a student or somehow treat students unfairly. For instance, if a professor arbitrarily changes the rules of the class midway through the semester, he or she could be sanctioned by the department or by the college. If the violation is egregious enough, the professor could be terminated from the school. This is just one example of how consensus and coercion operate continuously within every aspect of our lives, even when a person appears to be the authority figure in a situation.

In Weber's conception of law, the law contains three basic features that distinguish it from other normative orders, including **folkways** or **conventions**, and **customs** or **mores**. These three features are:

1. Pressures to comply with the law must come externally in the form of actions, or threats of actions by others, regardless of whether a person wants to obey the law or simply does so out of habit.
2. These external actions or threats always involve coercion or force.
3. Those who enact the coercion are individuals whose official role is to enforce the law. This corresponds to Weber's notion of legitimate authority. Legal authority is legitimate because it is based on rational grounds and is the right of those who have been elevated to positions of power to issue rules and commands (1947).

In contrast to laws, Weber said, were customs and conventions. **Customs** are general rules that members of a society follow, but they are not tied to any external sanction (Weber 1947). You will not be formally punished if you choose to break a custom. Similar to Weber's term *custom* is William Graham Sumner's use of the term **folkway**. Sumner (1840–1910) was an American sociologist who defined folkways as "habits of a group" (1907:2–3). Folkways are the small, daily behaviors that people tend to follow out of tradition and because doing so helps maintain the flow of social interaction, such as holding the door for someone or facing the door when you get on an elevator. You could face your fellow elevator passengers, but it would interrupt the daily routine of elevator travel.

Weber's use of the term **convention** also stands in contrast to law. Conventions are more binding than customs, but not so binding as to be written into law (1947). People conform to conventions not because they fear arrest, but because they will meet with the strong disapproval of their family and peers. Weber's conventions correspond to Sumner's **mores**, which are standards of behavior that are more important to the social structure than folkways, but not so important that they have been written into law (1907). Mores reflect the general welfare of the group such as looking out for small children or taking care of one's elders (Figure 1.1).

Laws are distinct from other norms or rules of conduct. They carry the weight of punishment; they are enforced by specialized people in offices with legitimate authority to do so. Laws reach into every part of our lives but not all laws are equal. Since the apparatus of law is so enormous, we will be looking at ways to make the study of law more manageable. One way to break law down into smaller parts is by using **typologies**. A **typology** is a system of classification that helps break a large concept into smaller categories, making it easier to grasp and apply to real-world scenarios.

CUSTOMS – Weber Folkways – Sumner	CONVENTIONS – Weber Mores – Sumner
• Rules of conduct generally observed without thinking • No real obligation to follow folkways, but most of us do • Manners, etiquette, unwritten dress codes	• Rules of conduct that involve a sense of duty or obligation but lack a specialized instrument of coercive power • Respect elders, take care of your parents into old age

Figure 1.1 Weber's Customs and Conventions & Sumner's Folkways and Mores

Weber also contributed to the study of society and law by using typologies of legal systems.

In his sociological examination of law, Weber made a distinction between **public and private law. Public Law** is the system of legal norms that directly regulate actions by the state, state officials, and people acting as agents of the state. The highest level of public law is constitutional law; it establishes the fundamental laws to which all others must conform. **Private law** is made up of all of the legal norms that regulate relations among individuals and among associations of individuals in social and economic relationships including marriage laws and other family law, labor contracts with private employers, and all other forms of civil law ([1905] 1978). A **crime** is a public wrong; a **tort** is a private wrong.

In contributing to our understanding of law Weber also constructed a typology of three general academic approaches to how the law can be studied. The purpose of Weber's typology is to provide different ways of analyzing the law. I will briefly discuss all three approaches, but the remainder of the book will focus mainly on the third approach, the sociological approach to the study of law (Figure 1.2).

1. The Moral Approach

The moral approach to law is based on the idea that law is rooted in some underlying beliefs about the nature of human beings and about what is right and what is wrong. Law is an expression of a common moral order on which there is general consensus. The moral approach is associated with claims of universality or commonality. Murder is against the law because we all agree it is bad, wrong, and immoral.

An example of the moral approach to law can be found in the writings of French philosopher Jean Jacques Rousseau (1712–1778). Rousseau believed that all people are born good and noble but if they become bad they have been corrupted by society. In *The Social Contract* (1762)

APPROACH	FOCUS	VALIDITY OF LAW
1. MORALITY	Moral grounds, collective agreement	Consistency of law with external ethical or moral values
2. JURISPRUDENCE	Independence of law; law as coherent body of rules	Internal consistency of law with its own rules, principles, practices
3. SOCIOLOGY	Law as a social construct; law and social action	Consequences of law for society

Figure 1.2 Weber's Approaches to the Study of Law

Rousseau wrote that "man is born free, and everywhere is in chains." According to Rousseau, the evils of social life are due to the constraints of society: the government, laws, and social institutions. Rousseau wondered how individuals retain their freedom within the social structure. He argued that morality exists outside the law and that law is an attempt to embody moral values but does not always succeed.

Along these lines American poet, naturalist, and philosopher Henry David Thoreau (1817–1862) offered another moral approach to law. Thoreau argued that people can and sometimes should *disobey* the law on the basis of moral principles. **Civil disobedience** is any act of lawbreaking intended to illustrate that the laws themselves are wrong and unjust ([1849] 2004). Examples of civil disobedience are acts of deliberate resistance, such as refusal to pay taxes which Thoreau did during the Mexican–American War. Other examples are refusal to join the armed forces as a conscientious objector, leaving the battlefield as a war deserter, and striking or taking part in other forms of work stoppages to highlight unjust practices of employers. In 1955 Rosa Parks carried out one of the most famous acts of resistance of the civil rights movement when she refused to give up her seat and sit in the "colored section" at the back of the bus. Acts of resistance are topics that could be studied using a moral approach to the law.

2. The Jurisprudence Approach

Jurisprudence is the scientific study of law. This approach argues that the law should be internally consistent, orderly, and logical. The law should be autonomous; it should be independent of religious, ideological, and political beliefs. Law is viewed as a coherent body of rules that are rational, logical, and meted out fairly. Law is the expertise of those within the legal profession, especially judges and legal scholars. These assumptions make it quite different from the moral approach.

The jurisprudence approach was discussed by Nicholas Timasheff in his 1937 article "What Is Sociology of Law?" Following Weber, Timasheff differentiates between the sociology of law and the jurisprudence approach to law, which he defines as the science of law. Timasheff also notes that jurisprudence has many branches or subfields including comparative/analytical jurisprudence, historical jurisprudence, and theoretical jurisprudence. Practitioners of the jurisprudence approach believe in the strict separation of legislative lawmaking and judicial decision-making and argue that the latter is the true arena of pure law (Figure 1.3).

For example, let's look at the definitions of negligence from a jurisprudence approach. Legal definitions of negligence require bipolarity, one of the legal constructs that defines the law on negligence. In a criminal case bipolarity means that one party is harmed (the victim) and another party caused the harm (the perpetrator or the defendant). In civil law awards of damages are based on the wrongfulness inflicted by the defendant. Legal theories of causation consider how directly the wrongful action of the defendant harms the plaintiff. Definitions of negligence and harm are legal constructs that have been established over time. They can be studied, and analyzed, and traced back to their origin. This type of academic exercise is the goal of the jurisprudence approach to the law.

3. The Sociological Approach

The third approach in Weber's typology takes a **sociological approach** to the study of law. This approach is concerned with the morality of law and its internal logic, like the first two approaches, but its primary concern

LEGISLATIVE LAWMAKING	JUDICIAL DECISION MAKING
e. g., Congress	e. g., Supreme Court
*influenced by morals, values, constituents, popular will, special interest groups, money	*where legal definitions are established *legal precedents are set *legal reasoning is used, and rules of evidence are used **
	In the JURISPRUDENCE APPROACH, judicial decision-making is the true arena of law

Figure 1.3 Legislative Lawmaking and Judicial Decision Making

is social: the effects of law on social action, how the law affects people's beliefs about the social world, and how social and legal institutions are organized and change as society changes. A sociological approach to law also examines how law is created, which social groups have access to law-making, and how various social groups are affected by the law's enactment. Sociologists are interested in how laws are created and the social conditions that give rise to new laws and changes in law.

To distinguish between Weber's three approaches let's take the example of how a sociological approach to law differs from the moral and jurisprudence approaches, using laws determining the legal age to drink alcohol in the United States. What would the moral approach consider on the issue of underage drinking? A moral philosopher of law might argue that drinking is dangerous and immoral for minors and that children need protection from the potential harm and corruption of alcohol. A moral approach could also look at the act of underage drinking as a form of resistance to a law deemed unfair or arbitrary by teen drinkers, not unlike Thoreau refusing to pay his taxes.

A jurisprudential approach to the topic of underage drinking might ask the following questions: What is the appropriate age of legality? How and when were these limits established and by what branch of the government? Why? Were there legal precedents? Are the laws establishing legal drinking ages consistent across time and place? Are those who sell alcohol to minors culpable for harms that occur while minors are under the influence? A jurisprudential analysis might also consider legal definitions of harm, risk, and liability associated with underage drinking.

What can a sociological approach add to the discussion of underage drinking? Despite the fact that laws forbidding this behavior have been in place for decades—and the legal definitions take into account harm, risk, and liability—we know that underage drinking is a widespread social phenomenon, particularly on college campuses and other places where teenagers and young adults congregate. Sociologically, we could look at the impact of the law on social behavior. For instance, what is the point of upholding a law that is so routinely broken? Maybe prohibition of under-age drinking is not harsh enough, and the legal drinking age should be 22 or 23. Sociologists can look at drinking as a teen ritual or rite of passage, or as a form of groupthink where group members seek consensus or una-nimity above all else, even to the point of suppressing their own personal opinions and silencing dissenters (Janis 1982). We could examine the social context of the laws, when were the laws constructed and why? Which states changed the laws first, and which ones waited until later? A sociolo-gist could conduct a cross-cultural analysis of teen drinking patterns in the United States compared to those in countries that do not have age limits. Do the laws deter teen drinking? How does drinking behavior differ in the

United States when compared to countries with more liberal approaches to young adults imbibing, such as France or Italy?

A development in the study of law dating to the mid-nineteenth century combines two of Weber's approaches to the study of law. Sociological jurisprudence brings together the sociological with the jurisprudential approach to study law, legal philosophy, and the use of law to regulate conduct. Roscoe Pound (1870–1964) founded the field of sociological jurisprudence. He argued that law should be studied as a social institution, and he utilized sociological theories and data in his work. Pound served as the dean of Harvard Law School from 1916 to 1936, and in those twenty years he developed his interdisciplinary approach to the study of law and society, viewing law as a dynamic, ever-changing system influenced by social forces, which in turn influence the larger society. As Pound stated in one of his most famous quotations, "The law must be stable, but must not stand still" (Pound 1922:19). We will look more closely at law and social change in Chapter 8.

Sociology and the study and practice of law do not always fit together perfectly. Each field has its own specialized language and methodologies. Lawyers are advocates and sociologists are scientists who should try to be as objective as possible. Sociologists view the law as an object of scholarly inquiry, not a tool to be used and practiced by social scientists. Increasingly, sociologists and lawyers are working together on problems that concern both groups, including jury behavior (social psychology), jury selection, conflict resolution, and consumer protection issues. Many lawyers and judges use sociological and criminological research in their work. The two professions certainly overlap and can complement each other.

In the next chapter, we will look more closely at the rule of law as well as different typologies of law and legal systems. As we have already seen in this chapter, there is no one way to define and study law. In Chapter 2: The Rule of Law and Major Legal Systems, we continue to examine some of the ways sociologists and other socio-legal scholars have taken up the task of defining law and studying how law affects the social lives of individuals. We also look at other typologies of law and different legal systems that exist throughout the world.

CHAPTER SUMMARY

◆ No aspect of our lives is untouched by law. Laws protect us, but they also control and even inhibit us. Laws uphold social interactions and social institutions, for example, marriage and the family. The law grants us freedoms and rights, but it can also hinder and control us.

◆ Law has many functions in society. Manifest functions are the obvious, intended functions, and latent functions are the unintended and not-so-obvious functions, or consequences of law. Some latent functions of law can prove dysfunctional. This means they can exacerbate the original problem they intended to address or create new social problems.

◆ Being a member of society involves submitting to its laws; the laws protect individuals, their rights, and freedoms. While all laws are supposed to apply to everyone equally, inequality is built into our legal system. Those with the power and resources make the laws to protect their interests.

◆ Law is a social construction—it varies from place to place and from one historical time period to another. Laws reflect the culture in which they are found. Definitions of law also vary and there is no one definition. A working definition is, "a body of norms and rules that regulate the actions and interactions of individuals, groups, and societies." Laws are codified social norms.

◆ Max Weber's sociological approach views law as a combination of consensus and coercion. Laws are distinguished from other norms such as customs, folkways, conventions, and mores.

◆ One way to make the study of law and society manageable is to use typologies, or systems of classifications, to put types of laws into different categories. Max Weber's three different approaches to the study of law, invovling morality, jurisprudence, and sociology is one such typology. I will present several typologies of law throughout this book.

KEY TERMS

civil disobedience   17
codify   13
coercion   14
consensus   14
conventions   15
crime   16
customs   15
dysfunctions   9
folkway   15
jurisprudence   17
law   13
litigious   1
manifest functions   2

latent functions   2
mores   15
negative sanctions   14
norms   13
private law   16
public law   16
social contract   10
sociological approach   18
tort   16
typology   15
working definition of society   13
working definition of law   13

CRITICAL THINKING QUESTIONS

1. A group of college and university presidents belong to an organization known as the Amethyst Initiative. They have argued that we should lower legal drinking ages or allow college students to drink alcohol in certain approved settings on college and university campuses. Do you agree with this approach, if not, why? What groups might benefit if this change becomes law? What groups would resist this social change?

2. Other than through legal changes, how could we deter underage drinking? Discuss a nonlegal (or extra-legal) approach to accomplish this.

3. How would the moral, jurisprudential, and sociological approaches analyze residency restrictions for sex offenders? What questions would a scholar working within each of these perspectives ask?

4. Does your state have residency restrictions for sex offenders? Are the restrictions addressing their intended goals?

5. In this chapter, we looked at laws that were successful in accomplishing their intended goals and laws that were not successful. Think of an example (1) a law that accomplished its manifest function, (2) a law that did not accomplish its manifest function. Why were these laws successful or not?

SUGGESTED MOVIE: *KIDS FOR CASH*

Kids for Cash Documentary. 2013. Robert May, Director.

Kids for Cash tells the story of a 2009 scandal that rocked the Luzerne County, Pennsylvania, juvenile justice system. The case involved a kickback scheme where minor youthful offenders were used as the raw material in a for-profit juvenile detention center. A juvenile court judge charged with upholding the law undermined the judicial system and the rule of law, all in the name of money. He got his just due in the end, but not before his actions had derailed the lives of thousands of children. The film covers a lot of legal ground and provides many key issues—such as zero tolerance policies, due process, right to counsel, the differences between adult and juvenile justice systems—to discuss as a starting point for a class on society and law.

Discussion Questions for *Kids for Cash*

1. Did your middle and/or high school have police officers, school resource officers—SROs—or probation officers inside the school? Did you know about "zero tolerance policies" in your schools, is so how? Did they make you feel safe?

2. Which story from the film made the biggest impression on you and why?

3. Were you surprised by Ciavarella's and Conahan's participation in the film, or not? Why do you think they agreed to be in the film?

4. In some states children as young as age 10 can be charged as adults. Do you think this is appropriate under any circumstance, or not? Under what circumstances?

5. When the Interbranch Commission on Juvenile Justice began its investigation into the "kids-for-cash" scandal, its members said they were looking into not only the action of certain parties, but the inaction of others that allowed the scandal to occur. What do you think they meant by this and to whom were they referring?

2

The Rule of Law and Major Legal Systems

WHETHER WE REALIZE IT OR NOT, law permeates all aspects of social life, from birth to death and everything in between. Laws protect us, but they also control and even inhibit us. Laws uphold social interactions, such as business deals between two corporations and property boundaries between two neighbors. Laws also regulate social institutions, including marriages, schools, and governments. Because laws are socially constructed, they vary greatly from society to society. For example, property laws are a preoccupation in capitalist societies such as the United States. Who owns what, who owns nothing (e.g., the "homeless"), where does one person's property end and another's begin? Who is responsible for property that was polluted at the turn of the last century before the Environmental Protection Agency (EPA) existed? These are not preoccupations in other noncapitalist countries or in developing countries where the majority of people do not own property.

THE RULE OF LAW

We are a society of laws. One can often hear politicians, lawyers, and judges from the United States and elsewhere utter phrases such as, "The rule of law will prevail," or "We must uphold the rule of law." Very recently you may have heard legal commentators say, "Even President Trump cannot defy the rule of law." As Dwight D. Eisenhower said in 1958, "In a very real sense, the world no longer has the choice between force and law; if civilization is to survive, it must choose the rule of law" (quoted in Glass 2012: n.p.). But what do we mean when we use the term *rule of law*?

"I don't know about you, but my confidence in the judge as an impartial guardian of the rule of law wasn't that high even before the Supreme Court ruling."

Source: Bob Mankoff/CartoonStock.com

Like the word *law,* the term *rule of law* is frequently used, especially by politicians, but it is not often explained or defined. The rule of law is a concept—it is a term that encompasses many ideas. The idea of the rule of law dates back to AD 1215 England and the *Magna Carta* (Great Charter), which used the term "the law of the land." The Magna Carta was drafted to protect the king's subjects from the king, at that time King John. The Magna Carta established basic rights and liberties for individuals. It protected people, even the king's subjects, from the unjust and arbitrary exercise of power. For the first time in English history, laws were written and the Magna Carta came to be seen as the law of laws. It allowed people access to justice and granted basic protection of their personal liberties. While some of the basic tenets of the document remain to this day, over 800 years since it was initially drawn up, the Magna Carta has also changed. King John went back on many of the promises he made in the original document, and the powerful land-owning barons of England forced his son, Henry III, to revise and reissue the Magna Carta in AD 1225. It has been upheld and modified since that time, and it lives on in England and other parts of

Magna Carta, 1215.

the world that were once colonized or otherwise influenced by England. (American Bar Association. Part I: What is the Rule of Law?; https://www. americanbar.org/advocacy/rule_of_law/what-is-the-rule-of-law/).

Some of the basic premises of the Magna Carta are found in the United States Bill of Rights which comprises the first 10 amendments to the Constitution, not the least of which is the idea that "No person shall be deprived of life, liberty, or property without due process of law ..." (Fifth Amendment, Constitution of the United States of America).

> If citizens cannot trust that the laws will be enforced in an evenhanded and honest fashion, they cannot be said to live under the rule of law. Instead, they live under the rule of men corrupted by the law. (Carpenter 2013:108)

So how does the rule of law play out in our daily lives? Think about the grievance procedure at your college or university; how does a student contest a grade? Typically, a student must take several steps in the college

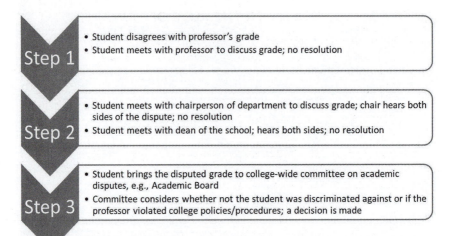

Figure 2.1   Steps in the College Grievance Process

grievance process. These steps tend to follow a path up the chain of command within the school. In most cases, a student is required to first discuss the grade with the professor. Second, if the matter is not resolved, the student would then bring the grade complaint to the chairperson of the department, who would attempt to mediate between the student and the professor. Third, if this step does not satisfy one or both parties, then the student and the professor discuss the contested grade with the Dean of the school (Figure 2.1).

If steps one, two, and three do not resolve matters, the student can then appeal to a college-wide committee on academic complaints. The committee, such as an Academic Board, is composed of faculty members and students who hold hearings to focus on any sort of procedural irregularities or discriminatory behavior on the part of a professor. For the student to win, one of two things would most likely have to occur. The student must:

a. demonstrate that he or she was discriminated against, or
b. demonstrate that the instructor violated either the course, department, or college/university policies or procedures.

While the procedures at every college or university are different, all schools should have a formal process in place that allows students to question their grades if they believe they were not graded fairly. These procedures may not meet any strict legal standard, but they do contain a number of features that meet the general **criteria of the rule of law.**

CRITERIA FOR THE RULE OF LAW

- The rule of law attempts to control the exercise of power by those in authority. It protects all citizens from arbitrary power and the abuse of authority.
- The rule of law is implemented through universal procedures. The procedures apply to everyone, from the president of the college to the people who clean the offices. Ideally, the procedures protect everyone.
- The rule of law affords equality before the law. In the example of the grade dispute, a student can challenge a grade, but a professor can also defend his or her grading decisions. Both parties are granted equal access to the law.
- The rule of law provides specific grounds or rationales for laws, and evidence must be used. To follow the contested grade example, the student cannot simply say, "My grade was unfair!" Nor can the professor simply insist that the grade must stand. Both sides must present some rationale or evidence for their position.
- The rule of law provides due process and guarantees that policies and rules are applied properly at all stages of the legal process. **Due process** is a somewhat flexible term for the compliance with fundamental rules for fair and orderly legal proceedings. Examples include the right to be informed of the nature and cause of the accusation, the right to be confronted with any witnesses against you, the right to have a process in place for obtaining witnesses in your favor, and the right to a fair and impartial jury (Turkel 1996).

Legal proceedings must observe rules designed for the protection and enforcement of individual rights and liberties.

Therefore, due process is the idea that policies and procedures have been applied properly and fairly at all stages of the legal system. If not, these improprieties provide grounds for appeal. Under the rule of law, relationships and actions are governed by codified, impersonal, and impartial rules and procedures that are meant to protect us all—they are applied universally and fairly. The rule of law stands as the ultimate source of authority and social control in a rational society.

Ideally, a democratic system governed by the rule of law should guarantee that the rules are generally known; laws should not be passed by a secret legislature or be carried out in secret courts. Legislatures and courts serve the public—they exist for all citizens. Laws should also not be passed retroactively; a law cannot punish someone who engaged in the outlawed behavior before the law was passed.

> **Legalese: Ex post facto**
>
> ---
>
> **Ex post facto** is Latin for "after the fact." Ex post facto law provides for punishment of people for an action taken before a law forbidding the action was enacted, or providing enhanced punishment for an offense that was in effect at the time of the act (Falcone 2005). In other words, the state cannot punish a person for actions that were *not prohibited by law* when the act took place.

The rule of law also necessitates that the laws be reasonably clear and not contradictory. Does this mean that citizens in a democracy know the details of every law that applies to them, from town ordinances to federal code? No, but it does mean the laws should be generally understandable and that one law should not prohibit behavior that another law allows. Laws cannot cancel each other out. Also, laws should not be impossible or unreasonable to uphold. Going back to the college, a professor cannot forbid sneezing in class. Sneezing is an involuntary act; it cannot be prevented. This idea is similar to **status offenses**. A police officer cannot arrest someone for being a drug addict, but they can arrest an individual possessing drugs. The first is a status; the second is an action. Does this mean that every person must know the criminal code and drug classification for all illegal drugs? Not necessarily, but people should know if they are carrying a drug that is illegal to possess. As the saying goes, "ignorance is no excuse." And, while we know that laws and rules change over time, the rule of law requires relative stability. Laws should not change on a whim; they should follow a fairly orderly legislative process.

THE RULE OF LAW IN THE UNITED STATES

In order to understand the sources of the rule of law in the United States, we must consider both classical liberalism and competitive capitalism. These constructs illustrate how the rule of law fits, or sometimes does not fit, the structural and cultural conditions of our political and economic systems—a representative democracy and a capitalist economy. Classical liberalism is the concept of individual liberty, the idea that we can take certain rights and freedoms for granted in our society. It first emerged in Europe and dates back to the 11th century, as we saw with the Magna Carta. In the United States, liberalism resulted from various struggles by people to gain freedoms from monarchs, such as the American Revolution, and from arbitrary state power, religious leaders, and the capitalist class—the powerful ownership class. The rule of law guarantees basic rights and freedoms that we all take for granted in this society, such as:

- The right to own property
- The right to a jury trial
- Religious freedom
- The ability to form associations, like unions, clubs, or sororities and fraternities
- The right to due process in criminal proceedings.

In the American experience, these liberties comprise the core of American independence and are protected by the Constitution. They have also been added to and modified over time as the result of major social changes brought about by the Civil War in the 1860s, the New Deal of the 1930s, and numerous social movements such as the civil rights movement of the 1950s and 1960s and the women's movement in the 1960s and 1970s.

The first 10 amendments to the Constitution exemplify the rule of law in our society; the Bill of Rights limits the powers of the federal government. Like the Magna Carta, the Bill of Rights establishes individual liberties as legal rights. Put very simply, the Bill of Rights guarantees our individual freedoms. However, according to critical legal theorists, in our society, a countervailing set of rules has grown up under our political and economic system of capitalism. Some argue that competitive capitalism is compatible with the rule of law, while others argue that liberalism and capitalism can work at cross purposes and are incompatible (Turkel 1996).

Early capitalism emerged as an economic system in Europe in the sixteenth century. Capitalism involves a class of people who own the means of production: the factories, the raw material needed to produce goods, and the land on which factories are built. The owners of capital need a working class—a group of people who will sell their labor in exchange for a wage. Early forms of capitalism, or competitive capitalism, also relied on competition—a competitive market. A competitive market economy is based on the following five features:

1. Private ownership of property that is spread throughout society, not just among the owning classes. Ownership can be found throughout all groups in society (ideally, there is no one owning class or monarchy).
2. The market is organized through the interactions of business owners buying and selling goods and services to one another. Therefore, the failure of one business, or group of businesses should not seriously damage the entire nation's economy under simple capitalism.

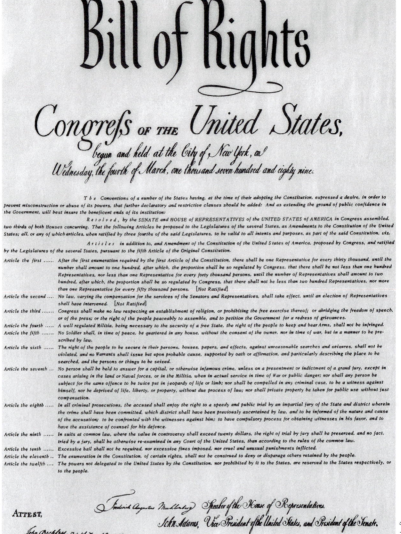

Bill of Rights, Congress of the United States, 1789.

iStock/leezsnow

3. Businesses are directly run by their owners, not by hired managers, groups of owners, or large boards of directors.

4. Workers are free to move from job to job. Workers sell their labor, so they do not have to stay with one company. They can move from job to job and sell their labor elsewhere for a better price.

5. The economy is self-regulating through the actions and decisions of owners, workers, and consumers. The so-called invisible hand of the market regulates all transactions (Turkel 1996:45).

This view of early or competitive capitalism is an ideal type; it is not necessarily how early capitalism worked in all settings in which it was found. Various legal scholars argue that capitalism is best served by a legal order based on the rule of law, since it is impartial and treats people with detachment and equality (Turkel 1996; MacPherson 1962). And, as we have seen, the rule of law is procedural and institutionalized; it has stable rules that are applied equally to all.

Because classical liberalism is also a set of beliefs that defines and promotes a type of individualism, it is also an ideology—a way of thinking. According to some legal scholars, the ideology of classical liberalism fits well with the ideology of capitalism. A capitalist ideology views individuals as independent; they relate to one another through free will and through markets. Therefore, according to some scholars, the rule of law, classical liberalism, and early market capitalism fit together well. As Gerald Turkel (1996) states:

> Classical liberalism understands society as relations among persons who interact on the basis of the power of their possessions for their individual gain. This view blends with and supports the logic of the competitive market and legal concepts such as individual ownership and contracts. (p.48)

Liberalism and competitive capitalism provided a modern world view that saw the individual as more important than the group or community. Economic activity is conducted through competition, markets, and contractual agreements. Property is privately owned and exchanged through the free will of individuals. The rule of law is the dominant means for settling disputes and controlling the actions of citizens.

Some critics see this world view as weakening community and discounting noncontractual ties and agreements. Ideally, the rule of law is supported by the political order and elected officials. Under these concepts, we are a government of laws not of people. Government officials' actions are conducted through legal procedures and institutions. They are not arbitrary, nor are they guided by individual interests. However, as we mentioned briefly in Chapter 1, there are many ways in which the law can be corrupted. The issue of elected judges and the case of the two Pennsylvania juvenile judges illustrates the potential for corruption. The judges received money to build a privately owned juvenile detention center and then received additional funding through kickbacks to ensure that the facility was filled with juveniles whose cases came before them. The judges were exchanging "kids for cash" (Ecenbarger 2012). Their abuse of power corrupted the rule of law and corroded citizens trust in the legal process.

There are many ways the rule of law can be undermined. The wisdom of the jury is not always legally rational, and even the Supreme Court justices are not always purely rational. They are human beings, and we all have our irrational moments. Irrationality and corruption may also sneak into the legal process through expert witnesses. Their testimony is not purely rational, and oftentimes the defense and the prosecution can find expert witnesses from the same field of study to provide opposing views in the same case.

Despite all of the possible problems with the institution of law, a society is characterized by the rule of law to the degree that it fulfills two conditions:

1. Law is the most pervasive source of social order. Social institutions such as schools, social service agencies, economic institutions, and businesses are defined and regulated by law. Contracts are resolved through law. People secure their property through law.
2. **Formal rationality** is dominant over other types of law. This is another term coined by Max Weber and is the autonomy of law over other social institutions such as the family or religion. Formal rationality exists when legal rules are organized around abstract principles and when procedures are followed and oriented toward finding the truth. While these elements contribute to the legal ordering of society, including knowledge and procedures based on science and tradition, formal rationality is dominant over all other types of reasoning (Turkel 1996:57).

Therefore, societies governed by the rule of law must be regulated through legal institutions that are above other institutions, including the family, the community, the religious order, and the monarchy.

Like any economic system, capitalism has changed—it has grown and spread across the globe. Late corporate capitalism hardly resembles the early competitive capitalism that emerged with classical liberalism. In liberal society, competitive capitalism and the rule of law are constantly changing as social relations become increasingly complex, technology advances, society becomes more productive, and new patterns of property and market relations develop under globalization and the global economy (Turkel 1996).

In the United States, legal scholars have argued that as our society modernized, and continues to do so, we have moved more and more toward **corporate liberalism** and **corporate capitalism**. The theory of **corporate liberalism** reinterprets liberalism and views it as the "movement of enlightened

ЅIPRESS

"If you prick a corporation, does it not bleed? If you tickle it, does it not laugh? If you poison it, does it not die?"

Source: David Sipress, New Yorker/CartoonStock.com

capitalists to save the corporate order" (Block 1977:352). The role of the government, in this view, is to serve the corporate leaders and to rationalize the economy and society (Block 1977). As a recent critic of corporate liberalism said, "a corporate liberal is someone who supports anything progressive that does not challenge corporate power" (Hirthler 2016: n.p.).

The term **corporate capitalism** denotes the shift from an early market capitalism to a late capitalism in which the economic system is dominated by large, multinational corporations that are protected by limited liability. Large corporations enjoy unfettered access to the government, allowing their desires and needs to supersede those of average citizens (Perrow 2005). The shift to corporate liberalism coincides with the transition from competitive early market capitalism to corporate capitalism, or late capitalism. Corporate capitalism is quite different from early, simple capitalism. It involves large multinational firms that develop huge amounts of power and wealth reaching across the globe. Corporate capitalism is global capitalism and it plays a central role in forming the economic, social, and political relations that guide our actions.

The Industrial Revolution, specifically at the turn of the twentieth century (late 1800s to early 1900s), was a period of widespread sweeping changes that brought about the rise of the modern corporation. A **corporation** is defined legally as a group of people who form an association endowed by the law with specific rights and duties, similar to individual rights, hence the term "corporate liberalism" (Clements 2009). A charter endows the corporation with its legal rights. This is a written contract that grants rights, privileges, and franchises by the state. Under these twentieth-century constructs, the following changes took place:

- Modern corporations amassed vast amounts of investment capital
- Corporations produced goods for mass consumption around the globe
- Property moved beyond small family ownership to large-scale shareholders and corporate capital
- The market became international and global
- Wealth and power became more consolidated.

In the transitional period between early capitalism and corporate capitalism, small business owners sought to limit the power of large corporations by using different legal statutes that tried to enforce strict competitive market conditions. Some of these were laws against price-fixing and monopolies, or shared monopolies.

At the other extreme, political leaders, state officials, and some business interests sought to maximize public control over corporations, making them accountable to the public. Examples of those efforts are federal licensing, reviewing of assets, and government oversight and certification of contracts and prices.

Eventually, due to the power of corporate capitalism, **a corporate legal approach** emerged that favored large corporations. It sought to allow corporations to determine market relations under a state system of regulative law that was enforced through the courts on a case-by-case basis. This approach relied on formal laws to define the corporation as a private, but socially responsible, actor that operated within the sphere of economic action. Through the use of state charters, states enable corporations to act as "bodies without souls." For critics of corporate capitalism, this was a huge and troubling development because corporations were allowed certain rights and freedoms similar to those that individuals were guaranteed under the rule of law. Conflicts emerged over who was to determine the pattern of market control and how the market should be organized. An example is the Sherman Antitrust Act of 1890 enacted under President

Benjamin Harrison. The Sherman Antitrust Act determined the boundaries of corporate power and governmental regulation. This act was the direct result of the transition of our society from an agrarian, traditional society to a more complex, industrial one. It was also a reaction to the expansion of corporate power.

When it was drafted, the Sherman Antitrust Act was primarily concerned with the power of banks and railroads in determining prices and access to credit. The act made market and industrial monopolies illegal, however, it was not well defined. It went through several revisions until the Supreme Court finally decided to give support to corporations. Corporations could contractually regulate the market within an environment of regulatory law decided by the courts on a case-by-case basis. After several shifts in antitrust laws, corporations were eventually given greater power in the marketplace, under regulatory agencies that had some measure of independence from Congress and the president. This compromise attempted to avoid the following two extremes:

1. Too many state interventions into the market.
2. The complete private ordering of markets through contracts dominated by large corporations.

For critics of corporate capitalism, the laws erred on the side of large corporations, giving them unfair access to laws governing, or failing to govern, their own corporate interests (Clements 2009).

More recently, the U.S. Supreme Court ruling on Citizens United brings to light the issue of corporate access to government and power. The ruling, which took place in January 2010, effectively overturned what had been limits on individual, group, corporate, and union spending for political campaigns. It allowed corporations and political action committees to spend unlimited amounts on political advertising and other tools to help elect or defeat individual candidates (Dunbar 2012). These pro-corporate rulings challenge the rule of law and hold the potential to undermine our democracy. Socio-legal scholars must remain vigilant in their analyses and critiques of how corporate capitalism operates.

"Law is but a response to social needs" (Hoebel 1954:293).

Every legal system reflects the intellectual, social, economic, and political climate of its time. Legal scholar Roscoe Pound (1877-1964) argued that law should be studied as a *social* institution, and he relied heavily on sociological theories in his work. Pound was a central figure of sociological jurisprudence. Proponents of sociological jurisprudence study law, legal philosophy, and the use of law to regulate conduct. But sociology and the study and practice of law do not always fit together perfectly; each field has its own specialized language and methodologies. Lawyers are advocates and sociologists are social scientists who should try to be as objective as possible. However, many sociologists and criminologists argue against pure objectivity and see the role of the social scientist as an informed activist. We will look more carefully at critical approaches to the law in the next chapter on modernization and theoretical approaches to the study of law. Conflict perspectives on law, critical legal studies, critical race theory, feminist legal studies, and the interactionist perspective all offer numerous ways to study law while also advocating for social justice.

The practice of law attempts to solve problems; it is geared toward specific needs and goals (Vago 2012). Sociologists view the law as an object of scholarly inquiry, not a tool to be used and practiced by sociologists. However, sociologists and lawyers are increasingly working together on problems that concern both groups, including jury behavior (social psychology), jury selection, conflict resolution, and consumer issues. Many lawyers and judges use sociological and criminological research in their work. Sociology and law overlap and there is quite a bit of give and take between the two professions.

TYPOLOGIES OF LAW

In defining law Oliver Wendell Holmes (1841–1935) said: "The prophecies of what the courts will do, in fact and nothing more pretentious, are what I mean by the law" (1897:461). This rather simple definition belies the fact that law is massive, convoluted, and often impenetrable. One way to make the law understandable is to break it down into types. A typology is a framework for classifying law and explaining the different types of law.

From a sociological perspective, one of the most influential conceptualizations of law is Max Weber's (1864—1920). As we saw in Chapter 1 Weber viewed law through the concepts of consensus and coercion. Weber argued that the law has three basic features that distinguish it from other norms: folkways (or conventions), mores, and customs. To review, Weber put forth several features of legal system.

Weber's Three Features:
1. Pressures to comply with the law must come externally in the form of actions, or threats of actions by others, regardless of whether a person wants to obey the law or simply does so out of habit.
2. These external actions, or threats, always involve coercion or force.
3. Those who enact the coercion are the individuals whose official role it is to enforce the law (legitimate authority).

ADVERSARIAL/ACCUSATORY – winner and loser

1. PENAL: violator should be punished

2. COMPENSATORY: contract, restitution

REMEDIAL – the law helps sort matters out

3. THERAPEUTIC: person needs help, e.g., rehabilitation

4. CONCILIATORY: social conflict in need of a resolution, e.g., marriage disputes

---

Figure 2.2 Donald Black's Four Styles of Law

Donald Black (1941–), a leading figure in law and society research, defined law simply as governmental social control. He also divided the law up into four styles: the first two are adversarial—they presume a winner and a loser. The second two are what he called remedial—they attempt to work toward a resolution to a problem, to sort matters out, and to restore order (Figure 2.2).

Elements of two or more of these styles may appear in a particular case. For example, a drug addict convicted of possession may also be granted probation, a lesser form of punishment than jail. The probation may be contingent upon the addict receiving help in a therapeutic program. Therefore, this case is resolved using both a penal and therapeutic approach.

As we saw in the discussion of the rule of law, a key function of the law is to regulate and constrain the behavior of individuals and groups in their relationships with one another. The law is, at its very basis, social. It would not exist without people interacting in relationships. When law is employed, other formal and informal methods of social control have not worked.

Finally, law can be distinguished from other forms of social control because it is a formal system embodying explicit rules of conduct. The planned use of sanctions to ensure compliance with the rules, and a group of authorized officials designated to interpret rules and apply sanctions to violators.

There are many typologies of law and we have already looked at those of Weber. Bear in mind that these different typologies of law are not necessarily mutually exclusive they can overlap. One way of typifying law is by its content, which can be either substantive or procedural. Substantive law covers rights, duties, and what is and is not allowed. Procedural law concerns how the laws are implemented and carried out (Figure 2.3).

SUBSTANTIVE	PROCEDURAL
Rights, duties, prohibitions	How substantive laws are to be
Administered by courts	administered and enforced and
What is allowed and what is not	changed and used
	e.g., how juries are selected, *voir dire*, how punishment is distributed, e.g., the recent changes regarding mandatory minimum sentences for crack v. powder cocaine

Figure 2.3 Substantive v. Procedural Law

Another typology of law is public and private law, a distinction made by Weber. Private law addresses relationships between and among individuals, such as marriage law, contract law, and adoption law. Public law establishes the structure of governments. An example is the establishment clause in the first amendment of the U.S. Constitution, which prohibits the establishment of government-sponsored religion, and states that no law can prohibit the exercise of religious beliefs. This part of the First Amendment has come to be known as the separation of church and state. The Constitution also established the three branches of the federal government: the legislative, the judicial, and the executive. These establishments of the structure of the federal government fall under public law (Figure 2.4).

A more common distinction in U.S. law is between civil and criminal law. Civil law is aligned with private law; it addresses torts. These are private wrongs, for example, when one party breaks a contract or when someone injures another in an accident. Criminal law defines laws that affect public citizens. Crimes are wrongs committed against the people and

PRIVATE	PUBLIC
The laws governing relationships between individuals; the law of torts and private injuries, e.g., contracts, wills, marriage, adoption	The structure of government; the duties and powers of government officials

Figure 2.4 Private and Public Law

CIVIL LAW (private)	CRIMINAL LAW (public)
Governs the conduct of individuals in their relationships with others	Defines crimes and prosecutes and penalizes offenders (consensus and coercion)
Violations of civil law statutes, called **torts**, are private wrongs for which the injured party may seek redress (usually monetary), e.g., medical malpractice	**Crimes** are wrongs committed against "the people" not just the individual victims of criminal cases. Crimes are public wrongs.
consumer law cases	They bring about the moral condemnation of the community at large (again, consensus)

Figure 2.5 Civil and Criminal Law

prosecuted on behalf of not just the victim of the crime alone but on behalf of the people, for example, *The People v. O.J. Simpson* (Figure 2.5).

Yet another typology is made between civil law and common law (Figure 2.6).

With its multitude of laws and multiple layers of law in the U.S., it is further broken down into five separate branches, each related but dealing with separate types of lawmaking and legal review (Figure 2.7).

We will look at each of these branches in greater depth in Chapter 4: The Organization of Law. Elements of some or all of the typologies of law can be fond in various legal systems throughout the world. Four major legal systems exist worldwide, as well as combinations or hybrids of these four.

CIVIL LAW	COMMON LAW
Legal systems whose development was greatly influenced by Roman Law, a collection of codes compiled in the Corpus Juris Civilis (Civil Law). Basic laws are found in codes.	In contrast to civil law, common law resists codification. Common law is based on case law, which relies on precedents set by judges.

Figure 2.6 Civil Law and Common Law

1. Constitutional	2. Case	3. Statutory	4. Executive Orders	5. Administrative
Concerned with the organization of the state and limits on power, namely, e.g., U.S. Supreme Court	Enacted by judges in the appellate courts	Legislated, law made by legislators— laws, statutes, and ordinances	Regulations issued by the executive branch at federal and state levels (the president and state governors)	Legal powers of government administrations. A body of law created by administrative agencies— regulations, orders and decisions, e.g., EPA, OSHA, FDA, Social Security Administration

Figure 2.7 Five Branches of U.S. Legal System

MAJOR LEGAL SYSTEMS

In addition to these various typologies of law, there are four major legal systems that we will consider, some more briefly than others. They are: Romano-Germanic (or Civil Law), Common Law, Socialist Law, and Islamic Law. There are more than four legal systems throughout the world, especially when you consider traditional legal systems in developing nations, but all established systems can trace their origin in one way or another to these main four.

Romano-Germanic System, or Civil Law

Romano-Germanic legal systems are found predominantly in most of Europe and many former colonies of France, Portugal, Spain, Italy, and Belgium, as well as in countries that became westernized during the nineteenth and twentieth centuries. These systems date back originally to the sixth century A.D. and to Roman Emperor Justinian. Civil systems are based on legal codes or bodies of laws.

Basic Features of Civil Law:

- Civil law is written into legal code
- Civil law does not officially recognize precedent
- Civil law is inquisitorial rather than adversarial; it focuses on inquiry to gather the truth, not necessarily on a contest that one party "wins"

- Civil law does not use juries in most cases
- Civil law uses judicial review sparingly; there is less reliance on appeals.

It should be noted that the form of civil law discussed here is not the same as the American civil law discussed in the typologies of law earlier in this chapter. In the American context, civil law means private law. Civil law in the Romano-Germanic tradition is also known as "code law" because it relies on written codes drafted by legal experts under Roman Emperor Justinian's direction. He wished to clarify and consolidate the numerous Roman laws into a clear, organized document, which came to be known as *Corpus Juris Civilis*, first published in A.D. 533.

Common Law Systems

The origins of English Common Law date to the Norman Conquest of England in 1066. Before this time England had a legal system that combined ancient custom, church law and remnants of the Romano-Germanic system found in most of Europe. After the invasion, the Normans set out to provide England with a law common to all, thus common law, as a means to unify England and increase royal power.

A 12-member jury.

Versions of English common law can now be found in the United States, Canada, Ireland, India, and other former or current British colonies.

Basic Features of Common Law:

- Common law is not written (traditionally)
- Common law relies on precedent, or previous cases decided by judges
- Common law is adversarial
- Common law uses petit (small) and grand juries (citizen bodies seen as coming between the state and the accused)
- Common law uses judicial review; it allows for appeals and for reviews of the legality of decisions by the executive and administrative officers of the government.

Common law systems rely on legal **precedents**—cases that were previously decided by judges. These cases become examples that are used to resolve similar cases. Common law is even referred to as "judge-made" law. The Latin term "*stare decisis*" means "let the decision stand" (Black 2001) or "stand by what is decided." The *stare decisis* doctrine is the principle of precedent; it is central to common law, where cases are decided based upon previous rulings and analogous, or similar, cases.

Legalese: Petit Jury versus Grand Jury

A petit jury is also known as petty jury; it is an ordinary jury used to determine issues of fact in criminal and civil cases and to reach a verdict. Petit juries are typically composed of 12 members, some jurisdictions allow six-person juries that are required to be unanimous.

A grand jury is a body of citizens summoned and sworn to determine whether the facts and accusations presented by the prosecutor warrant an indictment and trial. Grand juries are traditionally composed of 23 people. (Gifis 1996:277).

Socialist Legal Systems

Socialist legal systems trace their history back to the 1917 Bolshevik Revolution—the beginning of the Union of Soviet Socialist Republics (the U.S.S.R.). The collapse of the U.S.S.R. has been accompanied by the demise of, or at least the transition of, socialist law in Russia and its former Eastern European republics. Variations of socialist law still exist there and in many parts of the world, including China, North Korea, Vietnam, and Cuba.

Socialist law is based on Marxist-Leninist ideology. The term "Marxist-Leninist" means Karl Marx's political economy and communist ideology as translated through Vladimir Lenin (1870–1924). Lenin led the Russian communist revolution and established the one-party communist system in the Soviet Union in 1917. Lenin also served as its head of government from 1917 to 1918. Marx and his co-author Friedrich Engels (1848—2014) viewed socialism as a transitional system—one that had within it the seeds of its own demise, as it would no longer be needed in fully formed communist nations. This ideology argued that all aspects of the state would eventually "wither away." Many socialist legal systems are under transition, and each one is different based on the culture of the country in which it operates. For example, China's socialist legal system also incorporates elements of ancient Confucian philosophy. This would not be the case in Cuba.

Basic Features of Socialist Legal Systems:

- Communal values
- The popular will (as perceived by the Communist Party)
- No separation of powers
- Personal ownership (not *private* ownership) cannot be used as a means of producing income or profit
- Collective ownership is key—nationalized, with state-owned property, means of production, and raw materials.

Cuba's socialist legal system grew considerably under the Fidel Castro-led revolution of the 1950s. Castro's government enacted new laws that took private property from landowners and redistributed it to people who owned less. In many ways, Cuba's legal system is a transitional system that falls between a more traditional, localized form of law and a modern, established legal order. Transitional legal systems will be discussed further in Chapter 3: Modernization and Theoretical Perspectives on Society and Law.

Cuba's legal system involves small-scale legal tribunals found in neighborhoods throughout the country. These local tribunals attempted to make Cuban law the "people's law," and intended to be informal and small-scale with lay people acting as judges. The idea behind the tribunals was to bring citizens behavior in line and to deter citizens from stepping out of line. Because they are so informal, the tribunals have become unwieldy and too disorganized. As Cuba modernizes, it will likely move toward formalizing the people's law and handing over more of its administration to legal experts and professionals in the field of law.

Islamic Legal Systems

The last of the four main legal systems found worldwide is built around religious beliefs, also known as religious or theocratic law. While many types of religious laws are found in various belief systems, such as the Canon Law of the Catholic Church, religious laws tend to govern the church and its adherents. Canon law, for example, is a system of norms, rules, and legal principles made and enforced by the Catholic Church regarding the governance and mission of the church itself. Islamic law differs from this type of religious law because it is a form of religious law that governs the nation-states in which it is found.

Islam is the second-largest world religion. Islamic legal systems exist mainly in Middle Eastern, Arab countries, most of North Africa (Morocco and Egypt), and in the Pakistani and Bangledeshi regions of the Indian subcontinent. Over 1 billion people practice Islam globally. In Islamic systems, law is not independent of religion; law and religion are inseparable. The legal system, also known as *Sharia (or Shariah)*, is based on the *Koran* (Qur'an)—the word of God as given by the Prophet. Islam means submission, to surrender; *Sharia* means "the way, the path." Islamic Law derives from four principle sources:

- The *Koran* (the collected thoughts and revelations of the Prophet Muhammad)
- The *Sunna* (a companion book to the *Koran* containing statements, deeds, moral precepts, sayings, and other rules to live by from the Prophet)
- Judicial consensus (somewhat like precedents in common law)
- Analogical reasoning (used for unprecedented circumstances or instances not provided for in the Koran).

Islamic law covers a wide range of individual and social practices centered on preserving life, learning, family, property, and honor.

Basic Features of Islamic Law:

- Islamic law is written
- Islamic law is a hybrid of inquisitorial and adversarial systems
- Islamic law does not use juries

- Islamic law mandates rules of behavior in the areas of family relations and social and religious ritual, and it defines punishments
- Islamic law attaches religious rather than civil sanctions to the violation of law

When most Americans hear about Islamic law, they often attach negative connotations to it, especially when it is used with the words "radical" and "terrorist." Islam is not inherently radical or violent. Like many religions, it has fundamentalist groups within its ranks, but the radical fundamentalists do not define the entire belief system. Sharia law is also known for its harsh physical punishments. Punishments are associated with sin, and some sanctions involve the punishment of the body. For example, theft can result in the amputation of the thief's hand.

Sharia law is also known for its harsh treatment of women, strictly regulating everything from what they wear to what they are allowed to do in their private and public lives. Islam contains within it many different strands—from the very traditional, fundamentalist systems, such as those in Saudi Arabia and in Taliban-controlled Afghanistan, to the more liberal Islamic progressive systems found in the United States and elsewhere. Islamic feminists advocate for gender equality and social justice based around Islamic teachings. Linda Sarsour, one of the key organizers of the 2107 Women's March on Washington, D.C. supporting women's and human rights, is a Muslim (one who practices Islam). Sarsour argues that Sharia law is widely misunderstood and contains within it the seeds of equality and justice (Eicher 2017).

In the previous chapter we discussed the manifest and latent functions of a few individual laws, such as graduated driving laws for young drivers. In the next section, we look at the functions of law more broadly—at the macro level. Legal systems perform countless functions for the societies in which they are found. We consider three main functions of law in society: the social control function, the dispute resolution (or dispute processing) function, and the social change function.

FUNCTIONS OF LAW

Law grows increasingly central for defining and regulating relationships and actions. As societies modernize and grow in size, they also rely more heavily on laws to formally regulate all aspects of social life. Law performs many functions in societies, particularly in postmodern, post-industrial societies such as ours. We will look at four of the main functions of law in society, keeping in mind that there hundreds, even thousands, of manifest and latent functions of law. Later chapters in the book examine these main functions more closely, as well as discussing other purposes and uses of the law that may fall under these four main categories, or that may present an entirely new function of law.

Social Control

The social control function of law is most likely what comes to mind when one hears "law and order" along with the opening theme music to the television show *Law & Order*. The social control function of law denotes: "The principal laid down the law," or "I fought the law and the law won," or "You can't outrun the long arm of the law." The law makes us behave and punishes us when we do not.

Informal social control held sway in premodern societies and still operates in societies today. With informal social control, people adhere to social norms out of tradition, the need to "get along" and have relatively smooth social interactions. The fear of embarrassment and external group mechanisms of gossip, ridicule, humiliation, and ostracism control social interactions. In modern, and now postmodern, societies formal means of social control are needed in addition to informal ones. On a day-to-day basis, people are still controlled by socialization, the internalization of shared norms. We control ourselves and others through our daily interactions, our shared values, and the socialization processes that we have all been through—most of us have learned to follow the unwritten rules of conduct.

However, because of the size, diversity, and competition within and between societies, formal mechanisms of social control are needed. The law is called upon to bring order and to keep people in line.

Formal Social Control

Formal social control includes two key components:

1. Clear rules of conduct.
2. Planned use of sanctions and punishments to support the rules.

Lawrence M. Friedman, an American legal historian, studies the ways in which the law plays an integral role in social control: legal institutions are responsible for making and preserving the rules and norms that define deviance and crime (Friedman 2004). They announce which acts will be punished and how they will be punished. The legal system and criminal justice personnel also carry out the many roles of social control. Police, prosecutors, judges, prison guards, and parole officers—all of those people who make up the criminal justice system— enact the law. The topic of the law as an instrument of formal social control will be considered in more detail in Chapter 6: Law and Social Control.

Dispute Resolution

Law also functions to resolve disputes, or at least it attempts to do so. We live in a litigious society at litigious times. Disputes are everywhere, and law settles some and prevents others. Law cannot settle all disputes, but it is the main arena in which citizens, groups, companies, organizations, and the government process them. By settling disputes through an authoritative allocation of legal rights and obligations, the law provides an alternative to other methods of dispute settling, such as duals, dance-offs, or fisticuffs. We will consider the law as a forum for settling disputes in Chapter 7: Law and Dispute Processing. We will also look at some alternative methods of dispute resolution, such as mediation and arbitration.

Social Change

The third major function of law could be called a "social engineering" function. Law can initiate and guide social change. Keep in mind that law can also prevent or block social change. For instance, as we will discuss in Chapter 8: Law and Social Change, after the same-sex marriage law passed in Massachusetts, Congress passed the so-called Defense of Marriage Act (DOMA). DOMA defined marriage as a union between one man and one woman. DOMA was then overturned in the summer of 2013 when the Supreme Court of the United States ruled that all laws prohibiting same-sex marriage were unconstitutional. Laws either allowing same-sex marriage or banning gays and lesbians the right to marry exemplify the fluid nature of the law and social change. Change can go in either direction and can move in fits and starts. Social change is not always linear and one-directional. We will look more closely at the topic of law and social change in Chapter 8.

Law can also perform a watchdog function that is related to and supports the social change function. Watchdog function means that law and legal entities make certain that institutions are following the rules, regulations, and laws. For instance, the Southern Poverty Law Center (SPLC) monitors hate groups and other extremists in the United States (https://www.splcenter.org/what-we-do). Exposing hate activities to the public, the media, and law enforcement serves an integral function in a society built around individual freedom and liberty. Since hate groups prefer anonymity, groups like the SPLC and the Anti-Defamation League track their activities and broadcast them to the public, which then undermines the effectiveness of the groups.

Consumer watchdog groups protect citizens' rights and guard against unlawful or undesirable practices and products that can harm the public. The watchdog function of law can overlap with other functions of law. For example, consumer rights groups often employ the dispute resolution function by bringing lawsuits against corporations to fight for consumer rights. The monitoring function of law is important in its own right. As society grows increasingly complex, specialized monitoring groups are needed to guard against various potential infractions, including: human and civil rights violations, consumer safety violations, workers' rights violations, and First Amendment rights violations. In Chapter 9, we will explore the watchdog function of law and look at several legal watchdog groups in the United States.

CHAPTER SUMMARY

◆ The rule of law prevents those in power from abusing that power and exercising it arbitrarily. It protects all people before the law and is applied universally.

◆ In the context of the United States, the rule of law grew out of and supports classical liberalism and competitive capitalism. The Bill of Rights and the rest of the U.S. Constitution codify the rule of law for all U.S. citizens.

◆ Corporate liberalism and corporate capitalism have replaced classical liberalism and competitive capitalism. Both present new challenges to the rule of law in the United States and around the globe. Socio-legal scholars can monitor and critique these threats to the rule of law.

◆ Typologies of law help to make the vast institution of law understandable and manageable by breaking it down into smaller categories and types. There are many typologies of law, such as private and public, civil and criminal, and adversarial and remedial. The U.S. system contains five distinct branches of law: constitutional, case, statutory, executive, and administrative.

◆ Throughout the world, many legal systems exist that grew out of their sociohistorical contexts. The four major world legal systems are: Romano-Germanic or civil law, common law, socialist law, and Islamic law.

◆ Law performs many functions in societies. In this book, we focus on four major functions of law: the social control function, the dispute resolution function, the social change function, and the watchdog function. Each of these is addressed in later chapters of the book.

KEY TERMS

corporate capitalism   34
corporate legal approach   36
corporate liberalism   34

corporation   36
crimes   41
criteria of the rule of law   28

CRITICAL THINKING QUESTIONS

1. Look up the grade dispute procedures at your college or university. What are the steps in the process? Can you identify any of the criteria for the rule of law in the language of the grade dispute process?

2. Do a quick internet search on the term "the rule of law." How was the term used, by whom, and in what context?

3. How does administrative law operate? Find an example of a new rule or regulation that has been passed in the last few months. Which administration passed the law? What does it regulate and hat brought about the need for this new regulation?

4. How does the watchdog function of law overlap with other functions of law?

5. Do you think Citizens United should be upheld, or not?

SUGGESTED MOVIE: *THE CORPORATION*

The Corporation, Documentary. 2005. Mark Achbar and Jennifer Abbott, Directors.

The documentary critically examines the legal construct of the corporation—a body without a sole—that is responsible only to its shareholders. Using archive footage and interviews with journalists, academics, and even some CEOs, *The Corporation* asks if this legal entity of the corporation harms society. The filmmakers clearly believe the answer is "yes" and consider how society should respond to a "thing" that has legal rights, but very few legal obligations to the societies in which it operates. Because the film is organized into chapters, it provides a great resource to use throughout a semester or in its entirety to prompt discussion on Marxist perspectives on society and law, the dysfunctions of law, legal rights for institutions versus individuals, and the Fourteenth Amendment.

Discussion Questions for The *Corporation*

1. Should corporations be entitled to the same legal rights as individuals? Explain your answer.

2. How can law ensure corporations are held accountable for their actions? Should individuals (directors, employees, shareholders) bear any responsibility for the actions of a corporation? If so, to what degree?

3. Who benefits from the legal definition of a corporation? Why is the corporation defined as a person?

4. What safeguards should be in place to ensure consumers are aware of the risks associated with various products? Who should be responsible for testing products and ensuring their safety?

3

Modernization and Theoretical Perspectives on Society and Law

◆ ◆ ◆

NO SINGLE THEORY EXPLAINS SOCIETY AND LAW; rather, there are many theoretical approaches to these two vast and interrelated topics. Some of these approaches are opposed to one another; others overlap and are combined to explain various aspects of law in society. In this chapter, we consider several historical and contemporary theoretical perspectives on society and law. However, this chapter is by no means comprehensive. It provides a survey or overview of important theories in the field, many of which are discussed in other parts of this book. The focus of this chapter is on how the study of society and law emerged to examine the shift from traditional, premodern social organizations to modern, industrial societies. I also look at recent theoretical contributions to the study of law in society and in our everyday lives.

THE EVOLUTION OF LEGAL SYSTEMS

Formal, codified law emerges as societies grow in size and complexity. Historically, the development of legal systems and the process of modernization—including industrialization, urbanization, democratization, and stratification—are closely linked throughout the world. Legal structures emerge when the social structure of a given society becomes so complex that traditional regulatory mechanisms including folkways and norms, as well as other traditional methods of settling disputes, such as small-town hall meetings, no longer suffice. When societies can no longer depend on informal customs, mores, and conventions, nor can they call upon community, religious, or moral sanctions to regulate social life, people begin to construct formal legal structures to address social problems and keep citizens safe from harm, to control citizens, and to settle disputes between and among citizens. Formal and institutionalized regulatory mechanisms arise when other methods of controlling people's behavior are no longer sufficient.

Modernization and the Expansion of Law

Several interrelated and sweeping social transformations that emerged in the late eighteenth and the early nineteenth century necessitated changes in the number of laws and in the shape and importance of legal structures in different societies. The Industrial Revolution and the rise of capitalism, the process of urbanization, political revolutions and the democratization of the United States, France and elsewhere in Europe prompted social change in every area of social life. This brought about the need for new laws and entire legal systems to deal with modern social problems.

The Industrial Revolution

The Industrial Revolution began in the mid- to late-1700s and was in full swing by the mid-1800s. **Industrialization** first took hold in England and is still spreading globally. An industrial society depends on mechanization, or mechanical sources of power, to produce goods. Industrial societies are driven by inventions that facilitate new forms of agriculture and the production of goods and services. Industries also rely on new sources of energy, such as steam and gasoline. In the shift from farm-based, agrarian economies to those driven by manufacturing and mechanization, many societies experienced irrevocable shifts to new social relations and social structures. These changes affected every aspect of life: work, religion, family and child-rearing, homes, and schooling. The shift occurred very rapidly and in ways that must have seemed unrecognizable to those caught up in the massive changes. And, the law stepped into people's lives in ways that were completely new and increasingly pervasive.

Capitalism

Capitalism as a new economic system drove industrialization. In capitalist systems, factories, raw material, land, and tools are held in the hands of a relative few whose primary goal is to accumulate and expand their capital. **Capitalism** involves an owning class, the capitalists and a working class, the laborers. The working class, who own nothing but their labor, must exchange their ability to work for a wage. Under capitalism commodity is king. A **commodity** is any item: a tool, a stand of trees, or a cotton gin that can be exchanged for money. Therefore, in a capitalist economy labor power itself is a commodity. The capitalist brings together several commodities including the means of production, the raw materials, the laborers, and the machinery, to make something of greater value than each of those items is worth individually. With mechanization, goods can be mass produced. The owners of capital expand their holdings—they own more wealth and increasingly expand their production further.

Urbanization

Directly linked to the Industrial Revolution is the process of **urbanization**—the development of cities. **Urbanization** involves the wide-scale movement of people from rural, agrarian areas of the country to developing metropolitan hubs. Urbanization began long before the Industrial Revolution and dates back to the Middle Ages and the growth of early European cities. With industrialization, people in large numbers moved in search of paid employment, or wage labor, involved in the mass production of goods and rendering of services. Urban areas tend to be more diverse and heterogeneous than traditional, agricultural-based communities. They are more densely populated, and they present different social problems and challenges that call for centralized legal structures.

Political Revolutions and the Rise of Democracy in the United States (1775–1783), France (1787–1799), and Other Parts of Europe

Democracy simply means government by the people—rule by the citizens for the citizens. No two democracies are alike. The American Revolution of 1775–1783 gave rise to rapid and irrevocable social changes, which necessitated laws to address new social relations under a newly formed democracy. The establishment of individual rights, liberties, and the pursuit of happiness took priority and replaced the rule of the monarchy. In order to establish a newly independent nation, and state governments for the 13 original colonies, law proliferated. Law was called upon to establish territories and trade regulations, to institute property and tax rules, to build and maintain an independent army, and to generally formalize and codify what it meant to be an independent nation. These vast changes permeated all aspects of public and domestic life.

Many leaders of the French Revolution admired the American Declaration of Independence and drew inspiration from it. The French also participated in and supported the American fight for independence. In France, with the toppling of the French monarchy in 1789, changes proved to be so rapid that some social theorists, such as Friedrich Karl von Savigny an eighteenth- century legal scholar and August Comte, the so-called father of sociology, feared that chaos would replace the rule of the monarchy (Rodes 2004; Schaefer 2011). France was the most populated country in Europe at the time. The profligate spending of King Louis XVI brought the country to the brink of bankruptcy, and urban poor and rural peasants

George A. Hearn Fund, 1937

From Willamsburg Bridge, Edward Hopper, Met Museum.

alike were dying of hunger due to droughts, poor harvests, and soaring food prices. The French Revolution had many causes, but it was influenced by the American Revolution and by philosophers of the Enlightenment as well as scholars of law and government, such as Jean-Jacques Rousseau (1712–1778), Montesquieu (1689–1755), and Voltaire (1694–1778), all of whom emphasized individualism, as well as reason, logic, and science over tradition and religion.

Taken together, these major historical changes make up the process of **modernization**: the shift from traditional, agrarian-based economies to modern, industrial-based economic structures in which democracy prevailed. This massive, tumultuous period also saw the rise of modern systems of law. Figure 3.1 outlines the various changes in social structures in the shift from traditional, premodern societies to modern societies.

These major transformations occurred rapidly and caused people to think about the social world in new ways. Several new academic fields of study emerged during this period of modernization to grapple with and explain the massive social changes under way. Sociology developed to study the effects of modernization on the social structure and social relationships, and to try to understand social problems, the family, immigration, and racial and ethnic relations. Out of the larger field of sociology came demography: the study of population growth and transformations. Criminology

Economic Organization = Agrarian, farm-based economy with some small businesses	Economic Organization = Industrial economy Factories, mass manufacturing production; Capitalism–the selling of labor to owners of capital; Accumulation of capital
Rural, small villages and communities; face-to-face interactions	Urban centers with new social problems: crime; overcrowding, pollution; hygiene
Political Organization = Feudal, land-owning gentry and property-less peasants (serfs)	Political Organization = Democracy as political ideal— Individual Rights Liberty, Justice, Equality before the law
Primitive Legal Systems	Modern Legal Systems
Family organization = larger, more extended, with several generations working and living together on the farm; Children as economic assets;	Family organization = Smaller, nuclear; Children seen as emotional assets (not as workers)
Informal social controls, e.g., socialization, shaming, gossip, and simple legal structures	Formal social controls; complex, bureaucratic legal systems; law is codified; governmental control enters into every facet of life; Law becomes more and more prevalent and important in responding to social needs and settling disputes
Verbal agreements	Contractual agreements, Handshakes "paperized" relations;
Mechanical Solidarity	Organic Solidarity (Durkheim) The Rule of Law prevails;

Figure 3.1 Premodern/Traditional Society → Modern Society

and sociolegal studies emerged to study new issues related to law-making, lawbreaking, and the social consequences of both.

The development of legal systems can be viewed as works-in-progress. Legal systems begin as traditional; they are primitive and newly forming. They develop to fit the needs of the societies in which they exist. They grow and expand as societies grow in size and complexity (Figure 3.2).

A. Traditional Legal Systems →	B. Transitional Legal Systems →	C. Modern and Postmodern Legal Systems →

Figure 3.2 Transition from Traditional to Modern Legal Systems

Traditional Legal Systems

"To understand law one must view it in its social context and not as something which can be described by the analysis of a sample, however large, of cases alone" (Nader 1964:408).

Traditional or primitive legal systems are found in hunting and gathering societies as well as some simple, subsistence farming communities. The word "primitive" as used here means in the early stages of development. In traditional or primitive legal systems, there are some distinctions made between substantive law and procedural law. **Substantive law** addresses rights, duties, and prohibitions. **Procedural law** considers how law is to be administered, enforced, and changed over time. In traditional legal structures, judges are typically village chiefs, elders or religious leaders, or even people who community members see as capable legal listeners (Nader 1964). Courts might be held in town hall-like structures or they can be temporary; they are set up to address legal issues and then dispersed after the matter is settled (Nader 1964, 1965).

In traditional societies, no strict separation exists between law and religious beliefs. Laws are typically not written and are intertwined with customs, traditions, religious and spiritual beliefs, and ancient norms. Law is called upon to settle disputes, to coordinate social relationships, to control behavior, and to enforce kinship and other rules (Nader 1965; Hoebel 1954).

CASE IN POINT

Traditional Law in Haiti After the 2010 Earthquake

In 2010 the country of Haiti was struck by a 7.0 magnitude earthquake. At the time, the small nation on the island of Hispaniola was the poorest country in the western hemisphere (Quigley 2015). The quake killed over 220,000 Haitian citizens, injured approximately 300,000, and displaced 1.5 million (Simmons 2016; Quigley 2015). After the earthquake, voodoo priests were pressed into governmental service by the United Nations, which saw the priests as an important resource (MacQuarrie 2010). Long practiced in Haiti with origins dating back to the slave trade, voodoo became recognized as an official religion in the country in 2003, and approximately half of the country's nine million citizens practices some form of voodoo; there are about 60,000 voodoo priests (*hougan*) and priestesses (*manbo*) in Haiti (MacQuarrie 2010).

Boston Globe/Contributor

Haitians craft voodoo statues.

Voodoo beliefs revolve around family spirits to whom gifts are offered. The priests and priestesses mediate between the living and the spirits. Voodoo has no clear hierarchy of leadership, but it encompasses philosophy, spirituality, medicine, justice, as well as religion. It is an oral tradition with initiation rituals, feasts for the spirits, trances, animal sacrifice, and witchcraft (MacQuarrie 2010).

Because priests and priestesses are considered community leaders and often dispense unofficial justice and mediate disputes, after the earthquake, their informal roles as judges were expanded. They also acted as unofficial census takers, counting the dead (MacQuarrie 2010). These voodoo leaders who adjudicate disputes and dispense traditional forms of justice exemplify a traditional legal system. Even before the earthquake, the Haitian government was barely operating. The voodoo community leaders stepped into many roles that might normally be filled by lawyers, judges, and other governmental officials. In this traditional legal system, there is no strict separation between law and the belief system. Laws are not necessarily written, although some may be. Disputes can be adjudicated by a village or spiritual elder. There may or may not be a courthouse or central location for the law; law can be carried out in the community—in the village square or from the chair of the voodoo judge.

Transitional Legal Systems

Transitional legal systems are found in advanced agrarian and early industrial societies where the economic, educational, and political systems are increasingly separated from kinship relationships (Vago 2012). In transitional legal systems, there are basic legal structures including:

- Some written laws
- Courts
- Enforcement agencies
- Legislative structures
- Public/Private law distinctions
- Criminal law distinguished from torts (private wrongs)
- Procedural/substantive distinction.

But these structures are newly established and not as advanced and specialized as law under modern, industrialized nations. Transitional legal systems can take many shapes and forms; they are by definition transitory and thus are often unstable, as with the socialist legal systems discussed in the previous chapter. In addition, postcrisis transitional legal systems can arise anywhere in the world after wars or significant conflict. For instance, in 1999, both East Timor and Kosovo emerged from horrifying conflicts.

Istock/Claudiad

Aftermath of the Haiti earthquake of 2010.

In 1999, the Balkan country now known as Kosovo emerged from widespread and brutal ethnic cleansing campaigns by Serbian and Yugoslavia militia forces. In the same year, in the Southeast Asian state of East Timor, a vote for the country's independence from Indonesia after decades of brutal occupation sparked a campaign of "killing, burning, and looting" by forces that supported the integration of East Timor into Indonesia (Strohmeyer 2001). In both cases, the United Nations was called upon to quickly build transitional legal systems to fill the voids that years of conflict had opened. The transitional legal systems were called upon to restore order and to set each region on a path to nation-building (Strohmeyer 2001). Both cases highlight the importance of clearly defined legal systems, even if they are transitional and somewhat rudimentary. As legal scholar and humanitarian Hansjöerg Strohmeyer said of both regions:

> The experiences of the United Nations in Kosovo and East Timor have shown that the reestablishment, at a minimum, of basic judicial functions—comprising all segments of the justice sector—must be among a mission's top priorities from the earliest stages of deployment. Indeed, the absence of a functioning judicial system can adversely affect both the short- and long-term objective of peace-building efforts, including the restoration of political stability necessary for the development of democratic institutions, the establishment of an atmosphere of confidence necessary for the return of refugees, the latitude to provide humanitarian assistance, the implementation of development and reconstruction programs, and the development and reconstruction of an environment friendly to foreign investment and economic development. The lack of adequate law enforcement and the failure to remove criminal offenders can inevitably affect both the authority of the mission and the local population's willingness to respect the rule of law. (2001:60)

This excerpt illustrates the importance of examining the social context in which legal systems are constructed. A legal system born of brutal conflict and built by an outside body—such as the United Nations—looks quite different to one that has evolved over years of relative stability. The passage also highlights the importance of legal structures in bringing about stability and promoting the rule of law. Finally, Strohmeyer shows that formal, codified law must be backed by adequate law enforcement and sanctions for it to hold up in extremely difficult and contentious circumstances.

Modern Legal Systems

Modern legal systems contain all of the structural features of transitional systems but in greater numbers and in more complex, specialized arrangements. In modern societies, law grows in size, and it grows increasingly centralized and bureaucratized.

- There is a proliferation of public and procedural laws (or administrative law).
- Statutory law becomes more important than common law.
- Legislation becomes a more acceptable method of adjusting law to social conditions.
- There are clear hierarchies of laws and courts, from local/regional to constitutional law.
- Courts become more important and are used with increased frequency.
- The legal profession becomes more centralized and credentialized with licenses (e.g., the American Bar Association as credential-granter).
- Police forces are large and differentiated: town, county/parish, state, Federal (e.g., Federal Bureau of Investigation).
- Additional regulatory agencies emerge and proliferate, such as: the Food and Drug Administration, the Environmental Protection Agency, the Federal Trade Commission, Occupational Safety and Health Administration.

In modern legal systems, the rule of law prevails, and rules and regulations apply to everyone. Rights and duties stem from transactions or contracts, and legal norms are universal. Ideally, the law should be predictable, uniform, impersonal, and rational. Law is separated from religion and belief systems, kinship groups, and the monarchy. The nation-state administers law, and legislative, judicial, and executive functions are separate and distinct in modern law.

THEORIES OF LAW AND SOCIETY

As law was growing and changing in the process of modernization, theories of law and society also emerged and proliferated. These theories attempt to answer questions about the development of law in different societies, the various functions of law in societies, how law changes over time, and who benefits from laws and legal structures.

Early European Scholars of Law

For centuries in Europe, law was considered to be an absolute and autonomous entity unrelated to the social structure in which it existed (Deflem 2008). This idea was based on the notion of **natural law**—law viewed as a universal entity, applicable to all humans. The origins of natural law are traced back to ancient Greece. Aristotle maintained that natural law had a universal validity based on pure reason, free of passion, and subjectivity. St. Thomas Aquinas saw natural law as part of human nature and the way in which rational humans participate in the eternal laws of God (Vago 2012).

The idea of **natural law** is based on the assumption that, through reason, the nature of human beings can be known and that this knowledge can provide the basis for the social and legal ordering of human existence. Natural law is considered superior to law enacted by humans. Under the influence of natural law many European scholars believed that law in any given society was a reflection of a universally valid set of legal principles, and not socially constructed by humans (Deflem 2008).

Starting in the mid-eighteenth century, and through the mid-nineteenth century, the idea of natural law was called into question and largely displaced by evolutionary interpretations of law and legal positivism. **Legal positivism** is a scientific approach to law that examines objective social conditions, such as how culture and religious beliefs affect legal norms. Early European scholars of law and society employed legal positivism to make sense of the law as a human construction and not as a universally given set of standards. Legal positivism asserts that the law can be studied as any subject can be studied—through careful examination, collection of data, and theorizing.

Baron de Montesquieu (1689-1755)

Charles-Louis de Secondat, Baron de Montesquieu was a parliamentarian in Bordeaux, France, who argued against the absolutism of the French monarchy and also challenged the notion of absolute natural law. He believed that legal structures should be specific to a society's culture. Law must *fit* within its surroundings. He wrote *The Spirit of Laws* (1748) in which he argued that law results from a number of social and cultural factors such as customs, the economy, and the physical environment—the climate and the soil on which it stands (Vile 1998).

Montesquieu is most famous for his doctrine of the separation of powers: the legislative branch enacts new laws, the judicial branch interprets the laws, and the executive branch enforces and administers laws (Deflem 2008). While there is some debate over who first introduced the notion of the separation of powers, Montesquieu's name is most often associated with this important doctrine and he contributed significant ideas that lent to its longevity and power (Vile 1998).

In *The Spirit of Laws*, Montesquieu famously said, "Constant experience shows us that every man invested with power is apt to abuse it, and to carry his authority as far as it will go" (1748, Book 11:4). For Montesquieu, the separation of powers is necessary in a democracy wherein power should not become too centralized. Arranging law into three separate branches of governance kept the system in check and allowed for specialization within each branch.

Herbert Spencer (1820–1903)

Herbert Spencer was an English railway engineer turned social theorist of the mid- to late-1800s. His ideas were perhaps more popular in the United States than in his home country. In his book, *Social Darwinism in American Thought*, Richard Hofstadter points out that "England gave Darwin to the world, but the United States gave to Darwinism an unusually quick and sympathetic reception ... thinkers of the Darwinian era seized upon the new theory and attempted to sound its meaning for several social disciplines" (1969:4–5). The same could be said of Herbert Spencer.

Darwin's *On the Origin of the Species* was first published in 1859, and from that point on, popular magazines such as *Appleton's Journal, Popular Science Monthly*, and *The Atlantic Monthly*, as well as daily newspapers, published articles on natural selection and Darwinism (Darwin 1859; Hofstadter 1969:18–22). Spencer was strongly influenced by the evolutionary theories of Charles Darwin, so much so that he became known as a social Darwinist. Some argue that Darwin may have been influenced by Spencer. However, Spencer's social evolutionary ideas were circulated years before Darwin published *On the Origin of the Species* (Shapin 2007). While often attributed to Darwin, Spencer introduced the phrase, "survival of the fittest" (Howerth 1917:253). Spencer believed that societies evolve from primitive, barbaric forms to civilized social orders along natural, evolutionary stages. Spencer embraced social evolutionary theory and saw it operating everywhere—in the development of societies, of governments and commerce, in language and literature, in science and art (Shapin 2007). The language of evolution, progress, and natural selection—and Herbert Spencer's adage "survival of the fittest" —proliferated in subjects "quite remote from science" and became "a standard feature of the [American] folklore of individualism" (Hofstadter 1969:3–4, 50).

Spencer traveled to New York City in the 1880s as a guest of Andrew Carnegie, the Scottish-American steel tycoon and philanthropist. Carnegie saw Spencer as a friend but also a guru of sorts. Spencer's unyielding belief in laissez-faire capitalism was embraced by Carnegie and other American captains of industry because their success appeared as "natural"—or preordained.

Spencer believed in the free will of individuals above all else. Any effort to regulate industry or aid the poor would only interrupt the natural order of things. In Spencer's words, "idiots, imbeciles, lunatics, paupers, and prostitutes" would only proliferate and tax societal resources (Spencer

1884:132). Welfare degraded morals and overall fitness because it encouraged dependency.

While Andrew Carnegie has been called the father of American philanthropy (Theroux 2011), he did not believe in giving money to those he deemed unworthy, or unfit in Spencerian terms. He donated only to what he considered worthy causes, such as public libraries and educational foundations that could help people better themselves.

Spencer was a proponent of unregulated economic competition. He opposed most forms of public intervention into social problems; he believed they only interrupted evolutionary progress. Spencer argued that laws should uphold individual rights and the rights to private property. The law should not be seen as an equalizer in the survival of the fittest. Rules, regulations, and laws should be kept to minimum to allow the steady march of evolutionary progress in all aspects of society.

Sir Henry Sumner Maine (1822–1888)

Also influenced by evolutionary theory, legal scholar Sir Henry Sumner Maine was born in Scotland and died in Cannes, France. In his most famous work, *Ancient Law*, Maine was one of the first scholars to emphasize the study of law through history and historical methodologies (1861). In historical studies of different types of law, Maine saw the growth of the rights of individuals over the rights of the family, group, or community. This, he believed, was a basic component of the development of societies. Maine also saw the importance of the contract over customs and traditions. He viewed this progression as an evolutionary shift from status to contract (Figure 3.3) (Sutton 2001).

While influential, Maine's sociolegal theories have been criticized for assuming that all legal systems will develop along the same path and through the same stages as Western, developed law (Sutton 2001). His bias toward the type of modern legal system enjoyed by people of free will and individual rights may have prejudiced his view of less-developed, traditional legal systems.

Traditional Societies—Status	Modern Societies—Contract
○ Fixed condition	○ Voluntary social arrangements
○ Ascribed status	○ Achieved status
○ Caste determined at birth	○ Class based on merit
○ Group as primary social unit	○ Individual as main social unit
○ Feudal social orders	○ Modern social orders

Figure 3.3 Maine's Progression of Law

Classical Sociological Theories of Society and Law: Durkheim, Marx, and Weber

Sociology as a distinct discipline emerged in Europe in the early 1800s, a time when societies saw vast social changes and social upheaval related to the processes of modernization. French philosopher August Comte (1798–1857) is often credited with being the father of sociology since he first coined the term. For Comte, a positivist, sociology was the scientific study of society (Schaefer 2011). He believed that societies could be improved and made more stable by careful observation, examination, comparison, descriptive study, and experimentation.

Sociological discussions of law in society typically fall into two categories of macro-level conceptions: the consensus perspective and the conflict perspective (Figure 3.4).

CONSENSUS PERSPECTIVE Comte, Durkheim	CONFLICT PERSPECTIVE Weber, Marx
• Also known as functionalist paradigm • Society is seen as integrated, functional, stable, and held together by consensus over values, beliefs.	• Society is viewed as diverse, characterized by conflict, coercion, divisions, and special interests.

• Consensus Perspective Stresses:
  ◆ *Cohesion*
  ◆ *Solidarity*
  ◆ *Cooperation*
	• Conflict Perspective Stresses:
	  ◆ *Inequality*
	  ◆ *Competing groups*
	  ◆ *Unequal access to societal resources including law*

Law is viewed as a neutral framework for maintaining order and integration in a cohesive society.	Law is an instrument in social conflict and a tool wielded by the wealthy, owner classes.
Law is based on agreement, consensus.	Those in power, the ownership or capitalist class, create laws to support and protect their interests; law is a weapon for those already in power.
	The powerless do not have access to the law.

Figure 3.4 Sociological Perspectives on Society and Law

While this dichotomy between the two main paradigms is not exhaustive—it does not include all sociological approaches to society and law—it is a useful conceptual framework in which to view sociological theories. In other chapters of this book, I will discuss different theoretical approaches to laws, such as symbolical interactionism, and social constructionism will be covered in Chapter 5: Lawmaking and the Social Construction of Laws.

Emile Durkheim (1858–1917)

In sociological terminology, Durkheim was a consensus theorist, or a structural functionalist sociologist. Durkheim contributed a methodology for studying changes in social institutions and the larger social order. Influenced by Auguste Comte, Durkheim used a **positivist approach**—a scientific, rational approach to the social world—and was interested in establishing causality, in showing that one variable causes another to change. For instance, as societies grow in size, they also grow in complexity. Durkheim saw this as a **social fact**—an underlying pattern of social organization and moral beliefs that shapes our expectations of one another. Social facts are also reproduced through social institutions such as government, courts, and education. Durkheim believed the law performs several vital functions in society and as societies increase in complexity, law becomes more important, more pervasive, and increasingly differentiated and specialized.

Durkheim outlined his ideas about society and law in his book, *The Division of Labor in Society* ([1893] 1984). He viewed law as a measure of the type of **solidarity** found in society. **Solidarity** for Durkheim meant the persistent and ongoing expectations that people establish with one another that allow them to take their social world for granted. It is rooted in repetitive patterns of association in families, workplaces, and in the marketplace, as in a small, traditional village (Figure 3.5).

Repressive law in traditional society revolves around punishing the criminal for the crime but also for the harm caused to the social order—the collective conscience of society (Sutton 2001). **Restitutive law** corresponds to modern, industrialized societies. Durkheim viewed **restitutive law** as restorative, as bringing back social order and group cohesion after the upset of the crime (Sutton 2001).

Durkheim's distinction between mechanical and organic solidarity and repressive and restitutive law is not a strict dichotomy. Even today, in our modern, complex society, we seem to move more and more toward repressive forms of law and punishment. We imprison over two million people, often without any significant chance at rehabilitation; we treat juveniles as adults; we get tougher and tougher on crime. Many states still execute offenders. In other words, as with the earlier work of Sir Henry Sumner Maine, this seemingly clear, evolutionary progression from repressive

MECHANICAL SOLIDARITY	ORGANIC SOLIDARITY
Traditional	Modern
Simple division of labor	Complex division of labor
Similarity of tasks	Specialization of tasks
Agrarian	Industrial
Similarity, homogeneity	Diversity, heterogeneity
REPRESSIVE LAW	**RESTITUTIVE LAW**
◆ Penal law	◆ Reparations
◆ Punishment is main goal	◆ Rehabilitation of offender and compensation of victims
◆ Law is highly moralistic and repressive	◆ Restorative Justice
◆ The community is outraged by transgressions	◆ The law is also highly specialized
◆ Often involves sanctions that inflict physical punishment in public—the community takes part and it affirms the social norms	◆ Seeks to maintain general patterns of order and rights

Figure 3.5 Durkheim's Types of Solidarity and Corresponding Types of Law

to restitutive legal systems is perhaps not so clear and stage-like. Laura Nader's anthropological work on law in a traditional Zapotec village illustrates that restitutive law can be found in traditional communities and that repressive forms of law can be found in modern societies, such as our own punitive system (Nader 1964). As Durkheim himself wrote, " ... the essential elements of punishments are the same as they were in primitive societies. Punishment has remained, at least in part, a work of vengeance" (Thompson 1995:78).

In the United States, the juvenile justice system began over 100 years ago as a way to separate juvenile offenders from the adult population. The goal was to treat young offenders as capable of rehabilitation. Because of their youth, they were thought to be more amenable to rehabilitation and change. However, in the latter part of the twentieth century and into the twenty-first century, our societal approach has grown more repressive, treating children as young as 13, 14, and 15 as adults in the adult court systems and adult prisons (Ecenbarger 2012). Recently, we have seen a bit of a sea change back to the idea that young offenders must be treated differently. For example, several states have overturned life sentences without parole for juvenile offenders. Therefore, Durkheim's idea that as societies evolve and become more advanced they also grow more rehabilitative and reform-minded. This does not prove to be the case in many aspects of the U.S. criminal and juvenile justice systems.

Karl Marx (1818–1883)

Karl Marx studied law and literature at German universities. He was a philosopher, political economist, and historian, and has been claimed by sociologists as one of their own. Marx focused on the economic structure of societies and the modes of production of commodities—anything deemed valuable by society. Law is rooted in the material, economic forces of society. Marx's approach to law and society can be briefly summarized as follows:

Karl Marx, 1818–1883

SPUTNIK/Alamy Stock Photo

a. Law is the product of evolving economic forces.
b. Law is a tool used by the ruling class to maintain its property and its power over the lower classes.
c. In a true communist view of law, the idea of law as an instrument of social control will no longer be necessary and will eventually fall away.

To quote Marx and his coauthor, Friedrich Engels, in the *Communist Manifesto* [1848] 1993, "Your jurisprudence is but the will of your class made into the law for all, a will whose essential character and direction are determined by the economic conditions of your class" (p. 25). Marx's critical approach to law is rooted in a concern with freeing people from the burdens of unnecessary labor, poor material conditions of life, and patterns of thought that block their understanding of, and participation in, shaping their lives.

Marx focused on how law constructs social relations that separate people from one another, allowing for the exercise of power by those who own and control the resources over the people who work with those resources to make commodities (Marx and Engels [1848] 1993). Law defines and supports social classes on the basis of property, contracts, and their relationship to the means of production. **Contracts** and **property** are two main legal concepts under capitalism:

1. **Contracts** are written agreements between the owners and the workers and between the purchasers and the sellers of products. Contracts can also regulate relations between and among businesses.

2. **Property** is essential for capitalism to exist. Property is a relationship—a person or corporation owns a commodity, an item of value. Property must enhance in value; it must be exchanged. Property laws are enforced by the state to protect those who own it against those who do not.

Marx's influence on law and society can still be seen in critical studies of the sociology of law. For instance, William Chambliss' *"A Sociological Analysis of the Law of Vagrancy"* exemplifies a Marxist, conflict perspective (Chambliss 2004). Chambliss studied how vagrancy—homelessness in today's terminology—laws facilitated cheap labor for wealthy landowners during the period in England when the system of serfdom was collapsing. The first vagrancy law, passed in 1349, threatened criminal punishment for all those who were able-bodied and yet unemployed. The poor were forced to accept employment at a low wage or go to prison. The wealthy landowners were ensured an adequate supply of labor at cheap wages. Similar laws were passed to keep the poor and unemployed out of areas where labor was *not* needed so that certain areas, townships, or boroughs would not have to pay for alms for the poor—any form of welfare or social services for those in need (Chambliss 2004). Chambliss' study of vagrancy laws is one example among many illustrating Marx's influence on contemporary studies of society and law.

Max Weber (1864–1920)

Max Weber, also a German professor of economics, is most often placed in the conflict paradigm within sociology. Weber played a crucial role in the development of sociology as a distinct discipline and field of study. We have already discussed some of Weber's contributions to the study of law in Chapter 1, but his influence on the sociology of law bears further consideration here.

An important aspect of Weber's approach to the study of society and law is his distinction between **rational** versus **irrational dimensions of law,** along with his distinction between **substantive** and **formal dimensions of law.** These terms are based on Weber's notion of **ideal types,** or a conceptual framework or inventory of concepts describing the phenomenon being studied. Using Weber's two basic dimensions of law, we can classify legal decision-making from least rational to most rational. In addition, **formality** is the independence of legal institutions and procedures from all other social institutions, such as religion, family, politics, and economics. **Substantive law** is the opposite of formal law; it is tied either to a political order or a moral religious order. It is *not* autonomous and independent (Sutton 2001).

Rationality is the reliance on specifically legal principles and rules for making decisions that are logically applied to particular cases. **Rational law** requires the highest degree of institutional, procedural, and intellectual independence of law (Sutton 2001).

Rationality is:

- Systematically organized
- Rule-bound
- Based on logical interpretation of meaning
- Oriented toward intellectual pursuits of the truth.

Irrationality is:

- Not systematic
- Not written
- Based on customs, religious beliefs, or folk wisdom
- Informal.

Using formality and rationality, Weber constructed four types of law that can be used to analyze various legal systems (Figure 3.6).

Formally Irrational Law

- Law is ritually separated from other aspects of social life
- Judges are priests or magicians
- Procedures are ritualized and elaborate
- Dispute-settlement process is oriented toward fulfilling ritual requirements, not toward the logical search for the truth

Substantively Irrational Law

- No boundary between law and other aspects of social life Judges dispense folk justice; no specialized training
- Procedures are customary and informal
- Disputes are settled on the basis of popular wisdom, ethical maxims, and ad hoc analogies

Formally Rational Law

- The legal order is autonomous and professionally administered
- Legal rules are systematically organized around abstract principles
- Disputes are settled by applying abstract principles to concrete cases
- Procedures are oriented toward finding truth
- e.g., Supreme Court, ideally

Substantively Rational Law

- The legal order is secondary to religious or political orders
- Rules are systematically organized around extralegal principles, often in intellectually sophisticated ways
- Procedures are oriented less toward achieving religious, ethical, or political goals

---

Note: Table adapted from Sutton's *Law/Society* (2001:119).

Figure 3.6 Max Weber's Typology of Forms of Law

Weber has proven so influential to the study of law and society that some even consider him the founding father of the sociology of law (Deflem 2008). His typologies of law, methodological frameworks for the study of law, and theories about the roles of law in modern society provide rich intellectual ground that scholars are still sowing and reaping.

Sociolegal Theorists

Sociolegal theories are schools of thought within jurisprudence, the scientific study of law, that view law as integral to social life. For sociolegal theorists, law cannot be understood apart from the realities of social life. These theories are heavily influenced by the social sciences, most notably sociology, economics, and social psychology.

Albert Venn Dicey (1835–1922)

Albert Venn Dicey was an Oxford-educated English sociolegal scholar from a wealthy background. Dicey is best known for his doctrine of the **rule of law.**

In Dicey's Rule of Law:

   a. No one is punishable except for a distinct breach of law and therefore the rule of law is not arbitrary.
   b. The rule of law means total subjection of all classes to the law of the land, as administered by the court.
   c. Individual rights derive from precedents rather than from constitutional codes (Vago 2012:52).

In 1905, Dicey published *Lectures on the Relation between Law and Public Opinion in England During the Nineteenth Century*, which explored his ideas about the role of public opinion in shaping law and how citizens can take part in public life and even shape public policy (1905). He argued that public opinion tends to change slowly and the law should do so as well.

Oliver Wendell Holmes, Jr. (1841–1935)

Oliver Wendell Holmes, Jr. was Boston-born and bred. He attended Harvard Law School and then taught there as a professor. He was appointed to the Supreme Court in 1902 and remained there for three decades, making him unique at the time because he was a scholar of law before he was appointed as a Supreme Court Justice (Sutton 2001). Wendell Holmes was one of the founders of legal realism, a school of thought that argues that laws should be grounded in reality and should benefit the larger society.

Basic Tenets of Legal Realism

- Judges are responsible for formulating law, rather than just finding it in the law books.
- Judges make decisions based on what is right and just, before sorting through legal precedents, which can be found to support almost any decision.
- Values, personal background, and preferences are part of the process of legal decision-making.
- Judges must know the historical, economic, and political aspects of the law in order to fulfill his/her functions.
- There is no absolute certainty in the law (Holmes 1897).

Holmes argued for **legal pragmatism**, meaning he believed the law only made sense if it worked in its practical applications. Laws are enacted by human beings for human beings and therefore must make sense in their daily lives.

E. Adamson Hoebel (1906–1993)

E. Adamson Hoebel was born in Madison, Wisconsin, and attended the University of Wisconsin as an undergraduate. He earned his master's degree at New York University and his PhD from Columbia in the field of anthropology. Hoebel was president of the American Anthropological Association and was very influential in the field of anthropology of law and in the study of native North American groups. He wrote *The Law of Primitive Man* (1954) in which he noted that there is no straight line of development in the growth of law, unlike Spencer, Durkheim, and other previous theorists. For Hoebel, the law does not evolve in a simple linear, progressive fashion. Further, he was one of the first legal scholars to illustrate that law exists in even simple, primitive societies. Hoebel argued that the law does change and moves through stages, which are not arranged along a singular, evolutionary line. Legal systems grow out of the needs of the structure in which they are found (Hoebel 1954).

Hoebel outlined the following societies and corresponding legal systems:

Lower Primitive Societies, hunter-gatherer societies:

- Face-to-face relations
- Ridicule, taboo, and fear as forms of social control
- Physical violence as sanctions.

More Organized Hunter-Gatherer Societies with some settled agriculture (transitional societies):

- Size increases → Complexity increases
- Divergent interests → Conflict, tensions arise
- Private law emerges and spreads
- Tribes or groups develop hierarchies of power and authority (based on hereditary lines).

Gardening and Agriculturally Based Tribes (later transitional):

- Larger groups, societies
- Elaboration of law—more laws emerge and law grows in complexity
- Face-to-face interactions are not possible with all members of a society
- Many competing interests
- Allocations of rights, duties, privileges, powers, property (Hoebel 1954:316–319).

While these societies are arranged in increasing complexity, for Hoebel this is not a stage-like, linear progression. The trend of law is one of increasing growth and complexity in which the tendency is to shift the imposition of legal sanctions from the individual to the kinship group and then eventually to the larger community and then society. However, this does not mean that various systems are not found within a given society, there is overlap (Hoebel 1954).

Donald Black (1941–)

Donald Black is a contemporary sociolegal theorist. He received his doctorate in sociology at the University of Michigan in 1968. Black has taught at both Harvard and Yale law schools and now works as a professor of social sciences at the University of Virginia. His most notable books are: *Sociological Injustice* (1989), *The Behavior of Law* ([1976] 2010), and *The Social Structure of Right and Wrong* (1993). Black wrote, "Law is governmental social control" (1976:2). In his theoretical approach, he divided the law into four styles: penal, compensatory, therapeutic, and conciliatory. The first two, penal and compensatory, are adversarial forms of law with a winning and losing party. The second two, therapeutic and conciliatory, Black (1976) termed remedial. They help sort out or ameliorate social problems (Figure 3.7).

Elements of two or more of these styles may appear in a particular case, such as a drug addict convicted of possession and sentenced to jail time (penal law) who may also be granted probation contingent upon a attending a rehabilitation program (therapeutic).

ACCUSATORY/ADVERSARIAL – winner and loser

1. Penal: violator should be punished

2. Compensatory: contract, restitution

REMEDIAL – the law helps sort matters out

3. Therapeutic: person needs help, e.g., rehabilitation

4. Conciliatory: social conflict in need of a resolution, e.g., marriage disputes

---

Figure 3.7 Donald Black's Styles of Law

Like Hoebel, Black's research involves cross-cultural analyses of laws in different societies. Black views law as a quantitative variable—it can be measured objectively by the frequency with which statutes are enacted, regulations are issued, complaints are made, offenses are prosecuted, and damages are awarded; punishment is meted out in a given society (Vago 2012). The law's quantity varies from society to society and from historical period to historical period.

Modern, stratified societies possess more law than simple societies. Wealthy people have more access to the law than poor people and make use of it more frequently, and the poor are more often punished by the law. According to Black, all of these social issues can be measured quantitatively. Black also believes that law is a social process that is inherently biased. Differences in social status affect law at every turn, not just in terms of who is punished but also with regard to how lawyers are perceived, how jurors interact, and who has access to the legal process. Bias and prejudice are inherent in these social processes.

Since he viewed law as quantifiable, Black developed several propositions that explain the shape, quantity, direction, and style of law using five variables of social life:

- **Morphology:** shape of society—the aspects of social life that can be measured by social differentiation or degree of interdependence, e.g., division of labor
- **Stratification:** inequalities of wealth, power, privilege
- **Culture:** the symbolic aspect of social life—ideas, beliefs, etc.,
- **Organization:** capacity for collective action, degrees of centralized governance, economy
- **Social Control:** the normative aspects of society—how society responds to deviant behavior (Vago 2012).

According to Black, all of these elements of law are quantifiable and can be measured and studied as discreet variables using a scientific, positivist approach.

"Let's handle this the way neighbors do in an adversarial society such as ours...litigate."

Source: Chris Wildt/CartoonStock.com

CURRENT THEORIES OF SOCIETY AND LAW

Today there are many approaches to the study of society and law that draw influence and inspiration from earlier theorists discussed in this chapter. Each of these new approaches advances our knowledge of law in society while providing critique and pushing law and legal scholarship to do more in bringing about positive social changes. Among these are: providing more access to the law for poor and minority groups, guaranteeing equality before the law for all individuals, and recognizing the injustices that have been perpetrated in the name of law.

Critical Legal Studies (CLS)

The emergence of the new field of Critical Legal Studies, or CLS, is traced back to Yale Law School faculty and students of the 1960s. CLS is influenced by Marxism and legal realism. CLS scholars are critical of the power of law and the monopoly over the law that the American Bar Association and other professional organizations have in controlling expertise, accreditation and access to legal education.

Roberto Mangabeira Unger is a leading critical legal scholar. He teaches at Harvard Law School, where he is one of the youngest professors ever to have received tenure, and taught President Barak Obama when he was a student at Harvard. Unger was born in Rio de Janeiro and raised by a Brazilian mother and a German father in Brazil. Unger wrote *Law and Modern Society* (1976) in which he uses Max Weber's theories on rational legal systems. His main thesis is that the development of the rule of law—law committed to general and autonomous legal norms—can take place only when competing groups struggle for control of the legal system. For example, Unger contends that

> the unequal distribution of knowledge, power, and resources that employers have over employees, that producers have over consumers, and that leaders of corporations have over local communities become subject to state action because privately based inequalities have wide public consequences and no democratic justification (Turkel 1996).

Influenced by both Weber and Marx, Unger fears a dissolution of the rule of law under unbridled capitalism, where large corporations are allowed to take from society but not required to give back in return (Unger 1976).

Feminist Legal Theory

Feminist legal theory (FLT), or feminist jurisprudence, examines the interaction between law and gender. Topics addressed by feminist legal scholars includes workplace discrimination, reproductive rights and the body, domestic violence, sexual harassment, rape, prostitution and sex work, education, sports and Title IX, and the public private split in law and society (Levit and Verchick 2016). We will be looking more closely at feminist legal theory in Chapter 10: Gender, Inequality, and Law.

Critical Race Theory (CRT)

Critical Race Theory (CRT) addresses questions of law and racial discrimination, oppression, difference, and inequality. CRT also looks at the lack of diversity in the legal profession. The term CRT was coined in 1989 at a workshop on race theory held in Madison, Wisconsin. In Chapter 11: Race, Inequality, and Law, we will explore Ian Haney Lopez's (1996) *White by Law: The Legal Construction of Race* as well as other scholarship from the field of CRT.

Intersectional Approaches to Society and Law

Intersectional theory is a relatively new approach to studying and understanding social stratification. It is most often employed to analyze race along with other social positions, such as gender, class, and sexuality. In criminology, intersectional analysis has primarily been used to address the experiences of black women and girls in urban settings. However, more recent studies have applied intersectionality to other groups, such as rural women as both victims and perpetrators of crime (Carrington et al. 2014; DeKeseredy et al. 2016). In her 2015 book, *Intersectionality and Criminology: Disrupting and Revolutionizing Studies of Crime*, Hillary Potter notes that whiteness is rarely discussed in studies of crime. She states, "White is a race. Consequently, criminologists should, at least, contemplate how being white may influence individuals' experiences compared with those of other races" (2015:150).

Intersectionality recognizes that people are situated in differing locations within the social structural hierarchy that attach to disadvantages and advantages. Gender, age, race, socioeconomic status, sexuality, and disability affect one's location in the social structure, social identity, and access to power. "Intersectionality is strongly tied to real-world activism" (Potter 2013:314).

Potter (2013) notes that while intersectionality began with black feminist critiques of racial and gender discrimination, the perspective has now expanded to incorporate various social statuses. Kimberlé Crenshaw, the legal scholar who coined the term "intersectionality," stated that the concept of intersectionality "can and should be expanded" by factoring in issues such as "sexuality, nationality, and class, among other identities" (Crenshaw 1991; Potter 2013:309) In her 2015 book, *Intersectionality and Criminology*, Potter states, "I strongly believe the principal goals of intersectionality's origination are needed in considering all lived experiences, regardless of the identities individuals hold" (2015:79). Later in the same book Potter (2015:105) asserts, "*all* individuals can be considered from an intersectional framework. Simply because a research sample comprises only white men does not mean that race and gender and sexuality do not need to be considered" (2015:105). Crenshaw (2011:230) also argues that all individuals exist "within a matrix of power." She states, "Intersectionality represents a structural and dynamic arrangement; power marks these relationships among and between categories of experience that vary in their complexity" (2011:230). Similarly, sociologist Patricia Hill Collins (2009:21) uses the notion of matrix of domination to examine how "intersecting oppressions are organized" into domains of power that appear and "reappear across different forms of oppression." Collins (2009:26) highlights the "structural, disciplinary, hegemonic, and interpersonal domains of power" and how they control and oppress individuals and groups differently depending on intersections of race, class, gender, nationality, and sexuality. Intersectionality will be given a more thoroughgoing discussion in both Chapter 10: Gender, Inequality, and Law and Chapter 11: Race, Inequality, and Law.

CHAPTER SUMMARY

◆ This chapter examined several historical and contemporary theoretical perspectives on society and law, focusing on how the study of society and law emerged to examine the shift from traditional, premodern social organizations to modern, industrial societies.

◆ Formal, codified laws evolved along with other social changes of modernization.

◆ As societies grow in size and diversity, formal social control—including law—is needed along with informal social control to keep citizens safe, to regulate society, and to settle disputes.

◆ The modernization process included the Industrial Revolution, the expansion of capitalism and stratification, urbanization, the American and French Revolutions and democratization.

◆ Traditional legal systems were replaced with transitional legal systems, and then with modern legal systems.

◆ Early European scholars of law, such as Montesquieu, Spencer, and Maine, offered theories of society and law that challenge notions of natural law.

◆ Classical sociological theories of society and law from Durkheim, Marx, and Weber examined the role of law in the development of modern societies and the roles that law plays in those societies.

◆ Sociolegal scholars, such as Venn Dicey, Wendell Holmes, and Hoebel view law through the lens of science: they argue that law cannot be understood as separate from the social world in which it is embedded.

◆ Contemporary approaches to the study of society and law offer critical perspectives on law and view law as a tool to bring about equality and positive social changes.

◆ Critical legal studies, feminist legal theory, critical race theory, and intersectionality were discussed as current scholarly, theoretical approaches to society and law.

KEY TERMS

capitalism 54
commodity 54
contracts 69
Critical Race Theory 77
culture 75
democracy 55
feminist legal theory 77
formality 70
ideal types 70
industrialization 54
legal positivism 63
legal pragmatism 73
modernization 56
morphology 75
natural law 62
organization 75
positivist approach 67

procedural law 58
property 69
rational law 70
rational versus irrational
    dimensions of law 70
rationality 70
repressive law 67
restitutive law 67
rule of law 72
social control 75
social fact 67
solidarity 67
stratification 75
substantive and formal dimensions
    of law 70
substantive law 58
urbanization 55

CRITICAL THINKING QUESTIONS

1. How has Marxism influenced later theories of law such as CLS, FLS, and intersectionality?

2. How has law changed in your lifetime? Can you think of some ways that the law continues to modernize and change to fit the social structure in which it exists?

3. Can you think of a substantively irrational legal system according to Weber's typology? What would such a system look like?

4. A lot of young adult literature and films feature dystopian societies in which the laws of modern society no longer apply. Why do you think people in today's society are interested in themes of dehumanizing, unpleasant societies rife with totalitarianism, and brute force? What is the role of law in a dystopia? Is it seen as a positive or negative force?

SUGGESTED MOVIE: *LITTLE INJUSTICES: LAURA NADER LOOKS AT THE LAW*

Little Injustices: Laura Nader Looks at the Law, Documentary. 1981. Terry Rockefeller, and Michael Ambrosino, Directors. (available through Documentary Educational Resources–D.E.R.)

In *Little Injustices*, legal anthropologist Laura Nader explores a traditional legal system undergoing some small, gradual transitions toward modernization. She compares and contrasts the small-scale legal system in a traditional Zapotec Indian village in Oaxaca, Mexico, with the modern, large-scale legal system in the United States. One is face-to-face and the other is "face-to-faceless." Nader focuses on the dispute processing function of law in both settings and illustrates that a society based on consumerism—the United States—sees justice as an adversarial proposition. In Oaxaca, however, the legal system attempts to restore balance and order to relationships and to the larger village community.

Discussion Questions for *Little Injustices: Laura Nader Looks at the Law*

1. By the end of the film, small changes have started to modify the legal system in the Oaxacan village. Describe two of those changes. What do you think prompted these changes?

2. Have you ever had a consumer complaint? Describe one (or more) of these complaints. Was it resolved, if so, how? Was the legal system involved in this resolution?

3. Do you think consumers' approaches to product or service complaints have changed much since the film was made in the early 1980s, if so, how?

4. Other than writing complaint letters and suing in small claims court, what are some ways that consumers can object to shoddy products or bad service in this country?

5. Do you think corporations are taking consumer complaints more seriously today than they were in the 1980s? If no, why not? If yes, why? Provide examples of both.

4

The Organization of Law

WHILE "THE LAW" IS INTANGIBLE, the organization of the law is both tangible and visible. The law is organized into court houses and court systems, legislative bodies, various administrative agencies, as well as law enforcement agencies. These social institutions make up the structure of the legal system in the United States. The purpose of this chapter is to examine the structure of law and how the law operates—how law is carried out and made visible.

In early colonial America, the punishment part of law was public. It was visible in the town square through physical, corporeal sanctions that could range from people—most often women—forced to wear the scarlet letter "A" for adultery to the hanging of a person accused of witchcraft. The law was brought into sharp focus when someone convicted of breaking the law was punished before the whole community. Crowds of people would gather to witness the punishment of lawbreakers, to share in the experience, and to chat about it afterward.

Today, the punishment part of the law is much less visible—we no longer use the stockades in the center of town, nor do we hang people in public (or otherwise). Punishment in today's society typically involves fines and surveillance, for example, probation, parole, or some form of incarceration. This final step in the criminal law process is hard to see—most jails and prisons are located away from the public. People who are under criminal justice surveillance meet with their probation or parole officers privately. The court house represents the part of law that is open to public viewing in today's society—the courts represent the law in our public consciousness. The courts are where the action of the law occurs. The courts house the law and bring it to bear on our lives. Popular movies, television shows, best-selling novels, and podcasts are replete with courtroom dramas. We love to watch the law: to see it play out, to find out who the winner is and who the loser is, to see if the sentence fits the crime, and if the compensatory damages in civil court break a new record.

THE COURTS

The courts process **disputes—conflicts or disagreements** over opposing claims or rights. When disputes are brought before the court, judges, juries, or both try to decide between or among the competing claims of individuals and organizations. These organizations can be private organizations, such as a business. Governmental agencies, such as a city, can also stand as parties in a dispute. When the court renders a verdict in a criminal trial—deciding the guilt or innocence of the **defendant**, the offending party, or the person on trial—the case had been **adjudicated**. When the judge makes a determination in a civil case, this process is called **adjudication**. Adjudication is the "judicial processing of a case, the rendering of a final judgment" (Falcone 2005:3).

Courthouses represent the place of law—where the law is carried out.

Matters are brought before the court for resolution. Therefore, courts react to what has already happened. Ideally, the courts are public and available to all members of society. Courts apply and interpret the law; they are supposed to be impartial and impersonal.

Dispute Categories

Courts are organized by the types of disputes they process. Three categories of disputes make up most of the work of the judicial system in the United States: private disputes, public-initiated disputes, and public defendant disputes (Goldman and Sarat 1989; Sarat and Felstiner 1995) (Figure 4.1).

Private Disputes

Private disputes occur when there is a disagreement among individual citizens or private business entities. These disputes can include matters of family law, such as a divorce or a custody case. Private disputes can also involve cases brought to the courts by neighbors, as with a disagreement over a property line. Private disputes also include one business suing another. An example involves one of Kim Kardashian's companies, Kimsaprincess, Inc. The company is being sued over alleged copyright infringement regarding its self-illuminating phone case, which is supposed to help the user take better selfies. A person who claims he invented the product years earlier is suing Kardashian for $100 million. This is just one of many private disputes that have been brought against Kardashian-related businesses. In 2016, Kim

1. PRIVATE DISPUTES	2. PUBLIC-INITIATED DISPUTES	3. PUBLIC DEFENDANT DISPUTES
• No governmental party involved in the dispute • Family matters • Two business owners • Two people involved in a car accident • Many are settled or negotiated before they reach the court • Torts or private wrongs • Civil cases	• When the government seeks to enforce its laws or punish those who break the law • Brought to the court on behalf of the public, not just the individual victim of the crime • Criminal cases	• The government is a defendant in the case • Includes various challenges to review the action of the other branches of the government, such as when the government is not following its own rules and procedures

Figure 4.1 Typology of Disputes

and her sisters Khloe and Kourtney, were "hit with a $180 million lawsuit" (Dillon 2016:n.p.) over business dealings with Hillair Capital Management, a business partner involved with distributing the sisters' makeup line. The Hillair Company claimed breach of contract and fraud, saying the Kardashians did not hold up their end of the business deal because they did not promote the products (Dillon 2016). We could go down a rabbit hole of Kardashian-involved lawsuits, but I mention them here to illustrate how the word *private* is used in *private disputes*. While the Kardashians are very public figures and these lawsuits are playing out in the courts, which are public and governmental, the disputes themselves are still private because they involve privately-owned business entities.

Public-Initiated Disputes

Public-initiated disputes are brought about by the government itself. When the government seeks to uphold the law, or punish those who break the law, it takes part in a public-initiated dispute. The most common form of public-initiated disputes are criminal cases where the defendant is charged with breaking the law of the state, or the nation-state—federal laws—and the government brings that person to the attention of the court in a criminal trial. In a criminal trial, there may be an individual victim, for instance, a person who was robbed, but the case is brought on behalf of all citizens of the governing body—the public. For example, the famous O. J. Simpson trial in 1995 was known as *The People v. O. J. Simpson* because the entire state of California was represented. Simpson was accused of killing two people, but the crime was an offense against the community as a whole. Similarly, criminal law cases in Massachusetts are called "*The Commonwealth of Massachusetts v. Defendant X.*" Cases are argued by a **prosecutor** who works on behalf of the state of Massachusetts. A **prosecutor** is any individual lawyer who is hired to represent the interests of the state against a criminal defendant. At the level of state governance, there are district attorneys (DAs), assistant district attorneys (ADAs), and the attorney general (AG), who leads all state prosecutors as the chief legal officer. At the federal level, the United States attorney general (AG) is the top legal officer of the country. He or she heads the U. S. Department of Justice and holds legal authority over all U.S. attorneys general (Falcone 2005).

Public Defendant Disputes

In contrast, **public defendant disputes** involve a public, governmental entity as the defendant—the party being sued—in the trial. The civil rights movement's challenge to the separate but equal protection guarantee is one of the most famous of such cases in U.S. history. In the 1954 case *Brown v. the Board of Education of Topeka*, a group of citizens of Topeka, Kansas, sued the city's government over its segregated school system. They argued that racially segregated schools violated the Equal Protection Clause of the Fourteenth Amendment of the U.S. Constitution. The **plaintiffs**—the people who brought the complaint to the court—were 13 parents of 20 children. The parents worked together as a group in the **class action suit**. A **class action lawsuit** is a case brought to the court in the name of a group of people who share some grievance (Falcone 2005). Oliver Brown stood as the representative plaintiff in the *Brown v. Board* suit, therefore, his name will always be associated with the case. However, his name stood for, or represented, all of the plaintiffs.

CASE IN POINT

A Public Defendant Dispute on Behalf of Lowell, MA Teens

An example of a public defendant dispute in the state of Massachusetts highlights the types of trials that fall under the category of the government itself as the defendant. The Massachusetts Supreme Judicial Court, the state's highest court, threw out a juvenile curfew enacted by the city of Lowell in 1994. On **Friday, September 25, 2009,** the State Supreme Judicial Court ruled that a curfew on teenagers in Lowell violated both the U.S. Constitution and the Constitution of the Commonwealth of Massachusetts because it imposed potential criminal penalties on teens who had not committed any crime. Such arrests are known as **status offenses** and typically apply to juvenile offenders. Status offenses permit the arrest of youthful offenders for a wide range of behaviors that do not apply to adult offenders, such as running away from home, being a minor in need of supervision, being "incorrigible" or beyond parental control, and breaking a curfew (Chesney-Lind and Pasko 2013).

The Lowell case involved two teenagers who were arrested after midnight in 2004 because they were on the streets in violation of the city's "Youth Protection Curfew for Minors," which required everyone under the age of 18 to be home by 11:00 p.m. One teen was a 16-year-old boy from Somerville who was arrested at 12:15 a.m. while "attempting to visit a girl who lived in Lowell" (Saltzman 2009). The other teen was arrested when police broke up a group of young people after midnight; the boy could not run as fast as his friends who escaped.

The Massachusetts Supreme Judicial Court agreed that communities have a right to try to curb youth violence, but said they also need to be attentive to teenagers' rights. Their ruling stated:

> We conclude that the curfew itself is narrowly tailored to achieve its purposes. However, the criminal processes and punishments

provided in the ordinance for curfew violations are not the least restrictive means of accomplishing those purposes, and contradict well-established goals of rehabilitating, not incarcerating, juvenile offenders. Consequently, they are not sufficiently tailored to meet the strict scrutiny standard. (Saltzman 2009)

Therefore, you can fight City Hall in some cases—namely in public defendant cases.

Organization of the Courts

The American court system is a **dual hierarchical system**. Dual means that it includes both: (1) the state system and (2) the federal system. Hierarchical means it is ranked by importance. The courts system is ranked by whether or not the matter can be settled to the satisfaction of the parties involved in the legal matter. If a case is not settled in a state trial court, it will move up through the appeals process to a higher court. For example, the curfew case in Lowell, Massachusetts, began in a state trial court: it moved to an intermediate court of appeals and then to the Massachusetts State Judicial Supreme Court, where it was settled in favor of the teen plaintiffs. If it had not been settled to the plaintiffs' satisfaction at the State Supreme Judicial Court, it could have moved onto the second and higher court hierarchy: the U.S. District of Appeals. Therefore, the dual hierarchical system includes the 50 separate state court systems and the federal courts.

State Judicial Systems

No two state court systems are alike; each is made up of laws, procedures, and structures that have developed to accommodate the needs of each state as it was founded and expanded over time. However, some generalizations can be made. Most state systems have trial courts, intermediate courts of appeal, and state-level supreme judicial courts (Figure 4.2).

TRIAL COURTS	INTERMEDIATE COURT OF APPEALS	STATE SUPREME COURT
◆ Where most civil and criminal cases are originally heard, often before a jury ◆ Also called district courts	◆ The next level—if the loser in the trial case wishes to appeal, this is the next step ◆ Reviews cases from the trial courts	◆ The court of last resort at the state level ◆ Reviews the cases decided by the intermediate appeals courts

Figure 4.2 Typical State Court System

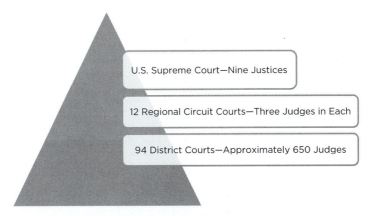

U.S. Supreme Court—Nine Justices

12 Regional Circuit Courts—Three Judges in Each

94 District Courts—Approximately 650 Judges

Figure 4.3 The Federal Court System Hierarchy

Federal Judicial System

The federal judicial system deals with questions involving the U.S. Constitution, such as free speech issues or religious freedom, as well as federal laws such as those dealing with racial and sexual discrimination. These are considered issues of national importance that exist beyond state boundaries. Federal district courts carry out most of the workload of the federal court system. At least one federal district court exists in every state and larger or more populous states are subdivided into several district courts. There are 94 district courts and approximately 650 district court judges (Vago 2012) (Figure 4.3).

The number of judges and case filings in the federal system can range from two district court judges with a caseload of approximately 600 cases, as in Vermont, to 28 district court judges with a caseload of over 11,000 cases, as in the state of New York (Vago 2012). Juries are used in approximately half of the 1 million or so civil and criminal cases decided by these lower federal courts. Based on the needs of the various courts, new court of appeals and district court judgeships can be created by legislation that must be enacted by Congress. New judgeships are based upon the number of court filings in a judgeship and other factors such as geography and the types of cases (http://www.uscourts.gov/faqs-federal-judges).

Circuit court judges, at the next level of the federal hierarchy, review decisions made in their districts. They are also empowered to review the decisions of federal regulatory agencies, such as the Federal Trade Commission or the Food and Drug Administration.

A typical court case begins with a trial court in the state court system. Most cases do not move beyond this initial level. However, some people, are not satisfied with the court's decision, this is where the appeal process begins (Figure 4.4).

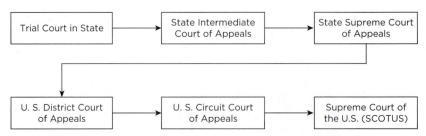

Figure 4.4 The Flow of Appeals in the Dual Hierarchical System

An appeal can take two forms; the first is a trial *de novo*, Latin for "as new." A trial *de novo* occurs when a case is heard for a second time as if it had not appeared before a court previously. A defendant can insist that a case be heard in a superior court when he or she was not satisfied with the verdict (Falcone 2005). The new trial "does not constitute an appeal, as there is no record to hand up to the appellate court .... Further, it does not constitute double jeopardy" (Falcone 2005:71). The second type of appeal is a more limited review of specific aspects of the previous proceedings. States have only one appellate court, the state's Supreme Judicial Court. State Supreme Court justices render final verdicts on all cases involving state law, both civil and criminal. The United States Supreme Court renders the final verdict on all matters involving federal law, as stated in the Constitution. In the lower courts, the burden of taking up the appeal process falls on the losing party. An appellate court's function is to correct errors made in the trial courts (Figure 4.5).

Trial Courts	Appellate Courts
Enforce laws on a case-by-case basis by applying relevant legal rules to the facts of the case	The party that loses at trial has the right to appeal the trial court's decision in appellate court
Handle both civil and criminal cases; in a civil case, the plaintiff's lawyer initiates the action; in a criminal case, a prosecutor begins the court action against a defendant	Composed solely of judges who base their decisions on the record of the trial court—do not consider new facts; they determine whether the law was applied correctly in the trial court
Focus on facts of the case—witnesses, documents, evidence	Focus on questions of law and procedures—rules of evidence, jury instruction; concerned with the boundaries of legal rules Decisions are published and become references for trial judges and lawyers

Figure 4.5 Two Types of Courts: Trial and Appellate

Another way to think about the court system is through the lower courts and higher courts. That system is illustrated in (Figure 4.6.)

In the lower courts, the burden of appealing a decision falls on the losing party. Once a case reaches the level of appeals, the appellate courts seek to correct errors in law at the trial court level, such as issues of evidence, procedure, judge's instruction, and other matters regarding how the trial was conducted. The higher courts do not retry cases or hear new evidence or cases, they decide on the legality of cases already adjudicated in the lower courts.

Participants in Court Processes

Many people work in the court system. Bailiffs are law enforcement agents who maintain peace and security within the courtrooms. Court reporters record the court proceedings, law or court clerks help the judge administer the duties of the court. Court commissioners are appointed professionals who have some of the same duties and powers of judges but who work on smaller, less important cases, in small claims courts. All of these personnel are support players in the theater of justice. The key roles in the courtroom are played by litigants, lawyers, judges, and members of juries.

Litigants

Litigants are the disputants—the people involved in the legal conflict. These can be individuals, organizations, government agencies, and other groups. According to legal scholar Marc Galanter, there are two general categories of litigants: (1) "one-shotters" who typically only enter into legal proceedings once in their lives, and (2) repeat players who use the courts

Lower Courts (a.k.a. Inferior Courts)	Higher Courts (a.k.a. Superior Courts)
Includes both civil and criminal courts and other specialized areas, e.g., family courts	Includes states' Supreme Courts and the Supreme Court system (including the district and circuit courts) as well as the highest court of the land and the final court of appeals—the Supreme Court of the United States
Also probate courts dealing with distribution of property, e.g., contested wills	
County and municipal courts, e.g., traffic courts	
Small claims courts usually for some set amount, e.g., $10,000 or less	All higher courts serve some appellate function

Figure 4.6 Lower and Higher Courts

often. Repeat players are usually companies that utilize the legal system as a matter of business, such as collection agencies, finance companies, and insurance agencies (Galanter 1974).

Lawyers

Ideally, lawyers are highly trained professionals who turn complaints into legal disputes. We will be looking at this group of professionals in more detail in Chapter 9: Gate-Keeping and the Law: The Legal Profession, so this section provides a brief overview of the roles that lawyers play in the organization of law. The majority of time, most lawyers work on nontrial activities—routine transactions that take place outside of court—such as filing legal papers and drafting and reviewing documents. Even some very highly paid lawyers in reputable firms rarely argue cases in courts of law. Those who specialize in arguing cases before judges and juries are known as trial lawyers.

"Save my seat."

Source: Trevor Spaulding/CartoonStock.com

Types of Trial Lawyers

Trial lawyers can be placed into different categories based on the work they do. There are representatives of particular interests, such as lawyers for a private business entity. There are also advocates for various issues, such as civil rights lawyers, consumer rights advocates, and environmental lawyers. Some trial lawyers represent specific private interests. Criminal defense attorneys are trial lawyers who specialize in specific types of cases, namely criminal cases. Criminal lawyers work for the defendants in criminal trials. Other lawyers serve individual clients who hire them for a particular purpose; they serve a case, not a business or a cause. They work in private practice and are hired on a case-by-case basis. They may specialize in a specific area of law, or they may be generalists who hang a sign in a small town square and serve whoever walks through their door.

Thus, most trial lawyers specialize in an area of law, such as environmental law, family law, or labor law. Others take on only particular clients, such as those in certain industries. Others work as in-house counsel for corporations, such as General Electric or Proctor and Gamble. Some lawyers are interested in activism—in attempting to bring about small or even widespread changes in the environment, housing, marriage law, or civil rights. Groups such as Neighborhood Legal Aid, Trial Lawyers for Public Justice, or the Southern Poverty Law Center work to bring about change for the public good.

Judges

Judges enjoy a lot of status and prestige in American society. They have reached a high point in their chosen profession; they determine the outcomes of important legal matters. Citizens assume that judges are honest, impartial, and "sober as a judge." Judges interpret the rules that govern the court proceedings; they provide instructions to the jury in a trial. While judges do not determine which cases make it to the court, they do run their courts—they appoint assistants and clerks, and administrate their courtrooms. They also hold pretrial conferences. Judges are typically highly educated professionals with middle- to upper-class backgrounds. In the United States, most judges start out as lawyers and work their way up the ladder to become judges. Relatively few lawyers do this.

State and Local Judges

State and local judges are chosen by a variety of methods: some are elected, some are appointed, and some are seated in a combination of both. For instance, in Pennsylvania and 38 other states, judges are elected to office. Pennsylvania judges serve 10-year terms; other states set terms anywhere from 6 to 15 years. Running for election to a judgeship is costly and time-consuming. Would-be judges must purchase advertising, hire consultants, meet with voters, and generally act as politicians running for election or reelection. Due to the money required to run such a campaign, the potential for corruption is great. Indeed, retired U. S. Supreme Court Justice Sandra Day O'Connor warned that judges running for election in political campaigns pose "a crisis of confidence in the impartiality of the judiciary .... Left unaddressed, the perception [that] justice is for sale will undermine the rule of law that courts are supposed to uphold" (Ecenbarger 2012:30). Best-selling novelist John Grisham dramatized just such a scenario in his 2008 novel *The Appeal*. The book offers a fictionalized account of the corruption of the judicial election campaign of Grisham's friend, Oliver Diaz. Diaz was a Mississippi Supreme Court Justice who won his seat on the court even though his opponent spent millions of dollars on advertisements opposing him and fouling his reputation. Because he was viewed as ruling against large corporations and in favor of protecting Mississippi citizens, he was vilified by large business interests in his state.

In the novel, a judge who received millions in campaign donations from corporate donors must decide on liability issues concerning just such business interests. He rules in favor of many big businesses until a tragedy strikes his own family, and he realizes that civil actions can and do protect consumers from unsafe products. While his personal tragedy gives him pause over his judicial ways, in the key case of the novel he ends up siding again with a big business—a multinational chemical manufacturer. After taking their money to fund his campaign, he is too indebted to them to turn back (Grisham 2008).

While Grisham presents a fictionalized version of the corruption that can come about from judicial campaigns, he is not far off the mark from what actually occurs. In the nonfiction book *Kids for Cash* author William Ecenbarger relays the true story of powerful Pennsylvania juvenile court judges who were influenced by money and special interests. The judges sentenced juvenile offenders to residential detention just so they could receive kickbacks from the private business entities that built the center in which the children were being locked up. As Ecenbarger states, "There is no perfect way to choose the men and women who preside over courts, but election is one of the worst. In an arena where integrity and independence are paramount, candidates are subjected to the corrupting influence of cash campaign contributions" (2012:30).

Some judges earn their seats on the bench by a combination of appointment and election. In some states, judges are initially appointed but then must run for office after their first term. For example, in California, the governor appoints judges to the State Supreme Court, and they serve an initial 12-year term (Vago 2012). Thereafter, they must run for re-election. In Oklahoma, state judges are selected through a nominating commission for an initial one-year term of office, but then must mount a retention election for a six-year term (Vago 2012).

Federal Court Judges

In accordance with the U.S. Constitution, Supreme Court Justices are nominated by the president, confirmed by the U.S. Senate, and appointed for life (http://www.uscourts.gov/faqs-federal-judges). Justices can only be removed by impeachment or conviction of a major crime. Typically, they retire of their own volition. Since the Supreme Court of the United States (SCOTUS) convened in 1790, only one justice has been impeached. In 1804 Associate Justice Samuel Chase was impeached by the House of Representatives due to what were seen as politically motivated charges. However, he was not removed from the bench because the Senate acquitted him. He served on the court until his death in 1811 (Nix 2016).

As with Supreme Court Justices, Court of Appeals Judges and District Court Judges are nominated by the president and confirmed by the Senate. The names of potential federal judges often come from members of the House of Representatives; usually recommendations are from members of the same political party as the president.

Juries

The jury system dates to AD 725 when it was established by the Welsh King Morgan GlaMorgan (Vago 2012). The jury system is part of the English common law tradition as carried down from Anglo Saxon and Norman conquerors. "Juror" means to tell the truth under oath (Falcone 2005:133). A jury is a group of citizens selected "according to the law and sworn to hear evidence in a trial and to render a decision based on the evidence presented" (Falcone 2005:133).

Before the twelfth century, both criminal and civil disputes were resolved by ordeal (Vago 2012). Trial by ordeal was an ancient practice that involved determining guilt or innocence by putting the accused through some type of unpleasant, painful, or dangerous experience. The ordeal could take many forms, such as:

- Ordeal by Water: If the accused sank, he or she was declared innocent (and sometimes dead); floating meant guilt (and sometimes a later death)
- Ordeal by Fire: The accused was forced to carry heated stones, for instance, or irons were placed on the skin; if the area was not infected within three days the accused was declared innocent

- Ordeal by Ingestion: the accused was forced to eat a poisonous substance; if he or she vomited, innocence was assumed; if the accused died, guilt was determined.

The jury system gradually replaced trials by ordeal in England, and other parts of Europe, and was part of the British colonization of what is now the United States. In 1607 the right to a jury trial was written into the U.S. Constitution. Juries are used in approximately half of the criminal and civil cases in the United States. Most civil cases are decided before the case goes to trial through some type of settlement. Some civil cases reach a settlement *after* a jury is empaneled, but *before* the jury hears the case—the seated jury acts as a chip in the bargaining process for the plaintiff's lawyers. As we will discuss in Chapter 7: Law and Dispute Processing, a **settlement** is a formal resolution of a legal dispute that occurs without the matter going before a judge or jury.

Legalese:

Empanelment is the process of selecting people to sit on a jury. A venireperson is the title for an empaneled juror (Falcone 2005).

How are juries selected by the court system? As with many topics we have discussed in this chapter, the answer to that question varies by state. Typically, potential jurors' names are placed on a master list of all prospective jurors; most states start with voter registration lists. A selection of names from the list is summoned to report to court at a certain date and time. These people constitute a jury pool and a selection from that group is chosen to serve on the jury. Ideally, the outcome constitutes a jury of one's peers, but many people never end up on juries.

Approximately 32 million people are called to jury duty annually, but only 8 million actually report for their civic duty (Martin 2015). Where do the rest go? Some attrition is due to the fact that the jurors' summonses are returned to the post office as "undeliverable"—accounting for about 4 million lost jurors (Martin 2015). Another 3 million potential jurors are excused because of financial or medical hardship (Martin 2015), others are excused because they are responsible for young children. Many would-be jurors show up and are later dismissed without being empaneled. Many—at least 3 million—simply fail to show up (Martin 2015).

What can be done about people who shirk their civic duty? The state of Massachusetts offers examples of some approaches to the problem of jury duty shirkers. In the past few decades, Massachusetts has been working to bolster jury participation among all of its citizens—to ensure that juries are more representative of the entire community (Saltzman 2004). One approach could be seen as a hard-line tactic: the state charges the worst offenders with criminal charges under its Delinquent Juror Prosecution Program (Saltzman 2004). If people fail to comply with juror summonses, they are issued a series of warnings. If they still ignore their call to serve, they are labeled jury delinquents and ordered to court to face criminal charges (Saltzman 2004). This "get tough" approach brought the state's jury delinquency rate down to approximately 6 percent, which, when compared to other states is very low—some states run as high as 40 percent (Saltzman 2004).

The urban poor are underrepresented on juries for several reasons: they cannot afford to miss work, they lack transportation to the court, the summonses never reach them because they tend to move often, they are homeless, they do not have an address, or they do not register to vote. Wealthier people find ways around serving on juries, and postponements are allowed. There are also permanent or long-term excusals in most jurisdictions for people over the age 70, for women and men in the daily care of children under the age of 12, for active lawyers, and for people who are teachers or supervisors at a school. Most fire and police personnel are also excused (Vago 2012).

Overall, approximately 1.5 million U.S. citizens are selected to serve on juries every year (Martin 2015). The length of jury service varies from state to state. Jurors can be called to sit on either petit or grand juries. A petit jury is a typical 12-person jury of one's peers. A grand jury is a group of 12 to 24 citizens empaneled to determine whether the government has enough evidence to indict a person—to bring a criminal defendant to trial (Falcone 2005) (Figure 4.7).

Criminal trials tend to use juries more often than civil cases, and juries must be utilized in all death penalty cases. In the 31 states that currently allow the death penalty, as well as in federal capital cases, no person can be convicted of a capital crime *except* by a unanimous verdict of a 12-member jury. A **death qualified jury** is a jury whose members have been questioned

Petit (regular) Jury	Grand Jury
• Six to 12 people who hear evidence, witnesses, etc., presented by both sides at trial • Civil or criminal cases • Determine facts in the dispute and make a decision	• Twelve to 24 people (varies by state, is sometimes 23) who consider the prosecutor's evidence • Criminal cases • Determine whether sufficient evidence exists to indict a person accused of a crime

Figure 4.7 Types of Juries

on their ability to determine guilt or innocence in a case that could result in the death of the accused. As a jury expert explains:

> Death qualification is a process unique to capital trials in which **venireper-sons** (prospective jurors) are questioned about their beliefs regarding the death penalty. In order to be eligible for capital jury service, a potential juror must be able and willing to consider both legal penalties (i.e., death or life in prison without the possibility of parole) as appropriate forms of punishment. A person who meets the ... standard is deemed "death-qualified" and is eligible for capital jury service; a person who does not ... is deemed "excludable" and is barred from hearing a death-penalty case (Butler 2008:1).

Voir dire is the jury selection process. *Voir dire* is French for "to see; to tell." Prospective jurors are questioned by the judge, and by the attorneys representing the defense and the prosecution in criminal cases, or by the opposing lawyers in civil cases.

"Your Honor, it would be a hardship for me to sit on a long, non-celebrity trial."

Source: Mike Twohy, New Yorker/CartoonStock.com

For the attorneys involved, *voir dire* can make or break a case, and several goals guide the process. Attorneys want to determine whether prospective jurors meet the minimum qualifications to sit as jurors, such as age and residency requirements. They also try to establish the impartiality of prospective jurors. This process involves obtaining sufficient information on prospective jurors to enable the attorneys to exclude any who may be prejudiced or biased against the defendant (Vago 2102). Two tools that lawyers use in the *voir dire* process are **peremptory challenges** and **challenges for cause**. **Peremptory challenges** are exclusions of potential jurors that a lawyer thinks will be unsympathetic to their arguments. In peremptory challenges, no explanation is needed for the exclusion; the lawyer simply asks that the potential juror be excluded and the judge excuses the person (Office of Jury Commissioner, Commonwealth of Massachusetts 1998:H-8). Each side has a fixed number of peremptory challenges, but usually the defense has more.

In the book *A Civil Action,* Jonathan Harr describes the use of peremptory challenges in the *voir dire* process for a civil trial in which two large corporations, W. R. Grace and Beatrice Foods, were sued by a group of parents whose children suffered from various illnesses, including leukemia. The cause of these illnesses was believed to have been chemicals that leached into the town's groundwater from the properties of the two corporations. The lawyer for the plaintiffs wanted some mothers of young children on the jury—he thought they could not help but sympathize with his side. The lawyers for the two corporations wanted no one of the sort—they preferred people who were not parents and who were not biased against big business. The *voir dire* process carried on for days as each prospective juror was questioned by the judge, the lawyer for the plaintiff, and the teams of lawyers for the two corporations. Harr writes:

> On a good day the judge would question as many as eighteen prospective jurors. Some days he got through only ten. By the fifth day Facher and Cheeseman [lawyers for W. R. Grace and Beatrice] had used all of their peremptory challenges, all but one on women with children. Schlichtmann [lawyer for the plaintiff], too, had used all of his, all on men—accountants, engineers, bankers. Then, on the sixth day, Schlichtmann had a scare. Into the judge's chambers came a man who manufactured chemical reagents for medical labs. The chemist said he had followed reports of the Woburn case in the professional journals with great interest. "I don't think they'll be able to prove that the materials these two companies disposed of caused leukemia." The judge thanked the man for speaking forthrightly and excused him. Then he looked at Schlichtmann and chuckled. "Having that fellow and no peremptories left?" Schlichtmann smiled gamely. "I was naked to the world." (Harr 1995:283).

The *voir dire* process in this complicated case took six days. Seventy-nine jurors were questioned, six were chosen plus six alternates.

Challenges for cause are used to keep potentially biased jurors off the jury. Challenges for cause are specific—a clear reason for the challenge must be given: the potential juror is related to the defendant, the person has been a victim of a similar crime, or he or she has read extensively about the case. Challenges for cause are unlimited, but a reason for the objection must be given (Adler et al. 1998). Jurors should be unbiased—even indifferent—to a case before deliberations begin. If they answer a question in a manner that seems biased, the lawyers for either side may ask for their excusal using a **challenge (or an excusal) for cause** (Office of Jury Commissioner, The Commonwealth of Massachusetts 1998:H-8).

Increasingly, trial lawyers have another tool in their toolboxes, especially in high-stakes, high-profile cases. That tool is **scientific jury selection**. Scientific jury selection has been around since the early 1970s but is growing in popularity. Scientific jury selection involves the use of paid experts, usually psychologists or social psychologists, to replace guessing, gut reactions, and lawyers' intuition. The goal of scientific jury selection is to attempt to make jury selection processes more predictable.

Scientific jury selection typically consists of three steps. First, consultants draw a random sample from the population, and a demographic profile of that sample is compared to that of prospective jurors. If there is over- or under-representation of any one group in the potential jury pool, the pool could be challenged. Second, after the consultants establish that the jurors represent the population at large, a random sample is drawn from the pool to determine the demographic, attitudinal, and personal characteristics considered to be favorable to whatever side is paying the jury selection consultants (Lieberman and Sales 2007). Finally, once consultants compose a psychological and demographic profile of a "favorable" juror, the social scientist can make recommendations to the client—either the lawyers for the defense or the prosecution (Lieberman and Sales 2007).

An even more elaborate technique used by scientific jury selection experts is the **shadow jury**. Lawyers use a shadow jury to gain feedback on how to try their cases. Shadow juries are attempted matches of the actual jury—people of the same gender, race, age, and income level are matched to each real juror in an attempt to predict the outcome of the trial and change course when needed (Lieberman and Sales 2007). Shadow jurors sit in on the actual trial and see and hear all the same information as the real jurors. They provide critiques of the trial as the proceedings unfold, giving feedback to the lawyers who hired them on their performances, the witnesses, and the evidence presented (Lieberman and Sales 2007). One of the largest scientific jury selection consulting firms, Courtroom Sciences, Inc. was founded in 1989 by Gary Dobbs and Dr. Phil McGraw, known on television as Dr. Phil. He is no longer associated with the firm, which has offices throughout the United States. Their slogan is "Positive Outcomes Are No Accident" (http://www.courtroomsciences.com/Home). However, the use of jury consultants such as Courtroom Sciences, Inc. has its critics. Opponents view these services as yet another way the wealthy can buy justice.

The jury system in the United States comes under attack because of various issues, such as the underrepresented groups who do not serve on juries, jury consulting firms that sway the jury one way or the other, and the concern that the average citizen cannot comprehend all of the potential evidence in complicated cases. The U.S. jury system does not seem to be going anywhere, because no serious alternatives have been considered to replace it. Juries are a basic component of the common law tradition.

LITIGATION IN THE COURT SYSTEMS

The processing of litigation differs for criminal and civil cases, and it differs in every case based on the machinations of the lawyers, prosecutors, judges, and juries involved. Some basic rules apply in the procedures of both civil and criminal cases.

Civil Cases

In civil cases, the plaintiff's attorney (or team of attorneys) brings the case to the court when he or she files the complaint. The plaintiff's attorney has some flexibility in choosing a court based on factors such as known biases of judges and convenience of location for the plaintiffs (Vago 2012). Bargaining and pretrial negotiations are common in civil courts. Pretrial conferences with judges may result in settlements. Only a small fraction of civil cases end up in court and even fewer of those ever reach a verdict. According to the American Bar Association:

> Relatively few lawsuits ever go through the full range of procedures and all the way to trial. Most civil cases are settled by mutual agreement between the parties. A dispute can be settled even before a suit is filed. Once a suit is filed, it can be settled before the trial begins, during the trial, while the jury is deliberating, or even after a verdict is rendered.
>
> A settlement doesn't usually state that anyone was right or wrong in the case, nor does it have to settle the whole case. Part of a dispute can be settled, with the remaining issues left to be resolved by the judge or jury. (https://www.americanbar.org/groups/public_education/resources/law_related_education_network/how_courts_work/cases_settling.html).

The point in civil cases is to settle—to avoid a trial altogether.

Criminal Cases

Anyone who had ever watched one of the thousands of episodes of *Law and Order* knows that criminal court proceedings can be unpredictable and rarely follow the same course of action. A full discussion of the criminal justice court system is beyond the scope of one section of one chapter of this book, so I will summarize a criminal court proceeding as briefly as possible.

Criminal litigation begins prior to court, when a crime is detected and brought to the attention of the police. Once an arrest is made, the case is made official and will enter into the court system. When a case reaches the court, the direction it takes depends on many factors. Sometimes charges are dropped and that is as far as the case goes. Whether the crime is a **misdemeanor**—a less serious transgression punishable by a fine or a year or less in jail—or a **felony**, which is a more serious offense subject to imprisonment for at least one year, determines the direction a trial can take. From there, other factors come into play, such as whether bail is set, whether plea bargaining occurs, or whether a defendant pleads guilty. The chart below illustrates the typical flow of a case through a criminal court (Figure 4.8).

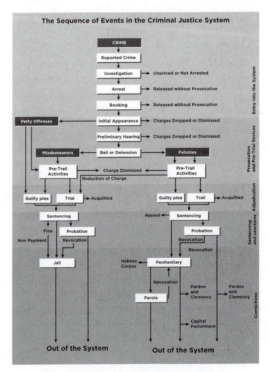

Figure 4.8 The Sequence Events in a Criminal Case

American Bar Association

As you can see from the diagram, multiple exits ramps are presented in the path of a criminal trial. If the case stays in the court system, the end of the adjudication process is sentencing.

LEGISLATURES

A **legislature** is a group of individuals elected as members of a formal law-making body as set forth by the state or federal constitutions. Legislatures are discussed in more detail in the next chapter, "Lawmaking and the Social Construction of Laws," thus this section provides a brief overview of the role of the legislature in the organization of law.

The main duty of legislatures is to make laws, but legislative bodies perform other functions as well. Ideally, legislatures attempt to resolve conflicts. Lawmaking is often contentious, and lawmakers are called upon to resolve, or at least manage, conflicts. The legislature of the United States is organized into two separate branches: the Senate and the House of Representatives (see Figure 4.9). The degree to which conflicts are resolved in Congress depends upon the makeup of these two branches. At present, it is difficult to point to a conflict that has been resolved in our legislature because we live in very partisan times. Republicans make up the majority in both the Senate and the House of Representatives; they rarely need to reach out to Democrats to get their laws passed. In other periods, these lawmaking bodies worked to resolve conflicts that arise in the lawmaking processes. Ideally, legislatures contribute to the cohesion or integration of the governing body by providing support for governmental systems. In the United States, the senate is authorized to make laws, but also to allocate funds, establish jurisdictions, and establish new administrative agencies (Figure 4.9).

As with any institution made up of individuals, the legislature follows both formal and informal codes of conduct. Political scientist Herbert Asher (1973) studied the Senate and the House and found that both bodies are influenced by both informal and formal rules. Informal rules include: newcomers serve a period of apprenticeship while learning their jobs, members become specialists in the work of the committees to which they are

Senate	House of Representatives
Two per state	Based on population of the state according to most recent Census data
Serve six-year terms representing the entire state	Serve two-year terms representing a district

Figure 4.9 The Branches of the U.S. Congress

assigned, members avoid ad hominem or personal attacks on each other, members reciprocate and compromise when possible (the conflict resolution function of lawmaking), and legislators do nothing that reflects poorly on the integrity of the legislative body as a whole (Asher 1973). Those are ideals, and are not always followed.

Three groups are important to the legislative process. Those groups are legislators, executives, and lobbyists. First are the **legislators**, the lawmakers—the senators and members of the House of Representatives. But who are they demographically speaking? Members of the 114th U. S. Congress share certain demographic characteristics:

- Male – 80%
- Middle- to upper-middle class
- Average age of 50
- Married
- Well educated
- White – 80%
- Christian – 92% (and most of those are Protestant)
- From professional and/or business backgrounds
- Over half of the members of Congress are lawyers (Bump 2015).

Our lawmakers are not exactly a cross-section of the U.S. population.

The second important group in the legislature is the **executives**: state governors and the U.S. President. They provide three main functions to the legislative branches of their respective governments. They serve as a source of ideas for the legislatures, and they make recommendations on what needs to reach the legislators. Executives function as catalysts; they strive to bring about support for their programs. They also officially enact new laws by signing bills into law and making public policy (Vago 2012).

Lobbyists comprise the third important group in the legislative process. Lobbyists are individuals and organizations that attempt to influence political decisions. They represent special interest groups. In general, who and what are these special interests? For the most part, lobbyists represent large business interests or professional groups, such as the health insurance industry as well as private health insurance companies, the American Medical Association, and the National Rifle Association. Some lobbyists represent causes, such as the League of Women Voters or Mothers Against Drunk Driving. Lobbyists are paid professionals who seek to influence the legislative process in favor of their clients—businesses, entire industries, or Political Action Committees. There are approximately 15,000 registered lobbyists in the District of Columbia, including many former members of Congress (Vago 2012). Lobbyists basically buy access to and influence over the legislative process.

ADMINISTRATIVE AGENCIES

Administrative agencies are sometimes referred to as the fourth branch of the government. In comparison to the legislature, administrative agencies have not been closely studied by social scientists, so we know less about how they operate. Generally speaking, these agencies perform social control functions through policies and regulations. In the twentieth and early twenty-first centuries—at the local, state, and federal levels—administrative agencies have grown in both the numbers of new agencies and the size of their bureaucratic structures.

The organization of administrative agencies varies by agency, but they are typically large bureaucracies. **Bureaucracy** is a term developed by Max Weber to denote a advanced formal organization in which power and tasks are distributed into a hierarchy based on a complex division of labor (Weber [1922] 1958). Further, "written records are kept and managers specialize in overseeing the system.... The accomplishments of organizational goals take precedent over the welfare of individual ..." (Johnson 2000:125). Some examples of administrative agencies are: the Environmental Protection Agency (EPA), the Occupational Safety and Health Administration, the Federal Communications Commission, and the Social Security Administration. Some agencies are called bureaus, departments, commissions, or offices. Most federal agencies have state counterparts; for instance, the Massachusetts Department of Environmental Protection is the EPA's state counterpart. At the federal level, all of these agencies are empowered by Congress, which created them under constitutional authority. This typically occurs when an issue or job is too big to be handled by the legislative branch. Therefore, they often emerge from a crisis.

The Administrative Process

Administrative agencies affect the rights and actions of individuals and organizations through investigation, rulemaking, and adjudication. They exercise control over individuals and, more often, over businesses and other organizations through their formal authority to regulate the specific areas they oversee.

Investigation

Investigation involves the gathering of information to regulate industry, prosecute fraud, collect taxes, or protect workers. Most administrations use formal and informal proceedings. The authority to investigate is one of the functions that distinguishes agencies from courts. Investigative power is conferred by Congress.

Rulemaking

Administrative agencies draw up rules and regulations to apply to the areas they oversee, such as worker safety regulations for the Occupational Safety and Health Administration (OSHA). The primary mission of these government agencies is to make rules or policies. These rules fall into three categories:

1. Procedural: outline the agency's organization, its methods of operation, and list the requirements of its practice for rulemaking and adjudicative hearings
2. Interpretive: issued by an agency (Vago 2012) to guide both staff and regulated parties on how the rules will be interpreted and carried out
3. Legislative: administrative statutes and written rules and regulations (Vago 2012) applied to the specific area within the administration's purview, for example, the EPA sets new coal emissions levels for the coal industry (Vago 2012).

The legislative statutes comprise the social control ability of administrations—the source of their control over individuals, businesses, or entire industries rests in their ability to make and enforce statutes.

Adjudication

Adjudication by administrative agencies occurs when administrations are called upon to settle disputes and mediate conflicts; it is akin to a trial in a criminal or civil case. As with civil cases, much of the business of administrations is handled informally, with settlements. When an issue goes to an administrative hearing, the parties must produce evidence, but the formal rules of evidence do not necessarily apply. In 1946, the Administrative Procedure Act was passed to permit a broader basis for judicial review of administrative decisions (Vago 2012). Courts can overturn decisions made by government agencies if the agency is found to have overextended its authority or misinterpreted the law. (Vago 2012).

LAW ENFORCEMENT AGENCIES

Police are the first step in the process of criminal law; they also protect the public and provide community service. **Police** are defined as:

> The governmental department, bureau, or agency of a city, township, county, or nation-state charged with the responsibilities of maintaining public order, preserving the peace, providing emergency services, preventing crime, detecting criminal activity, and enforcing the criminal law (Falcone 2005:197).

Police include local agencies, such as municipal departments in most townships in the United States. They include everything from Sheriffs' Departments at the county level to private police forces on college and university campuses. At the state level, state police agencies can range from Texas State Rangers to Massachusetts State Troopers, but all states have some form of state-level law enforcement agency.

Across the United States, local police agencies employ about 730,000 people; approximately 420,000 are sworn officers of the law (Schmalleger 2004). In addition to being one of the oldest police departments, the New York City Police Department (NYPD) makes up the largest municipal police agency in the country with over 54,000 full-time employees—approximately 36,000 of whom are sworn officers (http://www1.nyc.gov/site/nypd/about/about-nypd/about-nypd-landing.page). The NYPD is divided into bureaus for the purposes of enforcement, investigation, and administration, encompassing 77 patrol precincts covering the entire city, as well as 12 public transit districts policing the subway system. The NYPD also includes nine police service areas that cover the city's public housing developments (http://www1.nyc.gov/site/nypd/about/about-nypd/about-nypd-landing.page).

On the other end of the police department spectrum are rural and small-town departments that serve areas with low population density and, usually, lower crime rates. For instance, in Gaines Township, Michigan, one man, Mark Schmitzer, serves and protects all 7,000 citizens in a rural, agricultural community. He retired from a larger department in Flint, Michigan, but decided he was not done with police work. "One day you're an administrator, another day you're a detective, another day you're a patrolman here on patrol," says Schmitzer (Carlisle 2013:n.p.). While many small, rural communities rely on the state police, some, like Gaines Township, decide to keep a minimal police force to meet the community's needs. According to Brian Reaves of the Bureau of Justice Statistics, in 2013, municipal and township police departments comprised 98 percent of local police departments and employed an average of 2.1 full-time officers per 1,000 residents (2015:1). Approximately half of all municipal and small-town departments employ fewer than 10 officers (Reaves 2105:1). So small police departments are the norm, not the exception, in the United States (Figure 4.10).

In considering the police as the first point in the organization of law, an important feature of law enforcement is the discretionary power police officials use on the so-called "front lines," it is part of their daily routines. As Peter Moskos, author of *Cop in the Hood: My Year Policing Baltimore's Eastern District* (2008) noted, most police work is about common sense. Discretionary power is used to decide what violations, drug usage, or domestic disputes need attention. The use of discretion can take many

---

Federal Law Enforcement Agencies

Includes 34 different agencies from 11 government services spanning a wide range of departments. They are: (a) the Department of Agriculture (Enforcement Agency is the U.S. Forest Service), (b) the Department of Homeland Security (includes five different enforcement services, such as the Secret Service of the Bureau of Immigration and Customs Enforcement, and the U.S. Coast Guard, (c) the Department of Justice (enforcement agencies include the Federal Bureau of Investigation, the U.S. Marshals Service, and the Bureau of Prisons, to name a few), and (d) the U.S. Postal Service (Enforcement Agency is the Postal Inspection Service) (Schmalleger 2004:153).

State Law Enforcement Agencies

Includes State Police Departments, Fish and Wildlife Agencies, Highway Patrols, State Park Service Agents, State University Police, and Port Authorities.

County Level Law Enforcement Agencies

Includes sheriffs' departments—there are about 3,000 U.S. counties with sheriffs' departments, although some have been replaced or done away with because they were seen as redundant. Sheriffs' departments also operate local jails and oversee correctional officers. For example, the Los Angeles County Sheriff's Department oversees the L.A. County Jail System, the largest in the world (Schmalleger 2004:163). The L.A. County Jail System houses approximately 19,000 inmates in nine separate facilities and employs approximately 2,000 correctional officers and 1,200 civilians (Schmalleger 2004:163).

Cities, Townships, and Municipal Law Enforcement Agencies

City Police Departments, such as the NYPD or Town Police Departments, as well as Municipalities, such as Districts or Parishes (e.g., in the South and West).

Other

Villages, Boroughs, Ad Hoc Districts, Special-Purpose Forces;

Private Police Forces, such as campus police, mall police, and police that cover private residences (e.g., "gated communities") and businesses.

Figure 4.10 Hierarchy of Law Enforcement Agencies

forms, from investigation and confrontation to disposition and decisions about when to use force. As Moskos states:

In 1943, William Whyte was the first sociologist to describe what is now called police discretion. Building on Whyte and inspired by his time in the civil rights movement, the legal community documented the "problem" of police discretion in the 1960s and declared it illegal, immoral, and in violation of a democratic ethos. In 1967, Egon Bittner was the first to cast a positive light on police discretion, an underappreciated skill that allowed police to keep the peace on skid row. Law enforcement demands discretion. Every statute on the books cannot and should not be enforced. Departmental regulations say plenty about what police officers can and cannot do, but they offer little guidance as to *why* and *how* a situation should be handled. For this, officers rely on what they think is common sense, namely the law tempered by experience, the norms of their colleagues and the community, and potential for court overtime pay (2008:113–114; emphasis in original).

Police officers cannot do their jobs without some latitude and discretion. Moskos' book was written in 2008, and police discretion has come under increased scrutiny in the wake of several police shootings of unarmed black men and women in 2014, 2015, and 2016. The Black Lives Matter movement has led the charge to curtail police discretion and better train police on the use of force. Civil rights activists, such as those in the Black Lives Matter movement, members of the public, and criminologists and other academics offer suggestions for how to address police brutality against people of color, for example, civilian review committees that

Stephen Davies/Alamy Stock Photo

Protect and serve.

provide checks and balances from the public on controversial police actions. In 2016, Shaun King, a reporter for the *New York Daily News*, wrote a series called "Solutions for Police Brutality" in which he offers many potential ways to address police brutality, such as: diversifying police departments, decriminalizing addiction, requiring all police recruits to earn a four-year college degree before applying for police jobs, weeding out bad police and encouraging good police to speak up, and providing more training on deadly and non-deadly force (King 2016). Police cannot do their work without using discretion, but with better training and oversight discretion can be used as a positive tool and not a blunt instrument of force.

CHAPTER SUMMARY

◆ This chapter explored the organization of law including the courts, the legislatures, administrative agencies, and law enforcement agencies. Each plays an important role in how the law is carried out—how it is made visible and how it affects our daily lives.

◆ The courts process disputes, adjudicate cases, and render a final judgment in a dispute.

◆ There are three main types of disputes: private, public-initiated, and public defendant.

◆ Courts in the United States are arranged into a dual hierarchical system of state and federal courts. Cases that are not settled in the state courts may be brought to the federal system, which is made up of district courts, regional circuit courts, and the U.S. Supreme Court.

◆ There are many participants in the court system, including litigants, lawyers, judges, and juries.

◆ Litigation differs in civil cases and criminal cases, but in each, cases tend to follow a path through the court system.

◆ State and federal legislatures make new laws. They also allocate funds, establish jurisdictions, and support governmental systems.

◆ Administrative agencies make rules and regulations that apply to the areas that they oversee. They also investigate rule violations and can adjudicate cases.

◆ Law enforcement agencies are the first step in the process of criminal law—they are responsibly for upholding and enforcing the law at the level of the community.

KEY TERMS

adjudication   84
bureaucracy   105
challenges (excusal) for cause   99
class action suit   87
death qualified jury   97
defendant   84
disputes   84
dual hierarchical system   88
executives   104
felony   102
legislators   104
litigants   91
lobbyists   104

misdemeanor   102
peremptory challenges   99
plaintiffs   87
police   106
private disputes   85
prosecutor   86
public defendant disputes   86
public-initiated disputes   86
scientific jury selection   100
settlement   96
shadow jury   100
status offenses   87
venirepersons   98

CRITICAL THINKING QUESTIONS

1. Have you ever been called to serve on a jury? Did you actually serve? Why or why not? How do you think states could improve jury representation in your state?

2. Some legal scholars argue that the process of questioning potential jurors for a death-qualified jury brings bias into the process of deciding capital cases, since the potential jurors are asked whether or not they could decide on a death penalty case. People who are against the death penalty are automatically excluded from serving on capital juries. Do you agree that this process introduces a bias into a case? Can you think of a way to improve jury selection in capital cases?

3. Trial lawyers tend to specialize in specific areas of law, and new areas are emerging all the time. What are some recent areas that have developed in the last 5–10 years? Why are these new areas of law needed?

4. Some parts of the country, such as parts of New England, are rethinking the need for Sheriffs' Departments. Look into some of the arguments for and against dissolving sheriffs' offices. Which side do you agree with and why?

5. Do some additional reading of the suggestions by Shaun King on "Solutions for Police Brutality" in his series in the *New York Daily News* (2016). Select one of his solutions and make an argument on how and why it could work to reduce police brutality.

SUGGESTED MOVIE: *RUNAWAY JURY*

Runaway Jury, 2003. Gary Felder, Director.

Starring John Cusack, Rachel Weisz, Dustin Hoffman, and Gene Hackman, *Runaway Jury* resembles many big-budget, box office courtroom dramas *except* that it focuses on the jury and scientific jury selection. The film is a highly dramatized representation of how jury consulting firms can manipulate the jury from the selection process through to the final verdict. While the influence and methods of jury selection are greatly exaggerated throughout the film, *Runaway Jury* can prompt discussion of many of the key terms and topics covered in Chapter 4: The Organization of Law, such as: scientific jury selection, *voir dire*, peremptory challenges, and challenges for cause, empanelment, tort law, and the importance of a jury trial.

Discussion Questions for *Runaway Jury*

1. Have you been called to jury duty? Have you ever sat on a jury? What was the process like?

2. Before reading about scientific jury selection, did you know about this field? Do you think this new area of expertise is a positive development in our legal system? Why or why not?

3. The jury consultant, Fitch, states, "Trials are too important to be left up to juries." Do you agree or disagree? A perennial debate in this country is whether or not professional juries composed of specially trained citizens should be used instead of our current jury system. Using internet sources, look into this idea. Why do you think it has not gained much traction in the United States?

4. The fictitious film takes on one of the biggest debates of our time: whether gun companies should be held liable for their products. Why are gun manufacturers largely not held responsible for the harm guns cause? Are lawsuits such as the one depicted in the film a plausible way to approach the issue of gun violence? If not, why? (Note: This is a contentious issue, but we can remain civil even if we disagree.)

5

Lawmaking and the Social Construction of Laws

◆ ◆ ◆

TENS OF THOUSANDS OF LAWS ARE PASSED in the United States at every branch of government—executive, legislative, and judicial. The administrative arm of the government also crafts rules, regulations, and procedures that affect everything from the cars we drive to the food and drugs we ingest. Further, the various levels of government—municipal, state, and federal—also enact ordinances, rules, and laws. Taken together, the branches and levels of government churn out thousands of laws every year. This chapter focuses on the social construction of laws, lawmaking processes, and the social and cultural factors that affect lawmaking. As the sociologist Howard Becker said, "All social groups make rules and attempt, at some times and under certain circumstances, to enforce them. Social rules define situations and the kinds of behavior appropriate to them, specifying some actions as 'right' and forbidding others as 'wrong'" (1963:1).

In this chapter, we consider how social groups bring about new laws and who decides what is legally right or wrong.

Consider the following scenario: You are a woman on the subway, minding your own business. The weather is warm; you are wearing your favorite summer skirt. When you exit the subway car, a woman approaches you and asks if you realized that as you sat on the subway, a man was using his smartphone to take pictures up your skirt. She offers her own pictures as evidence. She had videotaped the man as he held his phone at an angle that pointed directly upward into your skirt. Stunned, you call the transit police and, with the help of the witness, you report this aberrant behavior. The police had received a previous report about similar behavior at the same time of the day and on the same subway route. They decide to conduct a sting operation. An undercover police officer—a female officer wearing a skirt—rides the same subway at the same time until she finds the man attempting to videotape up the skirt of another woman. The undercover officer arrests him. End of story, right?

A very similar scenario played out on a Massachusetts Bay Transportation Authority subway in 2012. And surprisingly, the arrest was not the end of this creepy story. It turns out that at the time of the arrest, there was no specific law against the behavior now known as "upskirting"—the clandestine taking of cellphone pictures or videos up a person's skirt. Massachusetts prohibits voyeurism, as do most states. A voyeur, also known as a "Peeping Tom," derives sexual pleasure from secretly observing the sex organs or sexual acts of other people. Criminal voyeurism statutes typically cover places in which people have a "reasonable expectation of privacy" (Grossman and Friedman 2014:1). The Massachusetts law covered *only* the photographing or videotaping of another person who is nude or in a state of undress, *and* in a place wherein the person has a reasonable expectation of privacy (Miller 2014). Therefore, in the Massachusetts case, the upskirter's lawyer was able to appeal his conviction to the Massachusetts Supreme Judicial Court (SJC), the highest court at the state level. His conviction was overturned. His actions on the subway did not fit the legal definition of voyeurism. The victim was not nude, nor partially nude, nor was she in a place where she had a reasonable expectation of privacy. As the defendant's lawyer argued, people are videotaped all the time in public and especially on public transit where transit authorities regularly use cameras to monitor riders and operators.

Istock/kasto80

Woman traveling on subway.

Wednesday 03/05/14 →	Thursday 03/06/14 →	Friday 03/07/14
MA Supreme Judicial Court Rules	MA State Legislature Passes	Governor Patrick Signs Bill
Against Voyeurism Law as	Bill Outlawing Upskirting	
Applied to "Upskirting"		Upskirting is Now
		Illegal in State of MA

Figure 5.1 Massachusetts Upskirting Law Timeline

However, the case did not end there. As Massachusetts State Senator William N. Brownsberger put it, "There was a sense of moral outrage that anybody might think that kind of behavior is OK" (Miller 2014:A11). The Massachusetts State Legislature acted quickly to pass a bill outlawing upskirting. In a matter of mere days (Figure 5.1), the state made upskirting a misdemeanor that could rise to the level of a felony if the photos or videos captured through upskirting were distributed (Miller 2014). The bill also "provides for enhanced penalties when the victim is a minor" (Grossman and Friedman 2014:4).

The Massachusetts House Bill settled matters of upskirting in Massachusetts, but other states are currently grappling with the same issue. In a Tennessee courtroom, another upskirter was set free because he took pictures in a mall—a public forum. In Washington State, a man took photographs up the skirts of young girls as they waited in line at a concession stand in a sporting arena. In this case, the Washington State Supreme Court decided "casual intrusions occur frequently ... in public" (Grossman and Friedman 2014:3). A similar ruling was reached regarding a case that took place at a county fairground in Virginia. The question of do we have the right to at least some level of privacy in a public space is by no means settled. Like many legal issues, this law varies from state to state. To further complicate matters, some states are asking: What about "downblousing" (photographing down a person's shirt)?!

The issue of upskirting brings to light several topics relevant to this chapter. As we discussed in Chapter 1, laws are socially constructed—they emerge through human interaction. They are created to address social problems. Governing bodies craft laws to protect citizens from harmful behavior. Harm can be physical, such as violence. Harm can also be emotional and psychological, such as an invasion of privacy. Harm does not simply apply to *individual* victims; harm can be *socially injurious*. Therefore, harm must be avoided or stopped through lawmaking. Laws prohibit injurious behavior. This is the assumption made by a **rationalistic approach to lawmaking**. The rationalistic model looks at how laws—mainly criminal laws—are created

Istock/ferrantraite

Voyeurs derive sexual pleasure from secretly observing others.

as rational, reasonable means of protecting people from harm. Crimes are socially, physically, and psychologically injurious and must be stopped. The rationalistic model is criticized as rather simplistic, since it fails to look at who makes the laws and why some actions are viewed as harmful in some places and time periods and others are not, such as gambling. Other practices that can be considered harmful are not against the law. For instance, avoiding taxes by hiding assets in offshore investments is perfectly legal and quite common among the very wealthy. The reasons for these differences in what is considered legal/harmless and illegal/harmful often revolve around money and power and who has access to legislative bodies.

Are laws simply a matter of prohibiting harm? Who decides what is harmful, and why are some detrimental behaviors not illegal? From a conflict perspective, as we discussed in Chapter 3, property laws are constructed to protect the dominant groups in society. Some groups and individuals are afforded more protection than others. A **conflict perspective on lawmaking** also asks: Why are some behaviors that people willingly engage in considered bad or harmful? Ever-shifting marijuana laws offer an example here. People choose to ingest marijuana and, as pro-marijuana advocates argue, they are not harming anyone, other than perhaps themselves, in the process. If marijuana users decide to drive or operate machinery while using, they are increasing the risk of harm to themselves and others. Why are marijuana sales and use prohibited in some states and not others, and why do laws pertaining to marijuana change from historical period to historical period? Laws prohibiting drug use will be addressed in more detail in Chapter 6: Law and Social Control. For the purposes of this chapter, laws vary from place to place and from time period to time period because laws are constructed to respond to ever-shifting social issues.

The case of upskirting also highlights the consensus notion of law. When Senator Brownsberger discussed a sense of outrage over upskirting, he spoke to a consensus over what "is OK" and what "is not OK" (Miller 2014:A11), as well as the outrage that an existing law did not properly prohibit this lewd behavior. This brings up TOBAL again—when bad behavior is detected, people say, "There Ought to Be a Law!" In this case, clearly, the transit police and state prosecutors thought there *was* a law—a voyeurism law. When that law did not suffice, state lawmakers stepped in to modify the law—to amend the preexisting voyeurism law to cover the behavior now known as upskirting. So sometimes, "There Ought to Be a *Better* Law!" becomes the rallying cry.

SOCIAL CONSTRUCTIONIST APPROACH TO LAWMAKING

The **social constructionist perspective** can help us to understand how certain behaviors under certain circumstances are made illegal. This perspective is also referred to as the social definitionist approach (Dello Buono 2004). And, to further complicate matters, this paradigm is sometimes called the moral entrepreneur approach (Becker 1963). I will use the term social constructionist perspective since that is the more common of the terms for this perspective. Social constructionism is an approach or set of approaches that views society and social knowledge as actively and creatively produced through human interaction (Berger and Luckmann 1966). From a constructionist perspective, social norms and laws exist because people have made them real through language and interaction, social conventions, habits, and etiquette.

In Chapter 3: Modernization and Theoretical Perspectives on Society and Law, we looked at two predominant sociological theories of law— functionalism and conflict approaches. Some contemporary sociologists argue that neither functionalism nor conflict perspective can explain "the subjective and interpretive aspects of social behavior" (Stout 2004:24). The development of the symbolic interactionist perspective in the 1930s and 1940s helped to address some of the gaps in sociological approaches to social problems. Symbolic interactionism views the social world as constantly created and recreated through the use of symbols: language, signs, and other cultural objects. Symbolic interactionism takes a micro-level view of society, examining how individuals and social groups make sense of the world around them through their interactions with others.

George Herbert Mead (1863–1931) is viewed as the founder of symbolic interactionism, although the term was not coined until after his death. Mead taught at the Chicago School—the Department of Sociology at the University of Chicago, which became so influential within the field of sociology in the first half of the twentieth century that it simply became known as "the Chicago School of sociology." Mead studied language, symbols, and shared meanings in social life. He also emphasized how people's positions or status shape their view of the world (Mead 1934).

Symbolic interactionism was not without its critics. Some argued that it was too myopic—that it could not be linked to the larger social forces of the political and economic order. Proponents of more macro-level approaches to society argued that symbolic interactionism is astructural, ahistorical, and noneconomic (Stout 2004:24-25).

Labeling theory is one approach to deviance and crime that grew out of the symbolic interactionist perspective and set the groundwork for the social constructionist approach to social problems. Emerging in the 1940s and 1950s, labeling theorists explored how and why some acts are defined as deviant while others are not and how and why some deviant acts are labeled as not simply *deviant*, but *criminal*. For labeling theorists, the *act* itself is not as significant as the *social reactions* to the act. Instead of seeing deviance and crime as unambiguous categories of behavior, labeling theorists posed new questions about why particular rules and laws exist in the first place, such as:

- What are the processes involved in identifying an act or a person as deviant or criminal?
- What are the consequences for individuals in applying a label to the act or the person?
- What are the societal consequences of the application of these labels?

Deviance is not the quality of the act itself; it is a consequence of the application of rules and labels to the act and the actor (Lemert 1951; Becker 1963). Edwin Lemert, a key theorist in the labeling paradigm, used the terms primary and secondary deviance to describe the labeling process. Primary deviance is the initial deviant acts that bring about some sort of societal response. Secondary deviance occurs when the person who has been labeled as deviant changes his or her self-concept based on the label (Lemert 1951).

Later social theorists, such as Stanley Cohen in his influential work, *Folk Devils and Moral Panics* (1972), developed the idea that secondary labeling can cause an amplification of the labeled behavior—an embracing of the label. Therefore, applying rules or laws to some individuals or groups may actually encourage the behavior that the laws are attempting to eliminate, a process known as amplification. Amplification can occur by constraining individuals who then actively use their deviant identity as a means of defense or an adjustment to their marginalized position. The label becomes their identity.

Social constructionism emerged by linking symbolic interactionism with more critical, conflict approaches in sociology. Social constructionism draws from labeling theory but broadens the scope of analysis. Instead of looking at how individual acts or people are labeled as deviant, constructionism explores how certain behaviors are constructed as illegal by people in positions of power. In this perspective the presence of an enterprising individual, group, or several groups can bring about new laws, or they can make changes to existing laws, as with the Massachusetts bill that amended voyeurism laws to include upskirting. A social constructionist perspective appeals to those interested in a critical approach to the study of society and law because it attempts to address the interconnections between and among power, social control, stratification, social movements, and the social organization of the law (Stout 2004).

Social constructionists call into question the objective, consensus notions of social problems and laws. For instance, in Chapter 1, we looked at underage drinking. An objective approach views young people consuming alcohol as fairly straightforward: it is bad for young people to drink alcohol, it is harmful to them, it is wrong, and it should be prohibited. Society agrees on these statements, so there is consensus around the issue. A constructionist perspective asks: Is there consensus? Whose morals are reflected in the law? Who benefits from the law? How did the government decide on the age of 21 as the threshold of responsible drinking? Despite existing laws in every state, these questions are not settled. Towns, states, and special interest groups continue to raise these questions. Illinois is considering a law that would allow people aged 18 or older to drink in restaurants if they have their parents' permission. Ten states already have similar laws: Connecticut, Kansas, Louisiana, Massachusetts, Mississippi, Nevada, Ohio, Texas, Wisconsin, and Wyoming. Further, some townships are now decriminalizing underage drinking. For instance, as of 2016, the town of Duxbury, Massachusetts, imposes fines on underage drinkers but does not arrest or criminally charge young people who are caught drinking alcohol in public.

Social constructionism looks at how some issues are labeled as social problems or crimes while others are not. Constructionism places issues within their social, cultural, and historical context. People working within a constructionist perspective study the role of claimsmakers in bringing attention to a particular issue in the social problems marketplace (Lowney and Best 1995). Thousands of social issues exist that could capture the public's attention, but not all succeed in doing so. Claimsmakers work to usher the social problem into the marketplace and draw attention, support, and resources to it.

The role of claimsmakers, sometimes referred to as moral entrepreneurs, in constructing social problems and laws to address social problems can be traced back to the work of Howard Becker, an American sociologist who in 1963 wrote the book *Outsiders*. In the book he looked at the development of criminal laws against marijuana. In 1937, the Narcotics Bureau defined marijuana as a social danger, and they used horror stories (Lowney and Best 2005), or what are also called atrocity tales, to build their case against marijuana. Becker noted that in 1930s Congressional Hearings, the Commissioner of Narcotics reported multiple crimes that were committed under the influence of marijuana, including a Florida mass murder (1963). These hearings led to the 1937 Marijuana Tax Act, which was intended to "stamp out the use of the drug" (Becker 1963) whose usage had also been linked to Mexican immigrants.

In a social constructionist study by Kathleen Lowney and Joel Best (1995) called "Stalking Friends and Lovers: Changing Media Typifications of a New Crime Problem," the authors look at a successful social problem construction that resulted in new laws against various types of problematic behavior that came to be defined as stalking. Unlike the swift response to upskirting in the state of Massachusetts, the legal changes against the behavior now known as stalking took place after a long and largely unsuccessful sequence of claimsmaking. Claimsmakers worked over several years to typify the social problem of stalking: to reframe, repackage, and offer new definitions in order for behaviors such as repeated following, harassing, unwanted calling on the telephone, and menacing to be defined as stalking and constructed as against the law. The behavior that we now legally define as stalking has been around for centuries. After all, Romeo stalked Juliet and Juliet stalked him right back. But Lowney and Best show that a social problem needs skilled claimsmakers to bring attention and resources to an issue and to remake harmful behavior into a crime. In social constructionism or moral entrepreneurship, one set of norms is viewed as better than others and emerges as the dominant one. Others that are perceived as outside the norm are degraded and often criminalized. In the next section of the chapter, I will use Lowney and Best's example of the social construction of stalking to illustrate how problematical behavior is constructed into illegal behavior. This analysis will help to answer the question of where new laws come from and who decides what is a crime.

LEGISLATION

As we saw in the previous chapter, **legislation** is the deliberate creation of legal precepts by a body of government that formalizes those legal precepts into written law. Legislation is separate from adjudication, which is the expression of legal rules by a judge or judges in the court system (Figure 5.2).

Legislation	Adjudication
Formulate laws	Process disputes
Modify existing laws	Decide specific cases
State rules	Set precedents

Figure 5.2 Legislation v. Adjudication

In general, legislators, or lawmakers, have more freedom to make significant changes and innovation in the law than do the courts. Courts are bound by legal precedent and principles. Legislatures are more responsive to public and private pressures than judges. Legislative lawmaking often represents a response to some kind of social problem—an issue that intrudes upon the well-being of a large number of individuals, organizations, or the well-being of the government itself. But an issue must first be defined as a problem and brought to the attention of the legislature.

The probability that some issue will be brought to the attention of a legislative body increases when special interest groups mobilize members. In the case of stalking, Hollywood actors emerged as a key powerful interest group when a young actor, Rebecca Schaeffer, was killed by a man who had repeatedly followed and attempted to contact her. This 1989 case galvanized the public and was followed by another headline-grabbing case: the attempted assassination in 1991 of President Ronald Reagan by John

Istock/MachineHeadz

Stalking was constructed as a criminal act in the 1980s.

Hinckley, who had previously stalked Jodie Foster. His attempt to kill the president was a bid to gain Foster's attention. These two celebrity stalking cases became typifying examples of the dangers of stalking. The disorganized public grew increasingly concerned with an issue that, as we learned, was not limited to celebrities. In the example of stalking, as in most cases of new laws being passed to address social problems, legislation is preceded by a series of prelaw-making stages that help to move the process along.

The Instigation and Publicizing Stage

At the instigation and publicizing stage, the mass media is a major player. News media outlets, such as all the major television stations, cable news, talk shows, and social media play a major role in getting the word out about a problem and, in many cases, stoking the public's anxiety or fear. Newspaper editorials are written. Senate investigative hearings are held. Books are published. Victims and survivors testify before Congress. Lifetime channel movies are produced. Senator Bob Krueger of Texas joined his wife, Kathleen Krueger, to bolster federal attention around stalking. Ms. Krueger experienced stalking and provided a victim's perspective to the national discussion on the issue. Further, the *Washington Post* reporter George Lardner won a Pulitzer Prize for a series he wrote on his daughter's murder by her stalker (Lowney and Best 1995). All of these events served to elevate stalking as an issue worthy of attention and solidified its place in the social problems marketplace.

Information-Gathering Stage

At the information-gathering stage, lawmakers collect data on the nature, significance, extent, and consequences of a problem. This stage often overlaps and is intertwined with the publicizing stage. In the stalking discussions, the figure of 200,000 stalkers nationwide was used by claimsmakers over and over again, but the origin of this statistic was not clear (Lowney and Best 1995). The point was to draw attention to an issue that could indeed affect you or someone you know. Lawmakers may also look at alternative approaches to solving the problem, or they may conduct a cost-benefit analysis on the effects of the problem and possible solutions. Lawmakers may even poll their constituents about the particular problem and their level of concern. The overall goal is to gather data on the issue and to put it to use in the formulation of new legislation.

Formulation Stage

In the formulation stage, legislators devise and put forth a specific definition of the problem and a legislative remedy for it. In 1990, due to the attention stalking received by the Screen Actors Guild and Hollywood in general,

California passed the nation's first anti-stalking law and the Los Angeles Police Department established a Threat Management Unit devoted to investigating stalking cases. By 1992, after national attention was drawn to the issue, several states followed California's example (Lowney and Best 1995). Today, every state in the United States has an antistalking law, and stalking has become part of the American legal and popular vernacular.

Interest Aggregation Stage

Interest aggregation is the process of bolstering the support of other legislators through cooperation and compromises. Proponents of the law mediate among groups in order to get their legislation heard. This stage can involve the bringing together of various special interest groups. In the stalking example, proponents of the new law worked with domestic violence advocates and the battered women's movement (Lowney and Best 1995). The interest aggregation gave stalking a wider domain of interest. This linkage helped establish stalking and move it along in state legislative proceedings. In Illinois, lawmakers "justified antistalking legislation by pointing to four recent cases of victims murdered by former husbands or boyfriends in Chicago suburbs" (Lowney and Best 1995:44). This stage connects and overlaps with the next stage of the process: the mobilization stage.

Mobilization Stage

In the mobilization stage legislators exert pressures, persuasions, or control on behalf of a measure by someone or some bodies who can take direct action to secure enactment. This might be someone with power within a particular policy area, such as then Senator William Cohen, Republican of Maine, who worked across the aisle with then U.S. Representative Joseph Kennedy II, Democrat of Massachusetts, to mobilize attention and resources around stalking. Special interest groups such as the National Victim Center and Victims for Victims, a group founded by stalking survivor and actress Theresa Saldana, also mobilized resources and lobbied in several states on behalf of new stalking laws (Lowney and Best 1995). Stalking became clearly linked to domestic violence, as a result advancing laws prohibiting the behavior.

Modification

In the modification stage, lawmakers alter the proposed law in a way that ensures it will be brought before the legislature and passed into law. The law may go through several drafts as the people who write the legislation try to ensure that whatever version makes it to the floor of the Senate passes. For instance, West Virginia's original stalking law only defined victims who had lived with or had intimate relations with their stalkers in the past. Since this definition excluded the types of cases that initiated the stalking debate in the first place, that is, people stalked by strangers who were obsessed with them, this definition was modified. Eventually, a stalking law was passed in West Virginia. As Lowney and Best illustrate, the "raw material for the stalking problem ... existed long before claimsmakers began talking about 'stalking'" (Lowney and Best 1995:48). The types of behavior we now recognize as the unlawful following, harassing, or menacing of another went through a process of typification, claimsmaking, and instigation, and this process was buoyed by the mobilization of cultural and organizational resources to bring it to the point of legislation. Now every state and the District of Columbia has enacted stalking laws and in 2013, the federal government passed 18 USC§2261A that prohibits interstate travel for anyone with "intent to kill, injure, harass, intimidate, or place under surveillance" another person (Federal Stalking Laws n.d.; https://victimsofcrime.org/our-programs/stalking-resource-center/stalking-laws/federal-stalking-laws#61a).

Administrative Rulemaking/Lawmaking

As we discussed in Chapter 4: The Organization of Law, administrative agencies comprise the so-called fourth branch of the government in the United States. Generally, these agencies perform social control functions through regulations. These agencies have experienced a huge amount of growth in the twentieth and early twenty-first centuries, at the local, state, and federal level. The Federal Registry monitors and records the daily activities of all of the agencies within the federal government, and it estimates that there are over 400 departments, agencies, and sub-agencies at the federal level (https://www.federalregister.gov/). The organization of administrative agencies varies from agency to agency, but it typically refers to large office bureaucracies, such as the EPA, Occupational Safety and Health Administration (OSHA), the Social Security Administration (SSA), the Food and Drug Administration (FDA), and the United States Department of Agriculture (USDA). Some are called bureaus, such as the Bureau of Alcohol, Tobacco, Firearms, and Explosives (ATF); others are called departments, such as the U.S. Department of Justice (DOJ). There are also agencies, such as the Agency for Healthcare Research and Quality (AHRQ), and others are called offices, as in the Office of Government Ethics (OGE). Taken together, this alphabet soup of government bureaucracies regulates everything from atomic energy to veterans affairs. Further, most federal agencies have state counterparts, for instance, the Massachusetts Department of Environmental Protection (MA-DEP) is the federal EPA's state counterpart.

At the federal level, all of these administrative agencies are empowered by Congress, which creates them under constitutional authority. When an issue or job is too big to be handled by the legislative branch, Congress forms an administrative agency to address specific issues that are often technical and specialized in nature. Therefore, these agencies often emerge from a crisis. Agencies can also be formed by executive order. The Federal Emergency Management Agency, FEMA, was created by executive order #12127 of President Jimmy Carter in April of 1979 in response to a request by the governors of the 50 U.S. states who saw the need for more centralized disaster aid and relief at the federal level (https://www.fema.gov/). FEMA was formed to coordinate government-wide relief efforts for all types of disasters, both natural such as floods, fires, hurricanes, and tornadoes, as well as human-made calamities, such as nuclear power plant leaks and gas and oil spills.

The Administrative Process

Administrative agencies affect individuals and organizations through **rulemaking, investigation,** and **adjudication. Rulemaking** is the most important function of agencies. It is the mission of any government agency to make rules, regulations, or policies. Generally speaking, there are three types of rules:

1. *Procedural*: Procedural rules identify the agency's organization, describe its methods of operation, and enumerate the requirements of its practice for rulemaking and adjudicative hearings.
2. *Interpretive*: Interpretive rules are issued by an agency to guide both its staff and its regulated parties as to how the rules will be interpreted and carried out.
3. *Legislative*: Legislative rules make up the body of law passed by administrations; they are administrative statutes. So if the EPA passes a new rule on lead levels in drinking water, that legislative statute is the law of the land (Vago 2012:133-134).

Taken together, these rules make up the bulk of administrative rulemaking.

Investigation involves the gathering of information to enforce the rules passed by these various administrations—to regulate industry, to prosecute fraud, to collect taxes, to fine employers who put their employees at risk. Investigative power is conferred by Congress and the authority to investigate rule-breaking is one of the functions that distinguishes agencies from courts. For example, an EPA investigator works on the frontline of enforcement of environmental rules. If the rules are put into place but no one checks to see if they are complied with, enforcement of those rules cannot occur. This lack of investigation and enforcement renders the rules "toothless"—they have no bite. Lack of investigation often results from a lack of resources. If an agency suffers cutbacks, they cannot hire and retain the staff to investigate rule-breaking. For instance, the Massachusetts Department of Environmental Protection, the state's equivalent to the EPA, experienced a 75 percent drop in fines collected by polluters in the state in the past decade (Abel 2017). This drop coincided with a nearly one-third reduction in the DEP department's workforce (Abel 2017). Fewer fines collected means even less money to hire investigative and inspection staff, which results in less enforcement of environmental rules and regulations and more pollution of water, air, and soil.

Administrative adjudication involves administrative agencies settling disputes and mediating conflicts. Most administrations use formal and informal proceedings.

Adjudicated powers are granted by Congress, and administrative adjudication is the process by which an administrative agency issues an order. It

Source: Bill Whitehead/CartoonStock.com

applies only to a specific, limited number of parties involved in cases before the agency. Administrative orders have a retroactive effect as opposed to lawmaking, which is proactive. The rule of *stare decisis*—the requirement that a precedent be followed—does not apply in administrative adjudication. Further, an agency does not have to wait for a case to come to it. Enforcement officials, also known as inspectors or investigators, can go looking for cases in the investigative process. Adjudication can be considered the administrative equivalent of a trial. However, much administrative adjudication is handled informally with fines and settlements. When an issue goes to a hearing, the parties must produce evidence, but the formal rules of evidence do not necessarily apply.

In 1946 Congress passed the Administrative Procedure Act, which provides a broader basis for judicial review of administrative decisions. Courts can overturn decisions made by government agencies if the agency is found to have overextended its authority or misinterpreted the law. The role of the courts in administrative adjudication is mainly procedural review and not to decide on matters of substance.

In the real-life legal thriller *A Civil Action* author Jonathan Harr (1995) chronicles a groundwater pollution case in Woburn, Massachusetts, that sickened several residents of the town—most of them children—in the 1960s and 1970s. After a long and costly trial, two major multinational corporations, W.R. Grace and Beatrice, agreed to settle with some of the survivors' families for $8 million, which amounted to less than half a million dollars per family (Harr 1995).

After the settlement, the EPA enforced its own rules and sanctioned W.R. Grace and Beatrice by fining them and filing a lawsuit against them to recover cleanup costs in the amount of almost $70 million. This part of the case is an example of administrative enforcement and adjudication. The case was the costliest environmental cleanup of its time in New England, and the environmental impact of the polluted aquifers is still being felt in Woburn today. Groundwater monitoring wells and reclamation technology are still in place in the town. W.R. Grace was also indicted by the United States Attorney for lying in its statements to the EPA. They received a $10,000 fine, which, for a huge multinational corporation like W.R. Grace, was a drop in the bucket (Harr 1995).

Administrative agencies can use both civil and criminal remedies to promote compliance with regulatory and administrative laws. One trend that has been occurring in the past few decades is to treat certain administrative infractions as criminal cases. There are examples in many states where employers who did not comply with Occupational Safety and Health Administration regulations were brought to criminal court and charged with crimes such as assault with a dangerous weapon or involuntary manslaughter.

CASE IN POINT

Two Workers Die in a South Boston Trench

In October of 2017, two employees of Atlantic Drain Services drowned when the 14-foot deep trench they were working in flooded. The men, Kelvin Mattocks and Robert Higgins, were working in South Boston when they were buried in clay and water within seconds (Ramos 2017b). Their coworkers tried their best to save the men's lives, but the water was "too deep and flowed too fast" (Ramos 2017b:A1). While this case could have been treated simply as a workplace accident with fines levied against the firm, Suffolk, Massachusetts District Attorney Daniel Conley decided to pursue two counts of manslaughter charges against the owner of Atlantic Drain Services. This case has not yet gone to trial, but the owner, Kevin Otto, faces up to 20 years in prison. After the two workers died, the company's previous safety infractions came to light, as did the fact that the company had violated 18 different workplace safety guidelines on the day the two men drowned in the South Boston trench (Ramos 2017a). The Occupational Safety and Health Administration had fined the company several times for conditions that could lead to cave-ins on their job sites, among other safety infractions.

When fines and other forms of administrative rule enforcements do not suffice, criminal indictments serve to enforce workplace safety laws and broadcast the importance of following the rules and regulations put forth by government agencies. Atlantic Drain Services also faces one of the largest workplace safety fines levied in New England in decades, almost $1.5 million (Ramos 2017), but the addition of criminal charges brings another level of punishment to workplace safety scofflaws.

And, sometimes the administrative officials who are supposed to be upholding the rules and regulations must be held criminally accountable. Several Michigan government officials have been charged with involuntary manslaughter in a 2014 case of a man who died of Legionnaire's disease, a type of pneumonia caused by water-borne bacteria. The charges came after an investigation into Flint's lead-contaminated water crisis. The man's death has been attributed to water quality issues that were not addressed by state environmental regulators and Department of Health and Human Services employees. In this case, the administrative agencies did not follow their own rules and regulations, endangered the public they were meant to serve, and are facing criminal charges as a result (Eggert 2017). Thus criminal charges can be a way of regulating the regulators for failure to do their jobs.

JUDICIAL LAWMAKING

The role of judges in the lawmaking processes has steadily increased in the United States. In many cases, legislators and administrators are willing to let judges decide on controversial actions. And some judges believe that the courts are the best arena for redressing social problems.

Lawmakers on both sides of the political aisle as well as many citizens criticize this increasing power of the judicial branch of the government. Critics argue that federal judges are not elected to the Supreme Court of the United States or to some state-level supreme courts. Detractors use the terms "activist judges" or "judicial activism." These terms are usually used disparagingly and are meant to conjure an image of all-too-powerful judges who are allowed to make decisions that affect the entire country, but who are not held accountable through the election process. Detractors argue that these judges justify law rather than interpret it.

Examples of decisions that have been criticized as judicial activism run the gambit, but have included:

- Gay marriage
- Inmate employment
- School expenditures
- Road and bridge construction
- Racial integration of schools
- The Miranda Warning (1966)
- Juveniles being treated as adults.

All of these issues and many others have been branded as forms of judicial activism, meaning the decisions of the judicial body are not accountable to the American citizens in the same way the elected legislative body would be. The term activist judges is most often levied against judges who make decisions with which particular groups are unhappy, and it has been used by critics from both the Republican and Democratic parties.

Lawmaking by Precedents

Stare decisis means that the court will stand by what has been decided. As discussed in Chapter 2: The Rule of Law and Major Legal Systems, *stare decisis* is a foundation of the common law tradition. When a court decides a matter of law—generated by the facts of a unique dispute—the decision constitutes precedent that should be followed by that court and all inferior courts. This tradition stands in contrast to codes in parliamentary law. Precedent is accumulated wisdom, and the legal premise is: like wrongs deserve like remedies. So what happens when there is no precedent? Judges search for similar cases and analogies, and sometimes make new law that will then become precedent.

The Interpretation of Statutes

A statute is an act of legislation. Statutes are enacted to prescribe conduct, define crimes, appropriate public monies, and promote the general public welfare. While lawmakers enact statutes, judges are often called upon to interpret what the statutes mean—what was intended in the statute. The interpretation of statutes determines the effects of legislative decisions. Not all statutes are clear-cut, and not all can be applied to specific cases before the court. And in some cases, the legislators who pass the law do not check their work. Recently in the state of New Hampshire, lawmakers passed a "fetal homicide bill" that was intended to define as a person a fetus that had developed beyond 20 weeks. This law intended to limit women's access to abortion by redefining it as fetal homicide, a legal strategy that has been attempted in many other states across the country. In New Hampshire, the law was so poorly worded that it accidentally allowed pregnant women to kill people without legal recourse. The bill's language read that "any act committed by a pregnant woman or a doctor acting in his [or her] professional capacity wouldn't apply in cases of second degree murder, manslaughter, or negligent homicide" (Graham 2017:n.p.). The bill passed in the state Senate and House of Representatives before anyone caught the error. Once the mistake was detected, the House passed an amendment correcting the wording to, in the words of one Democratic representative "make sure pregnant women don't go around killing people" (Graham 2017:n.p.). But even when there is no clear error, judges must sometimes step in to interpret the work of the legislature after a law has been passed. The wording may be vague, or the statute itself may be hard to apply to real-life cases since it is impossible to foresee all future situations to which a statute may be applied. Once the court interprets the statute, the clarified statute becomes law. Therefore, this is another form of judicial lawmaking.

The Interpretation of Constitutions

Judges interpret the Constitution at both the state level or the federal level. Controversial statutes, as well as a variety of controversial executive actions, are challenged in the courts on grounds of constitutionality. State Constitutions tend to be much more detailed documents, leaving much less room for judicial interpretations. When deciding the constitutionality of a government action, the courts have to decide what meaning they wish to give to the Constitution and which social objectives to pursue. For example, the Supreme Court has given quite different interpretations to the due process of law clauses of the Fifth and Fourteenth Amendments. Judicial lawmaking is usually directed at government agencies rather than private individuals. Courts have prohibited racial discrimination by government agencies, such as schools and parks and in elections, but not by private individuals. For example, an individual choosing a doctor based on skin color is not held to the same equal protection standards as a governmental body. Such a case would most likely not make it to the courts. In sociological terms, courts are more interested in fighting institutional discrimination than discrimination at the individual level.

INFLUENCES ON LAWMAKING PROCESSES

As we have seen throughout this chapter, various social forces can influence lawmaking processes. We have already looked at the role of special interest groups in bringing about laws against stalking. The techniques special interest groups use can vary. They can draw attention to their issue through political means, such as lobbies and political action committees. Usually, unified and coordinated efforts focused on one narrow topic tend to do best and financial backing is crucial.

Public interest groups are similar to special interest groups, but they tend to look beyond the interests of their own membership to promote issues of general public concern, such as the environment or basic human rights. From a conflict perspective, private interests are better represented than public interests in American society. The numbers of groups that claim to represent public interests are relatively small since it is difficult to agree on a "common good" in a plural society driven by capitalism. A few examples are: Common Cause, the Sierra Club, Public Interest Research Groups, and various public interest law groups. Common Cause, which began in 1973, promotes awareness of various issues from poverty to unemployment to racial injustice. All of these groups have access to lawmakers to provide a catalyst for legal change. The most prestigious and well-funded tend to have the greatest impact.

In addition to special interest groups and public interest groups, many other social forces can affect the lawmaking processes, such as: public opinion, science and detached scholarly analysis, protest activity and social movements, and the mass media. Public opinion is obviously often linked to special interest or public interest groups. In Chapter 2: The Rule of Law and Major Legal Systems, I noted that the socio-legal theorist Albert Venn Dicey (1835–1922) believed the influence of public opinion on lawmaking in the late 1800s was gradual and continuous. Venn Dicey believed that over time customs eventually become law. As societies grow and become more complex, the role of public opinion on lawmaking becomes more direct, and also in some cases, less gradual. Public opinion can bring about almost immediate changes in law, as we saw with the case of upskirting in Massachusetts.

In complex, diverse societies, such as the United States, there is no *one* public opinion; rather, there are many, many public opinions. So, whose opinion matters? This is a matter of perspective. A consensus perspective argues that there is generally a lot of agreement throughout public opinion—there is consensus. A conflict perspective views consensus differently: there is agreement among the ruling class, and their opinions tend to become the law of the land. Also, in the age of social media, there are various channels of public opinion. Countless social media platforms exist to allow the sharing and debating of opinions.

But public opinion is always tied to economic power. Children do not have the same power and ability to influence public opinion as does General Motors or the Halliburton Company. The conflict perspective on lawmaking looks at unequal access to resources that lead to structural breaks or divisions in society. These divisions are built into the very fabric of a capitalist society. Society is divided by income and wealth, racial and ethnic groups, gender, age, sexuality, and gender identity. According to a conflict perspective, laws emerge to protect the dominant group: their property and their interests. Their public opinions tend to be heard. As legal scholar Lawrence Friedman said in 1975, " ... 100 wealthy powerful constituents passionately opposed to socialized medicine outweigh thousands of poor, weak constituents mildly in favor of it. Most people do not shout, threaten, or write letters. They remain quiet and obscure unless a headcount reveals they are there" (p. 75). It is much more difficult for disadvantaged, subordinated groups to be heard.

There are three main types of public opinion: the first is direct constituent pressure. Constituents offer rewards or punishments to lawmakers, for example, they will not be reelected if their constituents feel as though their concerns have not been heard.

The second type is group public opinion, which coincides with special interest group pressure, such as the work of lobbying groups or political action committees—people who join forces to influence lawmaking.

The third form of influences on public opinion is indirect. This occurs when legislators act in accordance with constituent preferences because they either share those preferences or believe that they are doing what is best for their constituents. Public opinion polls in the United States attempt to gauge all three forms of public opinion and they can clearly influence what lawmakers do.

Science and all forms of scholarship can also influence lawmaking as well. Social science research theories and data can affect lawmaking. This can include the work of economists, sociologists, criminologists, and psychologists. Environmental science and ecology can affect laws concerning the environment. Medical science research can change health care laws. A scholar, or group of scholars, may study an issue or a social problem and present her or his research to either or both scholarly and popular audiences, or even directly to the legislature at congressional hearings.

There are many examples of controversies regarding how social science research is used to bring about new laws. For example, the publication in 1966 of *Equality of Educational Opportunity*, also known as the Coleman Report, reported on racial segregation in public schools in the United States. The report called for busing white and black students to different school districts to achieve racial balance in public school systems. James S. Coleman and his coauthors argued that integration was not simply equal money allocated to schools, but that true racial integration—black and white children learning together in the same setting—enhances the educational experiences of both minority and majority group members (Coleman 1966). Busing as a practice proved controversial because most people did not want their kids transported out of their own neighborhoods to other schools. Violence erupted in many parts of the country. Therefore sound scientific study and data do not guarantee a smooth course for new laws.

Writers of both fiction and nonfiction from inside or outside of academia can call attention to a problem or social condition. For example, Upton Sinclair's novel *The Jungle* (1906) was set in the stockyards and meatpacking industry of Chicago in the early twentieth century. Sinclair discussed pork ridden with tuberculosis, rancid meat being made into sausages, rats near meat processing, dead rats in the meat hopper, and even dead workers in vats later sold as lard. President Roosevelt read the book and sent officials to investigate and report on the meat industry. In the end, the book provided the impetus for meat inspection laws and other food safety measures. Similarly, Jonathan Harr's nonfiction book *A Civil Action* (1995) brought to light issues of groundwater contamination and cancer clusters in post-industrial cities.

Rachel Carson's 1962 nonfiction book *Silent Spring* offers another example of a lone writer influencing lawmaking, in this case, her book prompted the environmental movement in the United States and brought about the creation of the EPA and laws protecting the environment (Dunlap 2015). Specifically, Carson studied the effects of pesticides such as dichlorodiphenyltrichloroethane, or DDT, on insects, birds, and the entire food chain (Carson 1962). Her work prompted the prohibition of DDT in 1973.

Another example of a writer influencing law is Ralph Nader, a consumer advocate who looked at not just consumer safety issues but also general issues that affect consumers. In 1965 he wrote a book called *Unsafe at Any Speed*, which alerted the public to the auto industry's lack of concern for consumer safety. Nader's book provided the impetus for the 1966 Traffic and Motor Vehicle Safety Act. Nader's consumer advocacy has also provided the impetus for many other laws protecting the public's health and safety. The Natural Gas Pipeline Safety Act 1968; the Radiation Control Act, also in 1968; the Wholesale Poultry Products Act 1967; the Coal Mine Health and Safety Act 1969; and the Occupational Health and Safety Act of 1970 can all be attributed to Nader's work for consumer rights.

Protest activity is another impetus for lawmaking. Protests can take many shapes and forms: demonstrations, sit-ins, strikes, boycotts, Internet activism, sometimes called "hactivism," and various forms of civil disobedience. Rioting and other forms of violence can be used as tools by those who do not wish to engage in more conventional approaches to influence lawmaking, or those who are opposed to conventional lawmaking. Activism attempts to change social conditions, sometimes through changes in laws. In some cases, activism can take the form of *resisting* social change that is already under way, such as those who protested, sometimes violently, against busing in Boston and other cities.

Social movements are most often intrinsically connected to protest activity. A social movement is a type of collective behavior where a group of individuals organize to promote certain changes or alterations in behaviors or to bring about new procedures or laws. Many social movements or forms of collective action culminate in proposals for the creation of new laws and social policies. Indeed, changing law or bringing about new laws is often the ultimate goal of social movements.

Often, but not always, a social movement has a stated objective, a hierarchy of authority, and a clear ideology. New social movements, however,

Istock/william87

Social protest march.

are noted for not having any of those things—no hierarchy of authority nor clear membership, or maybe membership occurs only over the Internet or on websites. The term "new social movements," while imprecise, typically refers to forms of collective action that have emerged since the late 1960s. Unlike traditional social movements that focused on clearly defined goals and were comprised of people with clear common interests, such as labor unions or civil rights, new social movements often address issues of social identity or social values. In addition, they do not necessarily view the government as their ally in the fight for a better social world (Schaefer 2011), and often take part in protests against the government or specific government agencies or policies.

CASE IN POINT

Black Lives Matter: A New Social Movement

Istock/mauropedro1969

Black Lives Matter.

"The social justice movement spawned from Mike Brown's blood would force city after city to grapple with its own fraught histories of race and policing" (Lowery 2017:1). New social movements may not share one clear goal or objective, but they share their concerns or even their outrage over current social conditions. Black Lives Matter offers a case in point. Emerging in 2014 after a police officer in Ferguson, Missouri, shot a young, unarmed Black man named Michael Brown, the movement grew as more young Black males suffered the same fate. Anger within Black communities over police use of force, especially lethal force, fuels this new social movement. The movement does not have one stated purpose, nor does it have a clear membership or hierarchy. Journalist Wesley Lowery contrasts Black Lives Matter to the earlier civil rights movements. He notes:

> Ferguson would mark the arrival on the national stage of a new generation of black political activists—young leaders whose parents and grandparents had been born as recently as the 1970s and 1980s, an era many considered to be post-civil rights. Their parents' parents had been largely focused on winning the opportunity to participate in the political process and gaining access to the protections of promised them as citizens. Their parents focused on using the newfound opportunities and safeties provided by the Civil Rights and Voting Rights Act to claim seats at the table, with political and activist strategies often focused on registering as many black voters and electing as many black officials as possible. For at least two decades, the days of taking the struggle to the streets has seemed, to many politically active black Americans, to be a thing of the past (2017:3).

While the seeds of the movement existed before Michael Brown was shot in Ferguson—it was fomenting when Trayvon Marin was shot in Florida by a neighborhood watchman—Black Lives Matter erupted on the streets of Ferguson. It grew throughout the country and the world on social media—on Twitter and Facebook and other new social media platforms, a key component of new social movements. An Oakland, California, activist named Alicia Garza— one of the founders of Black Lives Matter—posted a "love letter to black people" that gave a name to the Black Lives Matter movement and quickly went viral. In in she says, "[s]top saying we are not surprised. [t]hat's a damn shame in itself. I continue to be surprised at how little Black lives matter. And I will continue that. [s] top giving up on black life. Black people. I love you. I love us. Our lives matter" (reprinted in Lowery 2017:8). Garza describes the movement as "an ideological and political intervention in a world where Black lives are systematically and intentionally targeted for demise ... an affirmation of Black folks' contributions to this society, our humanity and our resilience in the face of deadly oppression" (Lowery 2017:8). While Black Lives Matter may not be seeking to bring about a particular law or change in law, the movement is bringing attention to areas of civic life where African-Americans are not protected or served by the law. It seeks legal changes in the form of police reform and criminal justice system reform. Black Lives Matter continues and builds upon the long traditions of social protest, combining the tactics of new social movements to bring attention to issues affecting African-Americans and all citizens of the United States.

CHAPTER SUMMARY

◆ All social groups construct social norms, rules, and laws that attempt to determine what is right and what is wrong for their members.

◆ The social constructionist perspective links symbolic interactionism with more critical approaches in sociology to examine how individuals or groups of individuals can bring about new laws or changes to existing laws.

◆ Social constructionism addresses the interconnections between and among power, social control, stratification, social movements, and the social organization of law.

◆ Social constructionism looks at how some issues are labeled as problems or crimes while others are not. Claimsmakers typify social problems— they define and frame the issue and discuss how it should be addressed. Claimsmakers usher the social issue into the social problems marketplace and draw attention, support, and resources to it.

◆ Legislation is the creation of laws by a governing body. It involves several stages including instigation and publicizing, information gathering, formulation, interest aggregation, mobilization, and modification.

◆ Administrative agencies bring about rules, procedures, and laws to regulate specific areas of interest, such as a particular industry or natural resources. Most administrative adjudication is handled through fines, but some infractions bring about criminal charges to punish rule-breakers.

◆ Judicial lawmaking takes place through precedent-setting cases, through the interpretation of statutes, and through the interpretation of state constitutions and the constitutions of the United States.

◆ Law is not autonomous—law is very much affected by other social institutions in our society, special interest groups and public interest groups, public opinion, science and academic scholarship, lone fiction and nonfiction writers, social protests, and social movements.

KEY TERMS

adjudication   125
administrative adjudication   126
conflict perspective on
   lawmaking   116
investigation   125
legislation   120

rationalistic approach to
   lawmaking   115
rulemaking   125
social constructionist
   perspective   117

CRITICAL THINKING QUESTIONS

1. In this chapter we looked at stalking laws. How have these laws changed in the Internet age? Look up laws on cyberstalking in your state, when were they enacted and Why? What online behaviors do they cover? Do you think they cover every behavior or action that could be considered cyberstalking?

2. Social movements often bring about countermovements intended to counteract the work of the initial movement. What are some counter-movements that have arisen in the wake of Black Lives Matter? Are these countermovements seeking any specific legal remedy to a social issue?

3. As we have seen in this chapter, what is legal or illegal varies from place to place and from time period to time period. Can you think of a behavior that was legal 20 years ago but is now illegal? Conversely, can you think of a behavior that is legal now but was not legal 20 years ago? What do you think brought about these changes in law?

4. Do you think the trend in filing criminal charges against employers whose workers are harmed on the job makes sense? Why or why not? What might be some unforeseen or latent consequences to this approach to punishing employers?

SUGGESTED MOVIE: *FOOD, INC.*

Food, Inc. Documentary. 2008. Robert Kenner, Director.

   Food, Inc. critically examines corporate farming and agribusiness. Food writers Eric Schlosser and Michael Pollan take the audience through many of the pitfalls of industrialized food production and its deleterious effects on humans, animals, the environment, and small farming. Law is not the main focus of the film. However, the film sheds light on how the administrative agencies that are supposed to protect the environment (i.e., EPA) and our health (i.e., U.S. Department of Agriculture) have been co-opted by big business. It also looks at how large, multinational corporations have used money and power to write laws that benefit their interests, block laws that might curtail their profits, and mount legal cases against small farmers who challenge their practices.

Discussion Questions for *Food, Inc.*

1. The film shows that the food industry has largely been allowed to police itself. Why are government regulatory agencies such as the U.S. Department of Agriculture not doing a better job at regulating the food industry?

2. The film compares companies that produce unhealthful foods to tobacco companies. Is this a fair comparison? Why or Why not?

3. Who is responsible for 2½ year-old Kevin's death? Should law play a greater role in protecting people from dangerous food products, such as E-coli contaminated meat? How should it do so?

4. What role do consumers have in the food industry? What power do average citizens have, and how do they assert their power? Discuss ways that consumers could change the ways food is produced.

6

Law and Social Control

◆ ◆ ◆

SOCIAL CONTROL: WHY DO MOST PEOPLE BEHAVE MOST OF THE TIME?

The term **social control** means any methods or techniques used to prevent norm-breaking behavior. **Norms** are expected behaviors for members of a social group. Social control keeps people in line with the expectations of their social groups; these groups can range from your immediate and extended family to a group of friends, teammates, a religious order, a community, or an entire society.

Members of society are constantly being controlled, both informally and formally. Any time you stop yourself from doing something you want to do, or when someone or something prohibits you from taking some action, you have been socially controlled. For example, let's say you were very hungry when you woke up this morning, and you knew your roommate had one bagel left that she was saving for herself. Your roommate was still asleep and not able to stop you from eating her breakfast. You really wanted to eat her breakfast—doing so would have allowed you to skip going to the cafeteria, waiting in line, and paying for your own breakfast. Taking your roommate's food would have been the easier choice in the short term. But you stopped yourself from eating your roommate's bagel because you knew it was wrong. You also knew that doing so would most likely have caused problems between you and your roommate and you two need to live together for the rest of the school year. You controlled your immediate urge to eat her breakfast because it was the right thing to do, and it will make relations with your roommate easier in the long run.

Student thinking about taking her roommate's food.

When you arrived at your class, you had to take an exam. You were tempted to sit in the back of the class, wear a baseball hat to hide your eyes, and copy off of your smart friend who sits in front of you. Or perhaps you thought about using the cheat sheet that you carefully constructed last night when you should have been studying. But you did not cheat. You might have been able to pull it off, but if the professor caught you, you would have received an "F" on the test, or worse—you could have been kicked out of the class and received an "F" for the entire class. Your grade point average would have plummeted. In addition, when you arrived at the school you agreed to follow your university's honor code and in so doing, you pledged to follow the rules and ethical standards of the school.

Internalization of Norms

In both of these scenarios, you have been socially controlled. In the first case, when you stopped yourself from taking your roommate's food, you did so because you have **internalized** the social norms of the society in which you live (Clinard and Meier 2016). In the internalization of social norms, social control is the outcome of the **socialization process**—the lifelong learning of attitudes, behaviors, values, and beliefs appropriate to members of a particular society. By the time people have reached their late teens to early adulthood, most have learned the basic norms, rules, expectations, and laws of society and have decided to abide by them most of the time. Even most hardened criminals obey societal norms most of the time. The internalization process corresponds to consensus in Weber's definition of law. Weber defined law as a body of rules maintained through consensus and coercion. As we discussed in the introduction to this book, with consensus, people follow the norms of their society because they agree with and consent to them (Weber [1905] 1978).

Control through External Pressures: Sanctions

In the other scenario, where you did not cheat because you might have been caught, the second basic process of social control has taken place: **control through external pressure** (Clinard and Meier 2016). Social control through external pressure can involve both positive and negative sanctions. A **sanction** is a method of enforcing societal norms. Negative sanctions are punishments, such as an "F," or other penalties—school suspension, fines, jail, or prison time. Punishment corresponds to coercion in Weber's definition of law. **Coercion** is the enforcement of norms through the use of organized power, that is, the school's honor code and the professor's policies as laid out in the syllabus. Coercion includes all forms of **negative sanctions** or punishments for violations of the norms. In the above cheating scenario, negative sanctions could include an "F," expulsion from the class, or even expulsion from the college or university.

Positive sanctions reward people for good behavior, such as praise from your parents, approval from your teachers, an "A" on an exam, or a promotion at work. Official government sanctions, however, tend to be negative; one rarely receives positive reinforcement for abiding by the law, but the absence of negative sanctions stands as its own reward. If you abide by traffic laws and have a good driving record, you may receive a reward from your car insurance company—a safe driver discount. But these rewards rarely come from the government.

This chapter considers how law operates as a mechanism of formal social control—one of the key functions of law in society. The legal structure of a society is only one type of social control, however. As we saw in Chapter 3: Modernization and Theoretical Approaches to Society and Law, legal systems are the most prevalent and official form of controlling citizens in a complex industrial or post industrial society. Informal means of social control still operate in all social groups, but they do not have the governmental authority and power that formal means of control possess.

INFORMAL SOCIAL CONTROL

As we discussed in Chapter 1, norms vary in terms of their overall importance to society. Norms can be viewed on a continuum of importance—on how essential they are to the overall operation of society (Figure 6.1). William Graham Sumner, an American sociologist who wrote at the turn of the twentieth century, used the terms folkways, mores, and laws to discuss the levels of social norms in society (1907). A **folkway** is the least serious type of norm, usually involving matters of etiquette and manners, modes of dress, customs, and other social niceties. People generally follow folkways whether or not they give them much thought. Folkways make up the fabric of our every day interactions and help the social world run smoothly from social setting to social setting.

Mores are more serious behavioral expectations that govern important matters of right and wrong. Conventional wisdom tends to dictate mores; they correspond to a society's standards of decency. For example, the notion that you should respect your elders, especially your own parents, is a more. Folkways and mores are **informal means of social control**; they are techniques that we use to govern everyday behavior, but they fall short of laws. If you do not hold the door for someone and let it whack him or her in the face, you will most likely get a dirty look, or you might be spoken to, but you will not be arrested for breaking a folkway. If you do not take care of your parents into their old age, you may be a viewed as a bad person. However, you will not get arrested unless your behavior crosses over into elder abuse.

Many different techniques of informal control work to regulate our everyday behavior: gossip, ridicule, praise, reprimand, criticism, ostracism, honking horns, a thumbs-up gesture, or another gesture where a different finger is extended upward. Gossip—or fear of gossip—is one of the most powerful forms of informal social control in small groups. Gossip, or its possibility, is used to bring behavior into line. Think of gossip in your own life—when did you talk about others behind their backs? Was it because they did something you approved of? More often than not, you gossip about people whose behavior has transgressed a boundary of some sort. Or, think about a time when you were the subject of gossip. Did this talk make you think about changing your behavior?

Figure 6.1 Continuum of Norms

CASE IN POINT

Informal and Formal Control in Puritan New England

Informal social control mechanisms such as gossip tend to be more effective in small social groups where relations are intimate—a family, a tight-knit group of friends, or a small town. Deviant acts are quickly brought to the community's attention and dealt with informally. For example, in his sociohistorical study of colonial Massachusetts, *Wayward Puritans: A Study in the Sociology of Deviance* (1966), Kai Erikson conducted in-depth analyses of deviant acts, and reactions to those acts, in the seventeenth-century Massachusetts Bay Colony. In this close-knit village community where the population was fairly homogenous and strictly religious, many methods of informal social control were used to keep people from breaking the austere rules of this small, puritanical society. Informal social control mechanisms included surveillance by neighbors, gossip, ridicule, and even moral censure and ostracism (Erikson 1966). In traditional societies like early-colonial Massachusetts, informal social controls worked to keep most citizens in line. But, as the population grew and when serious norm-breaking occurred, formal social control mechanisms were called upon to punish deviant acts. As Erickson asserts, "A people who had trained themselves to police their own hearts and control their own impulses were now being asked to apply the same discipline to the community as a whole" (1966:72).

Plymouth Plantation in Massachusetts.

Further, he states:

> In a colony that depended on a high degree of harmony and group feeling, the courts were picking their way through a maze of land disputes and personal feuds, a complicated tangle of litigations and suits. Moreover, the earnest attempts at unanimity that had characterized the politics of [Governor] Winthrop's era were now replaced with something closely resembling open party bickering (1966:139).

The newly established judicial system was called upon to settle minor disputes between neighbors and fellow churchgoers, but it was also needed to address larger social problems. Indeed, in the first six decades of the settlement of the Massachusetts colony, the colonists withstood what Erickson called three serious "crime waves" that fell beyond the capabilities of informal means of social control (1966:67). While these events may not look like the types of crime waves we see in today's headlines, they were serious threats to the social fabric of the Massachusetts Bay Colony. Formal, legal social control was called upon to address these waves of dissent.

Since the Massachusetts Bay Colony was first and foremost a religious society, the infractions that shook it were religious in nature. The first was the Antinomian Controversy from 1636 to 1638—a period in which newcomers from England to the colony had reached a peak and new religious dissention threatened the established religious order (Erikson 1966). Antinomianism means discarding moral law and believing that faith alone is necessary for salvation (Hall 1990). Anne Hutchinson was perhaps the most well-known of the dissenters of this period; her beliefs broke from the Puritan doctrine that salvation is evidenced by good work. She also ministered to a small group of followers in her home—a clear break from strict gender roles and church doctrine of the period. Hutchinson was brought before the General Court of the Commonwealth where she was excommunicated from the church and banished to Rhode Island (Erikson 1966; Hall 1990). Hutchinson's case also presents an example of a transitional legal system that was still in the midst of being constructed—combining religious doctrine and punishment with criminal penalties.

The second "crime wave" saw Quakers threatening the religious and political power structure in the mid-1650s to the mid-1660s. The original colonists viewed the influx of Quakers to Massachusetts Bay as the "Quaker Invasion" and cast them as a "wild band of fanatics" (Erikson 1966:107–133). Like Hutchinson and her followers, the Quakers challenged Puritan beliefs and pushed for religious tolerance. It is no coincidence that the first two Quakers to arrive in Massachusetts were two middle-aged women, and one of the Quakers most outspoken members was a woman—Mary Dyer, who was also a loyal follower of Anne Hutchinson (Erikson 1966:120). While the Massachusetts religious leaders were concerned with their religious doctrine, they no doubt were just as concerned with maintaining the male power structure that they had so recently established. Overall, the formal Puritan response to the Quakers was brutal. Quaker adherents were banished from the colony, their children were sold into bondage, they were whipped and their tongues were burned with hot irons, they were imprisoned, and some were hanged (Erikson 1966:116–119).

The last of the three "crime waves" in the Massachusetts Bay colony was the most infamous: the witches of Salem Village. This episode of loosely organized deviance also centered on women as well as young girls. The witchcraft hysteria began in 1692 and lasted for about one year. The incidences involved girls and young women who regularly visited the home of Reverend Samuel Parris. Parris owned a slave named Tituba; she was brought from Barbados and she would entertain the young women with magic and stories. The girls and women began to act out—screaming and contorting their bodies. At the onset of these events, community members attempted to use informal social controls to bring the girls' behavior back into line—people gossiped about them, sermons were delivered, and physicians were called to administer remedies. Formal social control was eventually called upon to punish these deviant acts, which, in accordance with the religious standards of the day, were clear evidence of demonic possession. As such, they were handled by both religious and judicial authorities in a court of law. Hearings and trials were held, witnesses testified, and girls and women were sentenced to the gaol (jail), where at least two died. Several women were sentenced to hang; one man was sentenced to be pressed under a pile of rocks. Twenty-two people—all but two were girls or women—died in the witchcraft hysteria that ended almost as quickly as it began (Erikson 1966:149). Just as there was no clear starting point to the episodes of supposed witchcraft, neither was there a clear end—fear of witchcraft simply began to fade, and citizens balked at the idea of executing their own. When the hysteria spread and accusers began to point fingers at upstanding men of the community—pastors, church and government leaders, or their loved ones—the witchcraft scare died down significantly (Erikson 1966:152).

FORMAL SOCIAL CONTROL

As colonial Massachusetts in the later part of the 1600s illustrates, both informal and formal social control mechanisms operate simultaneously in social groups. Formal social control mechanisms are more prevalent and more important in maintaining order in complex societies with a greater division of labor and task specialization, and with diverse groups who hold competing values, interests, and ideologies. Formal social control arises when the methods of informal control no longer fully working to control social infractions. **Formal social control** includes specialized enforcement agencies, standard techniques of control, and sanctions that apply to all members of the group. State control is exercised primarily through the use or threat of punishment: negative sanctions.

CRIMINAL SANCTIONS

Criminal sanctions come into play when laws are broken. **Criminal sanctions** are penalties or other types of punishment used to promote obedience to the law. The federal penal codes at both the state and federal levels, combined with criminal justice systems, are the most highly structured formal systems of control used in the United States. **Penal (or criminal) codes** are documents that publish a jurisdiction's criminal laws and outline the corresponding penalties for breaking those laws. **Criminal justice systems** comprised police, courts, and corrections—all of the people and agencies involved in apprehending, prosecuting or defending, sentencing, and punishing those who break criminal laws (Bureau of Justice Statistics 2018a; https://www.bjs.gov/content/justsys.cfm).

Edwin Sutherland and Ronald Cressey (1974) examined the components of punishment as a form of formal social control. Sutherland and Cressey argue that social control is formal if it is inflicted by a group in the group's capacity, and punishment must be inflicted upon someone who is regarded as a member of the group. Therefore, punishment involves pain and suffering produced on purpose and justified by some value that the suffering is assumed to have by and for the group (Sutherland and Cressey 1974). Similarly, criminal justice professor Graeme Newman defines **criminal punishment** by five key factors:

1. Punishment must involve pain or unpleasant consequences.
2. Punishment must be a sanction for an offense against a specific rule or law.
3. Punishment must be executed upon the specific offender who has allegedly or actually committed the crime.
4. Punishment must be administered intentionally.

5. Punishment must be "imposed and administered by an authority constituted by a legal system against which the offense if committed" (Newman 2008:7–11).

How does punishment in the United States stack up to these key factors? The major forms of punishment used in the U.S. criminal justice system are: fines, surveillance—probation, parole or electronic monitoring, imprisonment, and in some locations and for particular cases the death penalty. In 2015, the number of Americans under the control of the criminal justice system was approximately 6.74 million (Bureau of Justice Statistics 2018c; https://www.bjs.gov/index.cfm?tid=11&ty=tp). This figure, also known as the **total correctional population**, includes approximately 1.5 million inmates in federal and state prisons and about 730,000 in local jails. (Bureau of Justice Statistics 2018c; https://www.bjs.gov/content/pub/press/p16pr.cfm). Additionally, the criminal justice system monitors approximately 3.78 million convicted criminals on probation and about 870,000 on parole (Bureau of Justice Statistics 2018b; https://www.bjs.gov/index.cfm?tid=11&ty=tp).

Legalese: What is the difference between probation and parole?

Probation is a sentence served outside of custody but under the supervision of the criminal justice system—the probation officer; or, "a sentence of imprisonment that is suspended" (Schmalleger 2004:445). **Parole** is the supervised release of an inmate from jail or prison, based on an "administrative decision by a legally designated paroling authority" (Schmalleger 2004:448). **Probation** is used in lieu of incarceration; **parole** is used after incarceration and can act as an incentive for good behavior during the period of confinement.

In American society, incarceration represents the main mechanism of formal social control. An oft-cited figure of the costs to U.S. taxpayers for correctional facilities is $80 billion annually (DeVuono-Powell et al. 2015; McLaughlin et al. 2016). However, as researchers from the Warren School of Social Work at Washington University in St. Louis, Missouri found, that number is an underestimation. When real costs are factored in, according to McLaughlin et al., the figure should be closer to $1 trillion per year (2016). This estimate includes indirect costs to prisoners, such as lost wages, lowered lifetime earnings, and physical and mental health costs from the trauma of imprisonment (Pager 2007; McLaughlin et al. 2016). The $1 trillion figure also attempts to account for losses to families and communities. Families must pay for expensive phone calls and transportation to and from visits to incarcerated family members, and they suffer a loss of income of the family wage-earner. Moreover, communities pay for social services that are needed due to all of these accumulated losses (McLaughlin et al. 2016). Unemployment benefits, housing assistance, Aid to Families with Dependent Children (AFDC), social security, and food assistance should be factored into the costs of imprisonment (Pager 2007; McLaughlin et al.). What do taxpayers receive for the costs of imprisonment? While it is impossible to estimate what U.S. citizens get in return for the money spent on incarceration, we can consider the goals of criminal punishment.

WHY WE PUNISH

In U.S. society, we tend to take punishment for granted. If someone commits a crime, he or she should serve the time, right? We rarely stop to think about why we punish and if the purposes of punishment are being realized. Punishment serves multiple purposes, so determining whether or not it meets its goals involves first establishing what those goals are. Three main purposes of criminal punishment in the United States are: (1) retribution, (2) incapacitation, and (3) deterrence (Neubauer and Fradella 2017). Some criminologists also add (4) rehabilitation and (5) restoration to the list of goals of punishment (Schmalleger 2004).

1. Retribution

Retribution is punishment for wrongs committed; it is also a form of public vengeance against the offender. Retribution, at its core, is the notion that the criminal should suffer in return for the suffering caused by the crime. Retribution is recognized as the oldest rationale for punishment, dating back at least as far as the Old Testament's "an eye for an eye" pronouncement (Schmalleger 2004:391). If taken literally, however, retribution offers a very brutal, medieval approach to wrongdoing. If society simply seeks revenge upon the criminal as an act of social satisfaction, then we are not advancing the idea of criminal or social justice. Retribution also emphasizes proportionality in punishment, integrating a "just deserts" formulation of criminal sanctions that takes into account two key characteristics of the crime and the offender: (1) the seriousness of the crime, and (2) the offender's prior criminal history. Indeed, these two key characteristics are the basis of state and federal sentencing guidelines. While the notion of retribution runs throughout the U.S. penal system and its "get tough on crime" rhetoric, there is very little evidence to indicate that social retaliation does much to deter criminals or make society safer. We will look more closely at the deterrent effect of punishment later in this chapter.

> ### Sidebar: President Trump Calls for the Death Penalty for Drug Dealers
>
> At a time when overall support for the death penalty in the United States is waning, and with the numbers of executions declining every year, President Trump heralded the idea that drug dealers should be executed for their crimes. The federal government has executed three people since 1963, however, and all were for murder (https://deathpenaltyinfo.org/federal-executions-1927-2003). Trump made this assertion on March 20, 2018, in a speech to citizens of New Hampshire who were concerned about the opioid scourge affecting their state and the entire country. Trump drew upon a rather obscure provision in a 1994 crime bill that has never been used. In the past year, Trump has praised the Philippines and Singapore for their extreme "get tough on drug dealers" approach; both countries have some form of the death penalty for drug dealing (Linskey 2018:A7). Trump stated: "Unless you have really, really powerful penalties, for the really bad pushers and abusers, I'm telling you we are going to get nowhere" (Linskey 2018:A7).

2. Incapacitation

The second goal of punishment attempts to protect the public from harmful offenders. To **incapacitate** means to remove the offender from society—to put the offender in jail or prison—to prevent that person from reoffending during the period of incarceration. Thus, incapacitation typically involves a jail or prison sentence but can also include probation, parole, or some form of monitoring. William Ecenbarger, a journalist who has studied the privatization of juvenile residential homes in Pennsylvania, calls the American dependency on incarceration as our main form of punishment our "lock-'em-up society" (2012:247). Encenbarger states: "We are a nation that sees imprisonment as the best means of controlling crime. And why should kids be any different? Retribution trumps rehabilitation every Election Day. Therefore, it is that America, with only 5 percent of the world's population, is home to 25 percent of its prisoners" (Ecenbarger 2012:260). This "lock-'em-up" mentality has led to mass incarceration and to the privatization of some prisons and even juvenile residential homes; people are profiting off of inmates. The problem with incapacitation as the main form of criminal penalty in our society is that we tend to forget that we cannot keep most offenders locked up forever. At some point, most incarcerated people leave prison. At least 95 percent of state prisoners will be released from prison at some point (Hughes and Wilson 2018). If incarcerated people are released back into society with no new skills or knowledge, the chances of their reoffending are high. The National Institute of Justice found:

> Within three years of release, about two-thirds (67.8 percent) of released prisoners were rearrested. Within five years of release, about three-quarters (76.6 percent) of released prisoners were rearrested. Of those prisoners who were rearrested, more than half (56.7 percent) were arrested by the end of the first year (National Institute of Justice 2014).

In order to bring about changes in behavior, offenders must be offered more than a jail or prison cell. We will look at this issue more carefully when we turn to rehabilitation as a goal of punishment.

3. Deterrence

To **deter** is to prevent bad behavior. As a goal of punishment, deterrence is the idea that people can be intimidated by the thought of imprisonment or some form of punishment. Deterrence can be **specific,** such as a police officer telling an individual drug dealer, "If I catch you on this corner again, I will lock you up." Or, deterrence can be more **general.** In **general deterrence,** by locking up the offender, the criminal justice system is broadcasting a warning to all people who could possibly break the law. For example, in the next chapter, we will look at the case of the first person in Massachusetts to be sentenced under the state's texting-while-driving laws. The teenager who was texting when he killed another driver was sentenced to two years in prison, and his driver's license was revoked for 15 years. While this punishment was meant to deter that individual driver from ever texting while driving again—specific or individual deterrence—the judge in the case said he wanted to send a message to other Massachusetts drivers. The judge saw the individual's punishment as a way to discourage this newly criminalized behavior—texting-while-driving—and broadcast the new state law for drivers who may not have been aware of the changes—general deterrence. In this way, the judge hoped to call upon both **the specific and the general deterrent effect of punishment.**

In terms of the deterrent effect of formal social controls, there does need to be some risk assessment involved—a cost/benefit analysis. Deterrence is based on the idea that people weigh the rewards and punishments before committing a crime. People will commit crimes when the gains outweigh the costs. Italian social theorist Cesare Beccaria revolutionized approaches to crime and punishment in eighteenth-century Europe. Beccaria presented a new way of looking at punishment. He argued that barbaric, cruel, and arbitrary forms of punishment, such as the various types of torture and execution that were common in his historical period, were not working to deter crime. This led him to argue:

In order that punishment should not be an act of violence perpetrated by one or many upon a private citizen, it is essential that it should be public, speedy, necessary, the minimum possible in the given circumstances, proportionate to the crime, and determined by the law (Beccaria [1764] 1872:161).

Punishment, according to Beccaria, should be just painful enough to outweigh the benefits that committing the crime might garner. Punishment should prevent crimes, not simply exact social revenge on those who break the law. In order to prevent crimes, punishment should be **swift**—it should follow shortly after the infraction. Punishment should be **certain**—the perpetrator should have no doubts that the punishment will be enacted. Punishment should be **proportionate** to the crime—the punishment should not be vastly worse than the crime itself (Beccaria [1764] 1872).

Drawing on the foundation laid out by Beccaria, contemporary legal scholar Lawrence Friedman (1977) argued that the efficacy punishment as a deterrent depends on several variables:

1. **Communication:** how well the law and the criminal penalty is broadcast to its target audience
2. **Certainty:** the belief that the violation will result in the application of the penalty
3. **Severity:** the punishment must be painful enough to stop most individuals from the prohibited behavior or action
4. **Speed:** the punishment should be applied in a timely manner
5. **Stigma:** there should be some public denouncement and shame involved in the punishment
6. **Procedural justice:** the law and the corresponding punishment should be seen as moral and enforced through due process and in a fair and equal manner (Friedman 1977:122–124).

In 1975 American criminologist William Chambliss (1933–2014) found that punishment may deter only *some* crimes and *some* offenders. Chambliss made a distinction between **instrumental acts** and **expressive acts** (Chambliss 1967). **Instrumental acts** are future-oriented, such as burglary, tax evasion, embezzlement, motor vehicle theft—activities that are a means to an end. The goal of instrumental acts is some type of personal gain. **Expressive acts** tend to be more emotional and impulsive—the so-called "crimes of passion"—such as murder and assaults between people who know one another. According to Chambliss, deterrence works better for instrumental crimes that involve some planning and weighing of risks. Fear of punishment and its deterrent effects might be ignored in some criminal equations, but this can be hard to measure. Some criminals may think they are above the law. Deterrence, according to Chambliss, works best on instrumental crimes committed by low-commitment offenders, not professional criminals (1967). A first-time tax cheater might be deterred by prison time, or deterrence may work on a lifelong criminal who realizes his next felony could land him in prison for life.

On the other hand, deterrence is least likely to work on cases of high-commitment people who engage in expressive crimes, such as an ex-husband who is committed to harming his former wife, or a school shooter who is determined to inflict as much harm as possible and may not expect to live beyond the rampage. For expressive crimes, the threat of criminal sanctions is less compelling (Chambliss 1967).

DOES THE THREAT OF DEATH DETER CRIMINALS?

Proponents of the death penalty argue that it deters the most heinous of crimes—murder. Yet, even as far back as the eighteenth century, Cesare Beccaria argued that the threat of loss of life did not deter violent criminals. As Beccaria stated, "… punishment should not be an act of violence perpetrated by one or many upon a private citizen …" ([1764] 1872). Beccaria argued against capital punishment, torture, and other extreme penalties that inflicted bodily pain.

In 1972, the U.S. Supreme Court decision *Furman v. Georgia* declared capital punishment unconstitutional as it was being administered at the time; the court deemed it arbitrary, capricious, and discriminatory. It also allowed juries unbridled discretion when imposing the death sentence. The *Furman v. Georgia* decision left the door open for some executions to be allowed at the level of the states, however. A number of states responded to the Court's ruling by modifying state laws to make the death penalty mandatory for certain offenses, such as multiple killings or the killing of police officers. Mandatory death sentences were then deemed unconstitutional by the U.S. Supreme Court in the cases of *Roberts v. Louisiana* and *Woodson v. North Carolina*, both in 1976. The Court's rationale was that mandatory death sentences did not allow for individualized consideration given to each offender or the offense before imposing the death sentence. In the case of mandatory death sentences, states had to go back to the drawing board. These revised statutes were held to be constitutional by the Supreme Court in 1976—only four years after *Furman*—when it voted in the case of *Gregg v. Georgia*. The Supreme Court of the United States voted seven to two in favor of reinstituting the death penalty. New procedural safeguards were put in place to reduce discriminatory imposition of the death penalty. Generally speaking, these safeguards include: (1) bifurcated trials must have separate guilty and sentencing phases, (2) juries must weigh aggravating factors against mitigating factors when making their sentencing decisions, and (3) there must be a direct appeal to the state's highest court when a death sentence has been imposed by a jury (Gershowitz 2007).

Since 1976, the United States has executed 1,472 people and another 2,817 are awaiting execution on death rows across the country. The United States remains one of the only democratic nations in the world to allow the death penalty. Although the country continues to use the death penalty, support for capital punishment is not universal. As of early 2018, 19 states in the United States did *not* have a death penalty: Alaska, Connecticut, Delaware, Hawaii, Illinois, Iowa, Maine, Maryland, Massachusetts, Michigan, Minnesota, New Jersey, New Mexico, New York, North Dakota, Rhode Island, Vermont, West Virginia, and Wisconsin. The District of Columbia also does not use the death penalty (Death Penalty Information Center 2018). All other states have some form of death penalty policy, as does the federal government and the U.S. military (Death Penalty Information Center 2018). The states that have death penalty laws differ in terms of which types of crimes are death penalty crimes, but all include some form of murder. For example, Louisiana also has the death penalty for aggravated rape of a victim under the age of 12.

Since the death penalty was reinstated in 1976, with *Gregg v. Georgia*, its use in the United States reached a peak in 1998, when 98 people were executed (Death Penalty Information Center 2018). Since 1998, the use of capital punishment has been declining, with some small upticks over the years (Death Penalty Information Center 2018). In the past few years, the number of executions carried out in the United States has been relatively low: in 2016, 20 people were executed nationwide and, in 2017 the number was 23.

Due to "evolving standards of decency that mark the progress of a maturing society," (*Trop v. Dulles* 1958) the U.S. Supreme Court recognized a few exceptions and placed restrictions on the use of the death penalty for certain offenders and for certain situations. For example, in the decision of *Atkins v. Virginia* (2002), the Supreme Court ruled that it will no longer execute those with intellectual disability, although states vary on how they define this term (Death Penalty Information Center 2018). A few years after *Atkins*, the U.S. Supreme Court again restricted the use of the death penalty in *Roper v. Simmons* (2005) by abolishing capital punishment for people who committed their crimes when they were under the age of 18, declaring it cruel and unusual punishment (Death Penalty Information Center 2018). The issue of the crime of rape as deserving of death came before the Court in *Kennedy v. Louisiana* (2008). The Court held that the Eighth Amendment prohibits states from imposing a death sentence for the rape of a child where the rape did not result in the child's death because there is no social consensus against it.

Over the past decade, the United States has been experiencing a steady decline in the use of the death penalty for a variety of reasons, including the constitutionality of lethal injection. There is mounting debate over whether lethal injection is cruel and unusual punishment in violation of the Eighth Amendment because of recent medical information showing a risk of great pain if poorly trained personnel mishandle the anesthetic that is supposed to render inmates unconscious (Ford 2014). Yet lethal injection is the most common means of executing criminals (Ford 2014; Death Penalty Information Center 2018). Further, in 2011, the European Union banned all exports of standard lethal-injection drugs to the United States, thereby cutting off the death row prisons from their large-scale suppliers of sodium thiopental (Ford 2014). The European Union took this step due to its opposition to the death penalty and the call for its universal abolition (Ford 2014). Following the European Union's lead, several smaller drug manufacturers in other parts of the world have also stopped selling sodium thiopental and other drugs used in lethal injections to U.S. states. The export ban's effects became visible in death penalty states around 2014 when states such as Ohio, Mississippi, and Tennessee began to run out of sodium thiopental and attempted to use new drug combinations to kill death-row inmates. Witnesses to executions reported seeing inmates struggle and suffer while waiting for the drugs to take effect (Ford 2014).

So does capital punishment deter crime? That is an ongoing debate, of course. Earlier studies such as Erlich (1978) found that the murder rate from 1933 to 1967 responded to changes in the likelihood of execution. Erlich's results indicated that between seven and eight murders were prevented by each execution that was carried out. His research has been highly criticized because of methodological problems and its inability to be replicated. Moreover, 88 percent of criminologists do not believe the death penalty is an effective deterrent (Radelet and Lacock 2009). In fact, some criminologists have found support for a "brutalization effect" rather than a deterrent effect, suggesting that the death penalty increases the rate of homicide. Bowers and Pierce (1980) argue that the death penalty illustrates to society that lethal violence is an appropriate response to those who offend, which, in turn, decreases people's respect for life. A short-term brutalization effect was identified in the months following an execution. In New York, data suggest a two-homicide increase in the immediate months following an execution (Bowers and Pierce 1980).

Although capital punishment does serve the purpose of retribution to the victims' families *if* the family is pro-death penalty and it does deter the person executed from ever committing another crime, the preponderance of empirical evidence suggest little to no deterrent effect of capital punishment in the United States. Capital punishment does not affect crime rates because it is so rarely used, and most people are not aware that an execution is taking place. Executions are no longer public spectacles, as they were in the Salem witch trials, and the life imprisonment sentence also deters the criminal from ever committing another crime—against the public, at least. Incarcerated people can still commit crimes within prison.

A 2012 report by the National Research Council found that any studies "claiming that the death penalty has a deterrent effect are 'fundamentally flawed' and should not be used when making policy decisions" (Death Penalty Information Center 2018). Data from the Federal Bureau of Investigations Uniform Crime Reports consistently show that murder rates are highest in the south, which accounts for over 80 percent of all executions (FBI, UCR 2016).

Most murderers are low-commitment offenders on drugs or alcohol at the time of the crime, and unlikely to think through the consequences of their actions. Studies of serial murderers have found that they do not see capital punishment as a deterrent (Kelleher and Kelleher 1998). The death penalty is seldom imposed and when it is imposed it is only after the convicted spend many years on death row. Therefore negating the swiftness and certainty effects of deterrence (Friedman 1998). Most death-row inmates spend an average of a decade on death row before they are executed (Death Penalty Information Center 2018). The nation's longest-serving death-row inmate died of natural causes in 2013 (Sullivan 2013). Sixty-six year-old Gary Alvord remained on death row in Florida for 40 years for a crime he committed in 1973 (Sullivan 2013). Alvord's execution was held up due to legal disputes over whether or not he was mentally ill and fit to be executed. As his lawyer, Bill Sheppard said, "I would love for the state of Florida to tell us how much money they wasted trying to kill a guy they couldn't kill. The death penalty is getting us nothing but broke" (Sullivan 2013:2).

Mr. Sheppard makes a good point. Capital cases receive more costly trials and they have more appeals, which further add to the cost to society. Looking at the death penalty from a purely financial standpoint, *Forbes* writer Kelly Phillips Erb states:

> It's true that the actual execution costs taxpayers fairly little: while most states remain mum on the cost of lethal injection because of privacy concerns from pharmaceutical companies, it's estimated that the drugs run about $100 (the Texas Department of Criminal Justice put the cost of the drug cocktails at $83 in 2011). However, the outside costs associated with the death penalty are disproportionately higher … capital cases … are more expensive and take much more time to resolve than non-capital cases. A report of the Washington State Bar Association found that death penalty cases are estimated to generate roughly $470,000 in additional costs to the prosecution and defense versus a similar case without the death penalty; that doesn't take into account the cost of court personnel (Erb 2014:2).

Death penalty convictions are also much more likely to be appealed than are life sentences, adding approximately $1.8 million per case (Erb 2014:3). Through all of the appeals, death-row inmates must be housed at costs that are typically higher than those of non-death row inmates (Williams 2009; Erb 2014).

CASE IN POINT

A White Supremacist with a Knack for Predicting the Future?

In 2009, *Los Angeles Times* reporter Carol J. Williams told the story of a white supremacist gang hitman named Billy Joe Johnson who asked his Orange County jury to sentence him to death because he believed the conditions on California's death row were more comfortable than in other prisons in the state and he did not think he would be executed any time soon (Williams 2009). California's capital punishment system had become "so bogged down in legal challenges as to become nearly an empty threat, say experts on both sides of the issue" (Williams 2009:A14). Death-row inmates in California live in single cells that are slightly larger than other maximum-security cells, have better access to telephones, and can visit with outside visitors in a more private setting than the general prison population (Williams 2009). While it is unclear whether or not Johnson weighed the costs of benefits of committing his crime, he was making a cost-benefit analysis of his sentence. Aged 46 when he was sentenced, he figured he would be about 70 years old by the time he exhausted his appeals and he did not want to live that long.

There is always the risk that an innocent person will be convicted and put to death, thereby increasing the human costs of capital punishment. Appealing to the idea that an innocent person could be executed has been the tactic of the Innocence Project, a nonprofit group that tries to exonerate death row-inmates based on DNA evidence. Since 1973, 161 individuals have been **exonerated**—found to be innocent and released—from death row as of 2017 (https://deathpenaltyinfo.org/innocence-list-those-freed-death-row). Further, poor and minority group members are more likely to end up on death row, especially if they are found guilty of murdering a white person. African-Americans currently make up just over 13 percent of the total population of the United States, yet they comprise approximately 34 percent of executed defendants since 1976 and "over 75 percent of murder victims in cases resulting in an execution were white, even though nationally only 50 percent of murder victims are white." (https://deathpenaltyinfo.org/race-death-row-inmates-executed-1976; Death Penalty Information Center 2018). We will consider the issue of disproportionate minority sentencing in more detail in the section "Who is Punished?"

4. Rehabilitation

A fourth goal of punishment attempts to bring about changes in offenders future behaviors. If a purpose of punishment is to reduce the number of criminal offenses, and therefore reduce the harm to society, rehabilitative approaches to punishment should be part of criminal sanctions. Rehabilitate means "to restore to a former state" (Merriam-Webster 1997:985), but in the criminal justice context, rehabilitation typically means any program or intervention that brings about positive changes in an offender's life while he or she is incarcerated. The term rehabilitation is often derided as a "hug-a-thug" approach to crime and punishment, but if a goal of punishment is crime reduction, rehabilitative approaches can offer a more humane and cost-effective approach, particularly for youthful offenders. Rehabilitation can encompass many approaches to criminal offenders including: basic life skills and other types of education and job training, alcohol and other drug counseling, psychological therapy and group therapy, anger management, parenting classes, and gardening. Some incarcerated people work with animals, such as training dogs that will become service or therapy dogs.

5. Restoration

The final purpose of punishment, **restoration**, attempts to place the crime within its community context and allow the offender to make amends—to repair the harm done to the victim and the larger community (Chambliss and Hass 2012). Restorative justice approaches to crime attempt to provide the offender with a second chance. Generally, restorative justice programs aim to:

1. Repair the harm caused through either restitution—pay the monetary costs of the damages, for instance—and/or community service, and/or a letter of apology to victim(s).
2. Encourage dialogue, that is, victim impact panels, victim empathy courses, or reparative boards made up of members of the community.
3. Transform the community and the government through programs such as prison tours, alternative dispute resolution collaborations with the courts, workshops on conflict mediation (Chambliss and Hass 2012:247).

Restorative justice programs are most often used for juvenile and adult non-violent offenders as an alternative to formal court proceedings (Chambliss and Hass 2012). Academic research on the efficacy of restorative justice approaches find "moderate to significant success in increasing offender accountability and reintegration into the community" (Chambliss and Hass 2012:247). Restorative justice can also help victims by allowing them to participate in the justice process; restorative justice also engages the community and can reduce recidivism (Bonta et al. 2002). Restoration focuses on healing, on making victims whole again, and on giving the victims and the larger community a say in what should happen to offenders.

WHO IS PUNISHED? DISPROPORTIONATE MINORITY SENTENCING

Criminal sanctions are not meted out equally in the United States. As we saw in the discussion of the death penalty, not all people are punished in the same numbers and in the same capacity. Due to disproportionate minority contact at every point of the criminal justice system, African-Americans are sentenced to prison in much higher numbers than their white counterparts. According to the Sentencing Project's report, "The Color of Justice: Racial and Ethnic Disparity in the State Prisons," African-Americans are incarcerated in state prisons at a rate that is five times that of Whites (Nellis 2016:3). African-Americans make up more than half of the prison population in 12 states: Alabama, Delaware, Georgia, Illinois, Louisiana, Maryland, Michigan, Mississippi, New Jersey, North Carolina, South Carolina, and Virginia (Nellis 2016:3). Latinos are also imprisoned at higher rates than whites—in Massachusetts that rate is about 4 to 1, in Connecticut it is about 4 to 1, and in Pennsylvania and New York it is closer to 3 to 1 (Nellis 2016:3).

While no one factor explains the higher rates of incarceration of people of color, the policies and practices put in place in the war on drugs of the 1970s, 1980s, and 1990s contributed to mass incarceration generally and disproportionate incarceration of African-Americans specifically. Mandatory minimum sentencing, longer sentences for drug crimes, and other "get tough" policies, as well as implicit biases in how these policies were carried out, has resulted in African-Americans being locked up at greater rates than all other groups. Structural disadvantages also play an integral role in why African-Americans come into contact with the criminal justice system. Race, class, unemployment, underfunded schools, and living in areas with higher crime rates intersect to place African-Americans at a disadvantage and put them in contact with the juvenile justice system and the criminal justice system (Nellis 2016).

Ta-Nehisi Coates, in his 2015 exposition on the mass imprisonment of African-Americans in the United States, "The Black Family in the Age of Mass Incarceration" notes:

> From the mid-1970s to the mid-'80s, America's incarceration rate doubled, from about 150 people per 100,000 to about 300 per 100,000. From the mid-'80s to the mid-'90s, it doubled again. By 2007, it had reached a historic high of 767 people per 100,000, before registering a modest decline to 707 people per 100,000 in 2012. In absolute terms, America's prison and jail population from

1970 until today has increased sevenfold, from some 300,000 people to 2.2 million. The United States now accounts for less than 5 percent of the world's inhabitants—and about 25 percent of its incarcerated inhabitants. In 2000, one in 10 black males between the ages of 20 and 40 was incarcerated—10 times the rate of their white peers. In 2010, a third of all black male high-school dropouts between the ages of 20 and 39 were imprisoned compared with only 13 percent of their white peers (https://www.theatlantic.com/magazine/archive/2015/10/the-black-family-in-the-age-of-mass-incarceration/403246/).

Coates clearly links incarceration rates to socioeconomic conditions, stating:

> The two are self-reinforcing—impoverished black people are more likely to end up in prison, and that experience breeds impoverishment. An array of laws, differing across the country but all emanating from our tendency toward punitive criminal justice—limiting or banning food stamps for drug felons; prohibiting ex-offenders from obtaining public housing—ensure this .... The American population most discriminated against is also its most incarcerated—and the incarceration of so many African-Americans, the mark of criminality, justifies everything they endure after (https://www.theatlantic.com/magazine/archive/2015/10/the-black-family-in-the-age-of-mass-incarceration/403246/).

Coates illustrates that the costs of imprisonment are steep. Beyond the costs to the taxpayers, incarcerating thousands of African-Americans every year causes poverty and disenfranchisement in families and entire communities. The term disproportionate implies that while some are punished for crimes in larger numbers; others are not punished to the same extent. Further, *some* crimes that are committed by *some* criminals are also not considered as dangerous or as harmful to society as others. While thousands of low-level nonviolent drug offenders are locked up, who is not being punished for other types of crimes?

WHO IS *NOT* PUNISHED PROPORTIONATELY? WHITE-COLLAR CRIME

The term white-collar crime was first coined in 1939 by the American sociologist Edwin H. Sutherland. He defined **white-collar crime** as illegal acts carried out by individuals in the course of their "respectable" occupations (1949:9–10). Sutherland was critical of what he called social pathology theories of crime that dominated criminology during his period. Pathology theories assume that crime is an individual problem—the belief that individual pathologies, depravities, or frailties lead people to commit crimes. Turning this notion on its head, Sutherland looked at the power and status dimensions of crime and considered how people abuse their power and privilege to commit illegal acts. Sutherland conducted research in the 1930s and 1940s at 70 large, reputable corporations where there were approximately 980 violations of criminal law in one year. The violations included false advertising, unfair labor practices, restraint of trade, price-fixing, stock manipulation, copyright infringement, and various swindles (1949).

Contemporary criminologists use the term **white-collar crime** to describe a wide variety of acts carried out in professional occupations such as acts of deception; concealment; and breaches of trust used to obtain money, privilege, and power, or to avoid losing those assets (Chambliss and Hass 2012). With advent of computers and other new technologies, the types and the magnitude of white-collar crimes have multiplied. The crimes that typically fall under the rubric of white-collar crimes are antitrust violations, bankruptcy fraud, bribery, computer and internet fraud, counterfeiting, credit card fraud, economic espionage and trade secret theft, embezzlement, environmental law violations, financial institution fraud, government fraud, health-care fraud, insider trading, insurance fraud, intellectual property theft, piracy, kickbacks, mail fraud, money laundering, securities fraud, tax evasion, phone and telemarketing fraud, and public corruption. (Legal Information Institute https://www.law.cornell.eduwex/white-collar_crime).

"I plead guilty, Your Honor, but only in a nice, white-collar sort of way."

Source: Charles Barsotti, New Yorker/CartoonStock.cim

Critical criminologists argue that white-collar crime poses a much greater threat to the well-being of society than do traditional street crimes (Sutherland 1949; Chambliss and Seidman 1971; Reiman and Leighton 2016). White-collar crimes include issues like pollution, workplace-related injuries and deaths due to health and safety violations, medical fraud and malpractice, and the financial burdens of corrupt business practices. An example of the last crime is the trillion-dollar bailout of the banks in the financial crisis of the early 2000s that was connected to corrupt mortgage loans. These crimes are more likely to affect U.S. citizens than are street crimes such as robberies and shootings. From a purely risk-assessment standpoint, we should all fear white-collar crime more than street crime.

However, the full extent of white-collar crime is hard to tally because we do not have accurate records; these crimes do not always end up on the FBI's Uniform Crime Reports or other crime data sources. Wealthy people can hide their crimes and/or avoid prosecution when detected. Many people may not even know where to report white-collar crimes. For example, if you are victimized by credit card fraud, you will most likely call your credit card company, but you will probably not call local police or any sort of federal authorities.

White-collar crimes are typically divided into two separate categories: occupational crimes and corporate crimes. **Occupational crimes** are committed by individuals on their jobs, where the jobs are occupations of the middle to upper-middle class. With white-collar crimes, people who have some sort of professional training or higher education commit crimes related to their jobs or their places of work, such as physicians who commit insurance or Medicare fraud or prescription drug fraud. Another example is accountants or financial managers who embezzle from their clients. Occupational crimes could be committed by a professor who sells grades. Occupational crimes benefit the immediate perpetrators, for example, the insurance cheat, the embezzler, or the professor on the take.

Corporate crimes are violations of the law committed through business activities to benefit the business operations—the corporation itself. A **corporation** is defined legally as a group of people who come together as a single legal entity (incorporate) to serve a purpose, such as making a product, providing higher education, and running a railroad. The corporation remains distinct from its individual members and maintains a separate legal "personality." A corporation can own property; it can sue or be sued (*Burton's Legal Thesaurus* 2007). With corporate crimes, the benefits go to the corporation—the business owners or the shareholders—and may not immediately or directly enrich any one individual. In the late 1880s, a U.S. Supreme Court decision granted to American corporations some of the same rights as those of U.S. citizens (Winkler 2018). Corporations enjoy freedom of speech and freedom of religion—in a sense, they are "people" without souls. The Supreme Court granted corporations this status under the Fourteenth Amendment, the same amendment that was adopted to protect the rights of freed slaves after the Civil War. Through some tricky legal machinations, corporations—beginning with the Southern Pacific Railroad Company—successfully argued that they should enjoy equal protection of the laws and should not be discriminated against based on their status as a corporation (Winkler 2018). This decision and other pro-corporation rulings in state courts and in the higher court system allowed corporations to act in ways that can threaten people's safety, health, and property.

Criminologist Craig Little (1989) outlines the gains to perpetrators and losses to victims in different types of illegal corporate actions. Little categorizes three types of **illegal corporate actions against customers**: antitrust violations, false advertising, and production and sale of hazardous goods. Each provides gains to the perpetrators, typically in the form of increased profits. These gains for the corporation are often attained at the expense of victims, usually in the form of increased costs to consumers or dangers to the health and safety of consumers (Little 1989). The 2016 case of the death of a child on a brand-new waterslide amusement in Kansas City, Kansas, provides a gruesome example. The owners of the waterslide—called *Verrückt*, German for insane—rushed the design and construction of the 170 foot tall waterpark ride in the hopes that the park would be featured on a television show about extreme waterparks and garner free publicity and advertising. The corporation's owners ignored safety concerns, and within days of opening, several people were injured on the slide. These dangers culminated in a 10-year-old boy being ejected from the ride; he was decapitated when his body hit a metal pole (Fortin 2018). This tragic and avoidable death brought to light the fact that the owners knew the ride was dangerous but opened the 17-story slide anyway (Fortin and Hass 2018). The case offers a clear and horrific example of a corporation placing its own profits before the safety of its customers. The waterpark and its former operations director have been charged with multiple criminal counts including involuntary manslaughter, aggravated child endangerment, and aggravated battery (Fortin 2018). The case has not yet gone to trial.

A second type of **illegal corporate action** is carried out **against employees**, such as occupational health and safety violations and labor law violations. The perpetrators gain through reduced costs or increased profits, but at a cost to victims who face, for example, increased danger at work or exposures to hazardous materials that may lead to health problems or death. Workers may also suffer reduced income (Little 1989). The late 1990s case of Consolidated Smelting and Refining Company of Sutton, Massachusetts, provides an example. Massachusetts Environmental Task Force investigators found that the company knowingly exposed its workers to very high levels of lead through repeated safety and health violations.

The case was one of the first in the state and the nation in which the owner of a corporation was charged with assault and battery with a dangerous weapon (Howe 1997). Even though the company's owner, Lowell Fiengold, was found guilty, he spent no time in jail and his company was fined $2,500 (Howe 1997).

A third type of **illegal corporate action places the entire public** at risk, such as when a corporation pollutes the air, the soil, or the water. Violations against the public can also include illegal political campaign contributions. Perpetrators benefit from these acts by reducing costs or increasing political power. The losses to victims include increased danger to the public that may lead to sickness, injury, and death or to long-term environmental threats such as global warming. In the case of illegal campaign donations, there are the less-tangible losses, such as loss of faith in the political process and in the government itself (Little 1989).

The fourth category of illegal corporate action is **crimes against corporate owners**, such as security fraud. The gains for the perpetrator in these types of illegal corporate acts are stocks and increased profits. The loss to the victim would be the owner of the security who holds worthless stock, similar to counterfeit money (Little 1989). In the United States, corporate malfeasance was not constructed as criminal until the nineteenth century. The end of the nineteenth century to the turn of the twentieth century saw more and more regulations and laws passed in an attempt to regulate some of the more obviously dangerous business practices.

Jeffrey Reiman is a philosopher and criminologist whose work asks readers to consider the question: Which is more costly to society, street crime or white-collar crime? His book *The Rich Get Richer and the Poor Get Prison* written with coauthor Paul Leighton, is now in its 10th edition (2016). These authors argue that white-collar crime is more costly to the entire society because it poses harm to all of us, not just to certain segments of society. Reiman and Leighton want us to rethink how we define harm and crime.

While it is difficult to estimate the costs to society incurred by white-collar and corporate crimes, most estimates place these infractions at around $300 billion annually, but even this is a very conservative estimate (Cornell Law School 2016; Healy and Serafeim 2016; Reiman and Leighton 2016). White-collar and corporate crime costs are hard to tabulate because we do not have one complete data set on white-collar crimes. The FBI's Uniform Crime Reports (2016) includes a data source titled "The Measurement of White-Collar Crime Using Uniform Crime Reporting (UCR) Data" but it does not capture all of the possible types of white-collar and corporate crimes. Rather it tabulates embezzlement, counterfeiting, bribery, fraud, and property crimes—all of which are costly to society. This reporting does not consider serious threats to human life, however. The waterslide tragedy would not end up in this data set, nor would many of the threats to human health that fall under the rubric of corporate crime.

Hundreds of thousands of workers are needlessly exposed to hazardous materials every year, ranging from poisonous chemicals to radioactive materials to lead. These types of exposures are allowed to occur because of corporate failure to obey safety laws and regulations, and/or the failure of administrative agencies to enforce regulations (Reiman and Leighton 2016). Why do so few corporate criminals serve significant prison time? There are many answers to that question. In American culture, we do tend to view corporate crime differently and treat it differently using fines versus prison and administrative rules and regulations instead of criminal law. In 1845, Friedrich Engels, a colleague of Karl Marx, wrote *The Condition of the Working Class in England*. He argued:

> If one individual inflicts a bodily injury upon another which leads to the death of the person attacked we call it manslaughter; on the other hand, if the attacker knows beforehand that the blow will be fatal we call it murder. Murder has also been committed if society places hundreds of workers in such a position that they inevitably come to premature and unnatural ends. Their death is as violent as if they had been stabbed or shot .... Murder has been committed if society knows perfectly well that thousands of workers cannot avoid being sacrificed so long as these conditions are allowed to continue. Murder of this sort is just as culpable as the murder committed by the individual (Engels [1845] 2009:108).

While Engels wrote this passage in 1845 England at the height of the Industrial Revolution, an event that took place in 2010 in West Virginia could have served as an archetype of the worker fatalities he describes. This was the setting for a mine explosion at Massey Energy coal mine in Upper Big Branch, West Virginia, that killed 29 men. The mine's owner, Don Blankenship, had continuously flouted mine safety regulations leading up to the deadly explosion. Indeed, in the years leading up to the massive mine explosion that killed 29 miners, many others had perished in other mines owned by Massey Energy. In a 2006 fire in which two miners died, Mine and Safety Health Administration inspectors found that several safety codes were not followed. There were no sprinklers or fire alarms, carbon monoxide detectors were not installed, emergency exits were unmarked, fire containment structures had been removed, and the company had never run a fire drill for the workers (Murphy 2015). The company paid about $2.5 million in fines and $1.7 million in civil penalties, but that was not enough for the corporation to change its ways regarding the safety of its workers (Murphy 2015). Massey Energy also exploited and damaged the environment, dumping coal mining sludge into surrounding towns and rivers. In a 2000 case, due to a Kentucky mine owned by Blankenship, townspeople lost access to drinking water because of coal waste contamination (Murphy 2015). Meanwhile, Blankenship, who owned a house near the site, installed his own waterline that drew water from a clean water source. This infraction ended up costing the company about $35 million in a lawsuit settlement, but Blankenship and Massey Energy appeared undeterred.

Blankenship was also known to give significant campaign donations to elected court judges who won seats on the West Virginia Supreme Court (Murphy 2015). He even vacationed on the French Riviera with one of the Chief Justices while a case against Massey Energy was before the Supreme Court in West Virginia. The Justice later voted in Massey Energy's favor.

As a result of the 2010 mine explosion, a criminal case was brought against Don Blankenship in 2016. He received one year in federal prison on one misdemeanor count of conspiracy to violate mine safety laws. He served his year in a minimum-security correctional institute in California; he also was ordered to pay a $250,000 fine. In January of 2018, Blackenship announced his bid to run for Senate in West Virginia. He also mounted an appeal of his conviction, but that appeal was rejected (Murphy 2015; Tripp 2018).

Reiman and Leighton argue that our legal constructions of harm need to be revised to look beyond the typical street crimes we have all been taught to fear through television, movies, and nightly newsreels. Harm is typically perceived as one-on-one—as direct—with a clear perpetrator and a clear victim. In current legal constructs, the *desire* to harm must be present. The *mens rea*, or guilty mind, requirement is a basic component of legal definitions of murder. Don Blankenship did not *want* to kill 29 mine workers in a violent explosion—that was not his intention. But he *did want* to maximize profits and minimize costs. He ordered his workers to cut occupational safety corners and cover their tracks. The legal problem with this type of action is that it is viewed as indirect harm, and this does not comport with our notions of murder, assault, or any type of physical harm. Because the criminal justice system tends to look at relatively direct notions of harm, we do not protect ourselves from a lot of harm that most U.S. citizens will encounter, such as medical malpractice, faulty products, pollution, unsafe rides, and injury or death on the job. These are all common occurrences in our society.

According to the Bureau of Labor Statistics, 5,190 people were killed on their jobs in 2016 (https://www.bls.gov/news.release/cfoi.nr0.htm). Is a person who assaults another person in a bar brawl more dangerous to society than a business executive who refuses to follow health and safety regulations that keep workers, consumers, and residents safe so he can make more money? In corporate crimes no one *wishes* to cause harm; the corporation is only *indirectly* responsible. Much of this type of corporate behavior is actually seen as legitimate because the economic goal of a for-profit corporation in a capitalist society is to maximize profits. We like to think that the criminal justice system protects us from danger. However, the criminal justice system does not even address some of the gravest dangers that most of us face (Reiman and Leighton 2016).

ADMINISTRATIVE LAW AND SOCIAL CONTROL

In addition to criminal law and the criminal justice system—the police, prosecutors, judges, juries, sentences, and prisons—there are other legal ways to control private business activities. Administrative law attempts to step in to control the various pursuits of businesses and industries in the United States, such as the production and marketing of electricity and natural gas; the operation of rail, air, and other transportation facilities; the construction of homes, buildings, and bridges; and the activities of other public facilities such as radio and television broadcasting and the Internet. All of these activities fall under the purview of the administrative agencies whose purpose is to regulate and socially control them. The main way these agencies operate to control activities is through licensing, inspection, and the threat of publicity.

Licensing

Administrative laws and rules set standards—for safety, for fair business practices, for environmental protection of our natural resources. Requiring and granting licenses to allow corporations to perform certain activities is a tool of social control. Local, state, and federal administrative agencies control businesses and occupations through licensing. Administrative laws generally specify the conditions under which a license is required, the requirements that must be met by the applicants, and the duties imposed upon the licensees the agency authorized to issue such licenses and the procedures in revoking those licenses.

Licensing applies to thousands of occupations, industries, and services. When you get your hair cut, your hair stylist holds a license; the same with a manicurist. Carpenters and builders must be licensed to work by the state. Licensing and certification are widespread and control a large portion of the labor force. In addition to requiring a license to practice various jobs and occupations, administrative law exerts control through the revocation or suspension of licenses. For example, pilots who fly planes while impaired can have their pilot licenses revoked. A lawyer who misleads his clients or fails to properly represent them can have his or her law license suspended or be disbarred—lose his license to practice law in a specific state.

Inspection

Administrative law also grants investigation and inspection powers to agencies, such the Mine Safety and Health Administration in the Massey Energy case. The EPA and/or its state-level equivalent would address the environmental issues from the mine waste runoff into the water. The Food and Drug Administration, U.S. Department of Agriculture, the EPA, the Occupational Safety and Health Administration, and countless other administrative agencies inspect businesses, but a lot of the work around following the rules is left to the businesses themselves. Generally speaking, most corporations are not good at policing themselves. While Blankenship's record at his mining operations is an extreme case of not enforcing safety rules, corporations are in business to make a profit and may not be the best candidates to protect workers, citizens, or the environment when left to their own devices.

Threat of Publicity

The threat of bad publicity can fill in where licensing and inspection fall short. Companies selling widely used products can be influenced by the threat of widespread bad publicity. The owners of the deadly waterslide can no doubt attest to the fact that not all publicity is good publicity. When the authorities caught up to Jeffrey W. Henry, one of the co-owners

United States Environmental Protection Agency.

of the Schllitterbahn Waterpark, in which the deadly waterslide was running, he was trying to escape to the Mexico. He was caught at the border between Texas and Mexico (Fortin and Haag 2018). His operations director hid or destroyed records of previous injuries to customers (Fortin and Haag 2018).

Thus one of the most important tools in any administrative agent's hands is the power to publicize. Sometimes, however, other sources do the publicizing rather than the agencies themselves. Consumer advocates, concerned journalists, and citizens can call attention to dangerous products, environmental concerns, and bad business practices. Consumer advocate Ralph Nader in 1965 published a book *Unsafe at Any Speed* that was a groundbreaking example of the power of bad publicity. He looked at a car, the Corvair, which posed serious dangers to drivers. His book contributed to be demise of that car. It was taken off the market because of bad publicity.

CHAPTER SUMMARY

♦ Social Control is any means used to prevent norm-breaking behavior. Norms are societal expectations. Social control keeps members of society in line with behavioral expectations.

♦ Social control operates through both the internalization of societal norms and external pressures. Sanctions are external pressures that can be positive or negative.

♦ Informal social control regulates everyday behavior through folkways and mores.

♦ Formal social control involves laws, the criminal justice system, specialized enforcement agencies, and negative sanctions.

♦ Criminal sanctions are penalties or other types of punishment used to promote obedience to laws and authorities.

♦ Punishment serves many purposes including retribution, incapacitation, specific and general deterrence, rehabilitation, and restoration.

♦ Social control through punishment is not meted out uniformly in the United States. People of color are sentenced more often and more harshly when they are caught committing crimes due to disproportionate minority sentencing and war on drugs policies that emerged and proliferated in the 1970s, 1980s, and 1990s.

♦ White-collar and corporate criminals are not punished as often or as severely as those who commit so-called "street crimes," despite the fact that their offenses are more costly to society and can pose serious physical harm to consumers, workers, and the general public.

◆ Administrative law enacts social control of industry and private business operations through licensing, inspection, and the threat of publicity.

KEY TERMS

certain (punishment)   153
certainty   153
coercion   143
communication   153
control through external
    pressure   143
corporate crimes   163
corporation   163
crimes against corporate
    owners   165
criminal justice systems   148
criminal punishment   148
criminal sanctions   148
deter   152
exonerated   158
expressive acts   153
folkway   144
formal social control   148
general deterrence   152
illegal corporate actions   164
incapacitate   151
informal means of social
    control   144

instrumental acts   153
internalized (social norms)   142
mores   144
negative sanctions   143
norms   141
occupational crimes   163
penal (or criminal) codes   148
positive sanctions   143
procedural justice   153
proportionate   153
rehabilitation   159
restoration   159
retribution   150
sanction   143
severity   153
social control   141
socialization process   142
specific deterrence   152
speed   153
stigma   153
swift (punishment)   153
total correctional population   149
white-collar crime   161

CRITICAL THINKING QUESTIONS

1. Can you think of a norm in today's society that was most likely *not* a norm 30 years ago? Conversely, can you think of a behavior that *was* a norm 30 years ago that we no longer allow today? What do you think has caused these shifts?

2. Do you think applying the death penalty to drug dealers would deter drug sales and purchases? Do you think Cesare Beccaria would agree with this idea? Why or Why not? Should this punishment apply to all drug dealers? Use material from this chapter to make an argument for or against this idea.

3. Does the best approach to corporate crime lie in the criminal justice system, the civil courts, or administrative law? What types (if any) of corporate crime should be handled in criminal courts and Why?

4. Some courts now include the costs of incarceration in their sentencing considerations. Do you agree that the amount that the taxpayers pay to keep a person in jail or prison should be part of jury considerations about the punishment for specific crimes? Why or why not?

SUGGESTED MOVIE: *THE THIN BLUE LINE*

The Thin Blue Line Documentary. 1988, Errol Morris, Director

Errol Morris's cult classic *The Thin Blue Line* follows the case 1976 case of Randall Dale Adams, who made the mistake of accepting a ride from a teenager named David Harris in Dallas, Texas. Unbeknown to Adams, Harris was driving a stolen vehicle. The two hang out for most of the day, smoking marijuana and drinking alcohol. When they get back on the road, Harris proceeds to kill a police officer who pulls the two over for a broken headlight. While guilty of some very poor judgment, Randall Dale Adams is not guilty of shooting and killing the officer. However, Harris claims Adams did it. Because this is a capital case in a solidly pro-death penalty state, Adams' life is at stake. The filmmaker retraces the steps of the two culprits and the investigations of the Dallas police to show that Adams is innocent. Along the way, Morris highlights the frailties of eyewitness testimony, the possibility that innocent people could be convicted of a capital crime and put to death; and the power of documentary filmmaking.

Discussion Questions for *The Thin Blue Line*:

1. Why do you think the film is titled *The Thin Blue Line*?

2. Discuss the role of eyewitness testimony in this case. What are some of the problems with relying on human observation and human memory in capital cases?

3. Discuss the role of the district attorney in this case. How do district attorneys exert their power and control over criminal cases?

4. Randall Adams is a working-class man with no college education; he is an out-of-towner who moves into town seeking work. He lives in a hotel with his brother. Does his status affect his access to the law? If he was the well-to-do son of a local oil tycoon, do you think he would have been treated differently? Explain how class status can play a role in criminal cases.

7

Law and Dispute Processing

◆ ◆ ◆

PRIVATE WRONGS AND PUBLIC OUTCRIES

In the past several decades, tort law, the law of private wrongs or injuries, has suffered some seriously bad press from popular print, television, radio news media, blogs, and websites highlighting the most outrageous lawsuits and depicting them as typical or "normal." For instance, every year the Chamber of Commerce's Institute for Legal Reform (ILR) publishes on its website a list of the "Most Ridiculous Lawsuits of the Year." The Chamber of Commerce is a special interest group that advocates for private businesses. The Chamber's tax-exempt Institute for Legal Reform's stated purpose is to advocate for civil justice reform (http://www.instituteforlegalreform.com/). The cases on the ILR list are presented as jokes, and the punchline almost always involves the legal system being used as a tool for unscrupulous people who would rather sue someone than work for a living. In 2017, the list featured a woman who sued a jellybean candy maker because she thought the candy was sugar-free, even though the label listed evaporated cane juice as a primary ingredient (http://www.instituteforlegalreform.com/). Another case involved a man who sued his date because she was texting on her phone throughout the movie he brought her to see (http://www.instituteforlegalreform.com/). What is not emphasized on the ILR website is the fact that many of these lawsuits never make it to court. For example, the movie-goer's date reimbursed him after the case made headlines in local and national news outlets. Further, the ILR scours the entire country to come up with these relatively few outlying examples every year. They then present these outlandish cases as typical of everything that is wrong with the civil law system in the United States. And cases that involve serious harm to individuals from

173

medical malpractice, dangerous products, or unsafe work conditions are left out of this discussion of "**tort reform**." Not to be confused with a *torte*, a delicious layered, cakelike dessert, a **tort** is a private wrong. The term **tort reform** entered the American legal and political lexicon in the 1970s and took hold in the 1980s and 1990s. **Tort reform** does not mean one singular thing; rather it is a collection of ideas that are geared toward changing the civil law system in ways that limit the number of civil lawsuits and the amount of damages that can be awarded in such suits. Indeed "**caps on damages**" represents one of the rallying cries of pro-tort reform groups, such as the ILR. **Caps on damages** means that there should be absolute maximums set on how much money can be awarded to the plaintiffs in civil lawsuits.

Calls for tort reform are a reaction to the notion that the entire American civil law system is misused by scoundrels who want to "make a quick buck" by bringing frivolous lawsuits to an already overburdened court system. Thus, civil law and the trial lawyers who practice it have come under fire by businesses big and small, as have entire industries, professions, and politicians—mainly by conservative Republicans who promote unfettered capitalism and pro-business agendas (Kuttner 2004). But should the civil law system be considered public enemy number one? Are all civil lawyers ambulance-chasing ne'er-do-wells out to make fast money for themselves and their clients? No. While there are always bad apples in any profession, the civil legal system plays an important role in processing disputes and protecting people from a variety of private wrongs, such as medical malpractice, environmental disasters, dangerous pollutants, defective products, and careless employers who endanger the lives of their workers. As Judge Learned Hand said in his 1951 speech to commemorate the 75th Anniversary of The Legal Aid Society, "If we are to keep our democracy, there must be one commandment: Thou shalt not ration justice" (http://www.legal-aid.org/en/las/thoushaltnotrationjustice.aspx). The opportunity to bring a matter to the civil justice system is a basic right of U.S. citizens. Since the average citizen is much more likely to be the victim of a dangerous product or a dangerous workplace than they are a dangerous crime (Reiman and Leighton 2017), attempts to curtail access to the civil justice system can affect everyone in the United States.

As a way to counter the negative image of tort law, in 2015 the well-known consumer rights advocate and one-time presidential candidate Ralph Nader opened the "world's first ever legal museum" called the American Museum of Tort Law, located in Winsted, Connecticut, Nader's hometown (Feeney 2015). The purpose of the museum is twofold: (1) to educate people on their right to a trial by jury, and (2) to teach citizens about the benefits of tort law (https://www.tortmuseum.org/). As the museum's director, Richard

L. Newman, states: "The thing that's cool about this place is that tort law potentially affects everyone. The museum is here to help people find that out (Feeney 2015:G7).

The museum features famous tort cases, such as the so-called "McDonald's hot coffee case" that became a cause célèbre for proponents of tort reform. The story perpetuated in the popular news media was that a woman was driving with hot coffee in her lap and spilled it on herself. She sued the fast-food chain and won over $2.5 million in damages. In reality, the woman, 79-year-old Stella Liebeck, was not driving the car; she was seated in the passenger side of a parked vehicle when the coffee, estimated to be about 180–190 degrees Fahrenheit, scorched her lap, causing third-degree burns that necessitated several surgeries and over two years of recovery (Burtka n.d.). Liebeck was willing to settle with McDonalds for the cost of her medical bills, but they only offered around $500. At the trial, a jury awarded Liebeck about $160,000 in **compensatory damages** and $2.7 million in **punitive damages**. The judge reduced the damages to about $500,000, and the parties later settled out of court for an undisclosed amount (Burtka n.d.).

Legalese:

In tort law, **compensatory damages** are also called actual damages; they cover measurable injuries sustained by the plaintiff, such as medical bills or loss of income (Falcone 2005; Gifis 1996). **Punitive damages** are rewarded to the plaintiff above and beyond the actual damages. Also known as exemplary damages, they punish the wrongful party and are typically awarded only in cases of "willful and malicious misconduct" (Gifis 1996:125).

This chapter examines the dispute resolution, or dispute processing, function of law in the United States. To understand this important function of law, we must first look at the term *dispute* and the types of possible disputes that law can process. A **dispute** is a disagreement, a controversy, or a debate; it can also be a quarrel. Disputes happen when two or more parties are in conflict over an event: a contract was breached, a patent was infringed upon, a personal injury was sustained, or perhaps a piece of property was encroached upon. These are just a few of the possible disputes that can be handled in civil courts.

Many terms are used to discuss the role of law in dealing with disputes. Some legal scholars use conflict resolution; others use conflict regulation.

Karen E. Hayden

A dispute can take many names.

Still others use the terms conflict management, or dispute settlement. We should note, however, that the courts tend to *process* or perhaps *sort out* disputes, but do not always *resolve* them. Dispute processing may be the best term to use because disputes are rarely fully resolved or settled in court or through the legal system. And legal disputes are seldom, if ever, settled to everyone's satisfaction because the legal system in the United States is adversarial—based on the notion of a winner and a loser.

STAGES OF DISPUTE PROCESSING

Two American anthropologists who work in the field of law are Laura Nader, sister of Ralph Nader, and Harry F. Todd. In the late 1970s, Nader and Todd identified three stages in dispute processing: the grievance or pre-conflict stage, the conflict stage, and the dispute stage (1978). Briefly, the stages involve:

- **Grievance/Pre-Conflict Stage**: individuals or groups perceive some form of harm, injustice, or problem
- **Conflict Stage**: the aggrieved parties confront one another
- **Dispute Stage**: the conflict is made public; it is brought to the attention of the court or some formal forum for processing disputes (Nader and Todd 1978).

When a third party is brought in to settle a dispute, then formal dispute processing begins. Law addresses disagreements that have been translated into legal disputes or conflicts.

METHODS OF DISPUTE RESOLUTION

Disputes can be found everywhere in our society, and they are often handed over to others to resolve. In more traditional, premodern societies, disputes were sometimes settled through violence, as in a fight, a duel, or a war. And, unfortunately, some disputes are still settled by force. Small-scale violence, such as a fight between two gangs, is an **extralegal** means of settling a dispute as old as time. Other traditional, informal types of dispute settlement were shaming, using rituals to clear the dispute, ostracism, or "lumping it," as in "like it or lump it," which means pretty much doing nothing about it—avoid or exit the conflict.

Legalese:

Extralegal may sound like it is "super legal"—as in extra-crispy fried chicken. But, it actually means the opposite. When one says "extra-legal," it means *not* officially sanctioned by law, existing outside of formal legal constructs.

In modern or postmodern American society, while violence is still all too prevalent, citizens often turn to the legal system to settle disputes. The United States has been called a **litigious** society, meaning we are prone to use lawsuits to settle disputes—in other words, we are "lawsuit happy" (Danzig 2012:n.p.). While U.S. citizens do use the courts as a form of settling countervailing claims, some legal scholars and commentators argue that the notion that Americans are more litigious than others is overblown. Yates, Creel Davis, and Glick studied torts in the United States over a 20-year period and caution against general claims of litigiousness (2001). They found that the tendency to use the courts to resolve disputes varies from state to state and is related to how well citizens feel the political system responds to their needs (2001). According to the Harvard School of Public Health, "fewer than one in 15 of the more than 750,000 patients who suffer injuries in a hospital each year ever file a lawsuit ... and only about a quarter of patients who sue ever receive money" (Allen 2005:A1). Similarly, Sadhbh Walshe, a legal reporter and commentator for *The Guardian*, looked into the idea of America's litigiousness and concluded:

> The truth is Americans don't sue that much at all .... According to recent data, only 10% of injured Americans ever file a claim for compensation and only 2% file lawsuits. All told, tort cases represent just 4.4% of all civil caseloads and that percentage has been declining steadily. (Walshe 2013:n.p.)

Maybe the fear of lawsuits on the part of business and property owners is driving this notion of American litigiousness in the same way that the fear of crime is often exploited to benefit politicians and private industries that build prisons or otherwise benefit from the fear of crime. So, while the idea that Americans turn to the courts for every small slight or injury is overblown, the courts are still a primary forum for dispute processing in our society.

Primary Resolution Processes

As we have noted in previous chapters, when societies grow in size and complexity, so too does the role of law. The law is often called upon to settle or at least process disputes. In order to manage the growth of disputes, legal institutions, lawyers, and other professionals have developed a variety of forums outside of filing a lawsuit through which parties can address their disputes. Each one is not necessarily distinct from the other; rather, they form a continuum (Galanter 1984; Turkel 1996). Primary dispute resolution mechanisms can be depicted on a continuum ranging from negotiation on one end to adjudication on the other. In between these two end points are mediation and arbitration (Figure 7.1).

We can also consider these forms of dispute processing as a hierarchy that rises in terms of legal formality and rationality. To review terms from Chapter 3, **formality** is the independence of legal institutions and procedures from all other social institutions, such as religion, family, politics, and economics (Sutton 2001). **Rationality** is the reliance on specifically legal principles and rules for making decisions that are logically applied to particular cases. **Rational law** requires the highest degree of institutional, procedural, and intellectual independence of law (Sutton 2001). **Rationality** means systematically organized, rule-bound, based on logical interpretation of meaning, and oriented toward intellectual pursuits of the truth (Sutton 2001) (Figure 7.2). As you move up the steps of the hierarchy, the process becomes more formal, more legitimate, and more legally binding.

A dispute can travel from one end of the continuum to the other until it is finally resolved, or the dispute can travel up the hierarchy. As they move up the hierarchy, disputes tend to become more structured, less voluntary, and more constrained by legal reasoning. They also become more adversarial, more public, and more rule-bound.

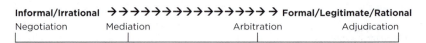

Figure 7.1 Continuum of Primary Forms of Dispute Resolution

Figure 7.2 Hierarchy of Dispute Resolution

In legal language, negotiation, mediation, and arbitration are called forms of Alternative Dispute Resolution or ADR. All are substitutions to adjudication, or suing someone in court. They can also be seen as methods to relieve overburdened courts and quicken the process of dispute settlement.

NEGOTIATION

At the first level of ADR, **negotiation**, participants enter into the process voluntarily. To **negotiate** means that the two parties work with one another to reach some type of settlement or agreement on a matter. The **negotiation** is arranged by the disputants, or the parties in the dispute, without a third party involved. The two parties attempt to settle a dispute through discussions, dialogue, compromise, and bargaining. Negotiations operate in both criminal and civil law. In criminal law, defense attorneys and prosecutors often engage in plea bargaining, a form of negotiation. In civil law, parties negotiate with the goal of settling their cases without having to go to court.

Negotiation is often predicated on unequal resources. For example, plea bargaining often occurs in criminal cases when a public defendant is too overburdened with cases to mount a credible defense. In civil cases, disparities in legal resources may force injured parties to settle too soon and for too little (Allen 2005). These criticisms of negotiation raise problems for legitimacy based on the legal norms of equality and universality. The inequality within the system can undermine the universal application of legal rules. Although it may lack normative legitimacy, negotiation tends to have cognitive legitimacy, meaning people who enter into the process voluntarily have some shared knowledge, beliefs, and goals about the power relations involved.

MEDIATION

When disputes are not settled by negotiation, they may move along the continuum to **mediation**, which aims at securing an agreement among disputing parties but still without formal legal procedures and rules. Unlike negotiation, mediation involves a neutral third party, known as the mediator. The mediator does not have power or resources to impose a settlement or to make a decision that either side must accept. Rather, the mediator acts as a facilitator and a go-between. In the United States, mediation has been around since the colonial period and has become more widely used since the 1960s (Vago 2012). It is used in a variety of legal settings including small claims court, housing courts, and family courts. Since mediators have no formal authority to settle a matter, they must rely on their own communication skills.

In mediation, the mediator is either appointed by someone in authority or chosen by the disputants. He or she tries to encourage the parties to come to an agreement by appealing to each side's interests. Mediators can

Source: Wiley Miller/CartoonStock.com

be lawyers, law students, or sometimes lay people with special training. As author Keith O'Brien states:

> In a civil dispute, going to trial is always risky. Verdicts can either force defendants to pay astronomical amounts or leave plaintiffs without a penny. And so people often decide they'd rather settle—if they can agree on a price. The parties then choose a mediator—both sides must agree on the person—and the process begins, behind closed doors, with both sides stating their cases and demands. The mediator separates the two sides into different rooms and begins shuttling back and forth between them .... What happens in a mediation is confidential. Mediators are prohibited from speaking about specifics (O'Brien 2009:24).

Since the early 1990s, the number of civil trials has dropped by about 75 percent in the nation's busiest courts (O'Brien 2009). At the same time, mediation has experienced a surge in popularity. People are turning to mediation to avoid spending the time and money involved in mounting civil cases (O'Brien 2009).

CASE IN POINT

Paul Finn, the Mediator Who Does Not Use the Word "Fair"

Boston mediator Paul Finn has become sought after for his mediation skills. Finn was trained as a lawyer at the New England School of Law, but turned to mediation full time in 1992 and is now president and CEO of the Brockton, Massachusetts-based Commonwealth Mediation and Conciliation, Inc. Finn has mediated some of the most high-profile cases in New England and across the country. He worked out a settlement in the Boston clergy sex abuse scandal, helped to settle the 2003 Station Nightclub fire in Rhode Island in which 100 people died, and also mediated a settlement in a 2006 case of a woman who died due to the collapse of a ceiling tile in a tunnel that was part of Boston's "big dig" project (O'Brien 2009). The key to Paul Finn's success is trust. Finn uses many of his own skills to gain the trust of both parties involved in the dispute. He disarms people with his humor; he is a straight talker and he perseveres, staying with a case until it is settled. As Finn himself puts it, "I'm the one who's going to stop it" (O'Brien 2009:24). And he is honest:

> If you're seeking justice, Finn tells the victims who come to see him, it's best to go somewhere else, because in his mediations, despite his sometimes course language, there is one four-letter word that he never uses. That word is "fair." (O'Brien 2009:22)

Finn acknowledges that victims and survivors of horrible accidents can never truly be compensated for their losses—how do you repair a lost limb or compensate for a lost love one? But once the disputants in a claim recognize this reality, Finn finds they can move toward a settlement.

Legal scholars Susan S. Silbey and Sally E. Merry analyzed various dispute processing strategies used by mediators (Silbey and Merry, 1986; Merry and Silbey, 1986). They employ the symbolic interactionist perspective to examine how the mediator uses the presentation of self in the mediation process. According to these two authors, successful mediation involves the control of information and the communication skills of the mediator. Mediators can control information in many ways:

- They control information about themselves; they present themselves as experts on settling disputes; they might talk about their extensive training and experience in mediating disputes; they bring up examples of other disputes they have resolved; they emphasize their connections to the court
- They control the communication between the disputants; the mediator meets with the two parties separately and does not reveal everything to each party
- They control the substantive issues in the case; they establish cognitive legitimacy by restating the dispute in ways that enable the disputants to agree on the important features of the conflict; they might rephrase the dispute or focus on what is resolvable
- They attempt to get the parties to articulate shared normative commitments and values; for example, in a dispute between neighbors, the mediator may try to get the two parties to agree on one simple idea, such as "neighbors need to live together and learn to get along" (Silbey and Merry 1986:18).

To summarize, mediation is a specific kind of communication in which a third party tries to move the disputing parties toward a settlement. To succeed, the mediator must establish authority and control the flow of information. A good mediator should demonstrate confidentiality, sympathy, and fair-mindedness for both parties.

ARBITRATION

The next step up the hierarchy of alternative dispute resolution is **arbitration**, a more formal process than negotiation and mediation. In **arbitration,** both parties argue their case to a third party, an arbitrator, who has the authority to make a decision or a settlement. Arbitrators are typically knowledgeable about the substantive issue of the cases that they hear, thus arbitrators often have their own specialties—such as labor disputes or contract disputes, for instance. There are different kinds of arbitration; some are more binding than others. In the 1920s, arbitration became a legally sanctioned form of dispute resolution. In 1920, New York passed a statute giving parties the right to resolve disputes through arbitration (Vago 2012). The U.S. Arbitration Act, enacted by Congress in 1925, recognizes the legality of arbitration when parties to commercial transactions have signed an agreement to arbitrate. The National Labor Relations Board is an empowered arbitrating body between labor and owners (McCammon 2004).

The American Arbitration Association, the largest professional organization of arbitration practitioners, has its own code of ethics, professional fees, and dues. In some cities, such as Philadelphia, a case that is under $10,000 is automatically assigned by the court to arbitration. The city has found that it costs about one-fifth the amount that litigation in the courts would cost (Vago 2012). Generally speaking, people who cannot settle disputes through mediation and negotiation may enter into arbitration for two reasons. First, they may have a contractual agreement to do so; many contracts, such as those between an employer and an employee, or between a cell phone carrier and a cell phone customer, stipulate arbitration (Fair Arbitration Now 2015 n.p). Second, the two parties may voluntarily agree to arbitrate a dispute rather than to litigate in court, which is more costly and time-consuming.

While it is more formalized than negotiation or mediation, formal rules of evidence do not apply in arbitration, and it is not subject to technical legal rules. The parties take on adversarial roles in the arbitration hearing. However, their communication is not completely formal, nor is it controlled by legal procedures—at least not to the extent that it would be in a court of law. Arbitration proceedings are not held in court and, unlike negotiation and mediation, the decision in an arbitrated case is final (Vago 2012). Typically, however, the proceedings are kept confidential, and there is no public record of what transpired.

FORCED OR MANDATORY ARBITRATION

Entering into arbitration on a voluntary basis offers people another way to avoid the time and money involved in the "I'll see you in court!" option. Many business, employee, and consumer contracts, however, include **mandatory arbitration clauses**. A **mandatory arbitration clause** forces the parties to go to arbitration and precludes or preempts their ability to enter into a lawsuit on their own behalf. Since the contracts are written by the corporations, the consumers or employees who enter into these contracts often do not realize that they have signed over their rights to sue in civil court, creating a clear imbalance of power and resources between the two parties. And typically, the arbitrator is arranged by the corporation, which brings in another layer of inequity between the two parties. While the arbitrator is supposed to be a neutral third party, he or she is more likely to be rehired by the corporation as opposed to an individual consumer, and therefore may favor the corporation's side in the dispute. For instance, consumer rights groups have criticized cellphone companies because of their forced arbitration clauses in consumer contracts. These clauses, often found in the very small print of the contract, prohibit users from pursuing legal action against the cellphone carriers in individual lawsuits or class actions. The consumer rights coalition Fair Arbitration Now found:

> In 2007, two groups of California T-Mobile customers challenged T-Mobile's $200 flat early termination penalty and practice of installing a locking device in its handsets to prevent consumers from switching services on the same phone. T-Mobile attempted to use its arbitration clause to shield the company from a class action lawsuit over the unfair terms of service. The California Supreme Court struck down the class action ban. The same year in Washington, Cingular customers brought a class action over improper long distance and/or out-of-network "roaming" charges, alleging that individual customers were overcharged up to $45 a month. Like California, the Washington Supreme Court also stuck down the class action ban in Cingular's arbitration clause. (http://www.fairarbitrationnow.org/cell-phone-arbitration/)

The right to sue someone in civil court is a basic right of all Americans. Large corporations, however, have quietly co-opted this right by adding mandatory arbitration clauses to contracts. According to the Pew Research Center, about 77 percent of American adults own a cellphone, so this marks a significant group of people who are unknowingly signing over their rights (http://www. pewresearch.org/fact-tank/2017/01/12/evolution-of-technology/). Similar mandatory arbitration clauses can be found in contracts between employers and employees, doctors and patients, banks and consumers, insurance companies and consumers, and nursing homes and their elderly patients. In short, these mandatory arbitration clauses tie the hands of the individual consumers and patients while benefitting the owners and shareholders of businesses.

If all of the forms of ADR fail to bring about a resolution to a dispute, the parties involved may turn to adjudication or litigation. Or, some disputants bypass ADR altogether and opt to bring a matter to the court system from the onset.

ADJUDICATION/LITIGATION

The terms **adjudication** and **litigation** are used interchangeably. **Adjudication** is the process of settling an issue through a formal court hearing (Falcone

2005). **Litigation** means a "suit … a judicial contest; a legal action … whether civil, criminal, or administrative" (Falcone 2005:150). This formal, public proceeding has the highest level of institutional legitimacy: legal procedures and patterns of reasoning determine how the dispute is defined as a case, how it is processed through the court, and how it is understood by legal professionals. Adjudication or litigation is an adversarial process; it is a win-or-lose scenario. Generally, adjudication as a form of dispute processing takes place in two types of lawsuits: **torts** and **contractual**. In **torts**, the plaintiff claims that the defendant acted wrongly and injured the plaintiff or damaged his or her property, such as in cases of medical malpractice or accidents. In **contractual disputes**, the plaintiff claims that the defendant broke a promise or an obligation prescribed in a legal contract; for instance, a construction company fails to finish a job or an employer reneges on a labor contract (Vago 2012).

In civil cases, the plaintiff must meet a standard of proof called **preponderance of the evidence**, which is not as strict as **beyond a reasonable doubt**, the standard in criminal cases. **Preponderance of the evidence** means that the plaintiff's side must present evidence that is more convincing than the defendant's evidence that the harm was likely caused by the defendant (Gifis 1996). **Beyond a reasonable doubt** in criminal cases "refers to the degree of certainty required for a juror to legally find a criminal defendant guilty …. It means simply that the proof must be so conclusive and complete … all reasonable doubts of the fact are removed from the mind of an ordinary person" (Gifis 1996:416–417).

In civil cases, adjudication begins when the plaintiff's attorney files a complaint in the trial court. The complaint lays out the facts of the wrongful action: any injuries or damages, or any monetary losses. The plaintiff also specifies the relief sought. The clerk of the court then issues a summons to the defendant, who is required to plead or respond by a specified time; if not, there may be a judgment based on default (Turkel 1996). The defendant's lawyer or lawyers can take numerous pretrial actions to try to delay or stop the proceedings, such as trying to claim faulty legal grounds, denial of the alleged misdoings, or filing motions for more specific allegations (Harr 1995).

Typically, the civil trial takes place in three phases. The first is discovery, where the lawyers must produce documents and evidence and depositions are taken. At this stage, there might be interrogatories, where written questions are posed by the opposing lawyers. The trial makes up the second phase. The plaintiff's attorney starts with opening statements, and then the defendant's lawyers take their turn at opening statements. A settlement can occur at any point to either preclude the trial or stop the trial as it is happening (Harr 1995; Turkel 1996).

Witnesses are examined by the side that called them and then cross-examined by the opposing side. There may be more questioning, redirect, and cross examinations by the judges. After all the evidence is presented, the opposing lawyers present their closing arguments. The judge charges the jury, giving them specific instructions on how to proceed. The jury moves to a private room and deliberates (Turkel 1996).

The verdict represents the final step in the adjudication/litigation process. If the verdict is against the defendant, either the judge or the jury determines a remedy or damages. The losing party can appeal the verdict. Appeals must be based on errors made by the trial judge and raised by the appellant's lawyer during the trial and in the trial record. The legal legitimacy of litigation as a form of dispute resolution rests in the following of procedures and compliance with the law. Litigation is formal, rational, public, and legally binding.

The four forms of primary dispute processing—negotiation, mediation, arbitration, and litigation—are not mutually exclusive; they overlap and are often combined. For example, divorce law almost always combines both mediation and litigation. In addition to these four traditional types of dispute resolution, there are several other forms of dispute processing, sometimes called hybrid or combined forms of dispute resolution.

HYBRID OR COMBINED FORMS OF RESOLUTION PROCESSES

Given the range and number of disputes that can emerge in advanced, industrial or postindustrial societies, new approaches to dispute processing have developed in the United States to address countervailing interests outside of the courtroom. These new approaches are sometimes called hybrid or combined forms of dispute resolution and can include: collaborative law, settlement counsel, partnering, rent-a-judge, and mini-trials.

COLLABORATIVE LAW

In an article titled, "Lawyers Who Just Say No to Litigation," attorneys David A. Hoffman and James E. McGuire look at what they call "a quiet revolution brewing in the legal community"—**collaborative law** (2001:E3). **Collaborative law** is a form of dispute processing in which both parties are represented by their own attorneys, but the parties enter into the process agreeing to settle the matter without litigation—without going to court (Hoffman and McGuire 2001:E1, E3). Practiced most often in the field of divorce and family law, and also in other areas of civil law, collaborative lawyers work "under the principles adopted by the Collaborative Law Council (an organization of 40 Massachusetts lawyers) and other similar organizations around the country, if settlement discussions fail, the collaborative lawyers must refer the case to another lawyer" (Hoffman and McGuire 2001:E1, E3). Collaborative law practioners view this new field as open, informal, private, and cooperative. It is also less expensive than having your day in court (https://blc.law/services-for-families/collaborative-law/).

SETTLEMENT COUNSEL

Within the field of business law, another shift away from litigation is the growing use of **settlement counsel**. **Settlement counsel** involves business lawyers who "specialize in negotiation and settlement techniques" between business interests (Hoffman and McGuire 2001:E3). Settlement counselors often work within large business law firms, but they have extensive training in "mediation and other modern dispute resolution techniques" (Hoffman and McGuire 2001:E3). Hoffman and McGuire explain the growing popularity of settlement counsel this way:

> First, even though most cases are settled without the need for a trial, the settlement usually occurs only after substantial resources are spent on pretrial preparations. Many clients, and settlement counsel, are looking to cut to the chase early in the process. Second, experienced lawyers know that durable and fair settlements can be reached only if the interests of all parties are thoroughly explored. Superficial attempts are usually unproductive (Hoffman and McGuire 2001:E3).

By shifting the focus away from a winner-and-loser proposition, settlement counselors and collaborative lawyers are moving toward new approaches to dispute resolution.

Collaborative law: A new approach in the legal community.

Istock/designer491

PARTNERING

Partnering, a form of mediation, typically addresses disputes in construction contracts (Hoffman and McGuire 2001:E3). The **partnering** process involves daylong discussions about the potential problems and pitfalls that could arise in large, complex building projects. It is a more open approach that some lawyers believe could be applied to other types of businesses (Hoffman and McGuire 2001:E3).

RENT-A-JUDGE

Rent-a-judge is a type of arbitration where people attempt to avoid entering into a formal court of law. Instead, they hire judges, sometimes a retired judge or one who works on the side—moonlighting—to hear the case and make a decision (Vago 2012). There is a winner and a loser in the rent-a-judge process; it is legally binding; and, unlike arbitration, the decision of the rented judge can be appealed (Goldberg et al. 2012). Rent-a-judge has grown in popularity among some groups—namely, large businesses that can afford to rent a judge. The process can cost anywhere from one to several thousand dollars per day (Terry 1982). Critics argue that it is a way to buy justice and outsource the rule of law, creating a segregated civil justice system (Terry 1982). The proceedings and outcomes are private, thus there is very little oversight of this private judging process. Proponents counter that rent-a-judge processes free up the courts to work on other matters and save taxpayers' money (Terry 1982).

MEDIATION-ARBITRATION OR MED-ARB

When mediation and arbitration are combined into one process, it is called **med-arb.** This dispute processing method is most often used in employment contract disputes. Typically, the same person serves as both mediator and arbitrator, and if the conflict cannot be resolved through mediation, he or she switches to the role of arbitrator (Vago 2012) or a different arbitrator takes over. This dispute processing tool is described by Harvard Law School's Program on Negotiation:

> A hybrid **mediation-arbitration** approach called *med-arb* combines the benefits of both techniques. In this increasingly popular process, parties first attempt to collaborate on an agreement with the help of a mediator. If the mediation ends in impasse, or if issues remain unresolved, the parties can then move on to arbitration. The mediator can assume the role of arbitrator (if qualified) and render a binding decision quickly, or an arbitrator can take over the case after consulting with the mediator …. In *med-arb*, parties first attempt to hammer

out a collaborative agreement, working together and in private sessions with a mediator or "med-arbiter," a neutral third party trained in *med-arb* (Harvard Law School, Program on Negotiation Staff 2017:n.p., italics in original).

Why do people turn to med-arb as opposed to one or the other? According to the Program on Negotiation at Harvard law School, "the threat of having a third party render a decision in a binding arbitration often inspires disputants to work extra hard in mediation to come to an agreement" (Harvard Law School, Program on Negotiation Staff 2017:n.p.). Med-arb can be quick and can smooth over relations in cases where the disputants may need to work together again. It saves "time and money by eliminating the need to start arbitration from square one if mediation fails" (Harvard Law School, Program on Negotiation Staff 2017:n.p.). Med-arb can be a win-win for disputants who agree to it and who have the money to pay for it. It is most often called upon for disputes between employers and labor unions.

"MINI-TRIAL"

A **mini-trial** is described by the American Bar Association as:

> a private, consensual process where the attorneys for each party make a brief presentation of the case as if at a trial. The presentations are observed by a neutral advisor and by representatives (usually high-level business executives) from each side who have authority to settle the dispute. At the end of the presentations, the representatives attempt to settle the dispute. If the representatives fail to settle the dispute, the neutral advisor, at the request of the parties, may serve as a mediator or may issue a non-binding opinion as to the likely outcome in court (https://www.americanbar.org/groups/dispute_resolution/resources/DisputeResolutionProcesses/mini-trial.html).

A mini-trial is quick—usually completed within one day. Mini-trials are most often used between and among corporations, such as two major oil corporations disputing offshore property agreements. Like the rent-a-judge approach, mini-trials represent another form of justice that is available to very wealthy people; it is usually used in matters of business and commerce, and is not widely used by the general public.

Taken together, hybrid forms of dispute resolution offer disputing parties various alternatives to settle matters outside of a court of law. By turning away from litigation and towards these alternatives, practioners of hybrid and alternative forms of dispute processing are "going against the grain of our legal, and popular, culture which glorifies the rigor of the courtroom battle through fiction, the news, and TV dramas" (Hoffman and McGuire 2001:E3). Some practioners of new forms of dispute processing are happy to avoid the drama of the courtroom and its winner-take-all, adversarial approach. As Chief Justice Warren Burger once said, "The entire legal profession—lawyers, judges, law teachers—has become so mesmerized with the stimulation of the courtroom contest that we tend to forget that we ought to be healers—healers of conflict" (quoted in Hoffman and McGuire 2001:E1). This "conflict healing" approach represents a profound shift in how we view disputes. While American society will always need the civil justice system to settle disputes, this quiet revolution within the field of dispute resolution presents a new way of thinking about how we handle disagreements that could end up in court (Hoffman and McGuire 2001).

WHO CAN SUE? JUSTICIABILITY AND STANDING

If opponents in disputes do end up in the court system, courts are a neutral and impartial place for dispute processing. Not every matter that is brought to the court system is viable as a legal dispute, however. Individuals and organizations who want to use the civil court system for dispute processing must meet certain legal requirements. To have their cases heard in a court of law, plaintiffs must demonstrate justiciability and legal standing (Vago 2012).

Justiciability means that the matter is "capable of being tried in a court of law ... it is feasible for a court to carry out and enforce its decision" (Gifis 1996:278). The courts must be able to provide a remedy. In this country, courts tend to be broken down into special areas. For example, you would not see a civil trial court ruling on a criminal matter, but most cases do find their court. Justiciability refers to a real and substantial controversy that is appropriate for adjudication—a matter that is concrete enough to be adjudicated in a court of law.

Legal standing represents another prerequisite to litigation/adjudication. **Legal standing** is the "right of a person or group to challenge in a judicial forum the conduct of another" (Gifis 1996:483). Standing means that the individual, groups, or organizations involved in the dispute have some legal status or stake in the outcome of the case. So, for instance, a daughter-in-law cannot sue her mother-in-law for divorce, even though there are undoubtedly some cases where that would not be a bad idea.

Earlier in this chapter, we looked at an example of a frivolous lawsuit involving jelly beans. That case brings to mind the Latin phrase *de minimis non curat lex*, meaning the law does not govern trifles (Vago 2012). Trivial matters are generally kept out of civil courts. Some smaller matters do find their place in **small claims court**, however. **Small claims courts** exist in all 50 U.S. states. They are a type of trial court that has limited jurisdiction to hear civil cases between private litigants involving, for instance, small business matters, debts, landlord-tenant disputes, motor vehicle repair costs, or small contract issues (Warner 2016). Small claims disputants usually represent themselves, although in some states disputants are allowed to bring lawyers. The monetary limit allowed in small claims courts varies by state, ranging from $2,500 in Kentucky and Rhode Island to $25,000 in Tennessee (https://www.nolo.com/legal-encyclopedia/small-claims-suits-how-much-30031.html). Most states have limits somewhere in between, typically in the $10,000 range.

TYPES OF PRIVATE WRONGS

Many different types of cases can wind up in civil litigation. The types of possible disputes brought to civil court are endless but can be categorized by the private wrongs involved. The first three we consider here are torts. While torts cover a wide range of possible wrongdoings, they can be grouped into the general categories of: intentional acts, negligent acts, and acts for which there is strict liability (Walsh and Hemmens 2016).

Intentional Acts

The first tort category—**intentional acts**—is more likely to be found in criminal courts but can also be adjudicated in the civil justice system. Intentional acts are just as the term sounds—when someone acts with intent to harm, such as harm to person or property (Walsh and Hemmens 2016). While these acts are crimes—assault and vandalism—they may also end up in a civil court if the harmed person decides to seek monetary damages. An example is two friends, Biff and Bo, get drunk and end up in a physical altercation. Biff breaks Bo's nose. While Bo decides not to press charges in criminal court, he later decides to sue his buddy for the medical care he needed to set his broken nose.

Legalese:

In the Biff and Bo scenario, instead of being called a criminal, Biff would be a **tortfeasor**: one who commits a tort, a private wrong (Gifis 1996:517).

Negligence

Negligence is defined legally as "failure to exercise the degree of care which a person of ordinary prudence would exercise under the same circumstances" (Gifis 1996:333). People should be able to assume protection against unreasonable risk. Legal definitions of negligence also contain several subcategories such as: slight negligence, ordinary negligence, and gross negligence—all of which involve the standard of care and the extent of the negligence. There is also comparative negligence, concurrent negligence, and contributory negligence—which address the extent to which the plaintiff and the defendant, or two or more defendants, may share some of the blame in the negligence. **Criminal negligence** is another form of neglect that brings about criminal liability, such as extreme recklessness or carelessness resulting in severe injuries or death (Gifis 1996:333–334). In a civil action, the plaintiff must prove that negligence exists. This proof includes:

1. the defendant had a duty to act in certain way
2. the defendant breached that duty
3. this breach of duty was the cause of the defendant's injury or loss (Walsh and Hemmens 2016:168).

Negligence cases also hinge on **causation**: did the defendant's actions or omissions cause the harm to occur? As social scientists know, causation is notoriously hard to establish, since many factors can cause an event to occur, but, in a tort case, a legal standard of causation, either actual or approximate, must be proved (Walsh and Hemmens 2016).

Strict Liability

Torts of **strict liability** address private wrongs in which the plaintiff does not need to prove that the defendant acted intentionally or negligently. Rather, the plaintiff must establish that he or she was injured and that the defendant caused the injury; the tort occurred and the defendant was responsible (Walsh and Hemmens 2016). For example, unfortunately for pet-lovers, owning an animal brings with it risk of strict liability. If your dog gets away from you on a walk and knocks someone over, you are strictly liable. Or, if your diseased livestock infects your neighbor's livestock, you are liable—something to think about at your next cattle auction.

PROPERTY DISPUTES

Another type of case that civil courts address is property disputes. **Property** is legally defined as anything that is "subject to ownership, has an exchangeable value, or adds to one's estate" (Gifis 1996:399). **Personal property** can range from a wedding ring, to a bicycle, to a television, to a sports team. **Real property** is more commonly referred to as real estate: houses, land, buildings. Ideas, inventions, and concepts developed by individuals or groups make up **intellectual property** (Walsh and Hemmens 2016).

Property is important in the United States. We are a capitalist society, and ownership of property is a key to capitalism. Each type of property has a subfield of law devoted to it, that is, intellectual property law and real estate law. And, because the possibilities for property disputes are endless, law is often called upon to settle everything from a quarrel about a fence between two neighbors to the decades-long standoff between Cliven Bundy and the federal government concerning whether or not Bundy can graze his cattle on federally protected land. This dispute has crossed over from a dispute between Bundy and the Bureau of Land Management—a federal administration—to a crime as the Bundy family also mounted an armed occupation of a National Wildlife Refuge in Oregon.

CONTRACT DISPUTES

Another type of dispute that can end up in the civil justice system is contract disputes. A contract is a formal agreement—a promise or set of promises that is legally enforceable (Gifis 1996). Contracts can be drawn between two individuals, an individual and an institution, between and among groups, between agencies, and between corporations (Walsh and Hemmens 2016). The possibilities for contract disputes are as numerous as the types of contracts: where an agreement exists; it can be broken. When an agreement is broken, a disagreement—dispute—is likely to occur. Some contract disputes are mediated or negotiated; others are arbitrated. And many make their way to court.

FAMILY DISPUTES

Families pose another potentially dispute-ridden area that the law is called upon to address. Family disputes are disagreements between related people. They can range from a divorce, to two brothers-in-law who fight when they have had too much to drink, to decades-long feuds between family members who together run a family business where there are millions of dollars at stake. Law enters into family life at the birth of a child—custody and parentage must be determined. Law also enters the family at the point of the marriage contract. A marriage contract is an agreement between the two spouses, but also with the state that issues the marriage license. It is a legal and governmental union. And law stays in the family after death, when wills and estates are contested and eventually settled. Every point along the way holds the potential for problems and disputes. And here again, these disputes may be brought to mediators, arbitrators, or lawyers. Or, a dispute could travel all along the continuum from negotiation, to mediation, to arbitration, to litigation.

"To be honest, I'm not sure if you marking your territory is legally binding in a boundary claim dispute."

Source: Marty Bucella/CartoonStock.com

For better or worse, law functions to address disputes. Individuals, groups, institutions, and corporations tend to turn to the law when things are not going well—a contract was breached, a product did not stand up to its promise, or worse, for instance, someone was harmed by a faulty product. Or, a worker dies on the job when an employer cut corners on safety to save money on the bottom line. When other types of dispute resolution fail, the dispute processing function of the law can step in and attempt to settle matters through formal litigation. Litigation holds the most legitimate legal authority and tends to be the final step in a dispute resolution process.

CHAPTER SUMMARY

◆ Tort law, the law of private wrongs, has come under criticism by pro-business special interest groups. They view the civil justice system as out of control due to frivolous lawsuits waged by unscrupulous trial lawyers and clients out to make a quick buck.

◆ The civil legal system plays an important role in processing disputes and protecting people from private harms. Average citizens are more likely to suffer from a private wrong than they are to be harmed by a criminal act.

◆ The dispute processing function of law makes up a large part of the civil justice system in the United States.

◆ In the stages of dispute processing, the grievance/pre-conflict stage occurs when individuals or group perceive some form of harm or wrong. When the aggrieved parties confront one another, the dispute reaches the conflict stage. And when the conflict becomes public in a court of law, the dispute processing stage begins.

◆ Many methods of dispute processing can be sought out to address or resolve disputes. Primary resolution processes include negotiation, mediation, arbitration, and litigation. The first three are also known as forms of ADR since they are alternatives to formal court proceedings.

◆ Forced or mandatory arbitration clauses are written into many contracts and often preclude individual consumers or workers from litigating a matter in civil court.

◆ Once a dispute reaches the litigation stages, formal legal rules and proceedings must be followed. The standard of proof in a civil trial is the preponderance of evidence, a lower standard than the beyond a reasonable doubt needed in a criminal trial.

◆ Hybrid or combined forms of dispute resolution have emerged to address disputes in new ways; these include collaborative law, settlement counsel, partnering, rent-a-judge, and mini-trials.

◆ For a lawsuit to be viable in a court of law, plaintiffs must demonstrate justiciability and legal standing. Justiciability means that the case is feasible and enforceable. Standing means the plaintiff has a right to challenge the conduct of another.

◆ Many types of disputes can end up in civil litigation. Torts are private wrongs grouped into intentional acts, negligence, and strict liability. Civil courts also hear property disputes, contract disputes, and family disputes.

KEY TERMS

adjudication   184
arbitration   182
beyond a reasonable doubt   185
"caps on damages"   174
causation   192
collaborative law   186
compensatory damages   175
contractual disputes   185
criminal negligence   192
dispute   175
extralegal   177
families (disputes)   193
formality   178
intellectual property   192
intentional acts   191
justiciability   190
legal standing   190
litigation   184
litigious   177
mandatory arbitration
   clauses   183

mediation   180
mediation-arbitration
   (med-arb)   188
mini-trial   189
negligence   191
negotiate/negotiation   179
partnering   188
personal property   192
preponderance of the
   evidence   185
property   192
punitive damages   175
rational law   178
rationality   178
real property   192
settlement counsel   187
small claims court   190
strict liability   192
tort reform   174
torts   174
tortfeasor   191

CRITICAL THINKING QUESTIONS

1. Do you think there are too many frivolous lawsuits in our society? Why or why not?

2. Have you ever purchased a product that you later found to be faulty, defective, or even harmful? What steps (if any) did you take to resolve the matter? Was it resolved to your satisfaction? Why or why not?

3. Do you own a cellphone? Did you read the contract you signed when you bought the cell phone and signed up for cellular service? Do you think that cellular service companies should be allowed to place mandatory arbitration clauses in their contracts? Why or why not?

4. Many professional sports teams have mandatory arbitration written into their players' contracts. Look up a player-owner dispute in professional sports and discuss it. What was the dispute? How was it processed? Was there a winner in the dispute? Are both parties protected with these types of arbitration clauses? Which side seems to be more protected?

5. Has anyone you know been involved in a property dispute? Describe the dispute and how it was handled. Who if anyone came out ahead? Would mediation have helped this dispute?

SUGGESTED MOVIE: *HOT COFFEE*

Hot Coffee, Documentary. 2011. Susan Saladoff, Director. HBO.

The McDonald's hot coffee case became a cause célèbre for people, institutions, and organizations fighting for reform of the civil litigation system. While deemed an egregious example of so-called jackpot justice, the film dispels the manufactured misconceptions about the hot coffee case and several others. The filmmakers also highlight the ways that the civil justice system can protect average Americans against dangerous products, medical malpractice, and mandatory arbitration clauses. The film opens the way for discussion of many legal terms and issues including, but not limited to: tort reform, punitive damages, caps on damages, judicial elections, and mandatory arbitration clauses.

Discussion Questions for the film, *Hot Coffee*:

1. What does the term "tort reform" mean? What do proponents of tort reform want?

2. Who were some of the "claimsmakers" in this tort reform movement? Why were they interested in changes to the civil justice system?

3. What are mandatory arbitration clauses (or "dispute resolution clauses")? Who benefits from these clauses?

4. How does our society define "harm"? How do we prevent it? How do we hold corporations responsible for harm?

8

Law and Social Change

◆ ◆ ◆

IN DECEMBER OF 1963, THE REVEREND Dr. Martin Luther King, Jr. addressed a crowd at Western Michigan University. He considered the relationship between law and social change and the ability of law to change the heart (http://www.letterstotheexiles.com/hearts-habits-men-mlk-law-morality/). He said:

Now the other myth that gets around is the idea that legislation cannot really solve the problem and that it has no great role to play in this period of social change because you've got to change the heart and you can't change the heart through legislation. You can't legislate morals. The job must be done through education and religion. Well, there's a half-truth involved here. Certainly, if the problem is to be solved then in the final sense, hearts must be changed …. But we must go on to say that while it may be true that morality cannot be legislated, behavior can be regulated. It may be true that the law cannot change the heart but it can restrain the heartless. It may be true that the law cannot make a man love me but it can keep him from lynching me and I think that is pretty important, also. So there is a need for executive orders … for judicial decrees … for civil rights legislation on the local scale within states and on the national scale from the federal government (http://www.letterstotheexiles.com/hearts-habits-men-mlk-law-morality/).

Dr. Martin Luther King, Jr. in 1964.

Alpha Historica/Alamy Stock Photo

The law *can* restrain the heartless; the law *can* keep one person from lynching another. Sometimes hearts and minds are changed first; but often, especially in matters of civil rights, the law must change behavior first and maybe hearts will follow.

LAW AND SOCIAL CHANGE

This chapter examines the relationship between law and social change. The question of "which comes first, legal change or social change?" has vexed philosophers, sociologists, and legal theorists for centuries. The relationship between these two social phenomena is not clear: Does the law bring about social change or do social changes in society bring about new laws? The easy answer is both. Law can lead social change or law can follow social change that is already well under way. Change is erratic and unpredictable. Therefore, the direction of change is not always discernable.

We should keep in mind that the term social change can encompass many, many aspects of our social world. Social change can be small, incremental modifications or massive social revolutions. Social change can involve organized social movements where people come together to bring about a specific social change or respond to something in society that they want altered, as in the discussions about TOBAL ("There Ought To Be a Law") in Chapters 1 and 5 of this book. Social change can also encompass the large-scale movements of human populations, such as immigration from one country to another. Migration can also be internal, as in the mass movement of people from rural settings to urban centers within one country in the process of urbanization. Social change includes cultural and economic revolutions, or the restructuring of all aspects of social life, such as the massive changes that took place during the Industrial Revolution. As we discussed in Chapter 3, industrialization changed how people worked, where they lived, what their families looked like in terms of size and shape; it also changed the role of education and religion in people's daily lives. The Industrial Revolution swept through all of parts of society, resulting in wide-reaching social changes.

When we discuss social change, we should also remember that societies are always changing; they never sit still. In this chapter, we consider whether law leads or follows social change. One way to think about this question is to look at two contrasting views on the relationship between law and social change: those of social theorists Jeremy Bentham and Friedrich Karl von Savigny.

Jeremy Bentham (1748–1832)

The first theoretical perspective on the relationship between law and social change comes from Jeremy Bentham, a British social theorist and reformer of the mid-eighteenth century. Bentham studied society and law at the beginning of the Industrialization Revolution and the urbanization processes that were taking place throughout Europe.

Sidebar:

Weird historical fact about Bentham: Upon his death, Bentham left a large part of his estate to the newly established University College, London. He also left clear instructions that his body be dissected, embalmed, dressed, and placed in a chair in the main corridor of the central building of the college. And there he still sits.

Bentham took a scientific approach to the study of making and breaking laws. He is most well-known for his theory of **utilitarianism,** which assumes that all human actions are calculated in terms of their likelihood of bringing happiness (pleasure), or unhappiness (pain). Bentham owed a great debt to an earlier Italian theorist, Cesare Beccaria (1738–1794), whose utilitarian theory shaped Bentham's. Bentham proposed a precise formula for this process of calculated pleasure and pain in lawbreaking. Indeed, Bentham saw people as what he called human calculators who put all situational factors into an equation to decide whether or not a particular crime is worth committing. His utilitarianism still influences many criminological theories today, most notably rational choice theory.

In accordance with his utilitarian principles, Bentham wanted to provide a plan for reforming the legal system in ways that would focus more on *prevention* than *punishment*. He believed preventing crime before it happened would serve a greater purpose and aid more people in society than punishing the crime after the fact; this approach provided more *utility* to society.

Jeremy Bentham, 1748–1832.

Luise Berg-Ehlers/Alamy Stock Photo

Bentham was among the first to argue that the certainty of punishment outweighs the severity of punishment as a deterrent to crime. Keep in mind that at the time Bentham was proposing his theory, the late 1700s to early 1800s, English law included over 200 capital offenses. As historian Douglas Hay noted: "The rulers of eighteenth–century England cherished the death penalty" (1975:17). Yet, all the while, crime rates in England continued to rise. The severity of various forms of punishment during Bentham's day was barbaric and outlandish from today's perspective. Branding, drawing and quartering, whipping, and, of course, hanging could await those who committed even minor infractions, such as poaching game or stealing a neighbor's sheep. Yet even the punishment of death, the most severe of all punishments, did not significantly deter criminals. As historian Peter Linebaugh stated:

> While terror, majesty, dread, and some pity ... were the emotions that the state sought to arouse in the multitudes witnessing the hanging, the slow slang and canting dictionaries that have survived to record the speech of the eighteenth-century London poor give us a different picture. In contrast to the solemn abstractions of the law the speech of the labouring class describes the hanging with irreverence, humour and defiance (1975:66).

Indeed, public hangings in England became a spectacle, a form of entertainment even, with thousands of people gathering—not in horror, but often in humor—to watch the condemned swing from the gallows.

In November of 1849, Charles Dickens witnessed the double execution of notorious husband and wife murderers, the Mannings at Horsemonger Lane. He described the circus-like nature of the crowd:

> ... I believe that a sight so inconceivably awful as the wickedness and levity of the immense crowd collected at that execution this morning could be imagined by no man, and could be presented in no heathen land under the sun. The horrors of the gibbet and of the crime which brought the wretched murderers to it faded in my mind before the atrocious bearing, looks, and language of the assembled spectators. When I came upon the scene at midnight, the shrillness of the cries and howls that were raised ... [by] boys and girls already assembled ... made my blood run cold .... When the day dawned, thieves, low prostitutes, ruffians, and vagabonds of every kind, flocked on to the ground, with every variety of offensive and foul behaviour. Fightings, faintings, whistlings, imitations of Punch, brutal jokes, tumultuous demonstrations of indecent delight when swooning women were dragged out of the crowd by the police, with their dresses disordered, gave a new zest to the general entertainment. When the sun rose brightly ... the two miserable creatures who attracted all this ghastly sight about them were turned quivering into the air, there was no more emotion, no more pity, no more thought that two immortal souls had gone to judgment, no more restraint in any of the previous obscenities ... they perished like the beasts. (Charles Dickens, November 13, 1849, Letter to the Editor of *The Times*, London)

Decades prior to this spectacle, Bentham argued against the death penalty and other barbaric forms of punishment. Bentham believed that legal reforms should respond quickly to new social needs and to the changes underway in society. He saw the relationship as: social upheaval comes first, new laws are quickly enacted to address social problems; and these new laws bring about necessary social changes to respond to social upheaval. Bentham turned the idea of punishment on its head. He argued that if punishment is certain, then it only needs to be slightly greater than the crime itself, or only slightly greater than the pleasure derived in committing the crime. The punishment should fit the crime, and sanctions need not be brutal if swift and guaranteed (Bentham 1789). For Jeremy Bentham, changes in law prompt social change—law leads, social change follows.

Friedrich Karl von Savigny (1779–1861)

The work of Friedrich Karl von Savigny presents an alternate theoretical view on law and social change. Born in 1779, Frederick Karl von Savigny descended from the landed nobility in Germany. He was a legal scholar who published his own ideas about the relationship between law and social change a few decades later than Jeremy Bentham.

Sidebar 8.2:

Strange historical fact about von Savigny: He was one of 13 children and all of his brothers and sisters and parents had died by the time young Friedrich reached the age of 13.

Savigny founded the historical school of jurisprudence, which viewed the law "not as something imposed on a community from above or without, but [as] an inherent part of its ongoing life, an emanation of the spirit of the people" (Rodes 2004:165). As von Savigny put it, "In the earliest times to which authentic history extends, the law will be found to have already attained a fixed character, peculiar to the people, like their language, manners and constitution" (as quoted in Rodes 2004:165). Von Savigny viewed law as evolving through consensus and long-standing traditions.

From von Savigny's perspective, legal change should be gradual and evolutionary; it should come after social change has occurred. He was critical of sweeping legal reforms that were brought

istock/gameover2012

Friedrich Karl von Savigny, 1779–1861.

about by the French Revolution and feared that they would drift into other parts of Europe. Von Savigny thought the law should come about from fully established social customs. In von Savigny's view, law was the codification of long-held folkways and mores and thus specific to the society in which they arise. The law does not *prompt* social change; law simply codifies societal changes that have already transpired. By this equation, laws change only after norms, customs, and mores have done so first. Savigny, a professor of Roman law, advocated what he called "historical continuity," or the idea that the law is driven by historical facts rather than legal precepts.

These two views on the law and social change should not be seen as in opposition to one another, but rather as varying points on the continuum (Figure 8.1).

In fact, both Bentham and von Savigny's perspectives highlight the difficulties in attempting to determine the direction of law and social change. For instance, one could argue Bentham's view assumes that social change comes first and then the law follows, since he put forth the idea that law must respond to social upheaval. Yet, Bentham was a legal reformer who argued that the law should be used as a tool to bring about necessary changes in society, such as legal reforms that would lower crime rates.

The role of law in bringing about or reacting to social change differs in every scenario, from society to society and from time period to time period. Viewing these two approaches as points on a continuum allows us to see that there are many different possibilities between two ends of the spectrum, and sometimes the direction of social change and law cannot be determined. Societal change is rarely linear and one-directional. The direction of change can turn, reverse, double-back. Once we put aside the attempt to determine which comes first, law or social change—a chicken and egg scenario, after all—we can examine specific scenarios to consider the role of law in bringing about or reacting to societal changes.

Thus the question is not simply: Does law drive societal change, or does social change transform laws? A better set of questions to ask is under what circumstances can law bring about social change, at what level, and to what extent? Conversely, we can examine the conditions in which social changes alter the law and at what level and to what extent.

For the purposes of discussion, we will break down this analysis by first examining social change that causes legal change, and then move on to look at legal changes causing social changes. But as we will see, oftentimes changes are concurrent; you cannot separate out which comes first.

Figure 8.1 The Law and Social Change Continuum

SOCIAL CHANGES AS CAUSES OF CHANGES IN LAW

In considering the first option, that social change causes legal changes, it is important to keep in mind that in a postmodern society such as ours, we are in a state of constant change, making it hard to determine the direction in which change flows. Society is in a constant state of flux, and sometimes even upheaval, in all areas of social life, such as:

- Demographics—birth rates, aging populations, death rates
- Immigration—internal and external
- Urbanization, suburbanization, exurbanization (the movement of beyond the suburbs in the search for affordable housing)
- Industrialization and post-industrialization
- New discoveries and inventions in sciences and technologies
- Transportation
- Agriculture
- Mass media
- Communication
- Commerce and industry
- Education
- Families
- Governance
- Multinational corporations
- Work and the economy

Changes in all of these areas, in turn, modify people's attitudes and ideas about the society in which they live. The culture is transformed along with social and economic order.

For instance, think about the notion of individualism as a major change in modern and postmodern societies. Individualism—the general idea that in a modern society the individual is more important than the group, or even the family—emerged during the period of industrialization. Industrialization transformed people's ways of working, giving rise to the notion that a person must sell his or her labor outside the home. The commodification of labor changed our ideas about the family. Families decreased in size, becoming more nuclear and more organized around wage earners. Changes in family structure transformed the gendered division of labor where one family member, often the man, was expected to leave the home every day to sell his labor for a wage. The woman of the household also worked—sometimes selling her labor as well, but more often the work was within the home and was unpaid. The remnants of this male wage-earner/female homemaker family structure are still very much with us today even though most women work outside the home.

These transformations in family structure also changed how family members viewed children. In traditional, agrarian societies, children are viewed as economic assets who contribute their labor and services to the economic unit of the family. In modern societies, children are viewed as emotional investments—you invest in your children and they reward parents and grandparents with their love, appreciation, and success. Changes in the labor force eventually brought about the need for Social Security and other benefits for older people. The traditional family structure where several generations lived together, and younger generations cared for elderly members into old age, is no longer the norm. Families have become more nuclear— typically with only two generations living under one roof. Extended families are often dispersed geographically. These transformations brought about other social changes and social policies: unemployment insurance, pensions, Medicare, and the Affordable Care Act. And all of these new institutions gradually replaced what previously had been functions of the family.

All the while, our ideas about the individual were also changing. The individual should be independent, self-sufficient, working for a living. The labor contract emerged as a legal mechanism to address various issues raised by new conceptions of work. A labor or employment contract is an agreement between owners/managers and employees in which the duties and obligations of each party are spelled out, such as wages and other benefits, work hours, and work conditions. This type of contract did not exist before the emergence of capitalism and wage labor.

NEW TECHNOLOGIES AS CATALYSTS FOR CHANGE

New technologies and inventions prompt changes in law in many different ways. New technologies emerge that change the way authorities can apply and enforce the law, such as the use of fingerprints and DNA testing. Recent technological changes in crime mapping and evidence-based policing use advanced computer modeling to predict, and even prevent, crimes before they occur. New technologies bring about new ways of processing arrests and keeping track of criminals and crime data. Computers allow police to track criminals and quickly share records between and among departments. So, if a person is pulled over for speeding, the officer can see if he or she had an outstanding warrant for a more serious crime. Computer technology allows the law to be applied in an efficient manner that could prevent future crimes before they happen. Jeremy Bentham could not have dreamed of this type of crime prevention.

Changes in technology also present new areas for laws to regulate, such as child pornography on the Internet and the vast array of cybercrimes. Cybercrime is a relatively new area of lawbreaking that encompasses numerous types of illegal behavior and activities that use computers and other new technologies and that are conducted over global electronic networks, such as the World Wide Web. Cybercrime can include anything from stealing people's identity, to using stolen credit cards to purchase items on the Internet, to trafficking human beings using global online networks, to hacking into private or governmental databases, to name just a few.

CASE IN POINT

Revenge Porn or Nonconsensual Pornography

Cases of "revenge pornography" or "revenge porn" provide examples of a recent type of cybercrime that did not exist even a decade ago but for which lawmakers and citizens have called upon legal strategies to remedy. Revenge porn involves the sharing of sexually explicit photos or videos of individuals without their consent on the Internet and new social media. The first cases of revenge porn to capture the popular media's attention typically involved a jilted boyfriend posting pictures of his ex-girlfriend online as a way to get back at her. Since not all cases are motivated by revenge, some jurisdictions use the term "nonconsensual pornography" to describe this illicit behavior.

A case described in *The New Yorker* magazine in 2016 exemplifies a typical revenge porn scenario. The author, Margaret Talbot, highlights the groundbreaking legal work of attorney Carrie Goldberg, who is leading the way in revenge porn prosecutions. The case involved a young New Jersey woman named Norma who broke up with her first boyfriend, Christopher, whom she met when she was 17 years old. While they were together, Norma shared with Christopher explicit photos of herself only after he promised to never show them to anyone else (Talbot 2016). When Norma broke off the relationship, Christopher continued to contact her, harassing her relentlessly. He threatened to post the intimate photos of her on websites, and eventually he followed through on those threats, sharing them on a site called PornHub. Not only did he post the photos, but he included instructions on how to contact Norma (Talbot 2016).

Despite this harrowing ordeal, Norma was lucky. She lived in New Jersey, the first state to pass laws against revenge porn. Under New Jersey's statute, this behavior amounted to "invasion of privacy in the third degree" (Talbot 2016:58). Thirty-eight states plus the District of Columbia now have some form of revenge porn legislation; seven have legislation pending. Norma was also fortunate to have Carrie Goldberg by her side when her case went to trial. Goldberg, who was once a victim of revenge porn, specializes in the new legal field of sexual privacy. She has helped people like Norma sue their online harassers, get the images off the Internet, and restore some semblance of normalcy to their lives. Goldberg also helps those being extorted for money to remove images, and she advises teenaged girls who have been sexually assaulted and found that their assaults have been recorded on cellphones and replayed at their schools and on social media (Talbot 2016). Norma's ex-boyfriend, Christopher, pled guilty to an invasion-of-privacy charge. He received five years of probation and 100 hours of community service and was ordered to stay away from Norma and her family.

Texting While Driving

In a time period of rapid technological changes, laws are also called upon to determine what should happen when different technologies are brought together in potentially dangerous ways. Laws attempting to prohibit texting while driving offer an example of states addressing two technologies—the automobile and the cellular phone—that have become linked in the twenty-first century. These laws also offer cautionary tales of what can happen when a law is difficult—sometimes impossible—to enforce.

Texting while driving is illegal in 47 states in the United States, in the District of Columbia, Guam, and in the U.S. Virgin Islands (National Conference of State Legislatures 2017). This law does not stop people, however. Massachusetts prohibited texting while driving in September of 2010; the law includes composing, sending, and reading any electronic message on any hand-held device connected to the Internet while operating a motor vehicle (Botelho 2013:B2).

The first person convicted of texting while driving in the state of Massachusetts killed another driver in a head-on collision. In February of 2011, just months after the law was passed, 17-year-old Aaron Deveau swerved into oncoming traffic on a major thoroughfare in Haverhill. The driver he hit, Donald Bowley, 56, died of injuries sustained in the accident. His girlfriend, Luz Roman, was critically injured in the crash but survived (Ballou 2012:B1). Deveau's phone records proved a key component of the prosecution's case. Prosecutors were able to establish that Deveau was texting his girlfriend right before the crash and that this behavior constituted negligence (Ballou 2012:B1). Deveau received the maximum sentence: two and a half years in jail for causing a motor vehicle accident. Yet the sentence was suspended for all but one year due to his young age and clean criminal record. He also received a 15-year driver's license suspension (Ballou 2012:B1). Deveau was aged 18 when he was convicted; he will not be able to drive again legally until he is 33 years old.

Because Massachusetts was one of the early adopters of texting-while-driving laws and because the case involved a fatality, Deveau's conviction made national news. It served to broadcast the changing laws around cell-phone use and driving, and this is just what the prosecutors hoped it would do. The Essex County, Massachusetts, district attorney said, "The Legislature rightfully passed this law because they acknowledge texting while driving is a very dangerous activity .... We're grateful the jury came back with the verdict they did, but there are no winners in this case" (Ballou 2012:B1). The presiding judge in the case, District Court Judge Stephen Abany, put it even more clearly, stating "Deterrence—that really seems to come into play in this case .... People want to be safe on the highways" (Ballou 2012:B1).

Deveau's case was fairly clear-cut—the district attorney was able to sub-poena his phone records because he was involved in a fatal car crash. What about cases where police are trying to *prevent* crashes and catch texting while driving *before* anyone gets hurt? This would truly deter the behavior and save lives. Catching people in the act of texting behind the wheel is not easy, especially when the both the law and the behavior can be murky. If the law does not prohibit certain cellphone activities, such as checking the weather or using navigational aids, then how can a police officer be sure that the driver was texting? If there are different age restrictions on cellphone use, such as no phone use for anyone under 18 and no texting for any drivers, as was the case in Massachusetts, how can a police officer detect who is doing what on their phones? Passing a law to react to new technologies does not necessarily make the change happen. Implementing and enforcing the law can bring about change, but that process can also be difficult.

When Massachusetts first passed its texting-while-driving ban, because it did not prohibit all types of cellphone use the state police found it hard to enforce the law. When pulled over, drivers said they were not texting: they were dialing their phones, using navigation, or even unlocking their phones. Some officers cited drivers for "impeded driving" instead, using an older law that prohibits doing anything behind the wheel that interferes with the task at hand—driving (Powers 2013). Lieutenant Stephen Walsh of the Massachusetts State Police acknowledged, "To put together a texting-while-driving case, you have to look at them for a long time and be able to see what they're doing on their phone .... You can do that sometimes, but it's difficult" (Powers 2013:A4). These ambiguities in texting-while-driving laws and their enforcement have led some states to modify the relatively new laws, adopting "hands-free" driving laws instead. New Hampshire's hands-free law went into effect in 2015 and prohibits drivers from using any hand-held device. Other states, such as Washington, have moved to "no distracted driving" laws that prohibit not just cellphones but any device or activity that takes the driver's attention away from the road.

These cases of new technologies in need of new laws point to instances where social change happens first, and legal change must follow. Laws often need to catch up to the rapid social changes that take place in our technological age. In the next section of the chapter, we turn to cases where the law acts as an agent of social change—where a new law is crafted to move society in a particular direction or where case law is decided in a way that transforms the society in which we live.

LAW AS A TOOL FOR SOCIAL CHANGE

There are many examples of laws enacting, or bringing about, social change—both deliberately and intentionally. In these cases, law is not simply a reflection of social reality; it is a powerful means of accomplishing a new social reality by making change happen. Wolfgang Friedmann (1907–1972), a German American legal scholar said, "The law—through legislative or administrative responses to new social conditions and ideas, as well as through judicial interpretations of constitutions, statutes or precedents—increasingly not only articulates but sets the course for major social changes" (1959:513). Similarly, Yehezkel Dror, a professor of political science at Hebrew University and scholar of law and society stated: "The use of law as a tool of directed social change is widespread in all contemporary societies whether underdeveloped or postindustrial, democratic or totalitarian" (1970:553). Both Friedmann and Dror argue that law can be a necessary and efficient way to bring about social change. Law can also be used in the opposite way; it can be a hindrance to social change or a tool to block social change.

In many areas of society, law is often called upon to bring about social changes, for instance, in education and race relations, transportation and energy use, housing, environmental protection, and, of course, crime prevention. These are all areas where the law can lead social change. In the mid-1950s and 1960s, the civil rights movement used law as an arena for social change to fight for equality for African-Americans in the United States. Civil rights workers used the courts to dismantle the racial caste system that was put in place for generations through slavery, through the Jim Crow post-Civil War era, and through laws that segregated Blacks and Whites and legally constructed blacks as second-class citizens. If we consider some of the major changes that came about during the civil rights movement, many of those were legal changes or were punctuated by legal decisions. Among these changes were the 1954 decision of *Brown v the Board of Education of Topeka, Kansas*; the 1964 Civil Rights Act; the 1965 Voting Rights Act; and *Loving v. Virginia*, 1967, which overturned anti-miscegenation laws—laws against interracial marriages that were enacted after the Civil War.

In some cases law brought about immediate changes. For example, with passage of the Voting Rights Act of 1965, voting rates increased dramatically in the southern states directly after the legal change took place.

Mississippi in 1964 had a 7 percent voting rate for blacks; by 1969 that rate had climbed to 60 percent (Sutton 2001). These changes illustrate an immediate and wide-sweeping social change brought about by law. Other changes, such as the integration of public schools after *Brown v. the Board of Education*, took much longer to implement, so long in fact that many argue that U.S. schools were never fully integrated.

Law can have direct and indirect effects on social change. In terms of the indirect effect of law on social change, law shapes social institutions that have a direct impact on society. An example is compulsory education. States mandate that all children attend school or receive some type of formal schooling, such as home schooling, up to a certain age, usually 16, but several states set the age requirement higher, at 17 or 18 (National Center Education Statistics 2015). Two manifest functions of compulsory education were to increase literacy rates and discourage child labor use. When compulsory education was enacted in the mid-1800s, during the period of late industrialization and mass immigration to the United States, it brought about many social changes, not the least of which was a literate and educated labor force. This in turn increased job preparedness and productivity, which in turn benefitted the wealthy owners of industries. It also erected one of the largest bureaucracies in the United States—the public school system. Some believed free, compulsory schooling benefited the lower classes, as well as the higher classes, by leveling the playing field between and among different social groups and social classes. Mandatory schooling also decreased crime rates, because it kept children off the streets. Thus compulsory education law prompted immense social changes to society—some foreseen and some unforeseen.

A prominent scholar of American law, Lawrence Friedman holds two views on how the law can act as a catalyst for social change. His two types of social change are: (1) law changes society through planning and implementation, and (2) law changes society through disruption. In planning, society can construct and implement new forms of social order and social interaction through law. In disruption, members of society can either block or ameliorate existing social forms and relations (Friedman 2005). The case of same-sex marriage in the United States offers examples of both of Friedman's views on laws as an agent of social change.

SAME-SEX MARRIAGE LAWS AND LAWS ATTEMPTING TO BLOCK SAME-SEX MARRIAGE

In 2015, the U.S. Supreme Court overturned all legal bans on same-sex marriage. To the casual observer, this legal change may have appeared abrupt. The struggle for gays and lesbians to legally marry in the United States, however, was not abrupt. It took over 40 years of legal wrangling, of fits and starts, of hopes dashed and victories won. It began in the late 1960s, stalled in the 1970s and 1980, and took some steps forward in the 1990s. The legal change was later blocked in the 1990s with the Defense of Marriage Act (DOMA), marched forward again in the early 2000s, and finally culminated in the 2015 U.S. Supreme Court ruling on *Obergefell v. Hodges* that granted same-sex couples the right to marry in the eyes of the law. This case offers an example of law being used to implement social change (Friedman's planning), but also to block both legal and social change that is well underway (Friedman's disruption) (Figure 8.2).

The U.S. Supreme Court's 2015 ruling on same-sex marriage illustrates that the law can indeed bring about social change. Overnight, gay and lesbian couples went from not being allowed to apply for marriage licenses in many states to being able to legally marry in any state in the United States. Both states and federal governments now recognize their marriages. A recent study also suggests that this legal change has had some unintended positive effects in reducing suicides among gay, lesbian, and bisexual young people (Guarino 2017). While no clear causation can be drawn between these two variables—same-sex marriage rights and reduced suicides among gay youths—a study by researchers at Johns Hopkins University and Harvard University published in the *Journal of the American Medical Association (JAMA) Pediatrics* indicate that there does appear to be a correlation (Raifman et al. 2017). The researchers used self-report data from more than 750,000 students. The study was conducted prior to the 2015 Supreme Court ruling on same-sex marriages, but the researchers were able to compare suicide rates from 2004 to January of 2015 in states that allowed same-sex marriages and states that did not (Raifman et al. 2017). For gay, lesbian, and bisexual youths, there was a 14 percent decline in self-reported suicide attempts in states that allowed same-sex marriage. During the same period, states that did not allow same-sex marriage saw no significant change in attempted suicides among gay, lesbian, and bisexual young people (Raifman et al. 2017). Researchers suspect that the acceptance of same-sex marriage reduced stigma for young gay, lesbian, and bisexual people and the very idea of having equal rights before the law is helping students think positively about the future (Guarino 2017). This is fitting given the language of Supreme Court Justice Anthony Kennedy's majority ruling in *Obergefell v. Hodges*. Kennedy said, "Their hope is not to be condemned to live in loneliness, excluded from one of civilizations oldest institutions .... They ask for equal dignity in the eyes of the law" (quoted in Ball 2015:n.p.).

While we have discussed same-sex marriage as an example of a legal change bringing about changes in society, one could argue that the change went in the opposite direction. Gays and lesbians have been fighting for

1967

- In *Loving v. Virginia*, the U.S. Supreme Court rules that anti-miscegenation laws (laws against interracial marriage) are unconstitutional. This constitutional decision is later used as a precedent for same-sex marriage laws in Massachusetts and other states.

1970s–1980s

- Several same-sex couples attempt to marry in different states using *Loving v. Virginia* as precedent, but with little success.

1993

- The state of Hawaii is sued in *Baehr v. Lewin* (later *Baehr v. Miike*). Baehr argued for equal rights to choose marriage partners without restrictions on gender. The Hawaiian Supreme Judicial Court remanded the case to the state, requiring it to demonstrate there was a "compelling state interest" in prohibiting same-sex marriages.
- This case turned into an extended battle and was finally dismissed by the Hawaii SJC in **1999** on the grounds that the legislature had passed a prohibition of same-sex marriages before the court could render an opinion.
- *Baehr* also sparked debates in many states about legislation to outlaw same-sex marriages. The Full Faith and Credit Clause in the U.S. Constitution requires interstate recognition of other states' laws. Legal marriages in one state would have to be recognized in others.

1996

- Same-sex marriages took center stage in national politics with DOMA. This federal legislation defines marriage as the "legal union between one man and one woman as husband and wife." It also provides that no state is obligated to recognize same-sex marriages performed in another state. In July 1996, senators voted 85–14 in favor of DOMA. President Bill Clinton later signed it into law.
- Critics argue that DOMA undermines the Full Faith and Credit Clause of the Constitution. Because of this contradiction, same-sex marriage advocates want the U.S. Supreme Court to decide a same-sex marriage challenge.

Late 1990s to 2000

- Same-sex marriage debate moves to Vermont, with the case of *Baker v. State of Vermont*. In 2000, Vermont becomes the first state to recognize civil unions between two people of the same sex. Civil unions allow almost all of the legal rights of marriage.

Vermont's Civil Union Law of 2000 allowed:

- the use of family laws, such as divorce, annulment, child custody, and property division

Figure 8.2 Timeline of Major Legal Decisions on Same-Sex Marriage in the U.S.

- the right to sue for wrongful death, loss of consortium, and any other tort or law related to spousal relationships
- medical rights, such as hospital visits
- family leave benefits
- joint state tax filing
- property inheritance without a will

It did not apply to:

- Any federal laws available to married couples, e.g., Social Security benefits for spouses, child tax exemptions, etc.

2001

- The same-sex marriage debate in Massachusetts begins in earnest when seven gay and lesbian couples are denied marriage licenses in Boston.

2003

- Two and a half years later, on November 18, 2003, the Massachusetts Supreme Judicial Court found no rational reason for prohibiting same-sex marriages under the state's constitution (*Goodridge et al. v. Massachusetts Department of Public Health*). Gays and lesbians were allowed to marry six months after the ruling.
- In the meantime, Massachusetts Attorney General Thomas Reilly finds a 1913 civil law prohibiting out-of-state residents to marry in the state if they are ineligible to marry in their home states. Then Governor Romney says it must be applied to same-sex marriages. The last time it was used, it was applied to interracial marriages.

May 17, 2004

- Same-sex couples apply for marriages licenses throughout the state of Massachusetts.

November 2, 2004

- Eleven states ban same-sex marriages (six states had already put such bans in place).

2005–2009

- Same-sex marriage laws passed in Connecticut; Washington, DC; New Hampshire; New Jersey; New York; Maine; Vermont; Iowa; Wisconsin; and Oregon.

July 9, 2009

- Massachusetts becomes the first state to challenge the constitutionality of DOMA, stating that it violates the U.S. Constitution.

Figure 8.2 Continued

February 2011

- President Obama orders his administration to stop defending DOMA and all pending cases are put on hold.
- Opinion polls indicate for the first time since polling on the issue began that more than half of Americans say they are ready to accept same-sex marriage.

November 10, 2011

- Massachusetts District Attorney General Martha Coakley asks the First Circuit Court of Appeals to uphold the 2010 district court finding that DOMA is unconstitutional and violates the Tenth Amendment of the Constitution (State's Rights: the Commonwealth has the sovereign authority to define and regulate the marital status of its residents).

July 2013

- DOMA is voted down by the U.S. Supreme Court.

June 2015

- The U.S. Supreme Court rules in *Obergefell v. Hodges* that same-sex couples can marry nationwide (5–4 ruling).

Figure 8.2 Continued

equality before the law in all areas of public life for decades. As Molly Ball, a journalist for *The Atlantic* put it, *Obergefell v. Hodges*:

> [w]asn't solely or even primarily the work of the lawyers and plaintiffs who brought the case. It was the product of decades of activism that made the idea of gay marriage plausible, desirable, and right .... The fight for gay marriage was, above all, a political campaign—a decades-long effort to win over the American public and, in turn, the court .... But what it achieved is remarkable: not just a Supreme Court decision but a revolution in the way America sees its gay citizens (Ball 2017:n.p.).

The gay rights movement finally brought about the legal change that the country witnessed in 2015, but the fight for full equality is not yet won. Thus, social change and legal change are best viewed on a continuum (See Figure 8.1). The definitive direction of change is not always discernable. Perhaps legal decisions and new laws *punctuate* social change that is already underway. Laws make change official, and then allow for further changes to follow. The case of gay marriage, and indeed all of the legal struggles discussed in this chapter, bring into sharp relief the difficulty in pinpointing which comes first in the law-social change equation. Social change is not linear. Change can be underway in the form of a social movement, but that change is given legitimacy when a law changes or a legal case is decided.

Marriage equality now

Legal change can also meet with resistance, countermovements, and legal machinations that block the change in its path, as we saw with DOMA. The legal case then moves ahead and forces more change, such as the increased acceptance of a previously marginalized group of citizens. This acceptance and recognition of rights can then bring about other positive effects, like improved mental health and fewer attempted suicides for young gay people. And yet, there are still challenges to the new law, sometimes at a very local level.

When Kim Davis, a Rowan County, Kentucky, Clerk, refused to issue marriage licenses to same-sex couples after the historic 2015 Supreme Court ruling, she became a folk hero on the right and a folk devil on the left. Her act of counter-resistance landed her in jail for five days, but she was allowed to stay on as county clerk, an elected position. Instead of Davis, her deputy clerks were allowed to issue marriage licenses to gay and lesbian applicants. By June of 2016, her argument was made moot when Kentucky removed county clerks' names from all state marriage licenses. Davis's actions, however, could cost Kentucky hundreds of thousands of dollars, as the state has been ordered to pay the legal fees for challenges to Davis's refusals. And, as of May 2017, two men are suing Davis personally for harm suffered when she refused to issue them a marriage license. Seeking change through law is rarely a clear and easy path (Figure 8.3).

Social change through litigation is an American phenomenon. The United States has entire segments of the legal profession devoted to changing various

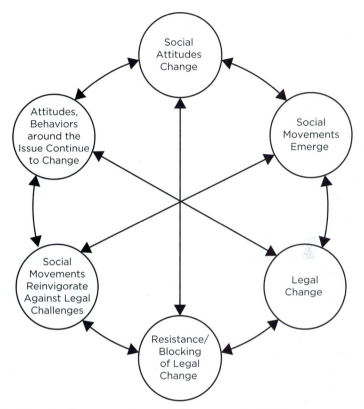

Figure 8.3 Social Change and Legal Change are Mulit-Linear.

aspects of our society. Environmental lawyers attempt to change laws to better protect our natural resources. Housing lawyers protect the legal rights to safe housing for the poor. Labor lawyers advocate for the rights of workers. Civil rights lawyers continue to fight for the rights and legal protections of racial and ethnic minorities, as they have done since the beginning of the civil rights movement. Social movements are often tied to legal movements, and those in power must expect a certain amount of disruptive litigation.

THE ADVANTAGES OF LAW AS A TOOL FOR SOCIAL CHANGE

So, how effective is law in bringing about social change? This is another question with no easy answer. According to the American legal scholar William M. Evan, there are two interrelated processes involved in utilizing law as an instrument for social change: the *institutionalization* of patterns of behavior and the *internalization* of patterns of behavior (1965).

Institutionalization of Patterns of Behavior is the establishment of a legal norm and the clear delineation of provisions for its enforcement.

Internalization of Patterns of Behavior is the incorporation of the value or values implicit in the new law, such as "marriage equality is good and beneficial to all." The law can be an effective mechanism for the promotion or reinforcement of social change, but not necessarily as an impetus for social change. Law alone may not be a driving force or an incentive for social change, but rather it punctuates change that is already underway. The extent to which law can provide an effective impetus for social change varies according to the conditions present in a particular situation.

In his 1965 work on the law as an instrument for social change, Evan suggests that a law is likely to be successful in inducing social change if it meets seven conditions:

1. The law must be issued from an authoritative and prestigious source.
2. The law must introduce its rationale in terms both understandable and compatible with existing values.
3. The advocates of change should make reference to other communities or countries with which the population identifies and where the law is already in effect.
4. The law must aim at making change in a relatively short time.
5. Those enforcing the law must be committed to the intended change.
6. The instrumentation of the law should include positive as well as negative sanctions.
7. The enforcement should be reasonable, not only in the sanctions used, but also in the protection of the rights of those who stand to lose by violating the law (1965:288–291).

According to Evan, the effectiveness of law as a mechanism of social change depends on a number of factors, such as the amount of information available about a given law, legal decision, or court ruling. When there is insufficient transmission of information, the law will not produce its intended effect. Ignorance of the law is not considered an excuse for breaking the law, but public ignorance of a law can limit its effectiveness. And, as we saw with texting-while-driving laws, some laws are limited if stated imprecisely or if their enforcement is difficult to carry out. Unclear laws permit multiple perceptions and interpretations. The language of the law should be unambiguous and limited in terms of multiple interpretations.

Social change is a complex and multifaceted phenomenon brought on by a host of social forces. Social change can be slow and disjointed or it can be abrupt and monumental. Revolution is the most drastic form of change but there are many others: rebellion, riots, coup d'états, protests, sit-ins and boycotts, strikes or other forms of "stop work," demonstrations, social movements, changes in the mass media, technological innovation, and discoveries, as well as public service campaigns and other government initiatives. Law as a form of social change is usually deliberative, rational, and conscious, and is generally not abrupt. The advantages of creating social change through law are that the law has legitimate authority, it is binding, and it carries sanctions.

Legitimate authority is a Weberian term meaning the expectation of obedience is based on appropriate, official rule. It is the authority of the government and its officers. **Rational-legal authority**, more specifically, derives from codified law enacted by governmental leaders. The authority of a state's governor resides in his or elected office; the same goes for the President of the United States. Governors and presidents are sworn in to office to uphold the laws of the state, and presidents swear to uphold the laws of the country. Rational-legal authority is a type of power; it is orderly, clear, and made legitimate through people's acceptance of it.

The binding force of law means that a law works because most people follow it. Why people follow the law can vary but is tied to the fact that it emanates from a legitimate, rational authority. People also fear punishment and most people tend toward order and civility most of the time. People are socialized into the cultures in which they are raised. We live in a multicultural, stratified society, but most people recognize the larger American culture—its customs, its rules, and its laws.

Directly linked to the first two advantages of law in creating social change are **sanctions**. Sanctions can be restrictive, such as limits placed on behavior or punishments for bad behavior. Or sanctions can be positive, such as permissions for certain behaviors or rewards for good behavior. Laws have force because they are backed by negative sanctions. As discussed in Chapter 6, in criminal law, negative sanctions are fines, jail, or prison, or some form of deprivation of freedom such as probation or parole or loss of privileges, such as a suspended driver's license. In civil law, negative sanctions might also be fines, but can also be lawsuits for compensation and damages.

THE LIMITS OF LAW IN CREATING SOCIAL CHANGE

Law as a vehicle for social change is by no means perfect. The law tends to favor the status quo and those groups that are already in power. As we have seen in the discussion of same-sex marriage, the use of law as a tool for social change can be met with many obstacles. Resistance to change can come from many sources including: social factors, psychological factors, cultural factors, and economic factors. In Chapter 10: Gender, Inequality, and Law, we look at the issue of sexual harassment in the workplace and how laws enacted in the 1970s and 1980s against harassment did not change the behaviors of men in the workforce. The #MeToo movement began in 2016 and picked up momentum in 2017. When it went viral on social media, it brought sexual harassment and sexual assault into the workplace and mainstream culture, and is now making inroads into an entrenched social problem. The laws were already in place, but a social movement brought the issue to the forefront and made it impossible to ignore.

Social factors are any social forces that may block or slow the pace of change. These could be groups that fear the loss of power or some other resource they value—people with vested interests in keeping things the way they are. When same-sex marriage was gaining momentum nationally, opponents argued on ideological grounds that it would devalue the institution of marriage. Since they were not able to prove that allowing same-sex couples to marry would change or devalue the legal institution of marriage itself, this argument did not win out in the end. But it was one of the reasons why DOMA was passed, so it did slow the momentum of same-sex marriage laws.

Social factors that resist social change include organized opposition, such as the National Rifle Association's opposition to any new gun control legislation, even in the wake of the Sandy Hook Elementary School shooting in Newtown, Connecticut on December 14, 2012. Twenty children, aged 6 to 7, and six adults were murdered at the school by a gunman armed with a rifle. Many gun control advocates believed this event would turn the tide and allow for more legal restrictions on guns. While some states, including Connecticut, were able to pass stricter gun control laws, the country as a whole did not embrace such laws. The National Rifle Association in the largest and most well-funded organized opposition group in the United States and it mobilized its considerable resources to block large-scale changes in gun laws.

Psychological factors also contribute to resistance to change. Minds are hard to change. Habits, prejudices, and selective perception can all inhibit social change. Much of the U.S. legal system presumes a winner and a loser, and that can carry over to all parts of law. Those who already have legal rights may assume that granting those same rights to others would somehow diminish their positions in the social order. For instance, when women suffragists fought for the right to vote, many men resisted this change, seeing it as a threat to their dominance in the public realm.

Psychologists who study habit acknowledge that habitual behavior is notoriously hard to change. Habits are involuntary, automatic; very little decision-making is involved. Indeed, recent research on cellphone use and driving points to one problem with laws against texting while driving: Most people know this behavior is wrong, but they are not *deciding* to text while drive; they do it out of habit. Researchers at the Max Planck Institute for Informatics found that research subjects in their study used their mobile for very brief periods, up to 60 times a day (Neyfakh 2013:K4). This fits the description of habitual behavior. People who use their cellphones habitually are more likely to text and drive. As *The Boston Globe* writer

Leon Neyfakh notes, "The tricky thing about fighting habitual behavior is that the brain's ability to form habits is one of its strengths. A habit is a powerful shortcut that helps us stay more productive" (2013:K4). And, if smartphone use has become so automatic, so mindless, solving the problem of texting while driving may require more than laws and public service announcements. It may require replacing one habit with another, like when a smoker replaces cigarettes with gum. With over 200,000 car crashes a year attributed to texting while driving, solutions are being sought from many different places: law, psychology, behavior modification, education, and public service campaigns.

Cultural factors can also slow change social and legal change. Customs, traditions, and folkways have been in place for many years and are difficult to change. When the proposed change threatens long-held beliefs, such as marriage is between one man and one woman, change can be threatening. Kim Davis, the county clerk in Rowan, Kentucky, based her opposition to upholding the same-sex marriage law on her religious beliefs. Davis belongs to the Apostolic Church, a conservative Christian sect that embraces a literal interpretation of the bible. Her beliefs, however, conflicted with the elected office she held, and a public servant is not allowed to cherry-pick which laws she wants to uphold.

Economic factors in a capitalist economy prove to be a formidable force in either implementing or blocking social change. Social resources, such as power, money, and access to lawmakers, often hold sway in matters of law and social change. From a Marxist perspective, the law is a tool for those in power, so if the capitalist-owning class wants change to occur, change will occur. If the owners of capital think the government should stay out of their business, they typically can block regulations that would hinder their business. The list of laws and regulations that have been blocked because of the special interests of large corporations or wealthy individuals are legion: environmental regulations, gun control laws, worker safety regulations, the right to unionize, and product safety regulations, to name just a few. Conversely, law can also grant unfettered access by the wealthy to the elections process. The ironically named 2010 *Citizens United* Supreme Court ruling allows corporations and unions to spend unlimited funds on political advertisements and other campaign tools to either elect or defeat individual candidates. So, while we are all equal before the law, some are more equal than others.

As we have seen in this chapter, the law can lead social change or it can follow social change. Often the two processes are so intertwined it is impossible to discern which comes first. In matters of granting rights and liberties, law is the arena for change, but often legal changes are prompted by long, hard struggles to bring change to the legislature or the courts.

In the immortal words of Dr. Martin Luther King Jr., as we saw at the beginning of the chapter, "... the law cannot make a man love me but it can keep him from lynching me and I think that is pretty important, also. So there is a need for executive orders ... for judicial decrees ... for civil rights legislation on the local scale within states and on the national scale from the federal government" (http://www.letterstotheexiles.com/hearts-habits-men-mlk-law-morality/. While law has allowed some of the worst atrocities in human history, it has also righted historical wrongs and expanded the rights of individuals throughout the world.

CHAPTER SUMMARY

◆ The question of which comes first, social change or legal change, has vexed sociologists, legal theorists, and philosophers for centuries. Sometimes the answer is both.

◆ Two scholars of law exemplify the two differing theories about law and social change. Jeremy Bentham represents the notion that law should be used to prompt social change. Friedrich Karl von Savigny argued that law should only be enacted after societal change was established; social change comes first and then law follows.

◆ Law and social change can be viewed as a continuum, with law leading social change on one end of the continuum and social change leading to changes in law on the other end. There are many possibilities for law and social change on the continuum. It is important to look at the context for change and ask under what circumstances law can bring about change, at what level, and to what extent?

◆ Social changes as causes of legal change is exemplified by the wide-sweeping changes that took place in the Industrial Revolution. All aspects of society changed—from the family, community, and households to work, the economy, governance, and culture.

◆ New technologies offer another example of social change, in the form of new inventions and new technologies, which bring about new areas of law. Cybercrimes such as revenge porn presented a new area for law to regulate. Texting while driving brought together two technologies, automobiles and mobile phones, in new and dangerous way. Law was called upon to address these new dangers, but this problem proves difficult to control through law alone.

◆ There are many examples of the law being used to prompt social change. Examples from the civil rights movement make a case for law leading social change. Same-sex marriage laws in the United States illustrate the efficacy of law in punctuating and codifying social change—the expansion of marriage rights to a segment of society previously excluded from the right to marry.

◆ Law can also disrupt or block social change as it is getting under way. DOMA demonstrates a legal change that stopped movement toward legalizing same-sex marriage in its tracks. When the Supreme Court overturned DOMA, legal change marched forward, again culminating in the 2015 Supreme Court decision on the *Obergefell v. Hodges* case that legalized same-sex marriage at the federal level.

◆ Law offers many advantages in enacting social change: it is based on legitimate authority; it is binding and codified; it is backed by negative sanctions.

◆ Law is not a perfect vehicle for driving social change, however. The law can meet several forms of resistance to change. Social factors, psychological factors, cultural factors, and economic factors can limit the efficacy of law as a tool for social change.

KEY TERMS

binding force of law   219
cultural factors   221
economic factors   221
institutionalization of patterns of
   behavior   218
legitimate authority   219

psychological factors   220
rational-legal authority   219
sanctions   219
social factors   220
utilitarianism   201

CRITICAL THINKING QUESTIONS

1. Review Evan's seven conditions under which the law can be an effective tool for bringing about social change. On each condition, address whether or not you think same-sex marriage met those conditions.

2. Can you think of a recent example where law was called upon to regulate a new technological innovation? What is it and what is the law/proposed law seeking to do?

3. Can laws deter texting while driving? What other methods or approaches could deter this behavior?

4. Dr. Martin Luther King, Jr. said that law can "restrain the heartless." Other than his example of lynching, what kinds of behavior do you think Dr. King was referring to in his speech on law and morality? Can you think of recent examples where a new law or legal change was called upon to restrain the heartless?

SUGGESTED MOVIE: *RBG*

RBG Documentary. 2018. Betsey West and Julie Cohen, Directors. CNN Films.

While the film *RBG* tells the life story of the unlikely cultural icon Ruth Bader Ginsburg—the second woman in the United States to win appointment to the Supreme Court—it also tells the tale of how law can bring about significant social change. Through the lens of women's rights, *RBG* illustrates how legal cases, both small and large, can gradually chip away at gender inequality in all its legal forms. The film illustrates Bader Ginsburg's legal finesse in picking winnable cases to bring to the court and her steely resolve in seeing these cases through to their logical conclusions. The topic of law and social change runs throughout the film, from the cases it follows to the fact that Bader Ginsburg's granddaughter recently graduated from a Harvard Law School class that was 50 percent male and 50 percent male. When Ruth Bader Ginsburg attended Harvard Law in the 1950s, she was one of only nine women out of about 550 students. The film also works for discussion of key issues presented in Chapter 4: The Organization of Law, such as the dual hierarchical legal system and the role of litigants, lawyers, judges, and juries in the judicial system.

Discussion Questions for *RBG*

1. At the beginning of the film, National Public Radio legal affairs correspondent Nina Totenberg states that Ruth Bader Ginsburg (RBG) "quite literally changed the way the world is for American women." Discuss three specific ways that RBG carried out change for American women.

2. After viewing the film *RBG*, do you believe that law brings about social change? Or, does social change bring about changes in law? Use examples to clarify your answer.

3. While Ruth Bader Ginsburg took on many cases of sex discrimination affecting women, she also took on cases in which men were discriminated against because of their sex. Discuss at least one of those cases. Why do you think she chose that tactic?

4. Ruth Bader Ginsburg famously said, "Being a woman was an impediment." What do you think she meant by this statement and is it still true today? If you believe it is true, discuss why. If you believe it is not true, why not?

9

Gate-Keeping and the Law: The Legal Profession

◆ ◆ ◆

IN THIS CHAPTER, WE EXPLORE THE LEGAL PROFESSION in the United States—how it evolved over time and where it stands today. As American legal scholar Lawrence M. Friedman stated, "In a society where 'law' is everywhere, there is everywhere a need for people who know how to use it or abuse it" (2002:165).

We examine the development of law schools in the United States and the part they have played in the establishment of law as a profession. And we look at the history and current role of the American Bar Association (ABA) as the primary gatekeeper of this monopoly of knowledge. As we discussed in Chapter 4: The Organization of Law, ideally, lawyers are highly trained professionals who turn complaints or wrongs into legal disputes, or defend their clients who are innocent until proven guilty in a court of law. Most of the time, lawyers work on nontrial activities—routine transactions that take place outside of court—such as filing legal papers and drafting and reviewing documents. All lawyers, including defense attorneys, prosecutors, and judges, however, have been trained in the profession of law.

A profession is, first and foremost, a monopoly of knowledge. The word monopoly is derived from the Greek *moños*, meaning singular, alone and *poleîn*, meaning to sell. To monopolize is to have market control over an area—an industry, a product, or a type of knowledge and expertise. Therefore, a profession stands as a form of monopoly. If you are involved in a lawsuit, whether it is civil or criminal, you will want a lawyer by your side. While you may sometimes hear of a defendant who defends himself or herself in court, acting as one's own lawyer is increasingly rare because lawyers possess specialized knowledge, and they keep a fairly tight grip on that knowledge (Larson 1977; Rothman 1984).

*"If you want justice, it's two hundred dollars an hour.
Obstruction of justice runs a bit more."*

Source: Leo Cullum, New Yorker/CartoonStock.com

There are many ways to define professionalization, but most schol-ars of the process highlight similar characteristics: the establishment of a body of expert knowledge, group solidarity within the profession, self-regulation and autonomy for practitioners, authority over clients, licensing the practice, and a code of ethics (Rothman 1984). Profession-alization, therefore, involves the establishment of special interest control over a field of expertise or a type of work (Marshall 1994). It typically entails the establishment of an organizational body, for example, the ABA, the American Medical Association, the American Sociological Association, the American Society of Criminology, or the Academy of Criminal Justice Sciences.

Professionalization often includes a code of conduct for members, management of knowledge and expertise, and oversight of the number of members—control over who belongs in the profession and who does not, as well as who should lose their right to practice the profession (Marshall 1994). In the legal profession, the loss of the privilege to practice law is known as being **disbarred**—being disqualified from the bar association of which one is a member and losing one's license to practice to law.

THE PRACTICE OF LAW: A BRIEF HISTORY

In one form or another, people have been practicing law for centuries but the legal profession as we know it is a relatively recent development. As we discussed in Chapter 3: Modernization and Theoretical Perspectives on Society and Law, when societies grow and diversify, the need for law and people who are well versed in the law also grows and diversifies. The first historical record of people practicing law, that is, arguing cases on behalf of others, was in ancient Rome (Brundage 2010). While not called lawyers at the time—they were called orators—these practitioners of law were prohibited from taking money for their services, and therefore were not professionals, per se. By the Middle Ages (about the fifth century to the fifteenth century), the practice of law became a profession, with lawyers acting as advocates and consultants for those who hired them. Also during this period, schools specializing in law emerged in Rome and other parts of Europe.

In order to understand the legal profession in the United States, we must first look to England and our colonial history. While many of our laws and approaches to legal education were transported from England, there are many aspects to the legal profession that are uniquely American.

The legal profession in England emerged around the 1200s. Lawyers advocated for clients as officers of the King's Court (Tigar 2000). From the late 1200s to the mid-sixteenth century, law schools did not exist in England. Practitioners of law, known as **barristers** if they argued cases in the courts and **solicitors** if they worked on legal matters outside the courts, learned as apprentices. Barristers wear the traditional white wigs in court; solicitors do not wear wigs, nor do they argue cases in court (Ruda 2001). Solicitors provide legal advice and act on behalf of clients outside of court. Legal apprentices learned under the tutelage of established lawyers—they worked in law offices, observed and took notes on court proceedings in an area called the "crib," and read legal documents and cases.

Legal apprentices also trained in London's Inns of Court—a group of four institutions that predates law schools and were responsible for legal education in England until about the 1600s. Today, the Inns of Courts are voluntary professional organizations that oversee such matters as legal reform and educational standards. Anyone who wishes to join the bar in England must join one of the Inns (https://www.barcouncil.org.uk/about-the-bar/what-is-the-bar/inns-of-court/). The Inns still provide support for barristers, solicitors, and students of law through a range of educational activities and through dining facilities, as well as access to common rooms and law libraries; they also afford access to grants and scholarships for students of the law (https://www.barcouncil.org.uk/about-the-bar/what-is-the-bar/inns-of-court/). Physically, the Inns of Court—Inner Temple,

Sidebar: Why do British Barristers Wear Those Weird Wigs?

Barrister wigs.

In a word: tradition. The wigs date back to the seventeenth century when it became fashionable to wear white, curly wigs to cover up hair loss, sometimes attributed to syphilis. The wigs were made of real human hair, sold by people in need of money, or bought or stolen from corpses. Other wig-makers used horse hair (*Lawyer Monthly* 2017). Since 2007, the tradition was dropped in all but the criminal courts (Reuters Staff 2007). While some barristers liked the authority and anonymity that the wigs provided, most surveyed reported that they agreed with dropping the tradition along with some of the more ornate parts of the barristers' robes (Reuters Staff 2007).

Middle Temple, Lincoln's Inn, and Gray's Inn—are located in the center of London and are made up of elaborate medieval buildings, gardens, and lawns (Ruda 2001).

By the mid-1700s, formal law schools at universities gradually replaced the Inns of Court in the teaching and training of English barristers and solicitors. Much of this shift can be attributed to the famous English jurist and author, Sir William Blackstone (1723–1780). Blackstone studied at Oxford and was admitted to the bar in England, although he did not practice law for long. He lectured in the law at Oxford. In the period between 1723 and 1780, he published *Commentaries on the Laws of England*, much

Lincoln's Inn Court, London.

of which was drawn from his Oxford lectures (Lucas 1962). In 1758, Blackstone was appointed the Vinerian Professor of Law at Oxford; in that same year, he delivered his inaugural speech entitled "On the Study of Law" in which he called for the reform of English legal education and the profession itself (Lucas 1962).

Blackstone did not approve of apprenticeship-style legal education or of the education provided at the Inns of Court (Lucas 1962). The class status and reputation of legal practitioners was a primary concern for Blackstone and he viewed the apprenticeship model as a form of indentured servitude. He believed that the law should be an academic pursuit for men of distinction—or as he said, "gentry learned in the law" (Lucas 1962:459). Similar to current American notions of lawyers as "ambulance chasers" and coarse people handing out business cards at funerals, English barristers in Blackstone's day were seen as unsavory characters whose education at the hands of practicing barristers and in the Inns was "unsystematic and unsupervised" (Lucas 1962:459). By moving the study of law to universities, Blackstone argued that law professors could guide their students in rigorous inquiry into the foundations and principles of law. He believed a degree from a major university should be a primary step toward the practice of law—a practice for those of "considerable property" who would become the "guardians of the English constitution" and the "makers, repealers, and interpreters of English law" (Lucas 1962:485). Since he saw a clear connection between those who practice the law and members of parliament, Blackstone was also concerned with who would be running the country. In short, Blackstone argued that only those of high status could properly guard the laws of England and thus they must be highly educated. Blackstone had his critics—including none other than Jeremy Bentham (see Chapter 8), who famously said that Blackstone "regarded merit as inseparable from high station" (quoted in Lucas 1962:486). But there is little argument about Blackstone's considerable role in transforming legal education and the legal profession in England.

In comparing the evolution of legal education and the profession of law in England to that of the United States, there are some similarities, but also some profound differences. In this country, education in law began with an apprenticeship model, as it did in England. However, the change from lawyers as apprenticed practitioners to lawyers as college-educated professionals—as *juris doctors* or J.D.s—came much more quickly on American shores. This is no surprise; America is a young country when compared to England. Our history is measured in only hundreds of years, not thousands. And, as with English barristers, practitioners of American law have also experienced some highs and lows in terms of their reputations—at times viewed as venerated professionals who fostered democracy in this new country and at other times perceived as crass opportunists out to make a buck off the misfortunes of others.

Like any profession, the legal profession in the United States is in a constant state of flux, growth and expansion, shifting perceptions, and changing fortunes. It continues to change to fit the needs of the society of which it is an integral part. When did the practice of law in the United States transition from an occupation that a person could learn on the job as an apprentice to a highly credentialed avocation bound by professional licensure, entrance exams, and codes of ethics? As with most transitions, these changes did not happen overnight, so it is difficult to pinpoint an

---

Legalese:

A *juris doctor*, or J.D., is a doctor of jurisprudence, the advanced degree earned after completion of law school. It is typically a three-year degree and the entry-level professional degree for aspiring lawyers who must also pass the bar exam in the state where they will practice law. All law school curricula differ, but most include classes in constitutional, civil and criminal law; contract law; torts; courtroom procedures; public law; property and real estate law, and business law, as well as other specialty areas, such as, intellectual property law and divorce law.

exact date at which the change occurred, but we can locate the shift to the late- eighteenth century. In this period, two important developments pushed the legal field toward professionalization: (1) the establishment and expansion of law schools in American universities, and (2) the establishment of the ABA.

THE EVOLUTION OF THE LEGAL PROFESSION AND THE PROFESSIONALIZATION OF LAWYERS IN THE UNITED STATES

Legal scholar Ronen Shamir notes that in modern American society, it is difficult to separate law from the lawyers who practice it. He states: "I start with the premise that law, whatever its sources are, is largely developed, shaped, interpreted, manipulated, and invoked by a specialized group of experts known as lawyers" (1993:361). The legal profession developed over time—indeed, up until the mid-nineteenth century, it was relatively easy to practice law in the United States (Friedman 2004). Until the 1750s, most lawyers learned through observation and hands-on work. They practiced under established lawyers and learned by reading cases and other legal documents. For instance, in the 1760s, Thomas Jefferson worked as a legal apprentice for George Wythe, an esteemed lawyer in colonial America. Licensing, exams, and specialized law schools emerged later and Jefferson played a key role in those developments.

LEGAL EDUCATION: THE GROWTH OF LAW SCHOOLS IN THE UNITED STATES

Thomas Jefferson was so passionate about the legal education he received under George Wythe that he established the first American law school at the College of William & Mary in Williamsburg, Virginia. William & Mary Law School opened its doors in 1779 when Jefferson, who was then the governor of Virginia, encouraged his former teacher and friend, Wythe, to fulfill his vision of law as an academic field of study (Douglas 2010). You could say that Jefferson played a similar role to England's Blackstone in the professionalization of legal education in America. Unlike Blackstone, though, Jefferson was not interested in preserving the law for the gentry, at least not overtly so, although law was still the purview of wealthy male U.S. citizens. Jefferson and his mentor Wythe saw law school as an arena to educate "citizen lawyers" ready to serve the new nation founded on self-governance (https://law.wm.edu/about/ourhistory/index.php). Wythe took up the task, becoming the nation's first law professor. His first law student, the author of the Declaration of Independence, went on to become the nation's third president.

Legalese: So Why Do We *Not* Call American Lawyers Barristers?

American practitioners of law are referred to as lawyers or attorneys. In the United Kingdom, there are different classes or categories of legal practitioners. **Barristers** go to court and argue cases before a judge. **Solicitors** give advice to clients and facilitate transactions, such as drawing up a will. In the United States, we make no distinction; this is most likely why the word barrister was dropped. All people licensed to practice law in the United States are lawyers or attorneys. And, just to complicate matters, while the term lawyer is derived from Middle English's *lawyere*, meaning a person versed in the law (https://www.etymonline.com/word/lawyer). The term attorney is derived from the French, whose legal system is not at all like our own—it is a Romano-Germanic or civil law system (see Chapter 2). Attorney comes from the French word *atorné* meaning "to turn in," which came to mean "to act in one's place" (https://www.etymonline.com/word/attorney).

Other schools of law quickly followed; there is even some disagreement over which came first. Harvard Law School, founded in 1817, lays claim to being the "oldest continually operating law school in the United States" since William & Mary closed during the Civil War and then reopened in 1920 (http://hls.harvard.edu/about/history/). But William & Mary Law School claims the title of "first law school on American shores" (Marshall 1994). But should it? Litchfield Law School in Litchfield, Connecticut, also claimed to be "the nation's first law school" and placed its genesis around 1774, when Tapping Reeve, who later became the Supreme Court Justice of Connecticut's State Supreme Judicial Court, began teaching students out of his home (http://www.litchfieldhistoricalsociety.org/museums/tapping-reeve-house-and-law-school/). The school ran until 1883, and many of its graduates went on to become noted lawyers, political leaders, and business leaders. So, which school was the first? That depends on who you ask, whose website you believe, and how you define "first." While Litchfield Law School predates the opening of William & Mary Law School, Litchfield was a small operation run out of a private residence. The school resembled a larger-scale apprenticeship model with Tapping as the main teacher and mentor. Thus, William & Mary was the first American law school attached to a major college or university. Why does it matter? Prestige—because law schools were new, not yet steeped in tradition as they were in Europe. The profession of law was just gaining a foothold among other established professions, such as medicine, art, architecture, and religion. The esteem attached to a school mattered and still matters.

Today there are 237 U.S. law schools, about 205 of which are accredited by the ABA. The number of accredited schools varies somewhat because the ABA grants provisional accreditation to some schools and can revoke its accreditation if it determines that a school is not meeting its standards. An example would be the school's graduates failing to pass the bar exam in sufficient numbers or having an insufficient number of full-time faculty. For instance, the Arizona Summit Law School was stripped of its accreditation in June 2018 due to low bar exam passage rates, low enrollment rates, and low employment statistics, to name just a few of its shortcomings (Zaretsky 2018a).

THE CURRENT PICTURE FOR LAW SCHOOLS IN THE UNITED STATES

In the 2017 academic year, 34,922 people graduated from ABA accredited law schools, down from 37,124 in 2016 (https://law.wm.edu/about/ourhistory/index.php). In the 2015 academic year, 39,984 people earned law degrees from ABA-accredited law schools, and in 2014, the number of new law school graduates totaled 43,832 (https://www.americanbar.org/groups/legal_education/resources/statistics.html). Law school graduation rates have been either flat or trending downward in the past decade or so (Figure 9.1). There are many reasons why the ranks of law students are waning at this period in our history (Schworm 2014). Several years after the Great Recession of 2008, law school numbers actually rose. The economic problems leading up to the recession started in 2006 and earlier, with subprime mortgage lending, interest-only loans, and stalled economic growth. Rebecca Ruiz, an education reporter for *The New York Times*, noted in 2010:

> It took longer than some experts expected, but the recession and the shortage of good jobs have spurred a jump in applications to law schools and a growing interest in graduate programs .... The number of people taking the Law School Admission Test [LSAT] for example rose to 20 percent in October [of 2010], compared to October of 2008, reaching an all-time high of 60,746. (Ruiz 2010:n.p.)

You might assume that people would not want to incur the kind of debt involved in paying for law school in a time of recession. But generally speaking, when jobs are hard to come by, people tend to turn to graduate and law schools to advance their future job prospects (Ruiz 2010).

Any bounce that law schools received postrecession appears to have plateaued around the period of 2013 to 2014, however. By 2015, the

YEAR	TOTAL NUMBER OF GRADUATES	PERCENT CHANGE
2017	34,922	–5.90
2016	37,124	–7.15
2015	39,984	–8.79
2014	43,832	–6.50
2013	46,776	+0.01
2012	46,364	+4.20
2011	44,495	+0.54
2010	44,258	+0.58
2009	44,004	+0.96
2008	43,587	+0.16
2007	43,518	–0.92
2006	43,920	–

Source: The American Bar Association, Legal Education Resources, Statistics, 2006–2017 https://www.americanbar.org/groups/legal_education/resources/statistics.html. And https://www.americanbar.org/content/dam/aba/administrative/legal_education_and_admissions_to_the_bar/council_reports_and_resolutions/August2018OpenSessionMaterials/18_aug_council_nalp_update_legal_emp_market.authcheckdam.pdf.

Figure 9.1 Law School Graduates by Year, 2006 to 2017

percentage of people graduating from law school dipped by 8.79 percent and that number continues to drop (Figure 9.1). There are several reasons for these declining numbers, and some of those law students who decided to wait out the recession in law school may have simply kicked the can down the road. Job prospects for new lawyers are uncertain, despite what the ABA's official statistics indicate. A 2011 article in *The New York Times* titled, "Is Law School a Losing Game?" highlighted the shortcomings—if not downright deception—involved in the ABA's publication of law school graduate and employment rates (Segal 2011). These ABA data are also used by *U.S. News and World Report*, and consistently report high levels of post-law-school employment for schools across the board, typically any-where from 80 percent to 90 percent employment rates at nine months after graduating (Segal 2011). The statistics do not indicate *where* the graduates are employed and whether or not a law degree is truly needed to do the jobs, however. The *New York Times* article states that since 2008, at least 15,000 attorney positions and legal staff-type jobs at large law firms have been eliminated due to layoffs, hiring downturns, and use of outsourcing and temporary employment for low-level legal tasks (Segal 2011).

Similarly, a 2017 article in *USA Today* warns potential law students about "Why You Might Want to Think Twice before Going to Law School." Reporter Greg Toppo argues that several small law schools are in danger of closing, as did Whittier Law School—the first ever ABA-accredited law school to shutter its doors. Other law schools have merged with larger schools, such as Hamline University and the William Mitchell School of Law in 2015, and the University of New Hampshire and Franklin Pierce Law School in 2010. Franklin Pierce had about 450 students at the time of the merger (Ramer 2010).

The rising costs of legal education and student debt have contributed to declining enrollment. In 2016, private-school law graduates had an average of about $135,000 in loan debt; for public-school law graduates, the average loan debt amounted to about $96,000 (McEntee 2018:12). In 2017, tuition for one year of law school in the United States cost anywhere from around $11,000, such as at the University of North Dakota Law School, to almost $63,000 at Columbia University—the highest law school tuition in the country (https://www.ilrg.com/rankings/law/tuition/3/desc/Tuition). The nationwide average tuition at a private law school in 2017 was $46,329; at public law schools it was $26,425 (https://data.lawschooltransparency.com/costs/tuition/?scope=national).

Therefore, another potential factor in the declining attendance at law schools could be knowledge about tuition costs, coupled with a difficult job market for graduates. While the ABA and law schools have long published data on employment rates for graduates, these data have been called into question by watchdog groups such as Law School Transparency (LST) and by the popular media. Two Vanderbilt University Law School graduates, Kyle McEntee and Patrick Lynch, founded LST in 2009. Among LST's key concerns are: increasing tuition, excessive enrollments, deceptive marketing and employment statistics from law schools, and overly generous student loan programs (Law School Transparency 2015). In 2010, schools under pressure from LST and potential students who wanted transparency about the high price of law school—when weighed against real employment opportunities in the field—agreed to release statistics to the LST. The organization now publishes yearly tuition costs and actual employment data on its website. In its 2011 "Law School Enrollment Report," LTS found:

> Between 1976 and 2000, law schools steadily enrolled between 40,000 and 44,000 new students each year. From 1976 to 1987, the average was 40,973. From 1988 to 2000, the average was 43,497—a little over 6% higher. But between 2000 and 2002, law schools increased first-year enrollment by 11.2%. In subsequent years, enrollment steadily creeped up, with minor ebbs and flows, until peaking in 2010 at 52,404. As law schools were pressured to become more transparent about job outcomes beginning in 2010, the media

and prospective law students took notice of inflated enrollment, inadequate job prospects, and high prices—and enrollment dropped. After 1L [first-year law student] enrollment peaked in 2010 at 52,404 new students, enrollment fell dramatically in each of the next three years, which was then followed by four years of even lower, but steady, enrollment [of] between 37,000 and 38,000 new 1Ls students. (https://data.lawschooltransparency.com/enrollment/all/?y1=2010&y2=2015)

Thus, law schools in the United States face many enrollment challenges. These include: high tuition costs that have outpaced inflation, uncertain job prospects, and pushback from recent graduates and potential students for more transparency about the actual costs of earning a law degree when measured against actual job prospects.

There may be a bright spot for American law schools since the 2016 election of Donald Trump to the U.S. presidency, however. Approximately a year and a half after Trump's election, many media outlets reported on a so-called "Trump Bump" at American law schools. This trend was parodied in the online humor news venue *The Onion*, which featured the photos of three Trump-employed lawyers—Michael Cohen, Ty Cobb, and Rudi Giuliani—with the caption, "Law School Applications Increase Upon the Realization That any F*&%ing Idiot Can Be a Lawyer."

While *The Onion's* take on this phenomenon may hold some truth, the ABA argued that the "Trump Bump" in law school applicants is real and significant (Ward 2018). Both the Kaplan Test Prep company and the

Michael Cohen.

Rudy Guiliani.

Law School Admission Test (LSAT) reported an uptick in people seeking to attend law schools after Trump's election. The *ABA Journal* reported that applications increased by 10.6 percent in 2018 when compared to 2017 figures (Ward 2018). This increase represents good news for laws schools; however, given the continued drop in the number of jobs for recent graduates, it is too early to tell if this bump will result in greater employment opportunities for new applicants. Over the past decade, approximately 60 percent of law school graduates "obtained full-time, entry-level attorney jobs" (Ward 2018:n.p.) and the remaining 40 percent did not.

The Kaplan Test Prep company surveyed over 500 recent law school applicants and found that almost one-third said that Trump's presidential win affected their decision to pursue law as a profession (Hawkins 2018). While some applicants reported being mobilized by their support of Trump, others indicated that they wanted to become lawyers to bring about change and perhaps join the ranks of more "level-headed leaders" (Hawkins 2018:n.p.). In other words, while it is not entirely clear if the bump is due to Trump's supporters or detractors, there does appear to be an effect.

One particular segment of recent law school applicants can be counted among Trump's detractors—women. In another survey by the BARBI Group, law students entering school in the fall of 2018 were asked about their political affiliations and motivations (Zaretsky 2018b). Almost 68 percent of female respondents said they were members of the Democratic Party and about 70 percent reported being very unhappy with President Trump (Zaretsky 2018b).

CASE IN POINT

Training Lawyers with a Sense of Purpose: The School for Justice in India

In the American setting, law schools train students to become practitioners of law. Not all people who attend law school go on to become practicing lawyers, but they will likely use their degrees in some professional setting. And many U.S. law schools specialize in specific types of law. For instance, the schools of law at Stanford, the University of Pennsylvania, and the University of New Hampshire specialize in intellectual property law. Harvard Law School, New York University School of Law, and Lewis and Clark Law School are renowned for business law. Southwestern University, Columbia University, and the University of California Los Angeles schools of law focus on entertainment law.

But what if law schools specialized in fighting *specific injustices* that the students themselves have experienced? The School of Justice in India does just that. Launched in April 2017 by the Dutch nonprofit group *Free a Girl*, the school provides training, funding, and other support for former victims of underage sex trafficking to pursue careers in the legal system (Ruiz-Grossman 2017). Nineteen young women made up the inaugural class; they are 19 of the millions of women and children sold into sex slavery in India. The School for Justice helps with the costs of school and also with housing, food, and transportation. Founders of the program acknowledge that they cannot change the problem with 19 young women, but see it as a start. The women will become public prosecutors and legal advocates, mentoring other survivors to do the same (Ruiz-Grossman 2017). And *Free a Girl* hopes to build the program in other locales, such as Brazil. As one student in the first class of the School for Justice stated:

> Being poor, I left my family at 9 years old to work in domestic service in a large house. The gardener, gatekeeper, the sweeper and other men abused me there .... I left the house, but I didn't realize that without money or directions I would not be able to find my way home. I asked [a woman begging on the street] for help, but she took me to a brothel and sold me to it. I was 13 years old .... I want to fight against child sexual exploitation and help others like me. I am excited about becoming a lawyer and this is why I joined the School for Justice." (Ruiz-Grossman 2017:n.p.)

Supporters of the school note that India's legal system has several laws prohibiting sex trafficking and child sexual exploitation, but very few cases are ever brought to conviction. Who better to train as lawyers with the skills to fight this abuse than those who have survived it?

Before we look more closely at the state of the legal profession in the United States, we will consider the second major development in the establishment of law as a profession: the ABA. As we noted, the ABA can grant or strip a law school of its accreditation—its right to operate as an ABA-approved law school. The ABA also publishes annual graduation and employment rates, so clearly laws schools and the association are interrelated. In the next section of this chapter, we look more closely at the ABA's impact on the legal profession in this country.

THE AMERICAN BAR ASSOCIATION

As we have seen, the first shift toward the professionalization of law involved the establishment of law schools in the United States. Closely connected to that development was the second—the founding of the ABA. The ABA is the largest voluntary professional organization of lawyers and legal professionals in the United States. In August 1878, 75 lawyers from 25 different states met in Saratoga Springs, New York, to start the ABA (https://www.americanbar.org/aba.html). As with many matters concerning law in the United States, the term *bar* derives from Old English; it originally referred to an actual railing or bar found in English courtrooms that separated the "barristers," or practitioners of law, from the part of the court where the judge or judges presided. Sheriffs or bailiffs also policed the separation of the two areas. When a person was "called to the bar," he—and in this period they were all "he's"—was allowed to make his argument or present his case. Thus, "passing the bar" meant being allowed to practice law (https://crosleylaw.com/blog/law-terms-etymology-history-passing-bar/).

The establishment of the ABA, which grew from its initial 75 members in its inaugural year to 289 the following year (1879) to now over 400,000 members, set in course many of the practices and standards to which American lawyers and law schools are held. And like the law itself, those practices and standards have multiplied and proliferated as the ABA has grown in numbers and in political power. Its most recent *Policy and Procedures Handbook* contains over 400 pages of rules, regulations, and standards upheld by the organization. The 400,000 ABA members are sorted into different sections based on their legal specialties and interests (https://www.americanbar.org/aba.html). Today, the ABA includes 21 different sections on specific areas of law ranging from administrative law to family law, taxation, and torts (Figure 9.2). Every August, the ABA hosts its annual meetings in a major U.S. city, with thousands attending (https://www.americanbar.org/aba.html).

The ABA's stated mission is "To serve equally our members, our profession and the public by defending liberty and delivering justice as the national representative of the legal profession" (https://www.americanbar.org/about_the_aba/aba-mission-goals.html). This mission includes four key goals and objectives (Figure 9.3).

The ABA has been at the forefront in establishing the law as a profession in the United States. It has also grown to become a large **lobbying group** that holds considerable political sway. According to the Congressional Research Service (CRS), lawyers represent the largest occupational

- Administrative Law and Regulatory Practice
- Antitrust Law
- Business Law
- Civil Rights and Social Justice
- Criminal Justice
- Dispute Resolution
- Environment, Energy, and Resources
- Family Law
- Health Law
- Infrastructure and Regulated Industries Section
- Intellectual Property Law
- International Law
- Labor and Employment Law
- Legal Education and Admission to the Bar
- Litigation
- Public Contract Law
- Real Property, Trust, and Estate Law
- Science & Technology Law
- State and Local Government Law
- Taxation
- Tort Trial and Insurance Practice (https://www.americanbar.org/groups/sections.html)

Figure 9.2 American Bar Association Sections: Areas of Specialization within the Practice of Law

group within the halls of Congress (CRS 2018:2). Lawyers can also be found outside the halls of congress as well—in the lobbies. **Lobbyists and lobbying groups** are people paid to represent special interests; they argue for or against legislation being considered in Congress. They are called lobbyists because they wait in the lobbies of the chambers of Congress, ready to grab the attention of the members as they walk out into the halls of the Capitol.

While there are no definitive numbers on how many lobbyists are lawyers, knowledge of the law is essential for lobbyists and many lobbyists are lawyers (Sullivan 2015). Additionally, many lobbyists are retired lawmakers (Lee 2014), so without any official statistics, it is safe to assume that lobbying and the legal profession are closely tied. And further, the ABA has its own lobby—the ABA Government Affairs Office—an advocacy arm of the organization that addresses matters concerning the legal profession before Congress (McMillion 2011). Describing the ABA's approach to lobbying, Rhonda McMillion, the editor of the ABA's *Washington Letter*, a publication of the ABA's Governmental Affairs Office, says:

Goal I: Serve Our Members

Objective:

1. Provide benefits, programs, and services that promote members' professional growth and quality of life.

Goal II: Improve Our Profession

Objectives:

Promote the highest quality legal education.
1. Promote competence, ethical conduct, and professionalism.
2. Promote pro bono and public service by the legal profession.

Goal III: Eliminate Bias and Enhance Diversity

Objectives:

1. Promote full and equal participation in the association, our profession, and the justice system by all persons.
2. Eliminate bias in the legal profession and the justice system.

Goal IV: Advance the Rule of Law

Objectives:

1. Increase public understanding of and respect for the rule of law, the legal process, and the role of the legal profession at home and throughout the world.
2. Hold governments accountable under law.
3. Work for just laws, including human rights, and a fair legal process.
4. Assure meaningful access to justice for all persons.
5. Preserve the independence of the legal profession and the judiciary (https://www.americanbar.org/about_the_aba/aba-mission-goals.html).

Figure 9.3 The American Bar Association's Goals and Objectives

While many organizations seek to wield influence through financial contributions, the nonpartisan ABA does not have a political action committee [PAC] and does not contribute to campaigns. The association instead depends on effective advocacy by its leadership, lobbying staff, and Grassroots Action Team, a group of ABA members who convey the association's views to individual legislators through personal contacts. (2011:n.p.)

These lobbying efforts no doubt help to further the ABA's stated number one goal: serve our members. Regarding the ABA's success in realizing its other goals, especially goal number three—to eliminate bias and enhance diversity in the field of law in the United States—we will look closely at those issues in the sections on stratification and diversity in the legal profession.

THE LEGAL PROFESSION TODAY

As we have already seen, the legal profession faces many challenges, including increased costs of legal education and decreased job prospects for new lawyers as well as competition from other professionals and lay people alike. In May 2018 a total of 1,338,678 people practiced law in the United States, a 2 percent increase from 2017 and a 15 percent increase over the past decade (https://www.americanbar.org/news/abanews/aba-news-archives/2018/05/new_aba_data_reveals.html). The average age of U.S. lawyers is 49, and 85 percent of lawyers are White (https://www.american-bar.org/news/abanews/aba-news-archives/2018/05/new_aba_data_reveals.html). In 2018, men made up 64 percent of U.S. lawyers; 36 percent were women. For law school faculty members, about 62 percent are male and 38 percent are female (Association of American Law Schools 2017).

Being a lawyer is, generally speaking, still a highly paid occupation with moderate projected job growth in the next decade. According to the U.S. Bureau of Labor Statistics, in 2017 lawyers earned a median salary of almost $120,000 and the job growth in the field for 2016 to 2026 is estimated at about 8 percent (https://www.bls.gov/ooh/legal/lawyers.htm). As the aforementioned numbers indicate, the legal profession is still predominantly male and White. The following sections of the chapter consider stratification and diversity within the field of law.

STRATIFICATION WITHIN THE LEGAL PROFESSION

The legal profession is stratified in many ways. Law schools are stratified by esteem and reputation—and of course—by tuition costs. Private law practices are sorted by power and prestige. The halls of government are populated by lawyers who have access to power and money in ways that average citizens do not. Law schools and the practice of law are stratified by race, gender, age, and socioeconomic background.

Stratified Law Schools

There are many ways to measure stratification within legal education in this country: by the LSAT scores, by the prestige and costs of the schools, by the demographic makeup of each school, by acceptance rates, or by the earnings of each school's graduates. By any measure, however, we see that a hierarchy of law schools exists and that hierarchy is reinforced and reproduced by hierarchies within the practice of law. Every year, *U.S. News and World Report* ranks all ABA-accredited law school in the United States. And every year, Ivy League law schools rank at the top, along with major university law schools—with some minor changes from year to year. In 2018, Yale ranked number one, Stanford number two, and Harvard came in at number three. The University of Chicago; Columbia University; New York

University; University of Pennsylvania; University of Michigan, Ann Arbor; University of California, Berkeley; and University of Virginia rounded out the top 10, in that order. The 11th through 15th rankings went to Northwestern University; Cornell University; Georgetown University; University of Texas, Austin; and the University of California at Los Angeles, respectively (https://www.usnews.com/best-graduate-schools/top-law-schools/law-rankings). These top-ranked schools are prestigious, costly, exclusive, and not accessible to most people in the United States. For instance, Yale University Law School only accepted 10 percent of all applicants in 2018; Stanford accepted 12 percent, and Harvard accepted 18 percent. While data on the gender and racial composition of each law school are not available, the Association of American Law Schools publishes aggregate demographic data on law students. Law school enrollment data for 2017 indicate that women now make up a slightly higher percentage of law students than do men: 51.27 percent female to 49.69 percent male. Minorities (unspecified) comprised 31.37 percent of all law school students in the same year (AALS 2017). Thus, women and minorities appear to be making gains in terms of law school attendance but have a lot of ground to make up in the legal profession. We will examine this issue more closely in the section on Diversity in Practice.

Stratified Law Practices

"Lawyering"—practicing law—is also stratified in terms of power, prestige, and access along racial, class, and gender lines. In the final two chapters, Chapters 10 and 11, we will examine inequality and law more carefully. In this section, however, we will briefly look at how stratification and inequality within the legal profession operate to keep the practice of law, in large part, a White, male, upper-class domain.

Big Law

Not surprisingly, the hierarchy of privilege and power that exists in law schools feeds into the legal profession. The top law firms recruit from the top law schools, thereby perpetuating the stratification by race, class, and gender over time. The top-earning law firms—so-called **big law**—appear quite similar in terms of location of the practices' headquarters, types of law practiced, and average salary for starting lawyers. *Vault*—an online career guidance website—has ranked the most prestigious law firms in the United States since the mid-1990s. *Vault* uses reviews from 17,000 law firm associates who are asked to rank firms on a 1-to-10 scale, excluding the firm at which they are employed. *Vault's* Top 100 rankings are used by media outlets, such as *Forbes Magazine*, and by students, colleges and universities, and employers (http://www.vault.com/company-rankings/law/vault-law-100/?sRankID=2).

Legalese: What is Big Law? Just How Big Is Big?

Big law is the legal profession insiders' nickname for the largest, most profitable law firms based in the United States. Big law typically denotes the size of the profits and not necessarily the size of the law firm. All of the top 10 law firms in this county count their profits in the multi-millions, with several in the multi-billions of dollars per year. Further, *The American Lawyer* magazine introduced the **profit per partner** measurement in 1985. This metric allows individual lawyers to weigh the profits they bring in against their partners within and outside of their firm, making the field even more competitive and dollar-driven (Gunderman and Mutz 2014).

The 10 top-earning law firms based in the United States—all have satellite offices in various locations in the U.S. and across the globe—employ anywhere from 265 to 2,000-plus lawyers; all but a few are based in New York City. Many of these top 10 Big Law firms trace their history to at least a century ago and the top firm, Cravath, Swaine, and Moore, LLC, is two centuries old. All of the top 10 firms specialize in some form of corporate/property law, such as: mergers and acquisitions, antitrust, real estate, intellectual property, private equities, or commercial law. Starting salaries at the top 10 range from $180,000 to $190,000 per year (http://www.vault.com/company-rankings/law/vault-law-100/?sRankID=2), making the starting pay for these elite few anywhere from $60,000 to $70,000 higher than the average salary for all lawyers in the United States, which, as we noted earlier, is about $120,000. (https://www.bls.gov/ooh/legal/lawyers.htm).

The American Lawyer also provides yearly rankings of the 100 and 200 top-earning law firms, respectively, in the United States. According to Roy Strom of *The American Lawyer*, 2017 proved to be a very profitable year for the top 100 law firms. They brought in $91.4 billion in revenue, making it the best earning year for the legal profession since before the recession of 2008. And, further pointing to the stratification within the practice of law, most of the $91.4 billion was earned by the top 25 earners (Strom 2018). The dominance of these top-earning practices can be attributed to mergers with other law firms, recruitment of top-earning lawyers (also known as "rainmakers"), and general revenue at the top staying at the top.

SMALL LAW OR PRIVATE PRACTICE

If big law makes up the top-earning 100 or so U.S. law firms, is there such a thing as "**Small Law**"? Not really; there are all of the other thousands of law firms that fall outside of the top 100 to 200, depending on which list of big law firms you consult. Some are small, some are large, but their earnings

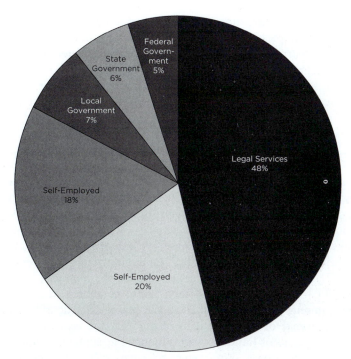

Figure 9.4 Where Lawyers Practice: The Largest Employers of Lawyers, 2016

are not high enough to qualify them as big law. The majority of U.S. attorneys are employed in small private practices. While there is no clear cutoff point for "small," a small practice typically employs about 20 lawyers. The smallest of law firms are comprised of solo practitioners—lawyers who hang a sign outside a small office or storefront and set up shop for themselves. According to the Bureau of Labor Statistics, lawyers held 792,500 jobs in 2016 (https://www.bls.gov/ooh/legal/lawyers.htm [Figure 9.4]).

The largest percentage, legal services—at 48 percent—includes anything from "big law" attorneys and **in-house counsel**—lawyers who work full-time for large businesses or other non-governmental organizations—to lawyers employed at smaller law firms. The self-employed category is made up of very small law firms in towns and cities throughout the country.

GOVERNMENT LAWYERS

As discussed earlier in the chapter, lawyers work in all areas of government: in the halls of congress as senators and representatives, in the courts as prosecutors and district attorneys, and, of course, as judges in both state and federal lower and higher courts, as well as in the executive branch. Further, government agencies hire thousands of lawyers to investigate and litigate on their behalf. Examples of agencies that hire lawyers are: the Department of Justice, the Department of Labor, the Department of Veterans Affairs, and the Department of Health and Human Services. One of the largest employers of government attorneys is the Social Security Administration, which employs over 25,000 lawyers (DeVelder 2011). And while not employed *by* government, lawyers also work in the lobbies of Congress as paid lobbyists.

ADVOCACY LAW/NONPROFIT LAW/PUBLIC INTEREST LAW

Advocacy law comprises another category of legal employment. Advocacy lawyers, also known as **public interest lawyers,** work on behalf of social causes, such as environmental issues, prisoners' rights, immigrants' rights, and animal welfare. The work—sometimes called "cause lawyering"—is undertaken for **nonprofit organizations.** Two examples of advocacy law are the Southern Poverty Law Center (SPLC) and the Juvenile Law Center (JLC).

In 1971, two civil rights lawyers established the **Southern Poverty Law Center (SPLC).** Morris Dees and Joseph Levin, Jr. wanted to use their legal skills and training to fight on behalf of the powerless. The SPLC works to "ensure the promise of the Civil Rights Movement" and uses litigation to fight against the remnants of Jim Crow segregation, white supremacy, and all forms of organized hate groups (https://www.splcenter.org/about). The SPLC also provides teaching resources through its Teaching Tolerance initiative and performs a watchdog role, tracking hate groups throughout the United States with its Intelligence Report and through the Hate Watch and Hate Map online tools.

The **Juvenile Law Center** (JLC) advocates for the rights, dignity, equity, and opportunity of young people, particularly those disenfranchised youth involved in the child welfare system and the juvenile justice system (https://jlc.org/about). Founded in 1975, this national nonprofit, public interest law firm "uses litigation, appellate advocacy, *amicus* (friend-of-the-court) briefs, policy reform, and consulting" to serve young people in need (https://jlc.org/about).

Both the SPCL and the JLC provide excellent examples of lawyers using their education, training, and skills to work for underrepresented groups. Advocacy law offers an alternative to the public perception of lawyers as sharks who feed off of others' misfortunes. Some people go into law because they want it to be more inclusive, and they wish to use the law as a tool to bring about social change for the better.

DIVERSITY IN PRACTICE? LAW AND DIVERSITY

In 2018, African-Americans comprised 5 percent of all U.S. lawyers; Asians, 3 percent; Whites, 85 percent; non-White, 15%; and Hispanics/Latinos, 5 percent. There were no Hawaiian/ Pacific Islander working as lawyers recorded in 2018; people identifying as multiracial comprised 1 percent of U.S. lawyers, as did Native Americans (ABA 2018a). The Association of American Law Schools reported that racial and ethnic minorities made up about 15 percent of faculty members at U.S. law schools, but did not provide any further breakdown of the specific racial and ethnic makeup of that percentage (AALS 2017).

In addition to ranking law firms by earnings, *The American Lawyer* website publishes its Diversity Scorecard every year. The Scorecard tabulates the average number of full-time-equivalent minority attorneys, including Asian-American, African-American, Latino/Hispanic, Native American, and self-described multiracial attorneys (Seal 2018). In 2017, the Diversity Scorecard ranked 227 of the top U.S. law firms; 43 firms had at least 20 percent minority attorneys and five firms had 20 percent minority partners (Seal 2018). These numbers mean that 18.9 percent of the top 227 law firms employ 20 percent minority lawyers and 2.2 percent of the top 227 law firms have promoted minority lawyers to the rank of partner. All of the remaining 227 firms employ less than 20 percent minorities, and less—often significantly less—than 2.2 percent of the minority lawyers have made it to the rank of partner. Except for those relatively few law firms with higher-diversity scorecard rankings, these numbers hardly seem a cause for celebration (https://www.law.com/americanlawyer/2018/05/29/the-2018-diversity-scorecard-the-rankings/). In an article about the 2017 Diversity Scorecard, Robert Grey, senior counsel at Hunton and William and then-president of the Leadership Counsel on Legal Diversity stated, "We get comfortable working with people we know, people that look like us, people that went to the same law schools [and] it becomes almost like inertia ... homogeneous societies are easier to deal with than diverse societies" (Tribe 2017:4). Grey sums up how institutionalized racism, sexism, and classism operate in this brief quotation. He also argues that legal clients—the customers—must drive change. If large corporations refuse to hire law firms without a proven record of hiring and promoting women and people of color, change will come. Some companies, such as Hewlett Packard, MetLife, and Macy's, are doing just that (Tribe 2017). This is another step toward diversity. But, the law profession itself needs accountability.

The headline of a recent *New York Times* article sums up the state of the legal profession for White women and women of color; it reads, "Lawyers Say They Face Persistent Racial and Gender Bias at Work" (Zraick 2018:B5). A study on bias in the legal profession conducted by the ABA in the spring of 2016 found the following:

- Women of color felt they were held to a higher standard than White men.
- Women reported they had to "walk a tightrope" in their behavior, that is, had to behave in feminine ways and ensure they were seen

as responsible for "office housework, such as taking notes, ordering lunch and comforting others."
- Many women reported being paid less than their male colleagues with similar experience.
- A quarter of female lawyers reported that they had experienced sexual harassment at work (Zraick 2018:B5).

Since women entered into the practice of law, female lawyers have encountered these types of obstacles and tightrope walks. They face higher hurdles in moving up the ranks of the profession. For some women, these hurdles prove insurmountable, and they end up leaving the profession (Pfeiffer 2007). And, as fewer women rise to the top of their chosen profession, the number of women available for leadership positions dwindles—resulting in fewer women qualified to work as judges, law partners, general counsels, law professors, and industry leaders. For example, in 2007, 1,000 lawyers in Massachusetts were surveyed about their experiences as lawyers (Pfeiffer 2007). Thirty-one percent of female law associates left private practice entirely, compared to 18 percent of male associates (Pfeiffer 2007). The report, "Women Lawyers and Obstacles to Leadership," conducted by the Massachusetts Institute of Technology found:

- Women comprise 17 percent of law firm partners.
- Women leave partnerships at much higher rates than men.
- Women stop pursuing partnerships due to difficulties around work and child care balance.
- About 40 percent of women lawyers with children have moved to part-time work compared to very few men, even though men in the legal profession have more children than women, on average (Pfeiffer 2007:A1, A15).

Supreme Court Justice Ruth Bader Ginsburg remembers how, as a young female lawyer, she was inevitably the parent called by her son's school when he misbehaved or was ill. Noting that her husband was an equal partner in their parenting, she asked the school to alternate which parent they called; she also noted that it was his turn. Ginsburg stated, "Women will only have true equality when men share with them the responsibility of bringing up the next generation" (Davis and Sherr 2001:18). For women lawyers who are single parents, the difficulties of work and child care are all the more pressing.

The ABA recognizes the challenges faced by women lawyers as they advance—or do *not* advance—in their field. Hilarie Bass, the 2017–2018 president of the ABA, undertook the President's Initiative, "Achieving Long-Term Careers for Women in Law." The initiative starts as a fact-finding and data-gathering mission, with the goal of making policy recommendations to advance women in the field of law. Women currently make up about 50 percent of all law students and about 45 percent of law firm associates (https://www.americanbar.org/content/dam/aba/administrative/office_president/Initiative_Overview.authcheckdam.pdf). Beyond the level of associate, however, women experience a precipitous drop, comprising only 19 percent of equity partners in large, private law firms (https://www.americanbar.org/content/dam/aba/administrative/office_president/Initiative_Overview.authcheckdam.pdf). Some examples of the Presidential Initiative's research plans are:

- Surveys of law firms and of female and male lawyers in practice from 20 to 40 years after law school to get a data-defined view of compensation, practice activities, and roles that women and men play at those stages of their careers.
- Focus group analyses to obtain more in-depth perspectives on the personal and structural factors that enhance or impede legal careers.
- A study of the long-term career trajectories of women lawyers; the factors that move them in one career direction versus another; and the personal, social and organizational factors that affect staying or leaving a particular work setting.
- Research on the particular challenges that women of color face, techniques to overcome obstacles, and what employers can do to even the pathways.
- An analysis of women lawyers who change career direction after age 55, exploring the nature of the changes, characteristics, reasons why, and rewards and challenges of taking a different direction (https://www.americanbar.org/content/dam/aba/administrative/office_president/Initiative_Overview.authcheckdam.pdf).

The ABA hopes to use the data gathered in the initiative to "help legal employers form the policies, practices and structures to promote retention of senior women lawyers and eliminate the attrition gender gap" (https://www.americanbar.org/content/dam/aba/administrative/office_president/Initiative_Overview.authcheckdam.pdf). This initiative certainly cannot

Balfore Archive Images/Alamy Stock Photo

Ada Kepley, 1842–1925. Suffragist, temperance activist, and first woman to graduate from law school and practice in a court of law.

hurt, but the problems faced by female lawyers, and especially those of color, have been around since the first woman entered the profession in the late 1800s.

In 1869, Arabella Mansfield (1846–1911) became the first women to pass a state's bar exam despite the fact that she was not allowed to enroll in law school. Mansfield was admitted to the bar in Iowa, which was the first state to allow women and racial minorities into the bar. The first woman to graduate from law school *and* practice in a court of law was Ada Kepley (1847–1925), a well-known suffragist and temperance activist. In 1870, Kepley graduated from Northwestern University School of Law but was not admitted to the bar until 1881 when the state of Illinois first allowed women to take the state's bar exam. The first African-American woman to practice law in the United States graduated from Howard University School of Law in 1872. Charlotte E. Ray (1850–1911) was admitted to the bar in the District of Columbia. Ray attempted to start her own practice in D.C., but due to the prevailing prejudices of the time, was unable to sustain her private practice. She moved to New York City to work as a teacher and joined the suffragist movement.

So, while the ABA's recent call for better data about the careers of women in the legal profession is laudable, the results and policy recommendations—and the action taken on these recommendations—cannot come soon enough. White women and women of color have been working as lawyers for nearly 150 years, but have yet to achieve anything close to parity with their male peers. The loss of educated, licensed, and trained female professionals from the occupational hierarchy affects women lawyers, their potential clients, and their employers, as well as the overall fight for women's equality.

In the final section of this chapter, we examine another trend affecting the legal profession. Deprofessionalization is a recent development in the field of law that threatens to change the very core of the field—the monopoly over legal knowledge and practice.

CRASHING THE GATE: DEPROFESSIONALIZATION AND THE PRACTICE OF LAW

Ironically, the legal profession is facing a threat to its monopoly on knowledge—a threat that could bring the legal field full circle. Earlier in this chapter, we looked at the professionalization of law, a process that began in the late 1700s and continued into the 1800s and mid-1900s. Could law now be dealing with *deprofessionalization*? Sociologists who focus on work and occupations define **deprofessionalization** as the loss of autonomy and control over one's professional life, as well as the larger loss of the monopoly on knowledge that the profession possesses (Rothman

1984). Sociologists have examined deprofessionalization in many areas of work, such as medicine, pharmacy, teaching, social work, library science, as well as law.

In an article published in *The Atlantic* in 2014, Gunderman and Mutz use the legal profession as a cautionary tale for medicine. The authors argue that the field of law has experienced a process of deprofessionalization and demoralization. They state:

> Simply put, the law is not well. U.S. law school applications are down nearly half from eight years ago [2006], and 85% of law school graduates now carry at least $100,000 in debt. More than 180 of the 200 U.S. law schools are unable to find jobs for more than 80% of their graduates. Median starting salaries for those who do find work are down by 17% and more than a third of graduates cannot find full-time employment. Tellingly, lawyers have higher rates of depression and alcoholism than the general public. (Gunderman and Mutz 2014:n.p.)

The authors provide several reasons for this dire prognosis, many of which have also been outlined by sociologists who have studied the occupation of law, such as Robert A. Rothman. According to Rothman, the professional dominance of lawyers in the United States reached its peak around the 1960s and 1970s. The process of deprofessionalization of law began in the late 1970s to the 1980s (Rothman 1984). The process has not only continued into the twenty-first century, it has also picked up steam. Rothman identified seven factors that have contributed to this deprofessionalization process.

The first factor is the **narrowing of the competence and education gap** between the general public and trained legal professionals. When the law became a profession, only the very wealthy could afford higher education—in fact, even in the late nineteenth century, fewer than 8 percent of the population earned a high school diploma (Rothman 1984). To most, the law, with its specialized language and practices, might as well have been a foreign culture. The American public, however, has become much more educated and today the high school graduation rate is about 83 percent (Strauss 2016). And if we add in those who have earned High School Equivalency Test/Graduate Equivalency Degrees, that number rises to 88 percent (Ryan and Bauman 2016). About one in three Americans (33 percent) have earned bachelor's degrees or higher (Ryan and Bauman 2016). Generally speaking, a more highly educated populace means we are closing the competency gap. Lawyers should not assume that they are the smartest people in the room and that their legal knowledge cannot be understood or challenged by lay people.

The second factor Rothman highlights in deprofessionalization is the **routinization** of expert legal knowledge (1984). **Routinization** means the breaking down of tasks and expertise into smaller, mundane tasks that can be accomplished by those without formal legal education and training. For example, wills and employment contracts can be reduced to fill-in-the-blank type forms. Legal advice can be found in easy-to-read, self-help style manuals. And, as we will discuss further, the age of computers and the Internet has brought about a new form of easy access to legal knowledge—legal facts, forms, cases, advice—are all at our fingertips.

Rothman (1984) also points to a third factor: **specialization** within the legal profession as contributing to the deprofessionalization of law. In contrast to routinization of tasks, the growth of very specific expert knowledge in particular subfields or sections within law can lead to lawyers becoming less unified and more differentiated (Figure 9.2 on page 240). Each of these subfields is further broken down into specific areas. The ABA's section on family law, for instance, has about 10,000 members who may focus on family law in general or on specific areas such as: adoption, divorce, custody, military law, alternative families, or elder law (https://www.americanbar.org/groups/family_law.html). A member of the ABA's Infrastructure and Regulated Agencies Section might further specialize in communications, cable TV, Internet, gas, oil pipelines, aviation, motor carriers, railroads, and water industries (https://www.americanbar.org/groups/infrastructure-regulated-industries.html). How does specialization within the legal field lead to its deprofessionalization? According to Rothman and others (cf. Heinz and Laumann 1978), this breaking down of a profession into smaller parts can weaken the group solidarity within the profession. There is strength in unity and numbers.

I would argue, however, that this intricate task specialization can also protect the legal field from deprofessionalization to some extent. So, while a lay person might be able to draw up a will or a contract without consulting an expert, one would be hard pressed to mount a high stakes legal case involving a natural gas pipeline running through a residential neighborhood. In other words, the more specialized an area of law becomes, the less likely it is that a nonspecialized lawyer or layperson will have the knowledge base and expertise to take it on.

A fourth area contributing to the deprofessionalization of law is what Rothman calls **consumerism** (Rothman 1984), or what I call **consumer advocacy**. Beginning in the 1960s, consumers began to question all forms of industries, businesses, and professions about their monopolistic hold over everything from the safety of products and market prices to expertise and knowledge. Consumers grew skeptical of the law's hold over its specialized knowledge and called for more governmental oversight into the legal profession, especially regarding issues like price-fixing and the competence of legal professionals (Rothman 1984:194).

Rothman summarizes the fifth potential threat to the legal profession this way: "Professional monopolies must be protected constantly from threats of encroachment by closely allied occupations seeking to enhance their own prerogatives and rewards by expanding into areas once reserved for existing professions" (1984:195). **Boundary maintenance** (Kronus 1976) is an issue in every occupation, especially one that traffics in expertise. **Boundary maintenance** involves any strategy a social system or institution—such as the legal institution— uses to keep the distinction between insiders and outsiders, that is, between lawyers and non-lawyers. Legal expertise can overlap with real estate expertise, banking expertise, insurance expertise, tax expertise, accounting expertise, and so on. Why pay a real estate agent *and* a real estate lawyer if you don't have to? Legal professionals must police the boundaries around their profession in order to maintain their monopoly on law. This task grows more and more difficult with the proliferation of competing professions and, as we will see, in the age of computer technology and easy access to all kinds of information.

Further, as we discussed in Chapter 7: Law and Dispute Processing, many legal consumers are turning to extralegal professionals to settle private disputes. Negotiators, mediators, arbitrators, and practitioners of collaborative law now make up new types of professionals who help people avoid lawyers in dispute processing, which, until fairly recently, was the purview of lawyers. Lawyers in this country face a lot a competition, and therefore boundary maintenance is an essential task of the ABA.

A sixth factor affecting deprofessionalization of the legal profession is **organizational employment** (Rothman 1984). As legal firms grow, they become more bureaucratized, which can limit professional autonomy. Lawyers' decision-making powers grow more centralized, time must be "billable," bureaucratic rules and procedures must be followed. The autonomy and expertise that drew lawyers to the profession are circumscribed by the bureaucratic structure. And as Gunderman and Mutz point out,

> Lawyers whose work is gauged by billable hours experience great pressure to make every minute count in the dollar column. Noble aspirations that may have drawn young people to the law in the first place—serving their fellow citizens, making the community a more just place, and securing democracy—evaporate thanks to this constant attention to money…. To professionals who choose careers in such fields as law, medicine, and teaching, it is demoralizing to be treated as a unit of production. (2014:n.p.)

If lawyers feel like they are simply service providers in a large-scale legal machine, the meaning of their work is lost. This is what Karl Marx called **alienated or estranged labor**—the loss of connection to the work one does (Marx [1844] 2007). If the work belongs to someone else and is unrecognizable to the person who produces it, then the worker derives no satisfaction from the work; the activity itself is devoid of meaning (Marx [1844] 2007). It is safe to assume that a person does not want to spend hundreds of thousands of dollars on law school only to become a cog in a huge legal services apparatus. This might be somewhat ameliorated for law partners who become stakeholders in their firms, but in "big law" firms only a small percentage of lawyers make partner.

Finally, Rothman points to **demographics and diversity** in the legal profession as a potential source of deprofessionalization. As we discussed in the section on diversity, increased minority representation within the legal profession is typically viewed as a positive development. Rothman, however, includes diversity as a potential source of deprofessionalization because it can lead to less overall solidarity within the field of law. Demographic shifts toward more diversity in the law have many benefits: they broaden the perspectives of lawyers, increase representation for all groups seeking justice, and lead to upward mobility for minority groups. Therefore, it is difficult to argue that it should be seen as a setback to legal professionalism. If you see the legal profession operating as one unified, homogeneous group, then diversity could be viewed as a threat to professionalism, however. Earlier in the chapter, we heard the sentiments of Robert Grey, an attorney at Hunton & Williams and an advocate for diversity in the legal profession. He stated, "We get comfortable working with people we know, people that look like us, people that went to the same law schools [and] it becomes almost like inertia ... homogeneous societies are easier to deal with than diverse societies" (Tribe 2017:4). One of the reasons why the law has been so slow to diversify is that homogeneity can provide solidarity, which can be perceived as strengthening the profession's monopoly. As legal clients become more diverse, however, law practices are now seeing heterogeneity as a strength.

In the early 1980s, Rothman and other scholars of occupations predicted the erosion of lawyers' professional privilege and monopoly of knowledge due to various factors, such as the emergence of consumer rights groups, specialization within the law, and various competing occupations. Several decades later, Rothman's prediction could not be more prescient. In addition to the forces identified by Rothman, there are fewer jobs for new lawyers, coupled with the high price of legal education. And, the field of law is also facing further deprofessionalization with the breaking down of legal tasks into smaller parts that can be carried out by temporary lawyers or outsourced to nonlawyers, a new step in the process of routinization (Rothman 1984). For example, in 2015, Washington became the first state to grant licenses to "legal technicians"—people who do not hold juris doctorate degrees but who are permitted to advise clients in some limited areas of law, such as contract law and family law (Toppo 2017). These legal technicians are compared to nurse practitioners in the field of medicine (Toppo 2017).

The Internet and new technologies also pose competition for lawyers, especially recent graduates. Tasks previously carried out by newly minted lawyers, such as legal research and low-level tasks like drafting wills and contracts, are now automated. Online sites such as LegalZoom®, Lawdingo, Inc., LegalShield®, and UpCounsel™ offer ways to complete legal tasks on your own computer or tablet without ever meeting (or paying) a lawyer. Or, you can consult with an attorney over the Internet. This process further deprofessionalizes the field of law, thereby loosening the grip on legal expertise and knowledge that was once held entirely by lawyers who had earned their juris doctorates at an ABA-approved school of law *and* passed the bar exam *and* were licensed to practice law.

Is the field of law returning to a type of practice that just about anyone can do, as with the legal apprentices of the 1700s? That would be an overstatement. The law has grown much more accessible and is having a "do-it-yourself" moment, though. From online law libraries, to blogs about the law, to online legal services, anyone from "jailhouse lawyers" who hope to have their criminal cases overturned to retirees who have the time to take on their age 55-plus home-owners' associations now has access to legal knowledge, case law, and legal forms.

CHAPTER SUMMARY

◆ This chapter explored the history of the legal profession in the United States and its roots in English law.

◆ Legal education in the United States began as an apprenticeship model and grew into formal training in law schools tied to major universities and other law schools.

◆ Today, law schools in the United States are experiencing declining application rates due to several factors, most notably high costs and uncertain job prospects.

◆ The ABA played a key role in the professionalization of the law. The organization oversees the entrance exam to the legal profession, as well as licensing, ethics, and standards of practice for the profession. It also approves, or does not approve, of the 200- plus law schools in the United States.

◆ The legal profession is stratified by money, power, and prestige, as well as by race, class, and gender.

◆ Lawyers are employed in many sectors of the economy, including large law firms, small practices, or in self-employment. Lawyers also work in all levels and branches of government.

◆ Advocacy or public interest lawyers work on behalf of various underrepresented groups and social causes.

◆ The legal profession is largely made up of White, middle-aged, and middle- to upper-class males. Law students have become more diverse; however, female and non-White lawyers are still underrepresented as lawyers, particularly at the higher ranks of the legal profession such as partners and general counsel.

◆ The deprofessionalization of the legal profession began in the 1970s. This process involves the loss of professional autonomy and decreased monopoly control over legal expertise.

◆ Several factors have contributed to the deprofessionalization of the legal field, including: the narrowing of the competency/education gap, the routinization of tasks, increased specialization, organizational employment, and diversity within the profession, as well as new technologies and increased access to the law.

KEY TERMS

advocacy law   246
alienated or estranged labor   253
barristers   227
big law   243
boundary maintenance   253
consumer advocacy   252
consumerism   252
demographics and diversity   254
deprofessionalization   250
disbarred   226
in-house counsel   245
juris doctor, or J.D.s   230
Juvenile Law Center (JLC)   246

lobbying group   239
lobbyists   240
narrowing of the competence and education gap   251
nonprofit organizations   246
organizational employment   253
profit per partner   244
public interest lawyers   246
routinization   251
solicitors   227
Southern Poverty Law Center (SPLC)   246
specialization   252

CRITICAL THINKING QUESTIONS

1. Have you thought about becoming a lawyer? According to information presented in this chapter, this may not be the best time to pursue a career in law. Using sources from the Internet, can you find an alternative viewpoint? Why might this actually be a good time to go to law school and join the legal profession?

2. Look into one of the sections of law on the ABA's website. What type of law most interests you and why?

3. Can you think of other reasons why the legal profession is experiencing a downturn in its popularity? Why do you think fewer young people are interested in the law as a profession? Explain.

4. *Vault, Inc.*, an online career information site known for its career and industry rankings, produces its yearly list of the top 100 most prestigious law firms. *Vault* also includes diversity data for each. Using the *Vault* website, compare and contrast the diversity records for the top five law firms on *Vault's* ranking. How is diversity measured and how are the top five Big Law companies performing on these measures?

5. Why do we need lawyers? Do you think we need so many lawyers? Why or why not? Do you think we need so many different types of lawyers? Why or why not?

SUGGESTED MOVIE: *A CIVIL ACTION*

A Civil Action. 1999. Steven Zaillian, Director

The film *A Civil Action*, based on the nonfiction 1995 Jonathan Harr book of the same name, tells the true story of a Massachusetts town whose water is contaminated by years of industrial waste dumping. An up-and-coming personal injury lawyer—Jan Schlictmann, played by John Travolta—takes on two large multinational firms on behalf of the families affected by the water contamination to provide some semblance of justice to parents who lost children to childhood cancers and other ailments. The film can be used to illustrate key concepts from Chapter 9: Gate-Keeping and the Law: The Legal Profession, such as the legal profession, legal education, and the stratification of law schools. The film also illustrates key terms and concepts from Chapter 4: The Organization of Law and Chapter 7: Law and Dispute Processing.

Discussion Questions for *A Civil Action*

1. Who are the plaintiffs in this civil action? What role do the plaintiffs play in a civil suit? Explain.

2. Who are the following lawyers: Schlichtmann, Facher, Cheeseman, and Mulligan? What were their roles in this case?

3. Who are the defendants in this case? Why are they named as parties to this case?

4. Why was the Woburn, Massachusetts case an especially risky civil action?

5. In Chapter 7: Law and Dispute Processing, we learn that law does not always *settle* disputes, but rather *processes* disputes. Do you think the law *settled* the case of contaminated water in Woburn, Massachusetts? Explain your answer.

10

Gender, Inequality, and Law

◆ ◆ ◆

IN MAY 2018, A WOMAN BY THE NAME OF Dovey Johnson Roundtree died at the age of 104. Roundtree was an ordained minister, an Army officer, and a lawyer. She was also an African-American woman who lived to see the end of the Jim Crow era, the beginning of the civil rights movement, and the election of Barack Hussein Obama, a lawyer and constitutional law professor, as the first African-American president of the United States of America (Fox 2018). In many ways, Reverend Roundtree's life highlights the changes in the rights and free-doms of African-Americans in the United States as well as the changing opportunities, roles, and rights for women in American society over the past century.

In this chapter, we examine the social and legal construction of gen-der in American society. While the final chapter of this book is devoted to issues of race and law, discrimi-nation based on gender and race is interrelated and difficult to discuss separately. In this chapter and the next, we will use **intersectionality** to analyze how different social posi-tions come together—intersect—to affect individuals and their positions in society.

Dovey Roundtree Johnson, 1914–2018.

Public domain

LAW AT THE INTERSECTIONS: INTERSECTIONALITY

Intersectionality recognizes that people are placed at interlocking disadvantages and advantages due to where they are located in the social structural hierarchy. Gender and race, as well as many other characteristics, such as socioeconomic status, ability or disability, sexuality, and age affect one's location in the social structure, one's social identity, and one's access to power (Hayden 2018).

Feminist criminologist Hillary Potter (2015) acknowledges that intersectionality began with Black feminist critiques of racial and gender discrimination. However, the perspective has now expanded to incorporate various social statuses. She notes that Kimberlé Crenshaw, the critical legal scholar who coined the term intersectionality, stated that the concept of intersectionality "can and should be expanded" by factoring in issues such as "sexuality, nationality, and class, among other identities" (Crenshaw 1991; Potter 2013:309). In her 2015 book, *Intersectionality and Criminology*, Potter states: "I strongly believe the principal goals of intersectionality's origination are needed in considering all lived experiences, regardless of the identities individuals hold" (2013:79). Crenshaw also argues that all individuals exist "within a matrix of power." She states, "Intersectionality represents a structural and dynamic arrangement; power marks these relationships among and between categories of experience that vary in their complexity" (2011:230).

In her examination of female African slaves on southern plantations of the antebellum United States, historian Jacqueline Jones notes:

> [I]t would be difficult to argue that racial prejudice superseded sexual prejudice as an ordering principal for this peculiar society. Rather than attempt to determine which was more oppressive, we would do well to remember that the two systems share a dense, common tangle of roots, and that together they yielded bitter fruit in the antebellum South. Black women bore witness to that bitterness in ways different from black men on the one hand and white women on the other. (1985:43)

Jones made this argument about a decade before the term intersectionality was in popular usage, but her observation of the compounding disadvantages borne by enslaved women provides a stark illustration of how multiple forms of inequality and oppression intersect in a "dense tangle of common roots" (1985:43). Similarly, sociologist Patricia Hill Collins uses the notion of a matrix of domination to examine how "intersecting oppressions are organized" into domains of power that appear and "reappear across different forms of oppression" (2009:21). Collins highlights the "structural, disciplinary, hegemonic, and interpersonal domains of power" (2009:26) and how they control and oppress individuals and groups differently depending on intersections of race, class, gender, nationality, and sexuality.

FEMINIST LEGAL SCHOLARSHIP/FEMINIST JURISPRUDENCE

This chapter also considers the work of feminist legal scholars to explain how gender has been legally constructed over time throughout American history. **Feminism** is awareness that women as a category of people are treated unequally and that their subordination was and is "socially created and maintained by a system that could be changed through collective action … feminism as a *paradigm* for explaining social relations and a *social movement* did not emerge until around the turn of the nineteenth century" (Renzetti 2013:3, emphasis in original). Feminist scholar Claire M. Renzetti says of the first wave or period of feminism—approximately from 1830 to 1920—that:

> In the United States, Great Britain, and Europe, early feminist activism focused largely on winning various legal rights for women given that they did not enjoy full citizenship the way men did. Initially, the goals included better legal protection of women and children from abuse, marriage and divorce reforms, equal access to education and improved employment opportunities, and revisions to property laws. As the movement grew, however, and encountered strong resistance from lawmakers, the focus narrowed, especially in the United States, to the right to vote, the argument being that if women had the power to elect law makers, the law makers would have to become responsive to women's demands. (Renzetti 2013:3)

We will examine this first wave of feminism in the United States as well as subsequent periods or waves of the feminist movement for social and legal equality (Figure 10.1).

We examine the split between the public and private realms in American society and culture—also known as the separate spheres ideology—and how this false dichotomy subordinates women. Using **feminist jurisprudence**, also known as feminist legal scholarship, we also consider how the notion of two separate spheres was reinforced and reproduced in several major legal decisions. **Feminist jurisprudence** is the study of the legal structure, legal cases, and legal reasoning using critical feminist perspectives. Philosopher Patricia Smith describes feminist jurisprudence, stating

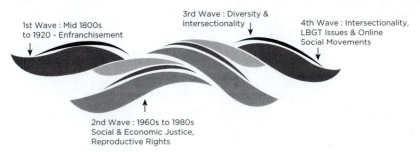

1st Wave : Mid 1800s to 1920 - Enfranchisement

3rd Wave : Diversity & Intersectionality

4th Wave : Intersectionality, LBGT Issues & Online Social Movements

2nd Wave : 1960s to 1980s Social & Economic Justice, Reproductive Rights

Figure 10.1 Periods or "Waves" of Feminist Movement in the United States

"[it] challenges basic legal categories and concepts rather than analyzing them as given. Feminist jurisprudence asks what is implied in traditional categories, distinctions, or concepts and rejects them if they imply the subordination of women" (1993:3). Feminist jurisprudence examines law and finds it infused with political and moral conclusions about the roles of women in all areas of society. Law also provides guidelines on how women should be treated in both private and public life. In the final section of this chapter, we look at the state of legal equality for women in the United States today. But first, we must trace our steps—we must first consider history and how law has shaped the lives and capabilities of women in the United States.

THE SOCIAL CONSTRUCTION OF GENDER

The social world around us constructs attributes that are organized into masculine and feminine. These socially defined characteristics are known as **gender norms** and are learned through behavioral expectations, standards of dress and appearance, daily interactions between and among members of society, and the societal institutions with which we must all contend: families, peer groups, schools, places of worship, sports teams, the media, economic institutions, governments, and law. Every day, individuals are taught, either implicitly or explicitly, how to behave according to their **gender norms**: the behavioral expectations that align with their sex. In most cases, one's sex is determined at birth. Gender, however, is learned over one's lifetime in a process of **gender role socialization**. Individuals can choose between and among the societal gender lessons that surround us (Figure 10.2). In other words, girls do not *have* to be caring

Female Gender Norms	Male Gender Norms
Submissive	Assertive
Passive	Active
Dependent	Independent
Gentle	Rough
Weak	Strong
Nurturing	Providing
Caring	Tough
Altruistic	Individualistic
Emotional	Stoic
Needing Protection	Protector

Figure 10.2 Dichotomous Gender Norms

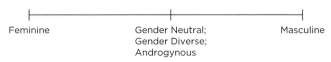

Figure 10.3 **Gender Norm Continuum**

and nurturing; they can choose to ignore or even subvert the gendered messages about femininity and nurturing that they receive on a daily basis. Boys can ignore the gendered lessons about toughness and independence as well.

The existence and reinforcement of gender norms does not simply mean that every girl will assume specific female gender roles and all boys will adopt specific masculine gender roles. Individuals can pick and choose among the gendered messages they receive—we are not predetermined to take on strict gender roles. Both girls and boys are able to forge their own **gender identities. Gender identity** means one's own perception of their gender, made through individual choices and viewed through one's own lived experiences (Butler 2015). Gender identity can change over time; it can correspond with societal gender norms, or it can resist or challenge those gender norms. And, our societal notions of gender also change over time. Today, girls and boys can select from a wide continuum of behaviors that may be traditionally feminine or traditionally masculine, or they may fall anywhere between those two ends of the spectrum. Where sociologists, legal scholars, and other academics, as well as the general public, once viewed gender norms as a dichotomy, we now see them as a spectrum or continuum (Figure 10.3).

While the gender norm continuum or spectrum analogy may not be perfect—it still includes two opposing ends, after all—it is more diverse than a binary view of gender and allows for movement and fluidity throughout one's life and even from one social situation to another. How you "do" your gender identity with your close friends may not be the same as how you act when you are with strangers.

THE SEPARATE SPHERES IDEOLOGY

While most Americans see gender norms around them on a daily basis, we do not always see just *how* those norms were codified into American law. What are now socially expected behaviors attached to girls and boys and men and women can be traced to legal language and rulings that dictated almost everything: who could own property, who could marry whom, who could vote, who could sit on juries, who could work outside the home and for how many hours a day, who could attend colleges and universities, and who could become members of professions. As feminist legal scholar Judith A. Baer states:

> In modern industrial societies, life has been structured by (a tiny minority of) men, for both men and women, around the (artificially created) dichotomy of the public and private spheres. Men preserve themselves in the "public" realm of paid work and political activity. Women, most of whom have been unable to earn a living wage and/or to participate in public life, have been forced to concentrate their energies within the "private" sphere of marriage and family. Outside of marriage, women's lot has been precarious; within it, their labor (formerly) ensured (marginally) that their needs would be met (minimally). (Baer 1999:6)

Historians note that the separate spheres ideology was most pronounced in the nineteenth century (Kerber 1988; Wright 2012); however, the notion that women occupy a more circumscribed, limited realm of home and hearth was by no means new to that era. Also, the concept of the two distinct, physically delineated worlds for men and women has been criticized as biased—it describes a White, middle- to upper-class ideal that very few families could attain. Women have worked outside the home in both unpaid and paid labor throughout the history of the United States. The separate spheres ideology was perhaps closest to reality for some middle- and upper-class families in the nineteenth century, however. And whether or not individual women, men, or families were able to fit into this ideal, they were judged by its assumptions nonetheless (Welter 1966; Coontz 1988, 1992; Kerber 1988). As we discuss below, women were also relegated by law to these gendered notions of what they could and could not do.

An **ideology** is a set of beliefs, thoughts, assumptions, and ways of thinking that shapes our understanding of the world around us. The **separate spheres ideology** was a set of assumptions and a way of viewing the world that sorted life into two realms: the public and the private. The **public sphere**—the world of men and masculinity—granted men access to paid employment and to all arenas of power. White men occupied the realms of the market, property, the economy, religious hierarchies, politics and governance, higher education and professions, and, of course, law: who could practice it, to whom it granted rights and protections, and to whom it applied. In the next chapter, "Race, Inequality, and Law," we will examine how race was also used to limit people's access to these arenas of power. White men's access to these institutions was assumed—it did not meet with legal restrictions or require legal challenge.

Women occupied the **private sphere**: the world of home and hearth, of childbearing and child-rearing. While women's work within this realm may

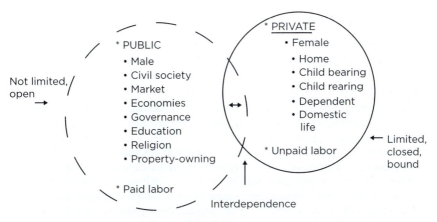

Figure 10.4 Separate Spheres Ideology

have been exalted on church pulpits and women's books and magazines (Welter 1966), it went unpaid and undervalued. In the domestic realm, due to the law of **coverture**, married women were "covered" by their husbands—their rights were subsumed by their husbands. **Coverture** was an English common law tradition transported from England to North America with the colonizers of the fifteenth and sixteenth centuries. As we will see below, coverture ran through most of U.S. history and continues to shape our notions of family and gender roles.

LEGAL CONSTRUCTIONS OF GENDER

In many ways, American law codified the separate spheres ideology that segregated women and men into separate spheres and assigned them specific gender roles. But law did much more than that; the legal structure also subordinated women to men, relegating them to an inferior status in the eyes of the law (Kerber 1988; Baer 1996; Taub and Schneider 1998; Wright 2012). In this section of the chapter, we examine just how the law excluded women from the public sphere and reified and legitimized discrimination based on sex. We follow an abbreviated history of laws pertaining to women's rights in the United States; we also examine how the law articulated the separate spheres ideology and then justified the unequal treatment of women based upon what were seen as natural differences between the sexes—how the socially constructed became legally constructed and how those constructions were made to appear "natural."

Early America: Women, Law, and the Colonial Era, 1630–1763

White women enjoyed very little legal status in Colonial America; African women and indigenous women enjoyed none. As historian Terri L. Snyder states:

> Everywhere across European and Indigenous settlements in 17th- and 18th-century North American and the Caribbean, the law or legal practices shaped women's status and conditioned their dependency, regardless of race, age, marital status, or place of birth…. Early American legalities, however, differed markedly for women of color—whether free, indentured, [or] enslaved, and whether Native or African in origin or descent—whose relationships to the legal regimes of early America were manifold and complex … women of color reckoned with a set of legalities that differed from those of their European counterparts. (2015:1)

While women of European descent dealt with the loss of their legal status under the law of coverture—when a woman married, her legal status and individual rights were transferred to her husband (Wright 2012)—Indigenous and African women suffered much more severe losses, depending on where they were located in the colonies. Generally speaking, there was a continuum for women in the colonies that ranged from "unfreedom to freedom" and one's placement on this continuum depended upon skin color, geographic location, and national origin (Snyder 2015:2). As Snyder states, "The three principal groups that populated early modern North America—Africans, Native Americans, and Europeans—all practiced varieties of slavery and captivity" (2015:2). Female migrants from Europe were able to use the courts to some extent, especially if they were single and owned property.

African women who were enslaved suffered not only the fact that they were bought and sold as property, but also knowing that their children inherited their status as slaves. Their masters owned their productivity—their labor. And slave women's reproductivity—their fertility—was also bought and sold (Jones 1985; Snyder 2015). The law also "provided economic incentives to encourage … their reproductivity" and further, the law "did not penalize owners who raped or otherwise sexually coerced their enslaved women" (Snyder 2015:5). The legal doctrine of *partus sequitur ventrem*—progeny follows the womb—was one of the first laws governing slavery, which it tied to maternal identity (Snyder 2015). Additionally, for any sort of transgression, enslaved women were subjected to severe punishments from their masters or mistresses as well as criminal penalties by law.

Native American women's legal status in the Colonial period varied depending on their indigenous status, in what region they lived, and to what extent they came into contact with White colonizers as well as other indigenous groups. Some Native American women and men were captured by Whites and sold into slavery as properties; these captured Native American women performed "domestic, artisanal, field, sexual, and reproductive labor" (Snyder 2015:3). Some were captured by other native groups in which their treatment varied. For instance, female captives among the Cherokee could be married or be adopted into clans, or they could be used as slave laborers. Some Native women were exchanged as a way to build trade ties and alliances between and among Native groups (Rubin 1975; Snyder 2015).

The Revolutionary to Post-Revolutionary Period, 1763–1815

Legal historians of early America have argued that the American Revolution did not significantly change the legal status of free women—it did not change the law of coverture, nor did it significantly unsettle the laws of domestic relations. As American legal scholar Lawrence M. Friedman states:

> It would be only a slight exaggeration to say that [family law] gave everything to the father, legally speaking, and very little to anyone else in the family. In 1800, for example, if a woman owned a piece of land—land she inherited, for example—when she married she lost title to the land; it passed into the hands of her husband. Husband and wife were, as the saying went, one flesh; but the husband was very much in charge of that flesh. And more than the flesh. The wife had, in many ways, as few rights as a newborn baby or a lunatic. (2004:60)

The post-Revolutionary period did not alter the separate spheres ideology. If anything, this notion became even more entrenched.

In July of 1848, suffragists Elizabeth Cady Stanton and Lucretia Mott organized the first-ever United States Women's Rights Convention in Seneca Falls, New York. Both women had fought for the abolition of African slaves and then applied their knowledge of human rights to consider the lack of legal rights for women. They addressed the question, How can one fight for the freedom of others when she also does not have the rights of full citizenship herself? The speeches and writings circulated at the convention highlighted the hypocrisies of a new republic organized around freedom, individual rights, and self-determination that *allowed* slavery and *did not allow* one half of the people to vote (Scott and Scott 1982).

The Declaration of Sentiments was a decidedly unsentimental view of the legal status of women in mid-nineteenth-century America. In a style and tone intended to mirror the Declaration of Independence, and in language borrowed from William Blackstone's 1765 *Commentaries on the Laws of England in Four Books*, Stanton clearly lays out the legal case for women's voting rights. In the Declaration of Sentiments and Resolutions, Stanton did not mince words, stating: "The history of mankind is a history

THE FIRST CONVENTION

EVER CALLED TO DISCUSS THE

Civil and Political Rights of Women,

SENECA FALLS, N. Y., JULY 19, 20, 1848.

———

WOMAN'S RIGHTS CONVENTION.

———

A Convention to discuss the social, civil, and religious condition and rights of woman will be held in the Wesleyan Chapel, at Seneca Falls, N. Y., on Wednesday and Thursday, the 19th and 20th of July current; commencing at 10 o'clock A. M. During the first day the meeting will be exclusively for women, who are earnestly invited to attend. The public generally are invited to be present on the second day, when Lucretia Mott, of Philadelphia, and other ladies and gentlemen, will address the Convention.*

———

* This call was published in the *Seneca County Courier*, July 14, 1848, without any signatures. The movers of this Convention, who drafted the call, the declaration and resolutions were Elizabeth Cady Stanton, Lucretia Mott, Martha C. Wright, Mary Ann McClintock, and Jane C. Hunt.

Declaration of Sentiments, The first convention ever called to discuss the civil and political rights of women. Seneca Falls, New York, July 19–20, 1848.

Photo 12/Alamy Stock Photo

of repeated injuries and usurpations on the part of man toward woman, having in direct object the establishment of an absolute tyranny over her" (Stanton [1848] 2015:3). To prove her point, Stanton lists a catalog of injustices endured by women because of their lack of franchise, including the following: "He has compelled her to submit to laws, in the formation of which she had no voice;" and "Having deprived her of this first right of a citizen, the elective franchise, thereby leaving her without representation in the halls of legislation; he has oppressed her on all sides." Further, Stanton states that "[H]e has made her, if married, in the eyes of the law, civilly dead"; and "He has monopolized nearly all the profitable employments, and from those she is permitted to follow, she receives but a scanty remuneration. Similarly, the author notes: "He closes her against her all the avenues to wealth and distinction, which she considers most honorable to himself. As a teacher of theology, medicine, or law, she is not known" (Stanton [1848] 2015:3–4).

As the Declaration of Sentiments clearly illustrates, the period between the American Revolution and the Civil War brought to light a host of inequities for women in the new republic. While America enjoyed its newly won freedom from British rule, women and enslaved Africans were just beginning their struggles for true liberty and justice before the law. As women involved in the abolitionist movement fought for the freedom of enslaved people in the United States, they came to realize just how few rights they themselves possessed because they, too, lacked any legal standing. The Seneca Falls Convention was by no means the beginning of the fight for women's suffrage. But because it was the first-ever public gathering for women's equality before the law, and because their demands for rights were written into the declaration, it was a very visible representation of that fight.

The Civil War and the Period of Reconstruction, 1861–1877

As we discussed earlier, women activists Elizabeth Cady Stanton and Lucretia Mott took on important roles in the abolitionist movement. Many women supported the Civil War as a struggle to emancipate slaves. Women activists also played key roles in the fight for post-Civil War amendments that they hoped would guarantee full civil rights to freed slaves *and* to women (Turkel 1996).

From the end of the Civil War in 1865 and well into the mid-twentieth century, African-Americans and women were afforded very little in the way of equal protection before the law. The U.S. Supreme Court's interpretation of the Constitution affirmed broader currents in American culture that maintained the separation of people by both race and gender. This legal separation applied to all aspects of public life: schools, occupations, and, in the case of race, housing, and public facilities. As we will discuss further in the next chapter, by the mid-1950s, the Supreme Court began to change its construction of race by overturning the "separate but equal" doctrine, which had served as the constitutional foundation for separating people on the basis of race. The court did not, however, extend its new construction of equality to women until almost two decades later. So, while the Supreme Court was establishing new standards for racial equality, it was still upholding the legal separation of women from men in certain areas of public life.

In the aftermath of the Civil War—the Reconstruction Period—three amendments were added to the U.S. Constitution; these were known as the Civil War Amendments. All were aimed at putting a clear, constitutional end to slavery and extending minimal rights to newly emancipated slaves. Thus, the Thirteenth Amendment of 1865 abolished the institution of slavery and involuntary servitude in the United States, except as a punishment for a crime.

The Fourteenth Amendment, added to the Constitution in 1868, granted a number of important rights. Section I of the Fourteenth Amendment stated that:

> All persons born or naturalized in the United States, and subject to the jurisdiction thereof, are citizens of the State wherein they reside. No State shall make or enforce any law which shall abridge the privileges or immunities of citizens of the United States; nor shall any State deprive any person of life, liberty, or property, without due process of law; nor deny to any person within its jurisdiction the equal protection of the laws.

The Fifteenth Amendment, adopted in 1870, granted that "the right of citizens of the United States to vote shall not be denied or abridged by the United States or by any State on account of race, color, or previous condition of servitude." The Fifteenth Amendment granted Black men the right to vote, but it also allowed states quite a bit of leeway. However, in determining voting rules, procedures, and practices, it led to some states enacting exclusionary practices such as poll taxes and "grandfather clauses" that turned African-American men away from the voting booths.

So, while women abolitionists and post-Civil War activists played important roles in the efforts to pass these Civil War Amendments, they were also acutely aware that the protections established in these laws did not yet extend to them. Suffragists held out hope that the equal protection clause of the Fourteenth Amendment was their best chance at extending legal equality to women. What stood in their way? American law still strongly upheld the separate spheres ideology and legally constructed women's place as in the home. One infamous case from this period brings the codification of separate spheres ideology into sharp relief.

In the 1870s, Myra Bradwell studied law under her husband's instruction. She founded and wrote for *The Chicago Legal News*, an influential law journal in the state of Illinois (Taub and Schneider 1998). When she applied for admission to the Illinois state bar, she was refused entry because she was a woman. She appealed her case to the U.S. Supreme Court. Her case, *Bradwell v. Illinois, 1873*, stands as a stark reminder of the legal ideology of sexual inequality (Taub and Schneider 1998), as well as the uneasiness that arose when women attempted to cross over into the public realm of work, law, and power. The legal language offered by the court in Bradwell's case clearly illustrates that women were viewed as unequal to men and that the law endorsed and enforced women's subordination. The ruling stated:

> [T]he civil law as well as nature itself, has always recognized a wide difference in the respective spheres and destinies of man and woman. Man is, or should be women's protector and defender. The natural and proper timidity and delicacy which belongs to the female sex evidently unfits it for many of the occupations of civil life .... The constitution of the family organization, which is founded in the divine ordinance, as in the nature of things, indicates the domestic sphere as that which properly belongs to the domain and functions of womanhood .... The paramount destiny and mission of woman are to fulfill the noble and benign offices of wife and mother. (*Bradwell v. Illinois*, 1973)

Using the separate spheres ideology, as well as opaque references to nature, the "natural order," and "divine ordinance," the court legitimized the notion that women belonged in the home as wives and mothers. Around the same period, for racial inequality, a different type of codified separation was also upheld.

Up until the very end of the nineteenth century, the Supreme Court upheld a race-based "separate but equal" doctrine established in the case of *Plessy v. Ferguson* (1896). In this precedent-setting case, the court saw no constitutional grounds for overturning a Louisiana law requiring separate railroad cars for Blacks and Whites, as long as the accommodations were comparable, or equal. This decision allowed for racial classifications and segregation in schools, hotels, restaurants, buses, drinking fountains, and other public facilities. In essence, the separate but equal doctrine allowed for legal discrimination. This legal form of discrimination held sway for over 50 years, when it was overturned in the case of *Brown v. the Board of Education of Topeka, Kansas* in 1954.

In *Brown v. the Board of Education*, Chief Justice Earl Warren used social science research to decide that requiring that Black children attend only all-Black schools imposed an inferior status upon them and therefore

CASE IN POINT

Linda Brown (1943–2018)

Linda Brown, 1943–2018.

While most readers have probably heard of *Brown v. the Board of Education*, many have probably not heard the story of Linda Brown. Linda was the girl whose father sued the Board of Education of Topeka, Kansas, for her right to attend a Whites-only school. While her father, Oliver, was the name attached to the famous case, it was Linda who had to walk across a rail yard and a busy road to catch a bus to her segregated school. Her parents objected to the distance and danger involved in Linda's walk. The Browns were recruited by the National Association for the Advancement of Colored People (NAACP) along with other families to test the separate but equal doctrine. NAACP Chief Counsel Thurgood Marshall argued the case before the Supreme Court. The Court threw out the separate but equal doctrine and set the stage for racially integrated schools throughout the United States (Genzlinger 2018). Linda went on to become an educational consultant and public speaker. She died in 2018 at the age 75 in Topeka, Kansas.

violated their equal protection of the laws. Why is the *Brown* decision significant for the fight for women's equal protection of laws? It marked the first acknowledgement by the Supreme Court that separate is never equal—that legal segregation always infers a lesser status on the minority group.

Separating out any group of people based solely on their membership to that group blocks opportunities and limits their abilities. Myra Bradwell tried to use the equal protection clause of the Fourteenth Amendment to argue that women should not be blocked access to occupations and professions. By the time the Fourteenth Amendment was ratified, however, citizens and voters were still defined as male. Women faced many years of struggle, many legal cases, and an Amendment to the U.S. Constitution to win before they reached anything close to equality to men in the eyes of the law. And, as we will see in the final section of this chapter, many feminist legal scholars assert that the fight for true women's equality is not over.

Myra Bradwell, 1831–1894.

The Picture Art Collection/Alamy Stock Photo

THE PROGRESSIVE ERA AND FIRST WAVE FEMINISM, 1890–1920

The struggle for the right to vote that began publicly at the Seneca Falls Convention in 1848 was not fully realized until 1920. In 1868, suffragist Elizabeth Cady Stanton foresaw a time when the right to vote for women would come down to a national party politics and a congressional vote (Scott and Scott 1982). Throughout the latter part of the 1800s and into the early 1900s, a period now known as the **first wave of feminism** (Figure 10.1), women's groups organized around enfranchisement. However, their efforts were interrupted during the Civil War and the post-Civil War period in which many women activists took up the fight for abolition of slavery and the extension of the rights of citizenship to newly freed slaves. It should be noted here, though, that not all women who were fighting for voting rights thought free slaves should be able to vote. Some suffragists were less than enthusiastic about the possibility that freed African men would be granted the right to vote before middle- and upper-class White women. As with all social movements, differing factions emerged. For first-wave feminists, those issues revolved around race and class, as well as women's positions on the issue of temperance and the prohibition of alcohol—another major legal debate of this era.

After Seneca Falls, several other women's rights conventions were held and, by the late 1880s, some states began to consider bills on women's suffrage at the state level (Scott and Scott 1982). By 1872, women began casting ballots—or, in some cases, attempting to cast ballots—in national elections. Many—most notably famed abortionist and former slave, Sojourner Truth—were turned away. Some were arrested: Suffragist Susan B. Anthony did vote in Rochester, New York, but was arrested, tried, and found guilty for doing so (Salam 2017). And, to illustrate just how difficult the fight for the right to vote was at this time, Anthony's case garnered only a short paragraph's coverage in *The New York Times* on November 6, 1872. The article characterized Anthony and the other women who voted with her as "a little band of nine ladies whose ballots were received by election inspectors ..." (Salam 2017:n.p.). The popular sentiment of the day was that most women did not truly *want* the right to vote, and it was only being sought by rabble-rousers such as Anthony and Elizabeth Cady Stanton. Further, as detractors such as Edward Rosewater, an Oklahoma newspaper editor, argued, "To give woman the ballot, provided woman wanted it, would be to bring desolation and distraction into multiple happy homes" (Salem 2017:n.p.). The separate spheres ideology was so thoroughly embedded in American culture that for many, to see women at the voting booth was absurd, if not downright dangerous to the very institutions of marriage and family.

In 1878, a Woman Suffrage Amendment was brought before the U.S. Congress. The Amendment was not acted upon until 1887 when the first vote for women's suffrage was taken in Senate; the Amendment was defeated (Scott and Scott 1982). During this period, there were several different women's groups and clubs, some of which had splintered from each other, but all working toward the same goal: the right to vote. By 1890, many of these groups put aside their differences and formed the National American Women's Suffrage Association, and from 1890 to 1915 several states began to recognize women's rights to vote in state elections (Scott and Scott 1982).

By 1915, women activists gathered over half a million signatures on petitions to Congress to fully support women's suffrage. In 1912, Theodore Roosevelt stated his support of women's suffrage, and, in 1916, Woodrow Wilson declared that the Democratic Party would support voting rights for women. In the next year, women visibly agitated for their right to vote, picketing in front of the White House and blocking traffic. Many were arrested and mounted a hunger strike, causing a public outcry and their subsequent release from jail (National Women's History Museum n.d.).

Seventy-two years after Elizabeth Cady Stanton wrote the Declaration of Sentiments and 52 years after she predicted that the fight would be won at the level of national party politics and within the halls of Congress, the battle was won (Scott and Scott 1982). In January of 1918, the House of Representatives passed the necessary two-thirds vote granting women the right to vote. After some give-and-take and another round or two of picket lines and protests, the Senate took up the vote on the Nineteenth Amendment to the Constitution. In June of 1918, the Senate passed the Amendment. And finally, in August of 1920, the constitutional amendment was ratified; the U.S. secretary of state proclaimed that women's struggle for the right to vote in all elections was over, that their "sacred right to the elective franchise" was won (Scott and Scott 1985:46).

SECOND-WAVE FEMINISM, 1960S TO 1980S

After winning the right to vote, women activists concentrated on making further inroads into the public sphere. These efforts gained steam in the second wave of feminism. The so-called waves of feminism are not distinct, individual periods in American history; rather, they are overlapping historical frames of reference that allow us to look at feminism in phases with specific focal issues. **Second-wave feminism** began in the 1960s and lasted until the late 1980s. The key focal points included social and economic justice, access to full employment and equal pay, and reproductive rights. Second-wave feminists won several important victories in these areas (Figure 10.5).

Second-wave feminists also made considerable gains in the halls of academe. Academic research and theory devoted to addressing male bias in scholarship flourished in this period, including in the areas of: feminist philosophy, feminist psychology, feminist sociology and criminology, feminist approaches within the sciences, and women's and gender studies as a field unto itself. Feminist jurisprudence emerged in this period as well, advocating for the laws, legal decisions, and academic approaches to law that would best benefit women's equality. Within these new feminist disciplines of the second wave, the cracks that affected the women's suffragist movement of the first wave were starting to reappear, and feminist legal scholars were no exception to these fissures. While all feminist jurisprudence involves a philosophy of law based in equality between the sexes, feminist legal scholars did not all agree on what the focal concerns should be, nor did they agree on how to get to true equality.

Generally speaking, second-wave feminists started to form loosely into two groups: (1) those seeking equal rights to those of men, and (2) a more radical group seeking to dismantle patriarchy and to recognize diversity among women in the United States. Within feminist jurisprudence, those two approaches fell into two groups: (1) reformist legal scholars, and (2) radical legal scholars (Baer 1999; Baer 2011; Bruchard, n.d.) (Figure 10.5).

Reformist	Radical

• Focus on sameness: women should be treated the same as men in the eyes of the law; changes can be made within the system
• Focus on differences weakens women's abilities to be treated equally or on par with men
• Also known as an assimilationist approach or a symmetrical approach to women's rights (Bruchard n.d.)
• Legal examples:
  ○ *Reed v. Reed* (1971): Supreme Court decided that sex-based classifications on who could administer wills violated the equal protection clause of the 14th Amendment; stated that women should be seen as individuals, not as a class of people.
  ○ *Frontiero v. Richardson* (1973): Supreme Court ruled that benefits given by the U.S. military to spouses of service members cannot be administered differently because of sex. Air Force Lieutenant Sharron Frontiero won this case, and her husband was allowed to collect spousal benefits
  ○ Equal Pay Act of 1963: Prohibits sex discrimination in wages
  ○ 1972 Amendment to the Civil Rights Act of 1964: Prohibits discrimination based on race, religion, sex, or national origin
	• Focus on difference: the differences between men and women must be recognized
	• The differences among women in terms of race, age, socioeconomic class, and sexuality should also be recognized
	• Also known as asymmetrical approach or essentialism (Bruchard n.d.)
	• Women and men are not the same and some rights should be based on the specific needs of women depending upon the situation
	• Women have special needs that men do not and to acknowledge these differences should not diminish their rights
	• Women should not be penalized for their differences, such as their ability to bear children
	• Legal examples:
	  ○ Sexual Harassment in the Workplace (MacKinnon 1979)
	  ○ First Step Act: Pending Federal Legislation that seeks to ban the shackling of pregnant women in custody of federal prisons (Cohen and Chang 2018)

Figure 10.5 Reformist Feminist Jurisprudence versus Radical Feminist Jurisprudence

FEMINIST JURISPRUDENCE: SAMENESS, DIFFERENCE, OR BOTH?

Feminist legal scholars who use a **sameness approach** believe that the legal system can be reformed from within and that for women to be seen as equal with men, their similarities to men must be emphasized. To focus on sex differences means seeing women as "less than" men and threatens to place women back into their separate sphere. An example of this approach is espoused by feminist legal scholar Wendy Williams, who sees special benefits for pregnant women workers as no better than earlier laws that sought to keep women out of the workplace because they *were*—or even could possibly *become*—pregnant (1981). For instance, the 1908 *Muller v. Oregon* Supreme Court decision argued that women were the weaker sex and that their maternal functions must be protected to preserve "the strength and vigor of the [human] race." The case involved a woman who wanted to work more than 10 hours a day in a job that required her to be on her feet. Specifically, the *Muller* decision read:

> ... that women's physical structure and the performance of maternal functions place her at a disadvantage in the struggle for subsistence is obvious. This is especially true when the burdens of motherhood are upon her. Even when they are not, by abundant testimony of the medical fraternity continuance for a long time on her feet at work, repeating this from day to day, tends to [have] injurious effects upon the body, and as healthy mothers are essential to vigorous offspring, the physical well-being of woman become[s] an object of public interest and care in order to preserve the strength and vigor of the race.... Differentiated by these matters from the other sex, she is properly placed in a class by herself, and legislation designed for her protection must be sustained, even when the legislation is not necessary for men and could not be sustained....
> (*Muller v. Oregon*, 1908:421–442)

The Court's focus on women's physical and biological constitution allowed for legal discrimination based on sex. Sameness legal scholars want to move away from any semblance of difference where it can be used to block access to paid employment and shore up age-old separate spheres ideologies that kept women's work unpaid (Taub and Schneider 1998).

But, what of women's differences? Feminist legal scholars who embrace a **difference approach** argue that gender-blind or strict gender equality approaches overlook the fact that men and women are different. The problem lies in the fact that those *differences* are used to place women at a *disadvantage* to men. If women have different needs that men do not have, women should not be punished for those differences. An example comes from the criminal justice system and its approach to punishment. By and large, prisons in the United States were built on the assumption that they would be filled with male prisoners. As women's ranks among incarcerated people grow—to date women make up about 7 percent of all adults in U. S. prisons—the differing needs for female inmates become increasingly apparent.

Federal prisons, as well as many state prisons and local jails, have rules and procedures regarding how prisoners should be transported outside the prison facilities. Outside the prison walls, because they are seen as flight risks, prisoners must be shackled by the hands and feet. Pregnant prisoners are typically taken off prison grounds to a medical facility for childbirth. Therefore, incarcerated women must give birth while shackled. The American College of Obstetricians and Gynecologists argues that being shackled while in labor and during delivery poses health risks for mothers and babies (Cohen and Chang 2018). The feet restraints increase the chances of tripping and falling and the hand restraints could prevent the use of hands to break the fall; shackles can get in the way of the obstetrician and nurses; and, in an emergency, a doctor may not have time to ask a guard to remove the shackles (Cohen and Chang 2018). While these medical reasons should be compelling enough, there is also the fact that unlike their male counterparts—who may or may not be planning an escape—pregnant women who are in labor pose very little risk of flight. A difference approach to feminist jurisprudence would argue that the specific needs of pregnant female inmates necessitate recognition of their differences and that those differences should not be held against them—it should not cause an undue burden or an extra form of punishment.

Another feminist jurisprudence approach that can be seen as an extension or subset of the radical feminist approach is the **empowerment model** (Bruchard n.d.). The empowerment approach to gender focuses on what is needed to balance power between historically unequal groups: women and men. Others take a similar approach but call it the **domination model of feminist jurisprudence** (MacKinnon 1987; Baer 1999). This approach looks at how rights have been defined and granted and argues that women

"It's a baby. Federal regulations prohibit our mentioning its race, age, or gender."

Source: Peter Steiner, New Yorker/ CartoonStock.com

have been historically excluded and given short shrift. For women to attain true equality, a redefining of rights and harms and a rebalancing of power is needed. (MacKinnon 1987; Baer 1999)

THIRD-WAVE FEMINISM, 1990S TO 2000S

The discussion of more recent developments in feminist jurisprudence brings us to the third wave of feminism. Third-wave feminism overlaps with the second wave—this is perhaps why a wave analogy has been used to describe feminism in the United States. As with waves in the ocean, you cannot always clearly distinguish where one ends and another begins. Water is fluid and waves tend to overlap. And so it is with feminism in general and feminist jurisprudence as well. **Third-wave feminists** pick up on topics that the second wave never fully realized. Or, they reinvigorate topics that the second-wave feminists addressed, but that did not fully take hold. They also address the failures of second-wave feminists, such as the lack of diversity and inclusivity among its ranks. Much of second-wave feminism took place in academia—a venue that tends to be predominantly White and middle to upper class. One of the most inclusive approaches to legal studies emerged from the groves of academe—namely, intersectionality. This critical approach came about in the third wave of feminism and called upon feminists in all areas of public and private life to recognize multiple statuses that intersect and grant some people rights and privileges while disadvantaging others.

FOURTH-WAVE FEMINISM?

While some feminist scholars and commentators see a fourth wave of feminism that emerged around from 2008 to 2012, others argue that today's resurgence in interest in feminism is more of a continuation of the third wave. Whether it is a fourth wave or still a third wave, in the current period intersectionality continues to expand into different areas and even into the popular lexicon. Indeed, intersectionality's entrance into popular culture and language is emblematic of fourth-wave feminism—it is inclusive and diverse; it embraces new social media like Twitter and Instragram as well as various online blogs such as *Vox*, *Bust*, and *Bustle*; it includes body positivity; it is queer- and trans-inclusive; and it aims to hold powerful men accountable for behavior and systems that harm girls and women.

#METOO

Sexual harassment law prepared the ground, but it is today's movement that is "shifting gender hierarchy's tectonic plates" (MacKinnon 2018:A19). An example of fourth-wave feminism and its connection to earlier waves

#MeToo.

comes from the legal field of sexual harassment and the #MeToo movement. The phrase "Me Too" was first used by African-American activist Tarana Burke in 2006. Burke is a survivor of sexual assault and wanted to help other girls and women of color who had experienced sexual violence (*The Chicago Tribune* Staff and Hawbaker 2018). In 2017, in response to widespread reports of sexual assaults and numerous forms of harassment in the entertainment industry, actress Alyssa Milano used the phrase to ignite an online movement. Milano urged people from all fields of public and private life to tweet "#MeToo" if they had been sexually harassed or assaulted (*The Chicago Tribune* Staff and Hawbaker 2018). Millions of women and men, as well as girls and boys, did so and a new social movement was born.

In her influential 1979 book, *Sexual Harassment of Working Women*, radical feminist legal scholar Catharine MacKinnon illustrated that most, if not all, American women who entered the workforce in the second wave of feminism met with sexual harassment or discrimination in some form. They were forced into sex by their male bosses, or given only menial tasks while their male coworkers were given the kind of jobs that would allow them to climb the occupational hierarchy. In addition, women were judged by male standards and given housework-type chores imposed on wives—tidy up the office, plan office parties, fetch coffee, and such. This subordination of women in the paid labor force did not have a name until about the mid-1970s when MacKinnon and other second-wave feminists coined it. MacKinnon's book *Sexual Harassment in the Workplace* paved the way for the legal system to address cases of sexual as a form of sex discrimination that creates a hostile work environment for women (MacKinnon 1979).

Workplace harassment is now covered under Title VII of the Civil Rights Act of 1964. It is also, as the #MeToo movement makes clear, still widespread. This is where fourth-wave feminism comes in.

In a February 2018 op-ed in *The New York Times*, Catharine MacKinnon addresses the #MeToo movement and how it is "accomplishing what sexual harassment law to date has not" (MacKinnon 2018:A19). As MacKinnon states:

> Sexual harassment law—the first law to conceive sexual violation in inequality terms—created the preconditions for this moment. Yet denial by abusers and devaluing of accusers could still be reasonably counted on by perpetrators to shield their actions. Many survivors realistically judged reporting pointless. Complaints were routinely passed off with some version of "she wasn't credible" or "she wanted it" .... Even when she was believed, nothing he did mattered as much as what would be done to him if his actions against her were taken seriously.... His career, reputation, mental and emotional serenity and assets counted. Hers didn't. (MacKinnon 2018:A19).

Because the #MeToo movement leveraged its access to new and old forms of media, it became impossible to ignore and made inroads into a problem that had been resistant to change for decades. As we discussed in Chapter 8: Law and Social Change, law is not always an ideal vehicle for social change, especially when those in power do not want real change. MacKinnon also acknowledges that law can be limited when it comes to bringing about social change, especially when new laws are enacted but not properly monitored or enforced. As she states, "It is widely thought that when something is legally prohibited, it more or less stops. This may be true for some exceptional acts, but it is not true for pervasive practices like sexual harassment, including rape, that are built into structural social hierarchies" (MacKinnon 2018:A19). Paying women less than their male counterparts for the same work has been illegal for decades under the Equal Pay Act, but equal pay for women is far from a reality.

MacKinnon concludes her op-ed on a hopeful note and gives credit to #MeToo and other similar new social movements that have broken the logjam "which has long paralyzed legal recourse for sexual harassment" (MacKinnon 2018:A19). Further, she states: "Structural misogyny, along with sexualized racism and class inequities, is being publicly and pervasively challenged by women's voices. The difference is, power is paying attention" (MacKinnon 2018:A19). She foresees a not-too-distant future where sexual harassment law can learn, grow, and transform because of the #MeToo movement (Manikonda et al. n.d.). The good news is that second wave feminists laid the legal groundwork for third- and fourth-wave activists to hit the ground running.

CASE IN POINT

Fight for Your Right to Party? The Case of Craig v. Boren, 1976.

When Sex and Age Intersect for Differential Treatment

In the 1970s, an Oklahoma law prohibited the sale of low alcohol content (3.2 percent) beer to males under the age of 21 and females under the age of 18. This type of beer was sometimes called "near beer," and it was a common item on college campuses. The Oklahoma law was based on the assumption that men are more likely to drink and drive and the state's goal was traffic safety. A young man, Craig, who was between the ages of 18 and 20, sued the state liquor commissioner on the grounds that the law denied males aged 18 to 20 equal protection before the law. The Supreme Court agreed and sided with Craig. In doing so, the court also established a new standard for judicial review in Fourteenth Amendment cases regarding sex discrimination: the **heightened scrutiny test**. This standard argued that there must be an important governmental reason to classify by sex and that the governmental objectives must be substantially related to the achievement of those objectives. In the case of Craig, the state of Oklahoma presented statistically evidence on male drivers and intoxication, but the court did not find the evidence substantial enough to discriminate on the basis of sex. (https://www.law.cornell.edu/supremecourt/text/429/190.) The different standards for judicial review are discussed further in Chapter 11: Race, Inequality, and Law. The *Craig v. Boren* case illustrates that sex-based equal protection challenges can benefit both males and females.

Despite numerous gains for women's equality before the law, feminist legal scholars still see work to do. Interestingly, some landmark cases around sex discrimination have been brought to the court by men; see for instance, the Case in Point above. The case of a young man, *Michael M. v. Sonoma County, CA*, 1981, brings to light two relevant issues: (1) males can bring sex discrimination cases before the U.S. Supreme Court and (2) one area that still confounds the court is sexual activity among teenagers.

Michael M. was a 17-year-old male from Sonoma County, California, who was charged with statutory rape for what he claimed was consensual sex with a female under the age of 18. Michael M.'s lawyers argued that he was denied equal protection before the law because he was held criminally liable for sex between two underaged people (Taub and Schneider 1998). The court upheld sex-based differences in Michael M.'s case and argued that the goals of the California law were to eliminate teen pregnancy, despite the fact that this goal was not explicitly written in California law. In upholding the law, the Supreme Court argued that since females can become pregnant, they need protection (Taub and Schneider 1998). The ruling read:

> We need not be medical doctors to discern that young men and young women are not similarly situated with respect to the problems and risks of sexual intercourse. Only women may become pregnant and they suffer disproportionately the profound physical, emotional and psychological consequences of sexual activity. (*Michael v. Superior Court of Sonoma County*, 1981)

Is this a case in which the differences between males and females need to be recognized as relevant to equality between the sexes? Feminist scholars may be divided on the sameness versus difference issues, but most would agree that the language of this ruling relies on age-old stereotypes of females as incapable of consent. California's statute also rests on assumptions that males are always the ones to initiate sex and that females must be protected from aggressive males. As with earlier cases where females were bound to the private sphere due their child-bearing abilities, the Michael M. case attempts to protect young women by limiting their freedoms (Taub and Schneider 1998). While many states have revised their statutory rape laws to protect all children under the age of consent—which varies from state to state—from sexual abuse, what constitutes abuse and victimization can still be gendered (Ellement and Ryan 2008). Additionally, most states have so-called "Romeo and Juliet" laws that treat consensual sex between teens less harshly (Ellement and Ryan 2009). Issues of sexuality, sexual freedom, and sexual equality are by no means settled in our state and federal legal systems. Fourth-wave feminists and feminist legal scholars still have plenty of work to do. If the #MeToo and other new social movements are any indication, the baton has been passed and feminist activists and scholars are off and running.

CHAPTER SUMMARY

◆ This chapter examined the social and legal construction of gender in American society.

◆ Intersectionality is a theoretical approach that looks at how issues such as gender, race, class, age, and sexuality affect people's positions within the social structural hierarchy as well as their access to power.

◆ Feminism is a paradigm for examining inequality between men and women and a social movement devoted to gaining equality for girls and women in all realms of society.

◆ Feminist legal scholarship, also called feminist jurisprudence, is the study of the legal structure, case law, and legal reasoning using critical perspectives that question gender inequality. Feminist jurisprudence rejects any legal categories, distinction, or concepts that imply or affect the subordination of women.

◆ The social construction of gender involves the sifting and sorting of roles, characteristics, and behaviors deemed feminine or masculine. Gender norms are learned through behavioral expectations, standards of dress and appearance, daily interactions between and among members of society, and social institutions in a lifelong process of gender role socialization.

◆ The separate spheres ideology structured men and women into two realms: the private and the public. Men in the public sphere had access to all forms of power; women in the private sphere did not. The separate spheres ideology was reinforced by laws and legal rulings that kept women in the private sphere and in subordinate positions to men.

◆ Coverture was a legal doctrine stating that when married, a woman's legal rights were subsumed under her husband. Laws such as coverture have constructed gender throughout American history and relegated women to an inferior status to men.

◆ Colonial America afforded very few rights to European women who settled in the colonies; African and Native women had no rights in the eyes of Colonial law.

◆ The Revolutionary and post-Revolutionary periods saw the rise of female suffragists. This period is also now seen as the first wave of feminism in the United States. The fight for the right to vote that began in this period was not won until 1920.

◆ The Civil War period and the period of Reconstruction was a time of significant change for freed African-American men, but women's legal advances during this time were still being challenged and fought.

◆ In the Progressive Era, first-wave feminists finally won the right to vote with the passage of the Nineteenth Amendment to the Constitution.

◆ Second-wave feminism emerged in the 1960s and concentrated on gaining access to other areas of public life, such as schools and universities, jobs and occupations, and government and academia. Feminists of this period split over what approach to equality was best: reformist feminists believed the system could be changed from within and radical feminists believed that patriarchy has to be dismantled completely.

◆ Within feminist jurisprudence, theoretical splits loosely aligned as sameness and difference approaches to gender equality. Sameness proponents argue that for true equality for women before the law, women must be viewed as the same as men.

◆ Difference scholars contend that men and women are different and that those differences should be recognized by law and not penalized.

◆ Third-wave feminists of the 1990s to early 2000s address some of the shortcomings and unfinished business of the second wave. The third wave is intersectional and inclusive; it recognizes and embraces multiple statuses, races, and sexualities. Some feminists see a fourth wave emerging in the present day; others view this as an extension of the third wave. In the fourth wave, diversity and inclusivity is highlighted even more, and feminists harness the power of new forms of social media such as Twitter and Instagram.

◆ The #MeToo movement exemplifies fourth-wave feminism: it uses new social media to bring widespread attention to sexual assaults and sexual harassment—an issue that had not been fully addressed by changes in laws from the second and third waves. #MeToo also illustrates how each wave of feminism have learned from earlier waves—both their successes and their mistakes—and have built upon each other.

KEY TERMS

coverture 265
difference approach 277
domination model of feminist
   jurisprudence 278
empowerment model 278
feminism 261
feminist jurisprudence 261
first-wave feminism 273
fourth-wave feminism 279
gender identity 263
gender norms 262

gender role socialization 262
heightened scrutiny test 282
ideology 264
intersectionality 259
private sphere 264
public sphere 264
sameness approach 277
second-wave feminism 275
separate spheres ideology 264
third-wave feminists 279

CRITICAL THINKING QUESTIONS

1. You have been asked to rewrite the 1848 "Declaration of Sentiments" to include issues related to the #MeToo movement. What new sentiments or statements would you include and why?

2. Can you think of an example wherein treating men and women as the same before the law benefits women? Explain.

3. Can you think of an example of an issue or area of law (other than pregnancy) where women should be treated differently from men to achieve fairness and equality before the law?

4. Describe/discuss another example of a new social movement that is bringing about, or has the potential to bring about, changes in laws regarding equality for women. What is it and what law or laws might it bring about or change?

5. Find an example online of writing about or from fourth-wave feminism. What are the key concerns discussed and how are they discussed?

SUGGESTED MOVIE: *NORTH COUNTRY*

North Country, 2005. Directed by Niki Caro.

    North Country, starring Charlize Theron, Woody Harrelson, Sissy Spacek, Frances McDormand, and Sean Bean, follows the story of Josey Aimes, a young, single mother from a working-class family in coal country, Minnesota. When Josey decides to follow her father into the mines in order to feed her family, she suffers constant harassment and abuse from the men in the mine. She decides to sue the mining company, and eventually is joined by other women who worked at the mine, in a class action lawsuit—the first class action sexual harassment suit of its kind. The legal case and specific scenes in the film illustrate the separate spheres ideology discussed in Chapter 10. The film can also illustrate and prompt discussions of intersectionality and the intersecting forms of discrimination in Josey's social positions, such as gender, class, single motherhood, and sexuality. Intersectional analyses push us to look at how social locations and social forces intersect in ways that work against some people and place them at a distinct disadvantage in the workplace, the legal system, and other systems of power. Josey's case can provide specific examples of how these intersecting inequalities affect her individual life and the lives of entire groups of people based on their membership in a group.

Discussion Questions for The Film *North Country*

1. What different positions or social statuses intersected in Josey's life?

2. How did these intersecting statuses affect Josey's life and the lives of her children?

3. What social forces worked against Josey as she tried to make a living wage and support her family? How were these intersecting forms of inequality made visible in Josey's legal case against her employer?

4. Josey's case turns into a class action lawsuit. What is a class action? In what types of cases do you think they are most often used?

5. Josey had been victimized in many ways leading up to her employment at the mine. Discuss the types of victimization she endured, and how these experiences shaped her decision to take on employment discrimination and sexual harassment in the mining company (and the entire industry).

11

Race, Inequality, and Law

◆ ◆ ◆

IDA B. WELLS, ALSO KNOWN AS Ida B. Wells-Barnett (1862–1931), was a suffragist, a journalist, a public speaker, an educator, and a mother. She helped to found the National Association for the Advancement of Colored People (NAACP), although she is not always credited with doing so. At a time in which women were not allowed to vote, she took on one of the most insidious and horrific issues of the post-Civil War era: the lynching of African-American men (mainly) in the South (Wells-Barnett 1895). Through her meticulous investigations and compelling storytelling, Wells illustrated that lynching was not simply a few abhorrent acts by rogue White supremacists. Lynching was a widespread practice in the late 1800s and, as Wells illustrated, it was used systematically to intimidate and oppress free African-Americans (Wells and Royster 2016). Further, the Whites who took part in this crime justified their actions by saying they had to quell race riots or protect White women from dangerous African-American men.

In her writings about lynching, Wells pointed out the victim-blaming and hypocrisy of this brutal practice, stating "It is with no pleasure that I have dipped my hands in the corruption here exposed .... Somebody must show

Ida B. Wells, 1862–1931. Journalist, suffragist, and civil rights activist.

NYPL Digital Collection/Willis, Oscar B.

289

that the Afro-American race is more sinned against than sinning, and it seems to have fallen on me to do so" (Wells quoted in Dickerson 2018:n.p.). Wells took on the task with great fervor, setting out to interview witnesses and uncovering records on dozens of cases. Because of her work, we now know that between 1892 and 1940, over 3,000 people, mostly Black and male, were lynched in the United States (Wells 1895; Kaba 2018) in the practice known as "lynch law"—which Wells stressed was an unwritten code that allowed for the extrajudicial killing of Blacks. She called it what it was: the barbaric subjugation of a group of people based on their race and gender. She told the stories of the victims and published their names for the historical record. An excerpt from her work, *The Red Record*, illustrates the force of her writing:

> Negroes were whipped, scourged, exiled, shot, and hung whenever and wherever it pleased the white man so to treat them, and as the civilized world in increasing persistency held the white people to account for its outlawry, the murderers invented a third excuse—that Negroes had to be killed to avenge their assaults on women .... Humanity abhors the assailant of womanhood, and this charge placed him beyond the pale of human sympathy ... the world has accepted the story that the Negro is a monster which the Southern white man has painted him (Wells-Barnett 1895:57).

Wells shows that this falsehood—that Black men posed a threat to the purity of White woman—was a way to stir old fears and cast all Black men in the role of the dangerous other.

Wells challenged notions of race and gender and she herself was victimized by violence. Due to her activism and writing, a White mob destroyed her newspaper's offices and presses in Memphis, Tennessee. She left the south for Chicago and continued her activism and writing there. Perhaps due to her radicalism, or her gender, or both, Wells became less prominent in the civil rights and suffragist organizations she helped to found. When she died in 1931 at the age of 68, she was working as a probation officer in Chicago (Dickerson 2018). Today, Wells' work is being brought back to the public's attention. In March 2018, *The New York Times* added Wells to their series on overlooked obituaries—a series that aims to correct for the fact that the paper's obituary section has been dominated historically by the death announcements of White men. A group of Chicago citizens, including some of her descendants, are trying to raise enough money to create a monument in her honor (Kaba 2018).

Wells' life, and her life's work, bring to light many of the racial and gender inequities that laws have sometimes caused and reified; sometimes ignored, and sometimes corrected. Using critical race theory, this chapter looks at social and legal constructions of race in American history. The chapter focuses on two areas of law that exemplify approaches to race in the American legal system: (1) naturalization and citizenship laws and (2) anti-miscegenation laws, or laws against mixed-race marriages. Through the lens of these two legal issues, we consider how race was *not* defined—or left undefined, how laws attempted to define it, and also how laws have redefined racial categories throughout American history. As we discussed in the previous chapter—and as we see in the work of Ida B. Wells— the legal construction of race and the rights and freedoms that people of color fought for were often parallel to and intertwined with those of women. Therefore, we will also consider an intersectional approach to race and gender in this chapter.

CRITICAL RACE THEORY

Critical Race Theory draws upon legal scholarship, sociology, Black feminist theory, and philosophy to raise questions about the construction of race in the United States and other modern societies. Critical race theorists argue that race cannot be understood without consideration of how laws have both *constructed* race and *subordinated* people of color. And, as with Ida B. Wells a century earlier, critical race theory proponents find racism is not the work of extremists on the fringes of society, but rather is built into the structure and culture of American society. Critical race theorists believe that Whites need to hear from people of color in order to learn from their experiences with racism in the legal system (Delgado and Stefancic 2012). Legal scholar Ian F. Haney Lopez describes critical race theory as "a new strand of legal scholarship dedicated to reconsidering the role of race in U.S. society …. Much of critical race theory scholarship recognizes that race is a legal construction" (Lopez 1996:12). Before we look more closely at race as a legal construction, we will first consider race as a social construction.

THE SOCIAL CONSTRUCTION OF RACE

A **racial group** is a **minority group**—a group that experiences unequal treatment compared to members of the dominant group. **Racial groups** are differentiated from the dominant group by perceived physical characteristics, such as skin color, hair texture, and facial features. These physical differences take on social significance in society. The main racial groups in the United States are: Whites—the dominant group, African-Americans, Asian-Americans, and Native Americans. Latinos or Hispanics are considered a White ethnic group. **Ethnic groups** are people who are set apart from the White dominant group by national origin, religious beliefs, distinct cultural patterns and/or language (Figure 11.1).

While **race** has historically been thought of as a biological or genetic classification, there are no clear biological markers that differentiate one

Race and Hispanic Origin	Percent of U.S. Population
White (alone)	76.6
Black or African-American (alone)	13.4
American Indian or Alaska Native (alone)	1.3
Asian (alone)	5.8
Native Hawaiian & Other Pacific Islander (alone)	0.2
Two or More Races	2.7
Hispanic or Latino (alone)	18.1

Source: U.S. Census Bureau. July 1, 2017. "Quick Facts."

Figure 11.1 Major Racial and Ethnic Groups, Percentage of U.S. Population

group from another, at least not in terms of behaviors, abilities, and propensities. **Race,** then, is a social construction, similar to gender as discussed in the previous chapter. So, while skin color tends to denote race in American society, what is more significant from a sociological perspective is the importance that members of a society place on skin color and other visible differences. As historian Barbara J. Fields states: "The idea that one people has of another, even when the difference between them is embodied in the most striking physical characteristics, is always mediated by the social context within which the two come into contact" (1982:148–149). We attach meaning to skin color in historical contexts, social interactions, and different situations. This is not to say that race is insignificant: the *meanings* and *assumptions* we attach to perceived racial differences are very important in a society that is stratified by race, class, gender, and other real or perceived differences.

Sociologists Michael Omi and Howard Winant use the term **racial formation** to denote the sociohistorical processes that have created and recreated racial categories over time (1994). Omi and Winant note that those in the dominant group have the power to define groups in accordance with the dominant group's needs. After the Civil War, when Africans were allowed to live freely among White Southerners, for the dominant group, racial constructions became even more important than they were under slavery (Fields 1982). Distinct racial differences that existed under slavery morphed into an "ideological medium through which people posed and apprehended basic questions of power and dominance, sovereignty and citizenship, justice and right" (Fields 1982:162). Similarly, the desire for territory and expansion led to racial constructions of Native Americans into one racial group, as opposed to many different groups or tribes. This racialized group was then forced off of their land and removed to new Indian reservations in the Indian Removal Act of 1830. And during World War II, the perceived need for security and protection from those who were constructed as enemies led to the internment of Japanese immigrants, as well as some Japanese-Americans in the Northwest.

Omi and Winant's racial formation approach allows us to see that race is not a fixed, immutable category; rather it is a moving target that can be shaped and reshaped for political purposes. These racial categories are never innocent of power and domination. As Barbara Fields argues, "physical impressions are mediated by a larger context, which assigns them their meaning, whether or not the individuals concerned are aware that this is so. It follows that the notion of race, in its popular manifestation, is an ideological construct and thus, above all, a historical product" (1982:149). Or as Ian F. Haney Lopez simply states, "race is not a measured fact, but a preserved fiction" (1996:102). Further, Lopez finds:

> Law is one of the most powerful mechanisms by which any society creates, defines, and regulates itself. Its centrality in the constitution of society is especially pronounced in highly legalized and bureaucratized late industrial democracies such as the United States. It follows, then, that to say race is socially constructed is to conclude that race is at least partially legally produced. (1996:9–10)

How were these preserved fictions, so slippery and mutable, codified into American law?

Throughout the nineteenth and twentieth centuries, courts in the United States struggled to pin down race. In this section of the chapter, we consider some of those legal efforts to define race, and how and why these attempts were significant.

Sidebar: What is Equal Protection? The Judicial Review Standards

As we saw in the previous chapter, the Fourteenth Amendment to the United States Constitution, added in 1868, granted a number of important rights to citizens. Its Equal Protection Clause guaranteed that "all persons born or naturalized in the United States, and subject to the jurisdiction thereof, are citizens of the State wherein they reside ... nor shall any State deprive any person of life, liberty, or property, without due process of law; nor deny to any person within its jurisdiction the equal protection of the laws" (U.S. Constitution, Fourteenth Amendment). How the equal protection clause was interpreted and applied to specific cases, however, became a matter of judicial review. Ideally these reviews ask, what is the governmental reason for classifying people by sex or race? Is it a public health reason? For safety? Does the matter involve the United States Census and gathering official governmental data?

Prior to the *Brown v. Board of Education* case in 1954, the Supreme Court used a so-called **rational basis test**, also known as "ordinary scrutiny," that simply stated that the court must illustrate *some* basis for differential treatment, even if that reason was simply tradition or custom. The court used the **rational basis** standard in *Plessy v. Ferguson,* 1896, arguing that it was legal to separate people in public facilities based on race if the facilities were equal. As far as sex segregation was concerned, all cases in which a woman challenged sex segregation up until about the 1970s needed only meet the rational basis test.

After the *Brown v. Board* case overturned the separate but equal notion, race-based cases moved to a higher level of scrutiny known as **intermediate scrutiny** or "heightened scrutiny." This standard of review states that an *important* governmental—federal or state—interest must be served in separating people by race or gender. For many years, most sex-based classifications stayed at the level of **intermediate scrutiny** because, as we discussed in the previous chapter, pregnancy and health of offspring are deemed an important governmental concern (Turkel 1996; Taub and Schneider 1998).

Strict scrutiny stands as the most rigorous judicial review. Under strict scrutiny, the government must illustrate a *compelling* interest to differentiate people. While most race-based cases must now meet this level of scrutiny, sex-based cases are still not quite at this level. What constitutes an *important* governmental interest versus a *compelling* governmental interest is open to interpretation and ongoing debate at the level of the federal judiciary (Turkel 1996; Taub and Schneider 1998).

LEGAL CONSTRUCTIONS OF RACE

After the Civil War, defining race became particularly urgent for the dominant group. Especially in the South, questions arose about how to redefine a group of people that had been defined as property, not as people. Many of these decisions revolved around United States citizenship—who was allowed to gain it and who was not. The *Dred Scott v. Sandford* decision in 1857 stands as the first in what came to be a long string of naturalization cases that made their way through the courts of appeal and eventually to the Supreme Court of the United States.

Legalese: Naturalization

Naturalization is "the process by which U.S. citizenship is granted to a foreign citizen or national after he or she fulfills the requirements established by Congress in the Immigration and Nationality Act (INA)" (United States Citizenship and Immigration Services). A naturalized U.S. citizen has all of the same rights and freedoms as a citizen born in the United States.

The *Dred Scott Decision* of 1857 occurred before the Civil War, but it set the stage for the legal battles over citizenship that came after the war. The Dred Scott case is rather convoluted, but it warrants consideration here. Dred Scott was an African slave born in St. Louis, Missouri, a slave state. Scott was sold to a new owner, John Emerson, who transported him to Illinois, a free state. He then went to the Wisconsin territory, which, at the time, was also free. In 1846, however, Scott and his wife—with their owner—returned to St. Louis, Missouri. He petitioned for his freedom on the basis that he had lived for years in free states. A Mis-

Dred Scott, 1799–1858.

NYPL Digital Collection/Fitzgibbon, J. H.

souri district court granted Scott's petition in 1850, but his owner's widow, Irene Emerson, appealed the decision to the Missouri Supreme Court. As we saw in Chapter 10, women had very few rights at this time, so Irene Emerson's brother, John Sanford, acted on her behalf in the legal proceedings. The case became known as *Scott v. Sandford*, which was a misspelling of Mr. Sanford's name. The higher court reversed the lower court's decision in 1852 (Lopez 1996). Mr. Scott was not granted his freedom and was thus not considered a citizen.

Scott appealed the decision to the Supreme Court of the United States. In the years leading up to the Civil War, the country was divided over the institution of slavery, and people on both sides of the *Dred Scott* case thought it might push the court to take a stand on not just Dred Scott's status but on slavery itself. Unfortunately for Scott and for all enslaved people, the Supreme Court's decision was lengthy—it involved matters of jurisdiction, statehood and states' rights, and constitutional intent, among other things—but clear in its intent. In sum, the court ruled that Scott had no legal rights to citizenship and thus no rights to sue for his freedom (*Scott v. Sandford* 1857; Lopez 1996). Specifically, Chief Justice Roger Taney's ruling read:

> A free negro of the African race, whose ancestors were brought to this country and sold as slaves, is not a "citizen" within the meaning of the Constitution of the United States;
>
> Since the adoption of the Constitution of the United States, no state can by any subsequent law make a foreigner or any other description of person citizens of the United States, nor entitle them to the rights and privileges secured to citizens by that instrument;
>
> Every citizen has a right to take with him into the Territory any article of property which the constitution of the United States recognizes as property (Transcript of *Dred Scott v. Sandford*, 1857).

The Dred Scott decision is dismissed today as one of the worst rulings ever to come out of the Supreme Court, but it was the law of the land in 1857 and stood for over a decade until it was ruled unconstitutional with the passage of the Fourteenth Amendment in 1868. It also mobilized the abolitionists' efforts and picked up the march to the Civil War (Ogletree and Wald 2007). The Fourteenth Amendment Equal Protection Clause, while not perfectly enforced for African- Americans or for women, did—as we saw in the previous chapter—lay much of the groundwork for both the civil rights movement and the second-wave feminist movement to continue the fight for equality before the law for all citizens of the United States.

RACIAL PREREQUISITE CASES: RACE AND CITIZENSHIP

While the *Dred Scott* decision clarified—rather arbitrarily—the citizenship of one racial group in the United States, it did not address the citizenship of other foreign-born people. As legal scholar Alexander M. Bickel noted:

> Citizenship is a legal construct, an abstraction, a theory. No matter what the safeguards, it is at best something given, and given to some and not others, and it can be taken away. It has always been easier, it always will be easier, to think of someone as a noncitizen than to decide that he is a nonperson, which is the point of the *Dred Scott* decision. (1975:53)

In 1790, Congress first addressed the issue of citizenship when it restricted naturalization to *white persons* (Lopez 1996).

The Naturalization Act of 1790

Specifically, the **Naturalization Act of 1790** stated that any alien (foreign-born), free white person could apply for citizenship, as long as he or she had lived in the United States for at least two years. At this time, indentured servants, free Blacks, and slaves were not regarded as citizens. This changed for free Blacks after the passage of the Fourteenth Amendment. In 1795, Congress changed the minimum residence requirement from two years to five years (U.S. Congressional Documents, 1774–1875). While the requirements for citizenship were continuously changing (Figure 11.2), the White racial requirement remained in place for 162 years until the Immigration and Nationality Act was passed in 1952. What Congress did not clearly establish, however, is how to define Whiteness. For over a century and a half, legal challenges to "Whiteness" were brought before the courts—State Supreme Judicial courts, Federal Circuit courts, and the Supreme Court of the United States. In each case, the court was pushed to define Whiteness and, as we will see in a sample of these cases, the courts were not able to do so.

Whiteness stood at the center against which all of the racial prerequisite cases bounced off of, but it was an ill-defined, nebulous center at best. How Whiteness was defined depended on when the court was asked. Some of the various answers and rulings focused on skin color and facial features, national origin, and language and culture; still others tried to rely on science to answer the question and ended up disappointed. As we will see later in this chapter, while many attempts were made to find a scientific definition and classification schema for races, these attempts fell apart when cultural anthropologists began to focus on races as social and cultural constructs. In many instances, the court fell back on common knowledge and public opinion to answer the question: Who is white? (Lopez 1996).

- 1790 Naturalization Act: Any alien, free White person could apply for U.S. citizenship
- 1870 Fifteenth Amendment: Black men permitted to vote as U.S. citizens
- 1882 Chinese Exclusion Act: Chinese declared ineligible for citizenship
- 1940 Nationality Act: Congress opened naturalization to descendants of races indigenous to the western hemisphere
- 1943: Chinese persons allowed to apply for citizenship
- 1946: Naturalization opened to people from the Philippines and India
- 1952 Immigration and Nationality Act, also known as the McCarron-Walter Act, abolished prerequisite laws (Sources: Lopez 1996; McLemore and Romo 1998).

Figure 11.2 A Brief Timeline of Naturalization Acts, 1790–1952

In re Ah Yup, 1878

After Dred Scott, other citizenship cases made their way to the federal court system. The case of *In re Ah Yup*, 1878, was decided in a Federal District Court in California. Ah Yup was a Chinese citizen who petitioned for citizenship to the United States. In 1878, Chinese were seen as "Mongolian" and Ay Yup asked the courts to decide if that constituted Whiteness. Using a combination of scientific knowledge, common knowledge, and congressional intent, the court determined that the members of "Mongolian race" were not White. Specifically, the ruling read: "Neither in popular language, in literature, nor in scientific nomenclature, do we ordinarily, if ever, see the words, 'White person' used in a sense so comprehensive as to include an individual of the Mongolian race" (Lopez 1996:210). The presiding circuit court judge, Judge Sawyer, even pulled out a *Webster's Dictionary* to note that Mongolian was classified as the "yellow race" and, therefore, not White (Lopez 1996:210).

In the years between 1878 and 1909, several other cases prompted the courts to define Whiteness; in each case they defined it by what it was *not*. Half-White and half-Native Americans were not White, Hawaiians were not White, Chinese were not White; neither were Burmese or Japanese people. Mexicans? Not White. A mixed-race person who was part Japanese and part Chinese? Definitely not White. Because of *In re Ay Yup*, most of these new cases relied on the precedent set in that case and did not move any closer to defining White.

Ex parte Shahid, 1913

Another challenge came to a district court in 1913 that once again attempted to push for clarity on the question of what is White. Faras Shahid was an immigrant from Syria who had lived in the United States for about 11 years when he applied for naturalization. He could not read or write in English. In three previous circuit court cases, courts had ruled that Syrians *were* White: *In re Najour*, 1909; *In re Mudarri*, 1910; and *In re Ellis*, 1910 (Lopez 1996:204–205). In Shahid's case, however, the court reversed this trend—and overturned precedent—when it refused his application for naturalization. Using common knowledge only, the court argued that "free White persons" were understood to be of European descent. The example of Syrians' attempts at U.S. citizenship illustrates just how murky the courts' notions of Whiteness were. In the end, a judge could decide that White is what we believe it is and should be.

Ozawa v. United States, 1922

A racial prerequisite case that made it to the U.S. Supreme Court was *Takao Ozawa v. United States*, 1922. Mr. Ozawa was born is Japan and arrived in the United States as a student. He attended the University of California, Los Angeles, and spoke English. His children attended American schools and his family attended American churches (Lopez 1996:218). Mr. Ozawa even argued that his skin was Whiter than the average Caucasian's skin, but to no avail. Using common knowledge and congressional intent, the court rejected his case and declared that Japanese people are not White and thus ineligible for citizenship.

CASE IN POINT

Korematsu v. United States, 1944.

During World War II, about two weeks after the attack on Pearl Harbor on December 7, 1941, Japanese and Japanese-Americans living on the West Coast of the United States were ordered to evacuate their homes and were relocated to internment camps. President Franklin D. Roosevelt issued the order, Executive Order 9066, claiming military necessity—that the entire Pacific Coast was under attack and the Japanese were our enemies (McLemore and Romo 1998). This mass evacuation took about seven months to complete. It involved removing people from their homes and building temporary shelters on racetracks and fairgrounds. The evacuees lived in horse stalls and tents surrounded by tall fences. Some evacuees were moved again, from what were called assembly centers to relocation centers away from the West Coast; some were in California; others in Arizona; still others in western states: Arkansas, Utah, Wyoming, and Colorado. For most evacuees, they had never traveled to these states and the areas were completely new to them.

Fred Korematsu was a Japanese-American, born in the United States. The 23-year-old did not speak Japanese and had never traveled outside of the country. He was ordered to leave his home in San Leandro, California. He tried to avoid this order, was arrested, and eventually convicted of violating a civilian exclusion order of the U.S. Army. He challenged his conviction in the U.S. Supreme Court, arguing the Executive Order was unconstitutional based on the Fifth Amendment right to due process (U.S. Courts, https://www.uscourts. gov/educational-resources/educational-activities/facts-and-case-summary-korematsu-v-us). The court decided against Korematsu, stating that he was evacuated because we were at war with Japan and military urgency demanded the internment of Japanese and Japanese-Americans, not because of their race, but because they were enemies.

In 1983, a legal historian named Peter Irons and a researcher named Aiko Herzig-Yoshinaga unearthed key documents proving that Japanese Americans had committed no acts of treason during WWII and that they were unjustly detained. A legal team reopened Korematsu's case on the basis of government misconduct. Mr. Korematsu's conviction was overturned in a federal district court in San Francisco on November 10, 1983 (http://www.korematsuinstitute.org/fred-t-korematsu-lifetime/). Mr. Korematsu went on to receive the Presidential Medal of Freedom from President Bill Clinton. Korematsu died in 2010 in the state of California. The Fred T. Korematsu Institute was founded to honor his legacy; to educate the public about the dangers of racial profiling; and to advance racial equality, social justice, and human rights (http://www.korematsuinstitute.org/fred-t-korematsu-lifetime/).

THE END OF RACIAL PREREQUISITES

This pattern of appeals continued; in case after case until the mid-1940s, Asian Indians, Filipinos, Afghanis, and "Arabians" were all declared not White by law. In 1952, all of the gray area around Whiteness and citizenship came to an end—but not because the courts or Congress found the magical definition for Whiteness. Rather, the 1952 Immigration and Nationality Act, or the Walter-McCarron Act, abolished prerequisite laws, stating: "The right of a person to become a naturalized citizen of the United States shall not be denied or abridged because of race or sex or because such person is married" (Lopez 1996:46). The inclusion of marital status highlights the intersection of race and gender in both naturalization and marriage law. As was the case with coverture, a married woman's citizenship was subsumed under her husband's; if *he* was a legal citizen, *she* was a legal citizen, but only because she had no real status as an individual. By the same token, until 1931, an American woman had to *terminate* her citizenship upon marriage to a non-citizen (Lopez 1996; Pascoe 1996). Here again is another example of how race and gender intersect to doubly discriminate against women.

There were many reasons for change in naturalization laws during this period. World War II challenged American restrictions on racial groups. In 1944, the outgoing U.S. Commissioner on Immigration and Naturalization, Earl G. Harrison, observed that other than Nazi Germany, the United States was the only country that used race as a deciding factor for naturalization and citizenship (Lopez 1996). At the same time, the country was also barring members of allied countries from becoming naturalized citizens of the United States (Lopez 1996). Overall, the fact that the United States was using the same type of racism our troops were fighting against became too hypocritical and, by 1940, Congress set to work on changing the citizenship laws.

What do these legal challenges to citizenship leading up to 1952 tell us about race? Clearly, they illustrate that race in America is both socially and legally constructed. The racial prerequisite cases also indicate that the White race was deemed valuable—it needed to guard and protect against encroachment. Indeed, legal scholar Cheryl I. Harris views Whiteness as a form of property in a country that very much values property—people build walls and gates around property; they surveil its boundaries; they protect what is rightfully theirs. She ties notions of Whiteness as property to the legal legacies of both the enslavement of African-Americans and the seizure of land from Native Americans. The law protected property interest in Whiteness, and Whiteness "shares the critical characteristics of property and accords with the many and varied theoretical descriptions of property" (Harris 1993:1724). Further, Harris argues, "Although property by popular usage describes 'things' owned by persons, the concept of property prevalent among most theorists ... is that property may consist of rights in 'things' .... Property is said to be a right, not a thing" (1993:1725). As the prerequisite cases illustrated, the law constructed and confirmed aspects of identity—who is and who is not White—*and* what privileges and benefits accrued from that identity, making it a status. Finally, Whiteness is property; legal entitlements have been granted due to people's Whiteness (Harris 1993). If property is anything that a society attaches value to, then Whiteness can be seen as a form of property.

RACE AND MARRIAGE: ANTI-MISCEGENATION LAW IN THE TWENTIETH CENTURY

Another area in which law policed the boundaries of Whiteness was marriage laws. **Miscegenation** is the mixing of races and, up until 1967, miscegenation was a criminal offense under various state statutes (Pascoe 1996). **Anti-miscegenation laws** prohibited intermarriage between Blacks and Whites and, depending on the state, other racial groups were specifically prohibited from intermarriage as well. Anti-miscegenation laws existed as far back as the 1600s; they were some of the first laws put in place in the colonies. Many states that did not have specific anti-miscegenation laws at the level of state governments adopted them after the Civil War. As with the naturalization cases, cases challenging anti-miscegenation laws were brought to states' Supreme Judicial Courts, to Federal Circuit Courts, and to the Supreme Court of the United States. In examining anti-miscegenation laws, we can see that law continued to define and redefine race by shaping marriage choices.

The late 1800s and early 1900s witnessed newly emerging theories about the presumed differences between and among racial groups, and the presumed superiority and inferiority of different groupings of people.

Just as the social and legal constructions of gender were made to appear natural and then subordinated women, social and legal constructions of race attempted to make the assumed differences between racial groups appear to be natural and then to subordinate people of color. Once people are separated and differentiated, they are easily stratified. Some groups are deemed fit for citizenship; others are not. Some people are sorted into marriageable categories; others are not. Some groups are eligible for voting rights; others are not. Many of these attempts at racial distinctions came from newly emerging sciences or pseudo-sciences of the twentieth century. Taken together, these attempts to recognize the science of racial distinctions are now seen as **scientific racism** (Pascoe 1996). Simply put, these newly emerging pseudo-sciences, such as **eugenics**—the science of human breeding—gave an air of legitimacy to plain old racism.

The period from the mid-1800s to the turn of the twentieth century was a time of scientific speculation; scientists and lay people theorized about human biology, hereditary traits, and intelligence. In 1859, Charles Darwin published *On the Origin of the Species*, in which he put forth his theories of human evolution, natural selection, biological inheritance, and reproduction. While Darwin did not make any overtly racist statements or hypotheses in his work, other theorists used Darwin's work to construct what are now seen as different types of scientific racism. As we discussed in Chapter 3: Modernization and Theoretical Perspectives on Society and Law, in the decades following the publication of *On the Origin of the Species* other scientists drew on Darwin's evolutionary biology to make claims about some groups of people as more evolved than others (Darwin 1859). For example, Francis Galton, Darwin's contemporary and half-cousin, was influenced by *On the Origin of the Species* and used it to put forth his ideas on heredity and human intelligence (Hofstadter 1969). Galton became known as the "father of eugenics" and argued that some groups of people should be encouraged to breed, while others should not, and that human hereditary traits should fall under the purview of social control (Hofstader 1969). By the 1870s, American eugenicists such as Richard Dugdale and Henry Goddard argued that certain traits, such as criminality and "feeble-mindedness" were inherited, and therefore governments were obligated to control marriage and breeding (Hofstadter 1969). While anti-miscegenation sentiments were not new to this historical period, they were given new life and new legitimacy with theories that had an air of scientific rigor attached to them. Notions of inherited traits and breeding for strong familial stock played right into miscegenation fears.

Anti-miscegenation laws were among "the longest lasting racial restrictions" in American law (Pascoe 1996:49). The laws were based on notions of racial purity, White supremacy, and the legitimacy of offspring. These laws also addressed property and inheritance—who could own what and who could inherit what from whom (Pascoe 1996; Friedman 2004).

While the Equal Protection Clause of the Fourteenth Amendment might seem like a good place to fight laws prohibiting individuals from legally marrying, from the 1870s to the 1920s many judges declared that laws against interracial marriages did *not* discriminate based on race. They were applied *equally to all races*—Whites, Blacks, and any other group that was legally constructed as a racial group (Pascoe 1996). By the 1920s, lawyers who challenged anti-miscegenation laws took a different tack; they tried to persuade the courts that racial classifications were in error (Pascoe 1996).

Kirby v. Kirby, 1922

The case of *Kirby v. Kirby*, 1922, presents an example in which the plaintiff attempted to convince an Arizona court that a marriage was invalid because the husband and wife were from two different races. A Mexican-American man, Joe Kirby, sought an annulment from his wife, Mayellen Kirby, whom he said was Black—or in the language of the day—a "negress" (Pascoe 1996). Ms. Kirby wanted to convince the judge that she was not Black, that she too was Mexican. At this time, courts were using various methods of defining races, and most of these were loosely based on vague appeals to "science" or "heredity." Genealogy, appearance, blood—all were brought into courtroom discussions of race in anti-miscegenation cases, as with naturalization cases. In *Kirby's* case, the judge settled on ancestry, which he surmised by her physical appearance. The judge said she had a "dusky countenance" and "characteristics of the African race and blood" (Pascoe 1996:51). These unclear racial characterizations were enough to deem the marriage in violation of Arizona's state anti-miscegenation law, and Mayellen lost her case. Since the marriage was deemed illegal and annulled, Mr. Kirby did not have to support his wife or share any of the marital property.

Up until about the 1940s, courts used various forms of scientific racism to justify racial restrictions on both claims to citizenship and marriage. Around the 1940s to the 1950s, scientific classifications of race began to be challenged. In naturalization cases brought before various courts, anthropologists were called upon to clarify racial distinctions. In many cases, however, anthropologists made better arguments for the people who were applying for citizenship because they were among the first social scientists to view race as a cultural and social construct. As Lopez found, "Despite their strained efforts, students of race could not plot the boundaries of Whiteness because such boundaries are socially fashioned and cannot be measured, or found, in nature …. The Court resented the failure of science to fulfill an impossible vow …" (1996:9). Thus, in most naturalization cases, the court used common knowledge—little more than the opinion of the "common man"—to uphold the Whites-only rulings for citizenship.

Historian Peggy Pascoe traced a similar disappointment with the sciences in the court's attempts to define race in marriage cases (1996). By the late 1800s, anthropologists such as Franz Boas (1858–1942) challenged scientific notions of race and turned to cultural views of race (Lopez 1996; Pascoe 1996). Boas was born in Germany and became a naturalized U.S. citizen. He is widely credited as the "father of American anthropology." Boas and his students argued that race was a cultural construction tied to language, customs, and region, but not to human biology (Pascoe 1996).

The Estate of Monks, 1941

Another noteworthy anti-miscegenation case highlights the tension between scientific notions of race and more cultural anthropological approaches. The *Estate of Monks, 1941*, like the case of *Kirby v. Kirby*, questioned the legality of a mixed-race marriage after the fact, rather than challenging whether or not a couple could marry. Marie Antoinette Monks of San Diego, California, married Allan Monks of Boston, Massachusetts. He was the heir to a fortune; she claimed to be a French countess. They married in Arizona and lived there after the marriage. When Mr. Monks died, he left two wills—one leaving his fortune to his wife and another leaving it to a friend. The friend, Ida Lee, challenged Mr. Monk's will and his marriage, saying Ms. Monks was a "Negro" and thus the marriage was invalid under Arizona's anti-miscegenation law. Several versions of racial definitions and categories were presented, some in favor of Lee and others in favor of Monk. The "experts" brought in to prove that Ms. Monks was Black included her hairdresser who talked of the "kink" in her hair, a physical anthropologist who said he could tell that she was at least "one-eighth negroid" from the shape of her face, and a surgeon who had only viewed Ms. Monks in the courthouse and claimed he could see she was partly negro because of the shape of her calves and heels (Pascoe 1996).

On Ms. Monk's side of the argument, her lawyer called upon an anthropologist who presented a culturalist position, stating that race was impossible to determine from physical characteristics. Unfortunately for Ms. Monks, this cultural approach proved too esoteric and undefined for the courtroom. It did not clarify any gray area around race, and the court sought clarity. The hairdresser and the casual observers provided more precision on race than the cultural anthropologist who studied race and, thus, Ms. Monks lost her case. Her marriage was deemed invalid, and her inheritance went to Ida Lee.

Loving v. Virginia, 1967

Miscegenation cases continued to rely on various forms of scientific racism to determine who was allowed to marry who until the most important miscegenation case in the history of the United States: *Loving v. Virginia, 1967*. Richard Perry Loving was a White man; Mildred Dolores Jeter was considered a "Colored" woman but was of both African-American and Native American ancestry. They were neighbors in a mixed-race neighborhood in Caroline County, Virginia. They legally married in June of 1958 in the District of Columbia and five weeks later, the county sheriff and two deputies entered their home in the middle of the night, dragged them out of bed, and arrested them for breaking the state's anti-miscegenation law, part of Virginia's Racial Integrity Act (Pascoe 1996). They were given the choice to leave the state and not return together for 25 years, or they could each spend a year in jail. The couple decided to move to Washington, D.C., and live as a married couple—the District of Columbia did not have an anti-miscegenation law. The Lovings traveled back to Virginia together and were arrested again. By 1963, Mildred reached out to United States Attorney General Robert F. Kennedy, who referred their case to lawyers at the American Civil Liberties Union.

The Lovings' lawyers did not rely on definitions of race to make their case, which, after appeals in the lower courts, made its way to the Supreme

Bettmann/Contributor

Mildred and Richard Loving.

Court of the United States in 1967. The Lovings' lawyers, Philp J. Hirsch-kop and Bernard S. Cohen, decided not to challenge the racial status of their clients, but rather to take the challenge to the anti-miscegenation law where they had started—with the Equal Protection Clause of the Fourteenth Amendment (Brown 2016).

After years of legal struggle, the Supreme Court unanimously ruled that it "cannot conceive of any valid legislative purpose ... which makes the color of a person's skin the test of whether his conduct is a criminal offense" (*Loving v. Virginia*, 1967). Further, the court found that laws against inter-racial marriage were "subversive to the principle of equality at the heart of the Fourteenth Amendment" and therefore were "unsupportable" (*Loving v. Virginia*, 1967). And, while not explicitly stated in the court's decision, the federal judiciary also acknowledged that the notion of "pure," determinable racial groups should be discarded.

For Mildred and Richard Loving, the ruling meant that they could move back to Virginia and live with their children among their families and friends. For the country, *Loving v. Virginia* meant much more. One of the last vestiges of legal segregation landed on the scrap heap of history. Marital assimilation is viewed by sociologists as the final step toward true acceptance between and among groups. The fact that people were legally prohibited from choosing marital partners from groups defined as other until just over 50 years ago greatly affected how groups saw each other and how they interacted with one another. Since 1967, the United States has experienced a steady rise in the numbers of interracial marriages, up from 3 percent in 1967 to 17 percent in 2015 (Pew Research Center 2017). The American public has grown more accepting of intermarriage, with 39 percent seeing it is good for society (Pew Research Center 2017). And, as we saw in Chapter 8: Law and Social Change, the *Loving v. Virginia* case stood as a precedent in the legal fight to allow same-sex marriage. The ripple effects of this important equal protection milestone are still being felt.

LAW AND SOCIAL CHANGE REVISITED

In Chapter 8 of this book, we looked at the social change function of law. Law can both lead social change and follow societal changes. Law can push social change along or disrupt it in its path. The *Loving v. Virginia* case offers further evidence that law can be a tool for both blocking social change—anti-miscegenation laws—and for bringing about positive social change—the overturning of marital restrictions with a Supreme Court decision.

Law also punctuates social changes that are already well under way in society. Ian Haney Lopez's (1996) work on naturalization and Peggy Pascoe's (1996) work on miscegenation illustrate that social scientists were already moving away from racial classifications based on biological notions of race and pseudo-scientific schema that categorized and stratified people into groups with innate intelligence levels, abilities, and proclivities. For the most part, the courts had not yet caught up with this academic discussion and legal changes around race lagged behind; different areas of law had to step in to settle the issues. For legal changes regarding citizenship, the legislative branch stepped in and passed the Immigration and Nationality Act. And for anti-miscegenation law, the issue needed to be defined as an equal protection issue, not as a matter of who belongs to what race and therefore who can marry who. In all of these instances, we are reminded of the pervasiveness and power of law in society.

EXECUTIVE ORDER 13769: THE TRAVEL BAN

In our society today, we see many challenges that are being—or will undoubtedly be—addressed by law. And, many of these challenges have a familiar ring to them—who is allowed to enter the United States? What groups should be granted citizenship in this country? In January 2017, President Trump signed Executive Order 13769, which he titled "Protecting the Nation from Foreign Terrorist Entry into the USA." The order is also known as the travel ban and "the Muslim ban" by those who object to its focus on mainly Muslim-populated countries (Liptak and Schear 2018). The original ban blocked people from Iran, Iraq, Libya, Somalia, Sudan, Syria, and Yemen from entering the United States. The third iteration of the list of banned countries included Iran, Libya, North Korea, Somalia, Syria, Venezuela, and Yemen (Bier 2018; Liptak and Schear 2018).

Legal challenges to this recent ban were numerous, but the most significant was the state of Hawaii's challenge based on religious discrimination. In *Trump v. Hawaii*, 2018, in a 5–4 vote, the Supreme Court upheld the travel ban. The majority held that since the ban did not specifically mention religion, it was constitutional. Further, Chief Justice John Roberts argued the ban was constitutional because it is based on legitimate purposes of "preventing entry of foreign nationals who cannot be adequately vetted" (Bier 2018; Liptak and Shear 2018).

The court withheld judgment on whether or not the policy itself was sound, however. Critics of the ruling saw it as a blow to religious freedom and civil liberties. In her dissenting opinion, Justice Sotomayor compared the case to *Korematsu v. United States*, writing:

> In the intervening years since Korematsu, our Nation has done much to leave its sordid legacy behind. [The Court's] formal repudiation of a shameful precedent is laudable and long overdue. But it does not make the majority's decision here acceptable or right. By blindly accepting the Government's misguided

invitation to sanction a discriminatory policy motivated by animosity toward a disfavored group, all in the name of a superficial claim of national security, the Court redeploys the same dangerous logic underlying Korematsu and merely replaces one "gravely wrong" decision with another. (*Trump v. Hawaii*, 2018)

It is too soon to tell if the *Trump v. Hawaii* decision will be challenged or if it will stand, if law will be used to build walls or tear them down. History has illustrated that the rule of law can adapt to changing realities and contemporary conditions in ways that foster equality and democracy. Law is an implement for social change and a tool for resolving disputes that arise between individuals, between institutions, and even between and among the branches of government. Law has never been a perfect tool for any of the functions it is asked to fulfill, but it is one of the best tools we have.

CHAPTER SUMMARY

◆ Critical Race Theory draws upon legal scholarship, sociology, Black feminist theory, and philosophy to raise questions about the construction of race in the United States and other modern societies. Critical race theorists argue that race cannot be understood without consideration of how laws have both *constructed* race and *subordinated* people of color.

◆ Racial groups are differentiated from the dominant group by perceived physical characteristics, such as skin color, hair texture, and facial features. These physical differences take on social significance in society.

◆ The main racial groups in the United States are: Whites—the dominant group, African- Americans, Asian-Americans, and Native Americans. Latinos and Hispanics are considered a White ethnic group. Ethnic groups are people who are set apart from the White dominant group by national origins, religious beliefs, distinct cultural patterns and/or language.

◆ Sociologists Michael Omi and Howard Winant use the term racial formation to denote the sociohistorical processes that have created and recreated racial categories over time (1994). Omi and Winant note that those in the dominant group have the power to define groups in accordance with the dominant group's needs.

◆ After the Civil War, defining race became particularly urgent for the dominant group. Especially in the South, questions arose around how to redefine a group of people that had been defined as property, not as people. Many of these decisions revolved around U.S. citizenship—who was allowed to gain it and who was not. The *Dred Scott v. Sandford* decision in 1857 stands as the first in what came to be a long string of naturalization cases that made their way through the courts of appeal and eventually to the Supreme Court of the United States.

◆ The Naturalization Act of 1790 stated that any alien (foreign-born), free white person could apply for citizenship, as long as he or she had lived in the United States for at least two years. At this time, indentured servants, free Blacks, and slaves were not regarded as citizens. This changed for free Blacks after the passage of the Fourteenth Amendment.

◆ The 1952 Immigration and Nationality Act, or the Walter-McCarron Act, abolished prerequisite laws, stating: "The right of a person to become a naturalized citizen of the United States shall not be denied or abridged because of race or sex or because such person is married."

◆ Miscegenation is the mixing of races and, up until 1967, was a criminal offense under various state statutes. Anti-miscegenation laws prohibited intermarriage between Blacks and Whites, and depending on the state, other racial groups were specifically prohibited from intermarriage as well.

◆ Anti-miscegenation laws existed as far back as the 1600s; they were some of the first laws put in place in the colonies. Many states that did not have specific anti-miscegenation laws at the level of state governments adopted them after the Civil War.

◆ As with the naturalization cases, cases challenging anti-miscegenation laws were brought to states' Supreme Judicial Courts, Federal Circuit Courts, and the Supreme Court of the United States. In examining anti-miscegenation laws, we can see that law continued to define and redefine race by shaping marriage choices.

◆ Attempts to recognize the science of racial distinctions are now seen as scientific racism. Simply put, these newly emerging pseudo-sciences, such as eugenics—the science of human breeding—gave an air of legitimacy to plain old racism.

◆ Up until about the 1940s, courts used various forms of scientific racism to justify racial restrictions on claims to both citizenship and marriage. Around the 1940s to the 1950s, scientific classifications of race began to be challenged.

◆ In the landmark case of *Loving v. Virginia*, 1967, the Lovings' lawyers did not rely on definitions of race to make their case. After appeals in the lower courts, *Loving* made its way to the Supreme Court of the United States in 1967. The Lovings' lawyers, Philp J. Hirschkop and Bernard S. Cohen, decided not to challenge the racial status of their clients but rather to take the challenge to anti-miscegenation law where it had started—with the Equal Protection Clause of the Fourteenth Amendment.

◆ The *Loving v. Virginia* case offers further evidence that law can be a tool for both blocking social change—anti-miscegenation laws—and for bringing about positive social change—the overturning of marital restrictions with a Supreme Court decision. Law also punctuates social changes that are already well under way in society.

◆ History has illustrated that the rule of law can adapt to changing realities and contemporary conditions in ways that foster equality and democracy. Law is an implement for social change and a tool for resolving disputes that arise between individuals, between institutions, and even between and among the branches of government. Law has never been a perfect tool for any of the functions it is asked to fulfill, but it is one of the best tools we have.

KEY TERMS

anti-miscegenation laws   301
Critical Race Theory   291
ethnic groups   291
eugenics   302
intermediate scrutiny   294
minority group   291
miscegenation   301
naturalization   295

Naturalization Act of 1790   296
race   291
racial formation   292
racial groups   291
rational basis   294
rational basis test   294
scientific racism   302
strict scrutiny   294

CRITICAL THINKING QUESTIONS

1. While we may like to assume that forms of scientific racism are a thing of the past, can you think of any examples where science is used in ways that promote or shore up racism or racist policies?

2. How did the *Loving v. Virginia*, 1967 case pave the way for *Obergefell v. Hodges*, 2015? (Review Chapter 8 on same-sex marriages in the United States.) How are these two decisions on marriages in this country similar? How are they different?

3. In the previous chapter, we looked at some cases in which legal scholars argue that it may be necessary to acknowledge the differences between men and women in order to ensure women are granted equality before the law. This is known as a "difference matters" approach. Can you think of an example wherein acknowledging difference between and

among racial groups is necessary before the law? If yes, what are they? If no, why not? Explain.

4. Supreme Court Justice Sotomayor compared *Trump v. Hawaii*, 2018, to *Korematsu v. United State,* 1944. How are the two cases similar? How do they differ? Do you agree with the comparison? Why or why not?

5. After reading this book, do you find law in the United States to be a force for positive social change or a force for blocking social change? Is it both? Use examples to strengthen your answer.

SUGGESTED MOVIE: *THE LOVING STORY*

The Loving Story, Documentary. 2011. Directed by Nancy Buirski.

As discussed in Chapter this chapter, Richard and Mildred Loving of Caroline County, Virginia, did not set out to change American history. They loved one another and married legally in the District of Columbia. When they moved back to their home state, however, their legal struggles began. They were roused from their bed in the middle of the night by county sheriff's deputies and arrested for being in a marriage that was considered illegal in the state of Virginia. Together with two civil rights lawyers, the Lovings take on the anti-miscegenation laws of the state of Virginia, and in so doing, they eventually overturn laws against interracial marriages in the entire country.

Discussion Questions for *The Loving Story*:

1. What was the Virginia "Racial Integrity Act"? What was the purpose of this act?

2. How did the Lovings' case make it to the U.S. Supreme Court? In what courts was their case considered before it was heard by the Supreme Court?

3. Which Amendment to the U.S. Constitution was called upon in this case? Why? Where else have we discussed this amendment in this book? Relate two of these cases to *Loving v. Virginia*, 1967.

4. How has the *Loving* case changed the United States of America?

Glossary

adjudication Adjudication by administrative agencies occurs when administrations must settle disputes and mediate conflicts; it is akin to a trial in a criminal or civil case. As with civil cases, much of the business of administrations is handled informally, with settlements. When an issue goes to an administrative hearing, the parties must produce evidence but the formal rules of evidence do not necessarily apply.

adjudication The judicial processing of a case; when the court renders a verdict in a trial, the case has been adjudicated.

administrative agencies Perform social control functions through policies and regulations; these agencies include the Environmental Protection Agency (EPA), the Occupational Safety and Health Administration (OSHA), the Federal Communications Commission (FCC), and the Social Security Administration (SSA). In the twentieth and early twenty-first centuries, at the local, state, and federal levels, administrative agencies grew in both number and bureaucratic structure.

administrative law A body of law created by administrative agencies—regulations, orders, and decisions; the legal powers of government administrations.

adversarial law An accusatorial legal system that presumes a winner and a loser.

advocacy law Another category of legal employment, also known as public interest law, that comprises lawyers who work on behalf of social causes, such as environmental issues, prisoners' rights, immigrants' rights, and animal welfare; the work—sometimes called "cause lawyering"—is undertaken for nonprofit organizations.

alienated or estranged labor The Marxist term that denotes the loss of meaning of a person's work and the loss of connection to the work one does; when the work of an individual belongs to someone else and is unrecognizable to the person who produces it, then the worker derives no satisfaction from it; the activity itself is devoid of meaning.

alternative dispute resolution (ADR) In legal language, negotiation, mediation, and arbitration are called forms of alternative dispute resolution—all are substitutions for adjudication, or suing someone in court; they can also be seen as methods to relieve overburdened courts and quicken the process of dispute settlement.

American Bar Association (ABA) Established in 1878, the ABA is the largest voluntary professional organization of lawyers and legal professionals in the United States.

anti-miscegenation laws Laws that prohibited intermarriage between Blacks and Whites; depending on the state, other racial groups were specifically prohibited from intermarriage as well.

appellate courts The party that loses at trial has the right to appeal the trial court's decision in appellate court; appellate courts are composed solely of judges who base their decisions on the record of the trial court; they do not consider new facts; they determine whether the law was applied correctly in the trial court, questioning law and procedures—rules of evidence and jury instruction; and are concerned about the boundaries of legal rules. Appellate court decisions are published and become references for trial judges and lawyers.

arbitration A form of alternative dispute resolution that involves both parties arguing their case to a third party, an arbitrator, who has the authority to make a decision or a settlement. In the 1920s, arbitration became a legally sanctioned form of dispute resolution.

arbitrator A third party who hears both sides of a dispute and is empowered with the legal authority to issue a decision; arbitrators are knowledgeable about the substantive issue of the cases that they hear and they often have their own specialties, such as labor disputes or contract disputes.

attorney general At the federal level, the United States attorney general is the top legal officer of the country.

barristers Practitioners of law in the United Kingdom who argue cases in the courts.

beyond a reasonable doubt The standard of evidence in criminal cases; the degree of certainty required for a juror to find a criminal defendant guilty; the proof must be so conclusive and complete that all reasonable doubts of the fact are removed.

solicitors Practitioners of law in the United Kingdom who work on legal matters outside the courts and learned as apprentices; solicitors provide legal advice and act on behalf of clients outside of court.

big law The largest, most profitable law firms based in the United States; typically denotes the size of the profits and not necessarily the size of the law firm; all of the top-10 law firms in this country count their profits in the multi-millions, with several in the multi-billions of dollars per year.

binding force of law This term means that a law works because most people follow it; law emanates from a legitimate, rational authority.

boundary maintenance Any strategy that a social system or institution—such as the legal institution— uses to keep the distinction between insiders and outsiders, i.e., between lawyers and non-lawyers; because expertise can overlap between and among professions, members of the profession must uphold the boundaries to maintain their monopoly on knowledge related to the profession.

bureaucracy A highly developed formal organization in which power and tasks are distributed into a hierarchy based on a complex division of labor.

capitalism An economic system in which the means of production—the factories, the raw material, the land, the tools—are held in the hands of a relative few whose primary goal is to accumulate and expand their capital; involves an owning class—the capitalists—and a working class—the laborers.

caps on damages Absolute maximums set on how much money can be awarded to the plaintiffs in civil lawsuits.

case law Law enacted by judges in the appellate courts.

causation In negligence cases, causation means that the defendant's actions or omissions cause the harm to occur; in a tort case, a legal standard of causation—either actual or approximate— must be proved.

challenges for cause These challenges are used to keep potentially biased jurors off the jury. Challenges for cause are specific; a clear reason for the challenge must be given, such as the potential juror is related to the defendant, the person has been a victim of a similar crime, or he or she has read extensively about the case. Challenges for cause are unlimited, but a reason for the objection must be provided. Ideally, jurors should be unbiased—even indifferent—to a case before deliberations begin. If they answer a question in a manner that the judge or lawyer(s) suspect is biased, the lawyers for either side may ask for their excusal using a challenge (or an excusal) for cause.

civil disobedience Any act of lawbreaking undertaken to illustrate that the laws themselves are wrong and unjust; examples of civil disobedience are acts of deliberate resistance, such as the refusal to pay taxes.

civil law Area of law aligned with private law; addresses torts—private wrongs—such as when one party breaks a contract or when someone injures another in an accident.

claimsmakers In the social constructionist perspective, claimsmakers work to usher the social problem into the marketplace to draw attention and support and to provide resources to it.

class action lawsuit A case brought to the court in the name of a group of people who share some grievance.

classical liberalism A set of beliefs that defines and promotes a type of individualism; it is also an ideology—a way of thinking; classical liberalism understands society as relations among persons who interact on the basis of the power of their possessions for their individual gain.

codify To write into legal code—to make official.

coercion The enforcement of norms through the use of organized governmental power.

collaborative law A form of dispute processing in which both parties are represented by their own attorneys, but the parties enter into the process agreeing to settle the matter without outside litigation; it is practiced most often in the field of divorce and family law.

commodity Any item—a tool, a stand of trees, a cotton gin—that can be exchanged for money or other resources.

common law Common law is based on case law, which relies on precedents set by judges.

Common Law systems Systems that date to the Norman Conquest of England in 1066; versions of English common law can now be found in the United States, Canada, Ireland, India, and other former or current British colonies; common law relies on precedent, or previous cases decided by judges, and is adversarial, relies on juries, and uses judicial review.

compensatory damages In tort law, also called actual damages, compensatory damages cover measurable injuries sustained by the plaintiff, such as medical bills or loss of income.

competence and education gap The difference in knowledge and skills between the general public and trained legal professionals; generally speaking, a more highly educated populace means we are closing the competency and education gap and lawyers cannot assume that their legal knowledge cannot be understood or challenged by lay people.

competitive capitalism An early form of capitalism that relied on competition—a competitive market economy based on private ownership of property spread throughout society; a market organized through the interactions of business owners buying and selling goods and services to one another; businesses directly run by their owners; workers who are free to move from job to job; an economy regulated through the actions and decisions of owners, workers, and consumers.

conflict perspective A sociological perspective in which society is viewed as diverse and is characterized by conflict, coercion, divisions, and special interests; stresses inequality, competing groups, and unequal access to societal resources, including law, which is seen as an instrument in social conflict and a tool wielded by the wealthy, owning classes.

conflict stage When the aggrieved parties in a dispute confront one another, a grievance enters the conflict stage.

consensus The notion that there are deeply held standards of behavior upon which people agree and to which they willingly consent.

consensus perspective Also known as functionalist paradigm; views society as integrated, functional, stable, and held together by consensus over values and beliefs; law is viewed as a neutral framework for maintaining order and integration in a cohesive society.

constitutional law Concerned with the organization of the state and limits on power, namely, e.g., the U.S. Supreme Court.

consumer advocacy Customers and special interest groups for people who question all forms of industries, businesses, and professions about their monopolistic hold over everything from the safety of products to market prices to expertise and knowledge.

contract disputes A type of dispute that can end up in the civil justice system; involves a grievance over a formal agreement—a promise or set of promises that is legally enforceable; contracts can be drawn between two individuals, an individual and an institution, between and among groups, between agencies, and between corporations, and disputes can arise among any of these.

contracts Written agreements between individuals, such as business owners and workers, and purchasers and the sellers of products or services; contracts can also regulate relations between and among businesses.

contractual disputes In this type of dispute, the plaintiff claims that the defendant broke a promise or an obligation prescribed in a legal contract.

conventions More binding than customs, yet not so binding as to be written into law.

corporate capitalism Denotes the shift from an early market capitalism to a late capitalism in which the economic system is dominated by large, multinational corporations protected by limited liability; the shift to corporate liberalism coincides with the transition from competitive early market capitalism to corporate capitalism, or late capitalism.

corporate crimes Violations of the law committed through business activities to benefit the business operations—the corporation itself.

corporate legal approach A legal perspective that favors large corporations and allows corporations to determine market relations under a state system of regulative law enforced through the courts on a case-by-case basis.

corporate liberalism A theory that reinterprets liberalism and the role of the government as to serve the corporate leaders and to rationalize the economy and society.

corporation A group of people who form an association endowed by the law with specific rights and duties, not unlike individual rights; a charter endows the corporation with its legal rights—it is a written contract that grants rights, privileges, and franchises by the state.

corporation Defined legally as a group of people who come together as a single legal entity (incorporate) to serve a purpose, e.g., to make a product, to provide higher education, to run a business.

coverture The legal doctrine that subsumed married women's rights under their husbands' rights; an English common law tradition transported from England to North America with the colonizers of the fifteenth and sixteenth centuries.

crime A public wrong; an act or behavior, or an omission of behavior, that violates a law.

criminal justice systems Composed of police, courts, and corrections—all of the people and agencies involved in apprehending, prosecuting or defending, sentencing, and punishing those who break criminal laws.

criminal law Laws that affect public citizens; crimes are wrongs committed against the people and prosecuted on behalf of all citizens, not just the victim of the crime.

criminal negligence Brings about criminal liability, such as extreme recklessness or carelessness resulting in injuries or death; in a civil action, the plaintiff must prove that negligence exists.

criminal sanctions Penalties or other types of punishment used to promote obedience to the law.

Critical Legal Studies (CLS) A new field of legal scholarship influenced by Marxism and legal realism. Proponents are concerned about the power of law and the unequal distribution of knowledge, power, and resources that employers have over employees, that producers have over consumers, and that leaders of corporations have over local communities as subject to state action; privately based inequalities have widespread public consequences and no democratic justification.

Critical Race Theory (CRT) Addresses questions of law and racial discrimination, oppression, difference, and inequality; also looks at the lack of diversity in the legal profession.

culture In Donald Black's variables of social life, culture is the symbolic aspect of social life— ideas, beliefs, and values.

customs General rules that members of a society must follow that are not tied to any external sanction.

cybercrime A relatively new area of lawbreaking that encompasses a vast array of illegal behavior and activities that take place using computers and other new technologies and are conducted over global electronic networks, such as the World Wide Web; cybercrime can include anything from stealing people's identity, to using stolen credit cards to purchase items on the Internet, to trafficking human beings using global online networks, to hacking into private or governmental databases.

death qualified jury A jury whose members have been questioned on their ability to determine guilt or innocence in a case that could result in the death of the accused.

defendant The offending party or the person on trial.

Defense of Marriage Act (DOMA) Federal legislation that defined marriage as the legal union between one man and one woman as husband and wife; it also specified that no state is obligated to recognize same-sex marriages performed in another state.

democracy Government by the people—the rule by the citizens and for the citizens.

deprofessionalization The loss of autonomy and control over one's professional life and the larger loss of the monopoly of knowledge that the profession possesses.

deterrence To deter is to prevent bad behavior; as a goal of punishment, deterrence is the idea that people can be intimidated by the thought of imprisonment or some form of punishment.

disbarred The sanction of being disqualified from the bar association of which a lawyer is a member and losing one's license to practice law.

disproportionate minority sentencing Not all people are punished in the same numbers and in the same capacity in the United States due to disproportionate minority contact at every point of the criminal justice system; people of color are sentenced to prison in much higher numbers than their White counterparts.

dispute stage When a conflict is made public: brought to the attention of the court or some formal forum for processing disputes.

disputes Conflicts or disagreements over opposing claims or rights. When disputes are brought before the court, judges, juries, or both must decide between or among the competing claims of individuals and organizations; these organizations can be private organizations, such as a business, or a governmental agency.

diversity Increased minority representation within a profession or institution.

domination model of feminist jurisprudence This approach looks at how rights have been defined and granted and argues that women have been historically excluded and given short shrift; the domination model argues that for women to attain true equality, rights and harms must be redefined and power rebalanced.

dual hierarchical system The legal system in the United States that includes both (1) the state system, and (2) the federal system. Each is ranked by importance and level of appeal; if a case is not settled in a state trial court, it will move up through the appeals process ranks to a higher court.

due process A somewhat flexible term for the compliance with rules for fair and orderly legal proceedings, e.g., the right to be informed of the nature and cause of the accusation; the right to be confronted with any witnesses against you; the right to have a process in place for obtaining witnesses in your favor; the right to a fair and impartial jury.

dysfunctions Unanticipated, negative consequences or outcomes that run counter to the intended purpose of individual actions, social structures, or social policies.

empanelment The process of selecting people to sit on a jury.

empowerment models A theoretical approach to gender that focuses on what is needed to balance power between historically unequal groups: women and men.

ethnic groups People who are set apart from the dominant group by national origin, religious beliefs, distinct cultural patterns, and/or language.

eugenics An example of scientific racism; the science of human breeding and the notion that the human race could be improved through controlled breeding.

ex post facto A law that provides for punishment of people for an action taken before a law forbidding the action was enacted, or for enhanced punishment for an offense that was in effect at the time of the act; the state cannot punish a person for actions that were not prohibited by law when the act took place.

executive orders Regulations issued by the executive branch at the federal level (the president) and state level (state governors)

expressive acts Criminal behavior that tends to be more emotional and impulsive—the so-called crimes of passion—such as murder and assaults between people who know one another.

extralegal Not officially sanctioned by law; existing outside of formal legal constructs.

family disputes Disagreements between related people.

federal circuit courts At the second level of the federal hierarchy, these courts review decisions made in their districts; they are also empowered to review the decisions of federal regulatory agencies, such as the Federal Trade Commission (FTC) or the Food and Drug Administration (FDA).

federal district courts The lower courts that carry out most of the workload of the federal court system; at least one federal district court exists in every state and larger or more populous states are subdivided into several district courts.

federal judicial system This system deals with questions involving the U.S. Constitution, such as free speech issues or religious freedom, as well as federal laws, such as those dealing with racial and sexual discrimination; these are considered issues of national importance that exist beyond state boundaries.

felony A serious criminal offense subject to imprisonment for at least one year.

feminism An awareness that women as a category of people are treated unequally and that their subordination was and is socially constructed and maintained by a system that could be changed through collective action.

Feminist Legal Theory (FLT) Also referred to as feminist jurisprudence; examines the interaction between law and gender; topics addressed by feminist legal scholars include workplace discrimination, reproductive rights and the body, domestic violence, sexual harassment, rape, prostitution and sex work, education, sports and Title IX, and the public-private split in law and society.

first-wave feminism In the latter part of the 1800s and into the early 1900s, women's groups fought for enfranchisement; first-wave feminists organized the Seneca Falls Convention and other women's rights conventions to fight for women's suffrage.

folkways The small, daily behaviors that people tend to follow out of tradition and because doing so helps maintain the flow of social interaction.

formal rationality Autonomy of law from other social institutions, such as the family or religion; exists when legal rules are organized around abstract principles; procedures are followed and oriented toward finding the truth.

formality The independence of legal institutions and procedures from all other social institutions, such as religion, family, politics, and economics.

formulation stage In this stage of lawmaking, legislators devise and put forth a specific definition of the problem and a legislative remedy for it.

gender identity An individual's perception of their gender, made through individual choices and viewed through one's own lived experiences; gender identity can change over time; it can correspond with societal gender norms or it can resist or challenge those norms.

gender norms Masculine and feminine attributes that are socially defined and learned through behavioral expectations; standards of dress and appearance; interactions between and among members of society; and societal institutions such as families, peer groups, schools, places of worship, sports teams, the media, economic institutions, governments, and law.

gender role socialization Lifelong social learning processes by which people come to understand the behavioral expectations that align with their sex.

general deterrent By locking up the offender, the criminal justice system broadcasts a warning to all people who could possibly break the law; punishment should prevent crimes, not simply exact social revenge on those who break the law.

grand jury A body of citizens summoned and sworn to determine whether the facts and accusations presented by the prosecutor warrant an indictment and trial; traditionally composed of 23 people.

grievance stage Also known as the pre-conflict state; occurs when individuals or groups perceive some form of harm, injustice, or problem.

higher courts (aka superior courts) Made up of state supreme courts and the federal supreme court system (including the district and circuit courts), as well as the highest court of the land and the final court of appeals—the U.S. Supreme Court; all higher courts serve some appellate function.

ideal type A conceptual framework or inventory of concepts describing a phenomenon being studied.

ideology A set of beliefs, thoughts, assumptions, and ways of thinking that shapes our understanding of the world around us.

incapacitation A goal of punishment in the criminal justice system: to remove the offender from society and place him or her in jail or prison to prevent that person from reoffending during the period of incarceration; typically involves a jail or prison sentence but can also include probation, parole, or some form of monitoring of the offender.

industrialization Social and economic changes that take place when an agrarian society shifts to an industrial society; depends on mechanization, or mechanical sources of power, to produce goods; industrial societies are driven by inventions that facilitate new forms of agriculture and production of goods.

informal social control Social norms that people adhere to out of tradition, out of the need to get along and have relatively smooth social interactions, out of fear of embarrassment, or because of external group mechanisms of control, such as gossip, ridicule, humiliation, and ostracism.

formal social control Clear rules of conduct and the planned use of sanctions and punishments to support the rules.

information-gathering stage At this stage, lawmakers collect data on the nature, significance, extent, and consequences of a problem; often overlaps and is intertwined with the publicizing stage; the overall goal is to gather data on the issue and to put it to use in the formulation of new legislation.

in-house counsel Lawyers who work full-time for large businesses or other nongovernmental organizations.

instigation and publicizing stage At this stage, the mass media is a major player. News media outlets—such as all the major television stations, cable news, talk shows, and social media—play a major role in getting the word out about a problem and, in many cases, stoking the public's anxiety or fear by elevating the issue as worthy of attention and solidifying its place in the social problems marketplace.

institutionalization of patterns of behavior The establishment of a legal norm and the clear delineation of provisions for its enforcement.

instrumental acts Criminal acts that are future-oriented, such as burglary, tax evasion, embezzlement, motor vehicle theft—activities that are a means to an end; the goal is to obtain some type of personal gain.

intellectual property Ideas, inventions, and concepts developed by individuals or groups.

intentional acts A tort category more likely to be found in criminal courts, but can also be adjudicated in the civil justice system; occur when someone acts with intent to harm a person or property; these acts may also end up in a civil court if the harmed person decides to seek monetary damages for the harm.

interest aggregation stage The process of bolstering the support of other legislators through cooperation and compromises. Proponents of the law mediate among groups in order to get their legislation heard.

intermediate court of appeals The first level of appeal court in a state court system; if the loser in a trial wishes to appeal, this is the next step.

intermediate scrutiny Also known as heightened scrutiny, this level of judicial review is higher than the rational basis test, and states that an important governmental interest—federal or state—must be served in separating people by race or gender.

internalization of patterns of behavior The incorporation of the value or values implicit in a new law, such as "marriage equality is good and beneficial to all."

interpretive rules Issued by an agency to guide both its staff and regulated parties as to how rules will be interpreted and carried out.

intersectionality A relatively new approach to studying and understanding social stratification that recognizes people are situated in differing locations within the social structural hierarchy that attach to disadvantages and advantages. Gender, age, race, socioeconomic status, sexuality, and disability affect one's location in the social structure, social identity, and access to power.

investigation The gathering of information by an administrative agency in order to, for example, regulate industry, prosecute fraud, collect taxes, or protect workers. Most administrations use formal and informal proceedings; the authority to investigate is one of the functions that distinguish agencies from courts; investigative power of government agencies is conferred by Congress.

irrational law A legal system that is not systematic, not written, and based on customs, religious beliefs, or folk wisdom.

Islamic legal systems Exist mainly in Middle Eastern Arab countries, in most of North Africa (Morocco, Egypt), and in the Pakistani and Bangledeshi regions of the Indian subcontinent; law and religion are inseparable; law is based on the *Koran* (Qur'an)—the word of God as given by the Prophet—and the *Sunna*, a companion book to the *Koran* containing statements, deeds, moral precepts, sayings, and other rules to live by from the Prophet; also based on judicial consensus and analogical reasoning.

judges Lawyers who have reached a high point in their chosen profession; determine the outcomes of important legal matters, interpret the rules that govern court proceedings, and provide instructions to the jury in a trial.

juries A group of citizens selected and sworn to hear evidence in a trial and to render a decision based on the evidence.

juries Citizen bodies seen as coming between the state and the accused.

juris doctor, or J.D. A doctorate of jurisprudence, the advanced degree earned after completion of law school; a doctorate of jurisprudence is typically a three-year degree and the entry-level professional degree for aspiring lawyers who must also pass the bar exam in the state where they will practice law.

jurisprudence The scientific study of law.

jurisprudential approach to law This approach argues that the law should be internally consistent, orderly, and logical; it should be independent of religious, ideological, and political beliefs.

justiciability If a matter is eligible to be tried in a court of law and it is feasible that the courts can provide a remedy, the matter is justiciable; refers to a real and substantial controversy that is appropriate for adjudication.

labeling theory An approach to deviance and crime that emerged in the 1940s and 1950s; grew out of the symbolic interactionist perspective; set the groundwork for the social constructionist approach to social problems; explores how and why some acts are defined as deviant while others are not, and, further, how and why some deviant acts are then labeled as not simply deviant, but criminal; the act itself is not as significant as the social reactions to the act.

latent functions The not-so-obvious and unforeseen functions of social phenomena.

law A body of norms or rules that regulates actions and interactions of individuals, groups, institutions, and societies; laws are the codified social norms of society.

lawyers Highly trained professionals who turn complaints or wrongs into legal disputes.

legal positivism A scientific approach to law that examines objective social conditions, such as how culture and religious beliefs affect legal norms.

legal pragmatism The notion that the law only makes sense if it works in its practical applications; laws are enacted by human beings for human beings and therefore must make sense in their daily lives.

legal realism A school of thought that argues that laws should be grounded in reality and benefit the larger society; judges are responsible for formulating law rather than just finding it in the law books; they also make decisions on the basis of what is right and just before sorting through legal precedents, which can be found to support almost any decision; values, personal background, and preferences are part of the process of legal decision-making; judges must know the historical, economic and political aspects of the law to fulfill their functions; there is no absolute certainty in the law.

legal standing A prerequisite to litigation/adjudication; the individual, groups, or organizations involved in a dispute have some legal status or stake in the outcome of the case.

legislative rules Constitute the body of law passed by administrative agencies; they are administrative statutes.

legitimate authority The expectation of obedience based on appropriate, official rule; legitimate authority derives from codified law enacted by governmental leaders.

litigants The disputants involved in the legal conflict; can be organizations, individuals, government agencies, or other groups.

litigation Adjudication and litigation are used interchangeably; both are the process of settling an issue through a court hearing—whether, civil, criminal, or administrative; this formal, public proceeding has the highest level of institutional legitimacy. Legal procedures and patterns of reasoning are used to determine how the dispute is defined as a case, processed through the court, and understood by legal professionals. It is an adversarial process: a win-or-lose scenario.

litigious Prone to engage in lawsuits to settle even minor disputes.

lobbyists Paid professionals, both individuals and organizations, that seek to influence the legislative process in favor of their clients; represent special interest groups such as large businesses or entire industries (e.g., health care, encompassing professional groups like the health insurance industry, private health insurance companies, and the American Medical Association). Some lobbyists represent causes, for example, the League of Women Voters, Mothers Against Drunk Driving (MADD), and the National Rifle Association.

lobbyists, lobbying groups Paid representatives of special interests, lobbyists argue for or against legislation being considered by Congress.

lower courts (aka inferior courts) Include both civil and criminal courts and other specialized areas, e.g., family courts and probate courts dealing with distribution of property such as contested wills; the lower courts include county and municipal courts and small claims courts.

mandatory arbitration clauses Often written into employment or service contracts; they force the parties to enter arbitration and preclude or preempt the parties' ability to enter into a lawsuit on their own behalf.

manifest functions The intended, obvious functions of individual actions, social structures, and social policies.

mechanical solidarity Persistent, ongoing expectations established in traditional, agrarian societies, with simple division of labor, similarity of tasks, overall similarity, and homogeneity.

mediation Aims at securing an agreement among disputing parties that cannot be settled through negotiation; does not have formal legal procedures and rules; involves a neutral third party, known as the mediator.

mediation-arbitration or med-arb Combined into one process called med-arb; a dispute processing method often used in employment contract disputes; typically, the same person serves as both mediator and arbitrator.

mediator A third party hired in a dispute resolution who does not have power or resources to impose a settlement or to make a decision that either side must accept; acts as a facilitator and a go-between, with no formal authority to settle a matter but must rely on their own communication skills.

#MeToo Movement Phrase first used by African-American activist Tarana Burke in 2006 to help girls and women who have experienced sexual violence; by 2017, in response to widespread reports of sexual assaults and numerous forms of harassment in the entertainment industry, the phrase with the hashtag was used to create an online movement against sexual assault and harassment in all areas of professional and social life.

mini-trial A private, consensual process in which attorneys for each party make brief presentations of their case as they would at a trial; a neutral advisor and representatives from each side observe the presentations; representatives attempt to settle the dispute with the help of the neutral observer.

miscegenation The mixing of races.

misdemeanor A less-serious criminal transgression punishable by a fine or a year or less in jail.

mobilization stage Stage of lawmaking in which legislators exert pressures, persuasions, or control on behalf of a measure by someone or some bodies who can take direct action to secure enactment.

modern legal systems Contain all of the structural features of transitional systems but in greater numbers and more complex, specialized arrangements; in modern societies law grows in size and becomes increasingly centralized and bureaucratized; in modern legal systems, the rule of law prevails.

modernization The shift from traditional, agrarian-based economies to modern, industrial-based economic structures in which democracy prevails.

modification Stage of lawmaking in which legislators alter the proposed law in a way that ensures it will be brought before the legislature and passed into law; the law may go through several drafts as the people who write the legislation try to ensure that their version makes it to the floor of the Senate and passes.

moral approach to law A perspective of law based on the idea that law is rooted in some underlying beliefs about the nature of human beings and what is right and what is wrong; the moral approach is associated with claims of universality or commonality.

mores Standards of behavior that are more important to the social structure than folkways, but not so important that they have been written into law.

morphology In Donald Black's variables of social life, morphology is the shape of society—the aspects of social life that can be measured by social differentiation or degree of interdependence, e.g., division of labor.

natural law A notion of law as a universal entity, applicable to all humans; based on the assumption that through reason, the nature of human beings can be known and that this knowledge can provide the basis for the social and legal ordering of human existence.

naturalization The process by which a foreign citizen attains U.S. citizenship after he or she fulfills the requirements established by Congress in the Immigration and Nationality Act; a naturalized U.S. citizen has all of the rights and freedoms as a citizen born in the United States.

Naturalization Act of 1790 Mandated that any foreign-born, free white person could apply for citizenship, as long as he or she had lived in the United States for at least two years. At this time, indentured servants, free Blacks, and slaves were not regarded as citizens.

negative sanctions Punishments for violations of norms that can include fines, community service, probation, or time in jail or prison.

negligence Failure to exercise a degree of care that a person should exercise under the same circumstances; people should be able to assume protection against unreasonable risk.

negotiation Participants enter into this process voluntarily; to negotiate means that the two parties work with one another to reach some type of settlement or agreement on a matter; arranged by the disputants or by the parties in the dispute, without a third party involved, who attempt to settle a dispute through discussions, dialogue, compromise, and bargaining.

norms Established rules of conduct.

occupational crimes Crimes committed by individuals on their jobs, where the jobs are occupations of the middle- to upper-middle class.

organic solidarity The persistent, ongoing expectations found in modern, industrialized societies with a complex division of labor, specialization of tasks, diversity, and heterogeneity.

organization In Donald Black's variables of social life, organization is the capacity for collective action, the degrees of centralized governance, and a centralized economy.

organizational employment As the number of professionals grows, they become more bureaucratized and decision-making powers grow more centralized; the professional autonomy and expertise that drew people to the profession are circumscribed by its bureaucratic structure.

parole The supervised release of an inmate from jail or prison based on a decision made by a legally designated paroling authority; used after incarceration and can act as an incentive for good behavior during the period of confinement.

partnering A form of mediation that typically addresses disputes in construction contracts; the process involves daylong discussions about the potential problems and pitfalls that could arise in large, complex building projects.

penal (or criminal) codes Documents that publish a jurisdiction's criminal laws and outline the corresponding penalties for breaking those laws; penal codes at both the state and federal levels, combined with criminal justice systems, are the most highly structured formal systems of control used in the United States.

peremptory challenges Exclusions of potential jurors who a lawyer thinks will be unsympathetic to his or her arguments; no explanation is needed—the lawyer simply asks that the potential juror be excluded and the judge excuses the person; each side has a fixed number of peremptory challenges, but usually the defense has more.

personal property Any item owned by an individual or family; personal property can range from a wedding ring, to a bicycle, to a television, to a sports team.

petit jury An ordinary jury used to determine issues of fact in criminal and civil cases and to reach a verdict; composed of 12 members—typically, some jurisdictions allow six-person juries—and required to be unanimous.

plaintiffs People who bring the complaint to the court in a civil trial.

police The first step in the process of criminal law; protect the public and provide community service; designated as the governmental department, bureau, or agency of a city, township, county or nation-state formally charged with the responsibilities of maintaining public order, preserving the peace, providing emergency services, preventing crime, detecting criminal activity, and enforcing criminal law.

precedents Cases previously decided by judges that become examples used to resolve similar cases.

preponderance of the evidence A standard of proof the plaintiff in a civil case must meet: present evidence that is more convincing than the defendant's evidence that the harm was likely caused by the defendant.

private disputes Occur when there is a disagreement among individual citizens or private business entities—torts or private wrongs; can include matters of family law such as a divorce or a custody case, cases brought to the courts by neighbors, or private disputes between businesses.

private law A branch of law that comprises the legal norms that regulate relations among individuals, and among associations of individuals, in social and economic relationships such as marriage law, contract law, and adoption law.

private sphere The realm of home and hearth, of childbearing and child-rearing that are unpaid and undervalued.

probation Used in lieu of incarceration; a sentence served outside of jail or prison custody but under the supervision of the criminal justice system by a probation officer, or a prison sentence that is suspended.

procedural law Concerned with how laws are implemented, enforced, carried out, and modified.

procedural rules Identify a governmental agency's organization, describe its methods of operation, and enumerate the requirements of its practice for rulemaking and adjudicative hearings.

professionalization The establishment of a body of expert knowledge, group solidarity within the profession, self-regulation and autonomy for practitioners, authority over clients, licensing the practice, and a code of ethics; special interest control over a field of expertise or a type of work.

profit per partner (PPP) A metric that law schools use to measure the amount of profits individual lawyers bring in against other lawyers within and outside of their firm.

property A commodity that can be owned or traded; an item of value that can appreciate in value.

property disputes Disagreements addressed by civil courts about any item that is owned, has an exchangeable value, or adds to one's estate.

prosecutor An individual lawyer hired to represent the interests of the state against a criminal defendant; at the level of state governance, there are district attorneys (DAs), assistant district attorneys (ADAs), and the attorney general (AG), who leads all state prosecutors as the chief legal officer.

public defendant disputes Involve a public, governmental entity as the defendant—the party being sued—in a trial. The civil rights movement's challenge to the separate but equal protection guarantee is one of the most famous of such cases in U.S. history. In the 1954 case, *Brown v. the Board of Education of Topeka, KS*, a group of citizens sued the city's government over its segregated school system. They argued that racially segregated schools violated the Equal Protection Clause of the Fourteenth Amendment of the U.S. Constitution.

public law Institutes the structure of governments, such as the establishment clause in the First Amendment of the U.S. Constitution.

public law The system of legal norms that directly regulate actions by the state, state officials, and people acting as agents of the state.

public sphere The realm of paid employment, civic life, and all arenas of power, such as the market, property ownership, the economy, religious hierarchies, politics and governance, higher education, professions, and law.

public-initiated disputes Brought about by the government itself to uphold the law or punish those who break the law; the most common form are criminal cases where the defendant is charged with breaking the law of the state or federal laws.

punitive damages Also known as exemplary damages; awarded to the plaintiff above and beyond the actual damages; punish the wrongful party and are typically awarded in cases involving willful and malicious misconduct.

racial formation Denotes the sociohistorical processes that have created and re-created race-based categories over time; the idea that those in the dominant group have the power to define groups in accordance with the dominant group's needs.

racial groups People who are differentiated from the dominant group by perceived physical characteristics, such as skin color, hair texture, and facial features.

racial prerequisite cases Legal challenges to race and citizenship under the Naturalization Act of 1790; while the requirements for citizenship were continuously changing, the White racial requirement remained in place for 162 years; Whiteness was not clearly established, thus, for over a century and a half, legal challenges to Whiteness were brought before State Supreme Judicial courts, Federal Circuit courts, and the U.S. Supreme Court.

radical feminist jurisprudence An approach to legal scholarship that acknowledges differences between men and women as well as differences among women in terms of race, age, socioeconomic class, and sexuality; also known as the asymmetrical approach or essentialism; radical feminists argue that women and men are not the same and that some rights should be based on the specific needs of women depending upon their situations.

rational basis Also known as ordinary scrutiny, this judicial review standard states that the court must illustrate some basis for differential treatment even if the reason is simply tradition or custom.

rational law A legal system that requires the highest degree of institutional, procedural, and intellectual independence of law; systematically organized, rule-bound, based on logical interpretation of meaning, and oriented toward intellectual pursuits of the truth.

rationalistic approach to lawmaking Looks at how laws—mainly criminal laws—are created as reasonable means of protecting people from harm; crimes are socially, physically, and psychologically injurious and should be prohibited by a governing body.

rationality Reliance on specifically legal principles and rules for making decisions that are logically applied to particular cases.

real property Large, tangible items that can be purchased and exchanged, more commonly referred to as real estate: houses, land, buildings.

reformist feminist jurisprudence Focuses on sameness, the idea that women should be treated the same as men in the eyes of the law; reformist feminists argue that changes can be made within the system and that focusing on differences weakens women's abilities to be treated equally or on par with men; also known as an assimilationist approach or a symmetrical approach to women's rights.

rehabilitation A goal of punishment that attempts to bring about changes in offenders' future behavior.

remedial law A type of law that attempts to work toward a resolution to a problem, to sort matters out, and to restore order.

rent-a-judge A type of arbitration where people attempt to avoid entering into a formal court of law; they hire judges, sometimes a retired judge or one who works on the side, to hear the case and make a decision; the proceedings and outcomes are private.

repressive law A legal system in which punishment is the main goal; norms and rules are highly moralistic and repressive.

restitutive law A highly specialized legal system that seeks to maintain general patterns of order and rights; oriented toward reparations, rehabilitation of offenders, and compensation of victims.

restoration A purpose of punishment; attempts to place a crime within its community context and allows the offender to make amends—to repair the harm done to the victim and the larger community; provides the offender with a second chance and is most often used for juvenile and adult nonviolent offenders as an alternative to formal court proceedings.

retribution Punishment for wrongs committed; also a form of public vengeance against the offender.

revenge pornography Also known as revenge porn, a type of cybercrime that did not exist even a decade ago; involves the sharing of sexually explicit photos or videos of individuals without their consent on the Internet and social media. Since not all cases are motivated by revenge, some jurisdictions use the term nonconsensual pornography or NCP to describe this illicit behavior.

Romano-Germanic legal systems or civil legal systems Legal systems whose development was greatly influenced by Roman Law, a collection of codes compiled in the Corpus Juris Civilis; found in most parts of Europe and many former colonies of France, Portugal, Spain, Italy, and Belgium, as well as countries that westernized in the nineteenth and twentieth centuries; civil systems are based on legal codes or bodies of laws.

routinization The breaking down of work and expertise into smaller, mundane tasks that can be accomplished by those without formal education and training.

rule of law A concept—or term—that encompasses many ideas; protects people from the unjust and arbitrary exercise of power; allows people access to justice; and grants basic protection of personal liberties.

rulemaking The most important function of an administrative agency; draws up rules and regulations to apply to the areas it oversees, such as worker safety regulations for the Occupational Health and Safety Administration; primary mission of these government agencies is to make rules or policies.

sanction A method of enforcing societal norms; negative sanctions are punishments such as jail or prison time; positive sanctions reward people for good behavior, such as praise.

scientific jury selection The use of paid experts, usually psychologists or social psychologists, to replace guessing, gut reactions, and lawyers' intuition in choosing jury members; attempts to make jury selection processes more predictable.

scientific racism Early twentieth-century sciences or pseudo-sciences that attempted to establish racial distinctions between and among groups of people.

second-wave feminism The second period of activism for women's rights; began in the 1960s and lasted until the late 1980s; key focal points included social and economic justice, access to full employment and equal pay, and reproductive rights.

separate spheres ideology The set of ideas that structured the world into a dichotomy, where men occupied the realm of paid work and political activity and women were expected to concentrate their energies within the private sphere of marriage and family.

settlement A formal resolution to a civil legal dispute that occurs without the matter going before a judge or jury.

settlement counsel A process within the field of business law; involves lawyers who specialize in negotiation techniques between business interests; settlement counselors often work within large business law firms but have training in modern dispute resolution techniques.

shadow jury An elaborate technique used by scientific jury selection experts to gain feedback for lawyers on how to try their cases; matches people of the same gender, race, age, and income level to each real juror in an attempt to predict the outcome of the trial and change course when needed; sits in on the actual trial and sees and hears all the same information as the real jurors; provides critiques of the trial as the proceedings unfold, giving feedback to the lawyers who hired them on their performances, the witnesses, and the evidence presented.

Sherman Antitrust Act A federal act passed in 1890 that determined the boundaries of corporate power and governmental regulation; primarily concerned with the power of banks and railroads in determining prices and access to credit; attempted to make market and industrial monopolies illegal.

small claims courts A type of trial court found in every state that has limited jurisdiction to hear civil cases between private litigants such as small business matters, debts, landlord-tenant disputes, motor vehicle repair costs, or small contract issues; disputants usually represent themselves, although in some states they are allowed to bring lawyers; monetary limit allowed varies by state.

social construction Anything that emerges through human interactions that takes place within linguistic, economic, political, and legal contexts.

social constructionist perspective Also referred to as the social definitionist approach and the moral entrepreneur approach; an approach, or set of approaches, that views society and social knowledge as actively and creatively produced through human interaction; believes that social norms and laws exist because people have made them real through language and interaction, social conventions, habits, and etiquette.

social contract The cornerstone of an organized society; the idea that individuals willingly enter into a state of governance in return for protection of their individual freedoms, rights, and general social welfare.

social control In Donald Black's variables of social life, social control refers to the normative aspects of society and how a society responds to deviant behavior.

social control through external pressure Occurs when behavior is brought in line through processes—both positive and negative sanctions—that lie outside of the individual.

socialist legal systems Systems of law based on Marxist-Leninist ideology; emphasize communal values, the popular will (as perceived by the Communist Party), no separation of powers, the idea that personal ownership (not *private* ownership) cannot be used as a means of producing income or profit, and nationalized state-owned property, means of production, and raw materials.

socialization process The lifelong learning of attitudes, behaviors, values, and beliefs appropriate to members of a particular society; the internalization of social norms.

society The largest form of human group; members share a common territory and governance, as well as a common culture and social institutions such as the family, the economy, and law.

sociolegal theories Schools of thought within the scientific study of law that view law as integral to social life; asserts that law cannot be understood apart from the realities of social life; heavily influenced by the social sciences—most notably, sociology, economics, and social psychology.

sociological approach to law A perspective on law primarily concerned with the social aspects of bodies of norms, such as the effects of a law on social action, how the law affects people's beliefs about the social world, and how social and legal institutions are organized and change as society changes.

solidarity Persistent and ongoing expectations that people establish with one another that allow them to take their social world for granted.

solicitors Practitioners of law in the United Kingdom who work on legal matters outside the courts and who learned as apprentices; provide legal advice and act on behalf of clients outside of court.

specialization The growth of very specific expert knowledge in particular subfields or sections within a profession.

specific or individual deterrence Punishment meant to deter a specific offender from reoffending.

stare decisis A Latin term meaning let the decision stand; the *stare decisis* doctrine is the principle of precedent and central to common law, where cases are decided based upon previous rulings and analogous cases.

state supreme court The court of last resort at the state level; reviews cases decided by the intermediate appeals courts.

status offense An act or conduct defined as a juvenile offense, such as truancy or running away, that would not be a crime if it were committed by an adult.

statutory law Laws made by legislators—laws, statutes, and ordinances.

stratification In Donald Black's variables of social life, stratification is the system of social inequalities of wealth, power, privilege, and educational attainment.

strict liability Torts of strict liability address private wrongs in which the plaintiff does not need to prove that the defendant acted intentionally or negligently; rather, the plaintiff must establish that he or she was injured and that the defendant caused the injury.

strict scrutiny This level of judicial review stands as the most rigorous; under strict scrutiny, the government must illustrate a compelling interest to differentiate people by race or sex.

substantive law A legal system tied to either a political order or a moral religious order; neither autonomous nor independent.

substantive law The area of law that covers rights, duties, and prohibitions—what is and is not allowed.

symbolic interactionism A sociological paradigm that views the social world as constantly created and re-created through the use of symbols: language, signs, and other cultural objects; takes a micro-level view of society and examines how individuals and social groups make sense of the world around them through their interactions with others.

third-wave feminists Women's rights activists who reinvigorated topics that the second-wave feminists addressed but that did not fully take hold; also addresses some failures of second-wave feminists, such as the lack of diversity and inclusivity among its ranks.

tort A private wrong or an infringement on a right.

tort law The law of private wrongs or injuries.

tort reform A collection of ideas geared toward changing the civil law system in ways that limit the number of civil lawsuits and the amount of damages that can be awarded in such suits.

tortfeasor One who commits a tort, a private wrong.

total correctional population The number of Americans under the control of the criminal justice system.

transitional legal systems Found in advanced agrarian and early industrial societies where economic, educational, and political systems are increasingly separated from kinship relationships; includes basic legal structures such as some written laws, courts, enforcement agencies, legislative structures, public/private law distinctions, criminal law distinguished from torts, and procedural/substantive law distinctions.

trial courts The place where most civil and criminal cases are originally heard, often before a jury; enforce laws on a case-by-case basis by applying relevant legal rules to the facts of the case and handle both civil and criminal cases; in a civil case, the plaintiff's lawyer initiates the action; in a criminal case, a prosecutor begins the court action against a defendant; focus on the facts of the case—witnesses, documents, evidence.

typology A system of classification that helps break a large concept into smaller categories, making it easier to grasp and apply to real-world scenarios.

upskirting The clandestine taking of cellphone pictures or videos up a person's skirt or other loose clothing.

urbanization The wide-scale movement of people from rural, agrarian areas of the country to developing metropolitan hubs, which tend to be more diverse and heterogeneous than traditional, agricultural-based communities; urban areas are more densely populated and present different social problems and challenges that call for centralized legal structures.

utilitarianism A philosophical theory that assumes actions are right if they benefit the greatest number of people; all human actions are calculated in terms of their likelihood of bringing happiness and pleasure, or unhappiness and pain.

vagrancy The condition of wandering from place to place without a job or occupation; homelessness is the more common term in modern language.

venireperson The term for an empaneled juror.

voir dire The jury selection process; French for "to see, to tell"; one of the most important jobs of the trial lawyer. Prospective jurors are questioned first by the judge, then by the attorneys representing the defense and the prosecution in criminal cases or by the opposing lawyers in civil cases.

voyeurism Deriving sexual pleasure from secretly observing the sex organs or sexual acts of other people; criminal voyeurism statutes typically cover places in which people have a reasonable expectation of privacy.

white collar crime Illegal acts carried out by individuals in the course of professional occupations.

References

"About NYPD." Retrieved February 20, 2018, from http://www1.nyc. gov/site/nypd/about/about-nypd/about-nypd-landing.page. "Attorney." https://www.etymonline.com/word/attorney. "Lawyer." https://www.ety-monline.com/word/lawyer.

Abel, David. 2017. "Cuts to Staffing at DEP Take Toll." *The Boston Globe,* March 9, A1.

Adler, Freda, William S. Mueller, Gerard O., and W. Laufer. 1998. *Criminology* 3rd ed. Boston: McGraw-Hill.

Allen, Scott. 2005. "Relief in Court Is Rare for Hospitals' Injured." *The Boston Globe,* March 13, A1.

American Museum of Tort Law. n. d. "A Museum with a Message." Winstead, CT: https://www.tortmuseum.org/about-us/.

American Bar Association. 2015. National Lawyer Population Survey. http://www.americanbar.org/resources_for_lawyers/profession_statistics. html

American Bar Association. "Mission and Goals." n.d. Washington, DC. https://www.americanbar.org/about_the_aba/aba-mission-goals.html.

American Bar Association. 2017, January. "A Current Glance at Women in the Law." ABA Commission on Women in the Profession." Washington, DC. https://www.americanbar.org/content/dam/aba/marketing/women/ current_glance_statistics_january2017.authcheckdam.pdf.

American Bar Association. 2018a, May 11. "New ABA Data Reveals [sic] Rise in Number of U.S. Lawyers, 15% Since 2008." Washington, DC. Author.https://www.americanbar.org/news/abanews/aba-news-archives/2018/05/new_aba_data_reveals.html.

American Bar Association. 2018b. "National Lawyer Population Survey: 10-Year Trend in Lawyer Demographics." Washington, DC. https://www. americanbar.org/content/dam/ aba/administrative/market_research/National_ Lawyer_Population_Demographics_2008-2018.authcheckdam.pdf.

American Bar Association. n.d. *How the Courts Work*. https://www.americanbar.org/groups/public_education/resources/law_related_educationnetwork/how_courts_work/cases_settling.html.

American Bar Association. n.d. "Presidential Initiative: Achieving Ling-Term Careers for Women in Law." Washington, DC. Author.https://www.americanbar.org/content/dam/aba/administrative/office_president/Initiative_Overview.authcheckdam.pdf.

American Bar Association. "Part I: What Is the Rule of Law?" Chicago. Retrieved May 9, 2019, from https://www.americanbar.org/advocacy/rule_of_law/what-is-the-rule-of-law/.

Asher, Herbert. 1973. "The Learning of Legislative Norms." *American Political Science Review* 67:499–513.

Association of American Law Schools. 2017. "Law School Demographics." Washington, DC.

Auden, W. H. 1983. "Law Like Love." pp. 1101–1102 in *The Norton Anthology of Poetry*, 3rd ed., edited by A. Allison. New York: Norton.

Baer, Judith A. 1999. *Our Lives Before the Law: Constructing a Feminist Jurisprudence*. Princeton, NJ: Princeton University Press.

Baer, Judith A. 2011. "Feminist Theory and Law." *The Oxford Handbook of Political Science*, edited by R. E. Goodin. New York: Oxford University Press. http://www.oxfordhandbooks.com/view/10.1093/oxfordhb/9780199604456.001.0001/oxfordhb-9780199604456-e-016?print=pdf.

Ball, Molly. 2015. "How Gay Marriage Became a Constitutional Right." *The Atlantic*, July 1. https://www.theatlantic.com/politics/archive/2015/07/gay-marriage-supreme-court-politics-activism/397052/.

Ballou, Brian R. 2012. "Haverhill Teen Convicted in Texting-While-Driving Case." *The Boston Globe*, June 6, B1.

Bar Council of the United Kingdom. n.d. "Inns of Court." London. https://www.barcouncil.org.uk/about-the-bar/what-is-the-bar/inns-of-court/.

Beccaria, Cesare. [1764] 1872. *On Crimes and Punishments*. Albany, NY: W.C. Little and Co.

Becker, Howard S. 1963. *The Outsiders: Studies in the Sociology of Deviance*. New York: The Free Press.

Bentham, Jeremy. 1789. *An Introduction to the Principles of Morals and Legislation*. London: Oxford at the Clarendon Press.

Berger, Peter L. and Thomas Luchmann. 1966. *The Social Construction of Reality*. New York: Doubleday.

Bickel, Alexander M. 1975. *The Morality of Consent*. New Haven, CT: Yale University Press.

Bier, David. 2018. "Trump Might Not Have Gotten His 'Muslim Ban' but He Sure Got His Extreme Vetting." *Washington Post*, December 10.

Bill of Rights Institute. Federalist Papers No. 51. Retrieved October 11, 2017, from https://www.billofrightsinstitute.org/founding-documents/primary-source-documents/the-federalist-papers/federalist-papers-no-51/.

Black, Donald. [1976] 2010. *The Behavior of Law,* Special Ed. Bingley: Emerald Publishing Group, Ltd.

Black, Donald. 1989. *Sociological Justice.* New York: Oxford University Press.

Black, Donald. 1993. *The Social Structure of Right and Wrong.* San Diego, CA: Academic Press, Inc.

Black, Henry Campbell. 2001. *Black's Law Dictionary,* 5th ed. Minneapolis, MN: West Publishing Co.

Blackstone, William. [1765] 2016. *Commentaries on the Laws of England in Four Books.* Oxford: Oxford University Press.

Block, Fred. 1977. "Beyond Corporate Liberalism." *Social Problems* 24(3):352–361.

Bluestein, Greg. 2009. "Sex Offenders Set Up Camp in GA." *The Boston Globe,* September 29, A11.

Bonta, James, Suzanne Wallace-Capretta, Jennifer Rooney, and Kevin Mcanoy. 2002. An Outcome Evaluation of a Restorative Justice Alternative to Incarceration." *Contemporary Justice Review* 5:319–338.

Boston Law Collaborative, LLC. n.d. "Collaborative Law." Boston. https://blc.law/services-for-families/collaborative-law/.

Botelho, Alyssa A. 2013. "Driver in Texting-Linked Crash Dies." *The Boston Globe,* June 18, B2.

Bowers, William J. and Glenn L. Pierce. 1980. "Deterrence or Brutalization: What Is the Effect of Executions?" *Crime and Delinquency* 26:453–484.

Bradwell v. Illinois. 1873. 83 U.S. 16 Wallace 131.

Brown, DeNeen. 2016. "He Helped Make Legal History in Loving v. Virginia. At 80, He's Still Fighting for Justice." *Washington Post,* December 10. https://www.washingtonpost.com/local/he-helped-make-legal-history-in-loving-v-virginia-at-80-hes-still-practicing-law/2016/12/10/e796f8a4-b726-11e6-b8df-600bd9d38a02_story.html?noredirect=on&utm_term=.4d4c42429d59.

Bruchard, Melissa. n.d. "Feminist Jurisprudence." *Internet Encyclopedia of Philosophy.* https://www.iep.utm.edu/jurisfem/

Brundage, James A. 2010. *The Medieval Origins of the Legal Profession: Canonists, Civilians, and Courts.* Chicago: University of Chicago Press.

Bump, Philip. 2015. "The New Congress is 80 Percent White, 80 Percent Male and 92 Percent Christian." *Washington Post,* January 5. https://www.washingtonpost.com/news/the-fix/wp/2015/01/05/the-new-congress-is-80-percent-white-80-percent-male-and-92-percent-christian/?utm_term=.5429b1fadd24

Bureau of Justice Statistics. 2018a. "The Justice System." March 14. https://www.bjs.gov/content/justsys.cfm.

Bureau of Justice Statistics, Office of Justice Programs. 2018b. "In 2016 State and Federal Prison Populations Declined for a Third Consecutive Year." January 1. https://www.bjs.gov/content/pub/press/p16pr.cfm.

Bureau of Justice Statistics, Office of Justice Programs. 2018c. "Total Correctional Population, 2016." March 14. https://www.bjs.gov/index.cfm?tid=11&ty=tp.

Bureau of Labor Statistics, U.S. Department of Labor. 2017. "Lawyers." *Occupational Outlook Handbook*. Washington, DC.

Bureau of Labor Statistics. 2017. "Census of Fatal Occupational Injuries Summary, 2017." U.S. Department of Labor. https://www.bls.gov/news.release/cfoi.nr0.htm.

Burtka, Allison Torres. n.d. "*Liebeck v. McDonald's.*" Winstead, CT: American Museum of Tort Law.

Burton, William C. 2007. *Burton's Legal Thesaurus*, 4th ed. New York: McGraw-Hill. https://legal-dictionary.thefreedictionary.com/corporation.

Butler, Brooke. 2008. "Caveats of the Death-Qualified Jury: Ways Capital Defense Attorneys Use Psycholegal Research to Their Advantage." *The Jury Expert: The Art and Science of Litigation Advocacy* 20(1):1–7.

Butler, Judith. 2015. *Undoing Gender*. New York: Routledge.

Carlisle, John. 2013. "One-Man Police Force Protects Small Michigan Town." *USA Today*, May 5. https://www.usatoday.com/story/news/nation/2013/05/05/one-man-police-force/2135569/

Carpenter, Dale. 2013.*Flagrant Conduct: The Story of Lawrence v. Texas*. New York: W.W. Norton & Co.

Carrington, Kerry, Joseph Donnermeyer, and Walter DeKeseredy. 2014. "Intersectionality, Rural Criminology, and Re-Imagining the Boundaries of Critical Criminology." *Critical Criminology* 22:463–477.

Carroll, Matt. 2008. "Teenagers Feeling Sting of Tougher Driving Laws." *The Boston Globe*. January 9, A1, A6.

Carson, Rachel. 1962. *Silent Spring*. Boston: Houghton Mifflin.

Chambliss, William J. 1964. "A Sociological Analysis of the Law of Vagrancy." *Social Problems* 12:45–69.

Chambliss, William J. 1967. "Types of Deviance and the Effectiveness of Legal Sanctions." *Wisconsin Law Review* 67:703–719.

Chambliss, William J. 2004. "A Sociological Analysis of the Law of Vagrancy." pp. 87–107 in *Social Problems, Law, and Society*, edited by A. K. Stout, R. A. Dello Buono, and W. Chambliss. New York: Rowman & Littlefield Publishers, Inc.

Chambliss, William J. and Aida Y. Hass. 2012. *Criminology: Connecting Theory, Research, and Practice*. New York: McGraw-Hill.

Chambliss, William J. and Robert Seidman. 1971. *Law, Order, and Power.* Reading, MA: Addison-Wesley.

Chesney-Lind, Meda, and Lisa Pasko. 2013. *The Female Offender: Girls, Women, and Crime.* Los Angeles, CA: Sage.

Chicago Tribune Staff and Hawbaker, K. T. 2018. "#MeToo: A Timeline." *The Chicago Tribune*, December 6. http://www.chicagotribune.com/lifestyles/ct-me-too-timeline-20171208-htmlstory.html.

Clements, Jeffrey D. 2009. "Beyond Citizens United v. FEC: Re-Examining Corporate Rights." Washington, DC: *American Constitution Society for Law and Policy.* Retrieved September 16, 2017, from https://www.acslaw.org/sites/default/files/Clements_Re-examining_Corporate_Rights_0.pdf.

Clinard, Marshall B. and Robert F. Meir. 2016. *Sociology of Deviant Behavior*, 16th ed. Boston: Cengage Learning.

Coates, Ta-Nehisi. 2015. "The Black Family in the Age of Mass Incarceration." *The Atlantic,* October. https://www.theatlantic.com/magazine/archive/2015/10/the-black-family-in-the-age-of-mass-incarceration/403246/

Cohen, Rachel and Ailsa Chang. 2018. "Federal Legislation Seeks Ban on Shackling Pregnant Inmates." National Public Radio, All Things Considered, December 5. https://www.npr.org/sections/health-shots/2018/12/05/673757680/federal-legislation-seeks-ban-on-shackling-of-pregnant-inmates.

Cohen, Stanley. [1972] 2002. *Folk Devils and Moral Panics.* New York: Routledge.

Coleman, James S. 1966. *Equality of Educational Opportunity.* Washington, DC: U.S. Government Printing Office.

Collins, Patricia Hill. 2009. *Black Feminist Thought.* New York: Routledge.

Congressional Research Service. 2018, July 11. "Membership of the 115th Congress: A Profile." R44762. Washington, DC.

Coontz, Stephanie. 1988. *The Social Origins of Private Life: A History of American Families, 1600–1900.* Brooklyn, NY: Verso.

Coontz, Stephanie. 1992. *The Way We Never Were: American Families and the Nostalgia Trap.* New York: Basic Books.

Craig v. Boren. 1976. 429 U.S. 190.

Crenshaw, Kimberlé. 1991. "Mapping the Margins: Intersectionality, Identity, Politics, and Violence against Women of Color." *Stanford Law Review* 43(6):1241–1299.

Crenshaw, Kimberlé. 2011. "Postscript." pp. 221–233 in *Framing Intersectionality: Debates on a Multifaceted Concept in Gender Studies*, edited by H. Lutz, M. T. H. Vivar, and L. Supik. Surrey: Ashgate.

Crosley Law Firm. "Law Terms: The Etymology and History of 'Passing the Bar.'" San Antonio, TX. https://crosleylaw.com/blog/law-terms-etymology-history-passing-bar/.

Curry, Allison E., Melissa R. Pfeiffer, Russell Localio, and Dennis R. Durbin. 2013. "Graduated Driver Licensing Decal Law: Effect on Young Probationary Drivers." *American Journal of Preventative Medicine* 44:1–7.

Danzig, Christopher. 2012. "Infographic of the Day: American Litigiousness Statistics That Will Make You Angry."

Darwin, Charles. 1859. *On the Origin of the Species.* New York: D. Appleton and Company.

Davis, Evan E. and Lynn Sherr. 2001. "A Conversation with Justice Ruth Bader Ginsburg." *The Record of the Association of the Bar of the City of New York.* Winter. 56:8–21.

De Tocqueville, Alexis. [1835] 1961. *Democracy in America,* edited by R. D. Heffner. New York: Mentor Books, p. 223.

Death Penalty Information Center. 2018. "Death Row Population by Race." https://deathpenaltyinfo.org/race-death-row-inmates-executed-1976. Updated October 1, 2018.

Death Penalty Information Center. 2018. "Fact Sheet." https://deathpenalty-info.org/documents/FactSheet.pdf. Updated March 28, 2018.

Deflem, Mathieu. 2008. *Sociology of Law: Visions of a Scholarly Tradition.* New York: Cambridge University Press.

DeKeseredy, Walter S., Amanda Hall-Sanchez, Molly Dragiewicz, and Callie M. Rennison. 2016. "Intimate Violence against Women in Rural Communities." pp. 171–179 in *The Routledge Handbook of Rural Criminology,* edited by J. F. Donnermeyer. New York: Routledge.

Delgado, Richard and Jean Stefancic. 2012. *Critical Race Theory: An Introduction,* 2nd ed. New York: New York University Press.

Dello Buono, Richard A. 2004. "Critical Perspectives in Law and Society: A Social Problems Approach." pp. 3–18 in *Social Problems, Law, and Society,* edited by Kathryn Stout, Richard Dello Buono, and William Chambliss. Lanham, MD: Rowman & Littlefield Publishers, Inc.

DeVelder, Carla. 2011, October 1. "Working for Uncle Sam: Government Jobs for Law School Grads." Washington, DC: American Bar Association. https://abaforlawstudents.com/2011/10/01/working-for-uncle-sam-government-jobs-law-grads/

DeVuono-Powell, S., C. Schweidler, A. Walter, and A. Zohrabi. 2015. *Who Pays: The True Costs of Incarceration on Families?* Oakland, CA: Ella Baker Center.

Dicey, Albert Venn. 1905. *Lectures on the Relation between Law and Public Opinion in England during the Nineteenth Century.* London: MacMillan.

Dickens, Charles. 1829. "The Execution of the Mannings." Letter to the Editor. *The Times,* November 13.

Dickerson, Caitlin. 2018. "Ida B. Wells, 1862–1931." *The New York Times*, March 8. https://www.nytimes.com/interactive/2018/obituaries/overlooked-ida-b-wells.html.

Dillon, Nancy. 2016. "Kardashian Sisters Hit with $180 Million Lawsuit over Alleged Blemishes in Kardashian Beauty Makeup Contract." *New York Daily News Online*, March 22. http://www.nydailynews.com/entertainment/gossip/kardashian-sisters-hit-180m-lawsuit-makeup-line-article-1.2573225.

Douglas, Davison M. 2010. "Jefferson's Vision Fulfilled." https://law.wm.edu/about/ourhistory/index.php.

Dred Scott v. Sandford, 1857. Transcript. www.ourdocuments.gov.

Dror, Yehezkel. 1970. "Law as a Tool of Directed Social Change: A Framework for Policy-Making." *American Behavioral Scientist* 13(4):553–559.

Dunbar, John. 2012. "The 'Citizens United' Decision and Why It Matters." Retrieved February 18, 2017, from https://www.publicintegrity.org/2012/10/18/11527/citizens-united-decision-and-why-it-matters.

Dunlap, Thomas R. 2015. *DDT, Silent Spring, and the Rise of Environmentalism*. Seattle, WA: University of Washington Press.

Durkheim, Emile. [1893] 1984. *The Division of Labor in Society*. New York: The Free Press.

Ecenbarger, William. 2012. *Kids for Cash: Two Judges, Thousands of Children and a 2.6 Million Dollar Kickback Scheme*. New York: The New Press.

Eggert, David. 2017. "Health Chief, 4 Others Charged with Involuntary Manslaughter in Flint." *The Boston Globe*, June 14, A1.

Eicher, Andrew. 2017. "Women's March National Co-Chair: Sharia Law is 'Reasonable,' and 'Misunderstood.'" CNSNews.com, January 25. Retrieved February 21, 2017, from https://www.cnsnews.com/news/article/andrew-eicher/womens-march-national-co-chair-says-sharia-law-reasonable-and.

Ellement, John R. and Andrew Ryan. 2008. "SJC Sees Possible Bias in Rape Case: Why Charge Only the Boy?" *The Boston Globe*, February 8, A1.

Engels, Friedrich. [1845]2009. *The Condition of the Working Class in England*. Oxford: Oxford University Press.

Erikson, Kai. T. 1966. *Wayward Puritans: A Study in the Sociology of Deviance*. New York: John Wiley.

Evan, William M. 1965. "Law as an Instrument of Social Change." pp. 285–293 in *Applied Sociology: Opportunities and Problems*, edited by Alvin W. Gouldner and S. M. Miller. New York: The Free Press.

Fair Arbitration Now. 2015. "Cell Phones." http://www.fairarbitrationnow.org/cell-phone-arbitration/.

Falcone, David N. 2005. *Dictionary of American Criminal Justice, Criminology, and Criminal Law*. Upper Saddle, NJ: Pearson/Prentice Hall.

Fang, Lee. 2014. "Where Have All the Lobbyists Gone?" *The Nation, February 19*. https://www.thenation.com/article/shadow-lobbying-complex/.

FAQs: Federal Judges, United States Courts. http://www.uscourts.gov/faqs-federal-judges.

Federal Bureau of Investigation. 2016. "Uniform Crime Reports." Washington, DC

Federal Stalking Laws. n.d. Retrieved June 23, 2017, from https://victimsofcrime.org/our-programs/stalking-resource-center/stalking-laws/federal-stalking-laws#61a.

Feeney, Mark. 2015. "Nader Museum: Informative at Any Speed." *The Boston Globe*, October 13.

Fields, Barbara. 1982. "Ideology and Race in American History." pp. 143–177 in *Race, Region, and Reconstruction: Essays*, edited by J. M. Kousser and J. M. McPherson. New York: Oxford University Press.

France, Anatole. 1923. *The Red Lily*. New York: Current Literature Publishing Company. Retrieved May 1, 2019, from books.google.com.

Ford, Matt. 2014. "Can Europe End the Death Penalty?" *The Atlantic*, February 18.

Fortin, Jacey and Matthew Haag. 2018. "Waterslide That Decapitated Boy Violated Basic Design Standards, Indictment Says." *New York Times*, March 27, A14.

Fox, Margalit. 2018. "Dovey Johnson Roundtree, Barrier-Breaking Lawyer and Officer, Is Dead at 104." *The New York Times*, May 22, A1.

Fred T. Korematsu Institute for Civil Rights and Education. n.d. "Fred T. Korematsu: Abbreviated Biography." San Francisco. http://www.korematsuinstitute.org/fred-t-korematsu-lifetime/

Friedman, Lawrence M. 1975. *The Legal System: A Social Science Perspective*. New York: Russell Sage Foundation.

Friedman, Lawrence M. 1977. *Law and Society: An Introduction*. Englewood Cliffs, NJ: Prentice Hall.

Friedman, Lawrence M. 1998. *American Law: An Introduction*, 2nd ed. New York: W.W. Norton & Co., Inc.

Friedman, Lawrence M. 2004. *Law in America: A Short History*. New York: A Modern Library Chronicles Book.

Friedman, Lawrence M. 2005. "Coming of Age: Law and Society Enters an Exclusive Club." *Annual Review of Law and Social Science* 1:1–16.

Friedmann, Wolfgang. 1959. *Law in a Changing Society*. Los Angeles: University of California Press.

Frontiero v. Richardson. 1973. 411 U.S. 677.

Galanter, Marc. 1984. "Worlds of Deals: Using Negotiation to Teach about Legal Process." *Journal of Legal Education* 34:268–276.

Galanter, Marc. 1974. "Why the 'Haves' Come Out Ahead: Speculations on the Limits of Legal Change." *Law and Society Review* 9(1):95–160.

Genzlinger, Neil. 2018. "Linda Brown, 75, Student at Center of Landmark Desegregation Case, Dies." *The New York Times*, A19.

Gershowitz, Adam M. 2007. "Imposing Caps on Capital Punishment." Faculty Publications. Paper 1251. http://scholarship.law.wm/facpubs/1251.

Gifis, Steven H. 1996. *Barron's Law Dictionary*. Hauppauge, NY: Barron's Educational Series, Inc.

Goldberg, Stephen B., Frank E. A. Sander, Nancy H. Roberts, and Sarah Rudolph Cole. 2012. *Dispute Resolution: Negotiation, Mediation, and Other Processes*, 6th ed. New York: Aspen Publishers.

Goldman, Sheldon, and Austin Sarat. 1989. *American Court Systems: Readings in Judicial Process and Behavior* 2nd ed. New York: Longman.

Governors Highway Safety Association. 2012. *Spotlight on Highway Safety: Teenage Driver Fatalities by State, 2012 Preliminary Data*. Washington, DC: Williams, Allan F.

Graham, Ruth. 2017. "N.H. Republicans Accidently Approve a Bill Allowing Pregnant Women to Commit Murder." June 22. Retrieved June 24, 2017, from http://www.slate.com/blogs/xx_factor/2017/06/22/n_h_republicans_accidentally_approved_a_bill_allowing_pregnant_women_to.html.

Green, Andrew. 2012. "Eisenhower Proclaims 'Law Day' May 1, 1958." *Politico*, May 1, n.p. Retrieved May 1, 2019, from https://www.politico.com/story/2012/05/eisenhower-proclaims-law-day-075750.

Grisham, John. 2008. *The Appeal*. New York: Doubleday.

Grossman, Joanna L. N. and Lawrence M. Friedman. 2014. "A Private Skirt in a Public Place: The Surprising Law of Upskirting." *Verdict*, March 12, 1–7

Guarino, Ben. 2017. "Legal Same-Sex Marriage Tied to Fewer Suicides." *The Boston Globe*, February 22, A2.

Gunderman, Richard and Mark Mutz. 2014. "The Collapse of Big Law: A Cautionary Tale for Big Med." *The Atlantic*, February 11. https://www.theatlantic.com/business/archive/2014/02/the-collapse-of-big-law-a-cautionary-tale-for-big-med/283736/.

Hall, David D., ed. 1990. *The Antinomian Controversy, 1636–1638: A Documentary History*, 2nd ed. Durham, NC: Duke University Press.

Hand, Judge Learned. 1951. "Speech to the Legal Aid Society." 75th Anniversary Celebration. http://www.legal-aid.org/en/las/thoushaltnotrationjustice.aspx.

Harr, Jonathan. 1995. *A Civil Action*. New York: Random House.

Harris, Cheryl I. 1993. "Whiteness as Property." *Harvard Law Review* 106(8):1707–1791.

Harvard Law School, Program on Negotiation Staff. 2017. "Undecided on Your Dispute Resolution Process? Combine Mediation and Arbitration with Med-Arb". Cambridge, MA. https://www.pon.harvard.edu/daily/mediation/deciding-on-arbitration-vs-mediation-try-combining-them/, November 27.

Harvard Law School. n.d. "History: A Brief Timeline of Our First Two Centuries." Cambridge, MA. http://hls.harvard.edu/about/history/.

Hawkins, Derek. 2018. "Did Law School Applications Get a 'Trump Bump'? Maybe." *Washington Post,* February 23. https://www.washingtonpost.com/news/morning-mix/wp/2018/02/23/did-law-school-applications-get-a-trump-bump-maybe/?utm_term=.81e12d259e9d

Hay, Douglas. 1975. "Property, Authority and the Criminal Law." pp. 17–63 in *Albion's Fatal Tree: Crime and Society in Eighteenth-Century England*, edited by Douglas Hay, Peter Linebaugh, John G. Rule, E. P. Thompson, and Cal Wilson. New York: Pantheon Books.

Hayden, Karen. 2018. "The Female World of Love and Ritual Violence: The Slender Man Case and Popular News Depictions of Female Adolescent Violence." pp. 72–89 in *Girls, Aggression, and Intersectionality: Transforming the Discourse of "Mean Girls" in the United States*, edited by K. McQueeney and A. Girgenti-Malone. New York: Routledge.

Healy, Paul and George Serafeim. 2016. "Who Pays for White-Collar Crime?" *Harvard Business School Working Paper* 16–148:1–48

Heinz, John P. and Edward O. Laumann. 1978. "The Legal Profession, Client Interests, Professional Roles, and Social Hierarchies." *Michigan Law Review* 76:1111–1142.

Helman, Scott. 2006. "Bill Asks for More Driver Training." *The Boston Globe,* June 16, A1.

Hirthler, Jason. 2016. "The Corporate Liberal in America." Retrieved February 18, 2017 from http://www.counterpunch.org/2016/07/20/the-corporate-liberal-in-america/

Hoebel, E. Adamson. 1954. *The Law of Primitive Man: A Study in Comparative Legal Dynamics*. Cambridge, MA: Harvard University Press.

Hoffman, David A. and James E. McGuire. 2001. "Lawyers Who Just Say No to Litigation." *The Boston Globe*, April 1, E1, E3.

Hofstadter, Richard. 1969. *Social Darwinism in American Thought*. New York: George Braziller.

Holmes, Oliver Wendell Jr. 1897. "The Path of Law." *Harvard Law Review* 10:457–478.

Howe, Peter J. 1997. "Firm Guilty of Assault in Lead Exposure." *The Boston Globe*. November 20, B1, B7.

Howerth, I. W. 1917. "Natural Selection and the Survival of the Fittest." *The Scientific Monthly* 5(3):253–257.

Hughes, Timothy and Doris James Wilson. 2018. "Reentry Trends in the United States." Washington, DC: Bureau of Justice Statistics. https://www.bjs.gov/content/reentry/reentry.cfm. Updated April 2, 2018.

Janis, Irving L. 1982. *Groupthink*. Boston: Houghton Mifflin.

Johnson, Allan. 2000. *The Blackwell Dictionary of Sociology: A User's Guide to Sociological Language*, 2nd ed. Oxford: Blackwell Publishers.

Jones, Jacqueline. 1986. *Labor of Love, Labor of Sorrow: Black Women, Work, and the Family from Slavery to Present*. New York: Vintage Books.

Kaba, Mariame. 2018. "Why I'm Raising Money to Build an Ida B. Wells Monument." *The Huffington Post* Opinion, May 2. https://www.huffingtonpost.com/entry/opinion-kaba-ida-wells-lynching_us_5ae9bfc6e4b022f71a03e4bc.

Kelleher, Michael D. and C. L. Kelleher. 1998. *Murder Most Rare: The Female Serial Killer*. Westport, CT: Praeger Trade/Greenwood Publishing Group, Inc.

Kennedy v. Louisiana, 554 US 407, 2008.

Kerber, Linda. 1988. "Separate Spheres, Female Worlds, and Woman's Place: The Rhetoric of Women's History." *Journal of American History* 75:9–39.

Kocian, Lisa and Frank Phillips. 2006. "Crash Report Cites Alcohol; Romney, Reilly Swap Accusations on Case." *The Boston Globe*, January 6, A1.

Korematsu v. United States, 1944. 323 U.S. 214

Kronus, Carol L. 1976. "The Evolution of Occupational Power: An Historical Study of Task Boundaries between Physicians and Pharmacists." *Sociology of Work and Occupations* 3:3–37.

Kuttner, Robert. 2004. "Now, Smearing the Trial Lawyers." *The Boston Globe*, August 25, A11.

Larson, Margoli S. 1977. *The Rise of Professionalization*. Berkeley, CA: University of California Press.

Law School Transparency. 2015. "*Law School Enrollment*." https://data.lawschooltransparency.com/enrollment/all/?y1=2010&y2=2015.

Lawyer Monthly. 2017, July 26. "Wednesday Wisdom: Why Do Barristers Wear Wigs?" https://www.lawyer-monthly.com/2017/07/wednesdaywisdom-why-do-barristers-wear-wigs/.

LeBlanc, Steven. 2008. "Measure Targets Archaic Blue Laws, Some Statutes Date to Colonial Times. *The Boston Globe*, March 5, B1.

Legal Information Institute, Cornell Law School. 2016. "White Collar Crime: An Overview." https://www.law.cornell.edu/wex/white-collar_crime.

Lemert, Edwin. 1951. *Social Pathology: A Systematic Approach to the Study of Sociopathic Behavior*. New York: McGraw-Hill.

Levenson, Jill S. and Leo P. Cotter. 2005. "The Impact of Sex Offender Residence Restrictions: 1,000 Feet from Danger or One Step from Absurd?" *International Journal of Offender Therapy and Comparative Criminology* 49:168–178.

Levit, Nancy and Robert R. M. Verchick. 2016. *Feminist Legal Theory: A Primer*, 2nd ed. New York: New York University Press.

Lieberman, Joel D. and Bruce Dennis Sales. 2007. *Scientific Jury Selection*. Washington, DC: American Psychological Association.

Linebaugh, Peter. 1975. "The Tyburn Riot against the Surgeons." pp. 65–117 in *Albion's Fatal Tree: Crime and Society in Eighteenth-Century England*, edited by Douglas Hay, Peter Linebaugh, John G. Rule, E. P. Thompson, and Cal Wilson. New York: Pantheon Books.

Linskey, Annie. 2018. "Death Penalty for Drug Dealers Is a Familiar Call." *The Boston Globe*, March 21, A1, A7.

Liptak, Adam and Michael D. Shear. 2018. "Trump's Travel Ban Upheld by Supreme Court." *The New York Times*, A1.

Little, Craig B. 1989. *Deviance and Social Control: Theory, Research, and Social Policy*, 3rd ed. Chicago: F. E. Peacock Publishers, Inc.

Lopez, Ian F. Haney. 1996. *White by Law: The Legal Construction of Race*. New York: New York University Press.

Loving v. Virginia, 1967. 388 U.S. 1.

Lowery, Wesley. 2017. "Black Lives Matter: Birth of a Movement." *The Guardian*, January 17.

Lowney, Kathleen S. and Joel Best. 1995. "Stalking Strangers and Lovers: Changing Media Typifications of a New Crime Problem." pp. 33–57 in *Images of Issues: Typifying Contemporary Social Problems*, edited by Joel Best. New York: Aldine de Gruyter.

Lucas, Paul. 1962. "Blackstone and the Reform of the Legal Profession." *The English Historical Review* 77:456–489.

MacKinnon, Catharine A. 1979. *Sexual Harassment of Working Women: A Case of Sexual Discrimination*. New Haven, CT: Yale University Press.

MacKinnon, Catharine A. 1987. *Feminism Unmodified: Discourses in Life and Law*. Cambridge, MA: Harvard University Press.

MacKinnon, Catharine A. 2018. "#MeToo and Law's Limitation." *The New York Times*, February 5, A19.

MacPherson, C. B. 1962. *The Political Theory of Possessive Individualism: Hobbes to Locke*. New York: Oxford University Press.

MacQuarrie, Brian. 2010. "Haiti Calls on Voodoo Priests to Help Battered Nation Heal." *The Boston Globe*, February 10, A1, A10.

Maine, Henry Sumner. 1861. *Ancient Law*. London: J. Murray.

Maine, Henry Sumner. 1954. *The Law of Primitive Man*. Cambridge, MA: Harvard University Press.

Manikonda, Lydia, Ghazaleh Beigi, Huan Liu, and Subbarao Kamb-hampati. Forthcoming. "Twitter for Sparking a Movement, Reddit for Sharing the Moment: #MeToo through the Lens of Social Media." *arXiv:1803.08022v1 [cs.SI]* 21 March 2018:1–7.

Marshall, Gordon. 1994. *The Concise Oxford Dictionary of Sociology.* New York: Oxford University Press.

Martin, Rachel. 2015. "Jury Duty: Who Gets Called, and Who Actually Served?" National Public Radio, Weekend Morning Edition, June 7. https://www.npr.org/2015/06/07/412633577/jury-duty-who-gets-called-and-who-actually-serves.

Marx, Karl and Frederick Engels. [1848] 1993. *The Communist Manifesto.* New York: International Publishers.

Marx, Karl. 1852. *The Eighteenth Brumaire of Louis Bonaparte.* Translated by Daniel De Leon. Chicago: Charles H. Kerr & Company.

Marx, Karl. [1844] 2007. *Economic and Philosophical Manuscripts of 1844.* Translated and edited by Martin Milligan. Mineola, NY: Dover Publications.

McCammon, Holly J. 2004. "Legal Limits on Labor Militancy: U.S. Labor Law and the Right to Strike since the New Deal." pp. 129–156 in *Social Problems, Law, and Society*, edited by Katherine Stout, Richard A. Dello Buono, and William J. Chambliss. New York: Rowman & Littlefield Publishers, Inc.

McEntee, Kyle. 2018. "Report with Iowa Young Lawyers." *Law School Transparency.* https://ecollections.law.fiu.edu/cgi/viewcontent.cgi?filename=2&article=1063&context=lawreviewsymposia&type=additional.

McLaughlin, Michael, Carrie Petus-Davis, Derek Brown, Chris Veeh, and Tanya Penn. 2016. "The Economic Burden of Incarceration in the U.S." Working Paper #AJ1072016. St. Louis, MO: Institute for Advancing Research and Innovation, George Warren School of Social Work, Washington University in St. Louis, Missouri, pp. 1–36.

McLemore, S. Dale and Harriet D. Romo. 1998. *Racial and Ethnic Relations in America.* Boston: Allyn and Bacon.

McMillion, Rhonda. 2011. "The ABA Adjusts Its Lobbying Efforts to Suit a New Climate on Capitol Hill. "*ABA Journal*, April. http://www.abajournal.com/magazine/article/the_aba_adjusts_its_lobbying_efforts_to_suit_a_new_climate_on_capitol_hill.

Mead, George Herbert. 1934. *Mind, Self, and Society*, edited by Charles W. Morris. Chicago, IL: University of Chicago Press.

Merriam-Webster, Inc. 1997. *The Merriam-Webster Dictionary*, 2nd ed. Springfield, MA: Merriam-Webster, Inc.

Merry, Sally Engle and Susan S. Silbey. 1984. "What Do Plaintiffs Want? Reexamining the Concept of Dispute." *The Justice System Journal* 9:151–178.

Merton, Robert K. [1949] 1957. *Social Theory and Social Structure*. New York: Free Press.

Merton, Robert K. [1976] 1996. *On Social Structure and Science*. Chicago: University of Chicago Press.

Michael M. v. Superior Court of Sonoma County. 1981. 450 U.S. 464.

Miller, Joshua. 2014. "Lawmakers Give Fast OK to Voyeurism Bill: Respond to SJC's Ruling on Taking Photos Up Skirts." *The Boston Globe*, March 7, A1, A11.

Misha, Raja, and Michael Levenson. 2006. "A Higher Age Vowed for Teen Drivers: Lawmakers Plan Bill with 17½ Minimum." *The Boston Globe*, March 26, A1.

Montesquieu, Charles de Secondat, Baron de. 1748/2007. *The Spirit of Laws*, Vol. 1. New York: Cosimo Books.

Moskowitz, Eric. 2010. "Steep Drop in Teen Driver Fatalities." *The Boston Globe*, April 18, A1, A19.

Muller v. Oregon. 1908. 208 U.S.

Murphy, Tim. 2015. "The Fall of King Coal." *Mother Jones*, October 1, 1–15

Nader, Laura and Harry F. Todd, eds. 1978. "Introduction." pp. 1–40 in *The Dispute Process: Law in Ten Societies*. New York: Columbia University Press.

Nader, Laura. 1964. "An Analysis of Zapotec Law Cases." *Ethnology* 3(4):404–419.

Nader, Laura. 1965. "Choices in Legal Procedure: Shia Moslem and Mexican Zapotec." *American Anthropologist* 67(2): 395–399.

National Center for Education Statistics. 2015. "Compulsory School Attendance Laws, Minimum and Maximum Age Limits for Required Free Education, by State: 2015." https://nces.ed.gov/programs/statereform/tab5_1.asp.

National Conference of State Legislatures. 2017, June 23. "Cellular Phone Use and Texting While Driving Laws." http://www.ncsl.org/research/transportation/cellular-phone-use-and-texting-while-driving-laws.aspx.

National Institute of Justice. 2014. "Recidivism." Washington, DC.

National Women's History Museum. n.d. "Women's Suffrage Timeline." http:/ www.crusadeforthevote.org/woman-suffrage-timeline-18401920/.

Nellis, Ashley. 2016. "The Color of Justice: Racial and Ethnic Disparity in State Prisons." Washington, DC: The Sentencing Project, pp. 1–21.

Neubauer, David W. and Henry Fradella. 2017. *America's Courts and the Criminal Justice System*. Belmont, CA: Cengage.

Newman, Graeme. 2008. *The Punishment Response*, 2nd ed. New York: Routledge.

Neyfakh, Leon. 2013. "Why We Can't Stop: Texting While Driving Is Just the Tip of the Iceberg, Say Researchers. The Real Problem Is Our Phones Are Programming Us." *The Boston Sunday Globe*, Ideas Section, October 10, K1, K4.

Nix, Elizabeth. 2016. "Has a U.S. Supreme Court Justice Ever Been Impeached?" History Website. http://www.history.com/news/ask-history/has-a-u-s-supreme-court-justice-ever-been-impeached#.

NOLO. 2017. "50-State Chart of Small Claims Court Dollar Limits." https://www.nolo.com/legal-encyclopedia/small-claims-suits-how-much-30031.html. November 7.

O'Brien, Keith. 2009. "The Closer." *The Boston Globe Magazine*, April 12, 22–25.

Office of the Jury Commissioner, Commonwealth of Massachusetts. 1998. *Trial Juror's Handbook*. Boston: Commonwealth of Massachusetts Trial Court.

Ogletree, Charles J. Jr. and Johanna Wald. 2007. "Lessons of Dred Scott." *The New York Times*, April 5, Op-ed.

Omi, Michael and Howard Winant. 1994. *Racial Formation in the United States*, 2nd ed. New York: Routledge.

Pager, D. 2007. *Marked: Race, Crime, and Finding Work in the Era of Mass Incarceration*. Chicago: University of Chicago Press.

Papachristou v. City of Jacksonville. 405 U.S. 156 (1973).

Pascoe, Peggy. 1996. "Miscegenation Law, Court Cases, and Ideologies of Race in Twentieth-Century America." *The Journal of American History* 83:44–69.

Perrow, Charles. 2005. *Organizing America: Wealth, Power, and the Origins of Corporate Capitalism*. Princeton, NJ: Princeton University Press.

Pew Research Center. 2017, May 18. "Intermarriage in the U.S. 50 Years After Loving v. Virginia." Washington, DC.

Pfeiffer, Sacha. 2010. "Many Female Lawyers Dropping Off Path to Partnership." *The Boston Globe*, May 2, A1, A15.

Plessy v. Ferguson. 1896. 163 U.S. 537.

Potter, Hillary. 2013. "Intersectional Criminology: Interrogating Identity and Power in Criminological Research and Theory. *Critical Criminology* 21:305–318.

Potter, Hillary. 2015. *Intersectionality and Criminology: Disrupting and Revolutionizing Studies of Crime*. New York: Routledge.

Pound, Roscoe. 1922. *An Introduction to the Philosophy of Law*. New Haven, CT: Yale University Press.

Powers, Martine. 2013. "State Police Hone Ways to Catch Texting by Drivers." *The Boston Globe*, September 27, A1, A4.

Quigley, Fran. 2015. "Haiti's Earthquake Was Devastating. The Cholera Epidemic Was Worse." *The Nation*, October 16.

Radelet, Michael L. and Traci L. Lacock. 2009. "Do Executions Lower Homicide Rates: The Views of Leading Criminologists." *Journal of Criminal Law and Criminology* 99: 489–508.

Radin, Max. 1938. *Handbook of Anglo-American Legal History*. Columbus: Ohio State University, College of Law.

Raifman, Julia, Ellen Moscoe, Bryn Austin, and Margaret McConnell. 2017. "Difference-In-Difference Analysis of the Association between Same-Sex Marriage Policies and Adolescent Suicide Attempts." *Journal of American Medical Association Pediatrics* 171(4):350–356.

Ramer, Holly. 2010. "Franklin Pierce Law Center to Merge with UNH." *Seacoast Online, March 17.* http://www.seacoastonline.com/article/20100317/NEWS/3170370.

Ramos, Nestor. 2017a. "Citing Trench Violations, U.S. Levies Large Fine." *The Boston Globe*, April 13, B1.

Ramos, Nestor. 2017b. "Drain Firm Charges in Deaths of 2 Workers." *The Boston Globe*, February 9, A1.

Reaves, Brian A. 2015. "Local Police Departments 2013: Personnel, Policies, and Practices." *U. S. Department of Justice, Bureau of Justice Statistics Bulletin*, May 2015, NCJ 248677:1–21.

Reed v. Reed. 1971. 404 U.S. 71.

Reiman, Jeffrey and Paul Leighton. 2016. *The Rich Get Richer and the Poor Get Prison,* 10th ed. New York: Routledge.

Reiman, Jeffrey and Paul Leighton. 2017. *The Rich Get Richer and the Poor Get Prison: Ideology, Class, and Criminal Justice,* 11th ed. New York: Routledge.

Renzetti, Claire M. 2013. *Feminist Criminology.* New York: Routledge.

Reuters Staff. 2007. "Wigs Off as Britain Ends Courtroom Tradition." *Reuters News Agency*, July 13. https://www.reuters.com/article/us-britain-wigs-idUSL1287872820070713.

Roberts, Sam. 2016. "Alcohol, Gens, and Golf: The Long History of Blue Laws in New York." *The New York Times*, June 16, A21.

Rodes, Robert E., Jr. 2004. "On the Historical School of Jurisprudence." Scholarly Works. Paper 858. http://scholarship.law.nd.edu/law_faculty_scholarship/858.

Rothman, Robert A. 1984. "Deprofessionalization: The Case of Law in America." *Work and Occupations* 11:183–206.

Rousseau, Jean-Jacques. [1762] 1893. *The Social Contract, or the Principles of Political Rights.* Translated by Rose M. Harrington, with Introduction and Notes by Edward L. Walter. New York: G. P. Putnam's Sons, the Knickerbocker Press.

Rubin, Gayle. 1975. "The Traffic in Women: Notes on the 'Political Economy' of Sex." pp. 157–210 in *Toward an Anthropology of Women*, edited by R. Rayna. New York: Monthly Review Press.

Ruda, Richard. 2001. "A London Walking Tour That's Strictly Legal. *The New York Times*, February 17, Travel Section.

Ruiz, Rebecca R. 2010. "Recession Spurs Interest in Graduate, Law Schools." *The New York Times*, January 1. https://www.nytimes.com/2010/01/10/education/10grad.html).

Ruiz-Grossman, Sarah. 2017. "This 'School for Justice' Trains Sex Trafficking Survivors to Be Lawyers." *The Huffington Post*, July 13. https://www.huffingtonpost.com/entry/free-a-girl-school-for-justice-india-sex-trafficking-lawyers_us_5967868de4b0d51cda60ad74.

Ryan, Camille L. and Kurt Bauman. 2016, March. "Educational Attainment in the United States: 2015." United States Census Bureau, pp. 1–12.

Salam, Maya. 2017. "When Susan B. Anthony's 'Little Band of 9 Ladies' Voted Illegally." *The New York Times*, November 5.

Saltzman, Jonathan. 2004. "Mass. Gets Tough on Jury Delinquents." *The Boston Globe*, September 26, A1, B4.

Saltzman, Jonathan. 2009. "SJC Sharply Limits Youth Curfew Laws: Bars Criminal Charge, Allows Civil Penalty." *The Boston Globe*, September 26, A1.

Sarat, Austin and William L. F. Felstiner. 1995. *Divorce Lawyers and Their Clients: Power and Meaning in the Legal Process*. New York: Oxford University Press.

Schaefer, Richard T. 2011. *Sociology: A Brief Introduction,* 9th ed. New York: McGraw-Hill.

Schmalleger, Frank. 2004. *Criminal Justice: A Brief Introduction*, 5th ed. Upper Saddle River, NJ: Pearson/Prentice Hall.

Schworm, Peter. 2014. "Waning Ranks at Law Schools." *The Boston Globe*, July 6, A1, A9.

Scott, Anne Firor and Andrew MacKay Scott. 1982. *One Half the People: The Fight for Woman Suffrage*. Chicago: University of Chicago Press.

Seal, Ben. 2018. "Diversity Scorecard: The Rankings." *The American Lawyer*, May 29. https://www.law.com/americanlawyer/2018/05/29/the-2018-diversity-scorecard-the-rankings/.

Segal, David. 2011. "Is Law School a Losing Game?" *The New York Times*, January 8. https://www.nytimes.com/2011/01/09/business/09law.html.

Shamir, Ronen. 1993. "Professionalism and Monopoly of Expertise: Lawyers and Administrative Law, 1933–1937." *Law and Society Review* 27(2):361–398.

Shapin, Steven. 2007. "Man with a Plan: Herbert Spencer's Theory of Everything." *The New Yorker*, August 13, 75–79.

Sheldon, Ken. 2016. "Blue Laws? Blame the Puritans." *Yankee* 80(6):n.p.

Silbey, Susan S. and Sally E. Merry. 1986. "Mediator Settlement Strategies." *Law and Policy* 8:7–32.

Simmons, Ann M. 2016. "Haiti Earthquake: $13.5 Billion in Donations, but Is Any of It Working?" *Los Angeles Times*, April 8, A1.

Sinclair, Upton. 1906. *The Jungle*. New York: Doubleday.

Skipp, Catharine and Arian Campo-Flores. 2009. "A Bridge Too Far." *Newsweek Web Exclusive*, July 25. http://www.newsweek.com/id/208518/outprint/print.

Smith, Aaron. 2017. "Record Shares of Americans Now Own Smart Phones." Pew Research Center, Fact Tank: The News in Numbers. Washington, DC.

Smith, Patricia, ed. 1993. *Feminist Jurisprudence.* New York: Oxford University Press.

Snyder, Terri L. 2015, September. "Women, Race, and the Law in Early America." pp. 1–26 in *Oxford Research Encyclopedia of American History.* New York: Oxford University Press. http://oxfordre. com/americanhistory/view/10.1093/acrefore/9780199329175.001.0001/ acrefore-9780199329175-e-12?print=pdf.

Spencer, Herbert. 1884. *The Man versus the State.* Indianapolis, IN: Liberty Classics.

Spoto, MaryAnn. 2012. "N.J. Supreme Court Upholds Decal Law for Young Drivers." *The Star-Ledger.* August 6.

Stanton, Elizabeth Cady. [1848] 2015. *A Declaration of Sentiments and Resolutions.* Carlisle, MA: Applewood Books.

Stout, A. Kathryn. 2004. "Law and Social Change: Bringing Social Movements into the Dialectic." pp. 19–40 in *Social Problems, Law, and Society,* edited by A. Kathryn Stout, Richard A. Dello Buono, and William J. Chambliss. Lanham, MD: Rowman & Littlefield Publishers, Inc. A.

Strauss, Valerie. 2016. "U.S. Graduation Rate Is Up but There Is a Warning Attached." *Washington Post,* October 27. https://www. washingtonpost.com/news/answer-sheet/wp/2016/10/27/u-s-high-school-graduation-rate-is-up-but-theres-a-warning-label-attached/?utm_term=.fbf14d5c02a8.

Strohmeyer, Hansjörg. 2001. "Collapse and Reconstruction of a Judicial System: The United Nations Mission in Kosovo and East Timor." *The American Journal of International Law* 95(1):46–63.

Strom, Roy. 2018. "Despite Anxiety-Inducing Trends, Am Law 100 Rose to the Challenge in 2017." *The American Lawyer,* April 24. https://www. law.com/americanlawyer/2018/04/24/despite-anxiety-inducing-trends-am-law-100-rose-to-the-challenge-in-2017/.

Sullivan, Casey C. 2015. "Forget Being a Lawyer, Become a Lobbyist Instead. FindLaw, August 24. https://blogs.findlaw.com/greedy_associates/2015/08/forget-being-a-lawyer-become-a-lobbyist-instead.html.

Sullivan, Dan. 2013. "Nation's Longest Serving Death-Row Inmate Dies in Florida." *The Tampa Bay Times,* May 21, 1–2

Sumner, William Graham. 1907. *Folkways: A Study of the Sociological Importance of Usage, Manners, Customs, Mores, and Morals.* Boston: Ginn and Company Publishers/ Athenaeum Press.

Sutherland, Donald H. 1949. *White-Collar Crime.* New York: Dryden.

Sutherland, Edwin H. and Donald C. Cressey. 1974. *Criminology,* 9th ed. Philadelphia: Lippincott.

Sutton, John. 2001. *Law/Society: Origins, Interactions, and Change*. Thousand Oaks, CA: Pine Forge Press.

Talbot, Margaret. 2016. "The Attorney Fighting Revenge Porn." *The New Yorker*, December 5, 56–65.

Taub, Nadine, and Elizabeth M. Schneider. 1998. "Women's Subordination and the Role of Law." pp. 328–355 in *The Politics of Law: A Progressive Critique*, edited by D. Kairys. New York: Basic Books.

Terry, Sara. 1982. "Rent-a-Judge: A Fast Way to 'Day in Court.'" *The Christian Science Monitor*, February 9. https://www.csmonitor.com/1982/0209/020935.html.

The Onion. 2018, August 20. "Law School Applications Increase upon the Realization That Any F*%&ing Idiot Can Be a Lawyer." https://www.theonion.com/law-school-applications-increase-upon-realization-that-1828464779.

Theroux, Karen. 2011. "A Century of Philanthropy: Carnegie Corporation and New York." *American Libraries Magazine*, September 13. Retrieved September 17, 2017, from https://americanlibrariesmagazine.org/2011/09/13/a-century-of-philanthropy-carnegie-corporation-of-new-york/.

Thompson, Ken. 1995. *Emile Durkheim*, Revised Ed. New York: Routledge.

Thoreau, Henry David. [1849] 2004. *Walden and Civil Disobedience*. New York: Pocket Books.

Tigar, Michael E. 2000. *Law and the Rise of Capitalism*. New York: Monthly Review Press.

Timasheff, Nicholas S. 1937. "What Is Sociology of Law?" *American Journal of Sociology* 43:225–235.

Toppo, Greg. 2017. "Why You Might Want to Think Twice before Going to Law School." *USA Today*, June 28.

Tribe, Meghan. 2017. "The Diversity Scorecard." *The American Lawyer* June. ALM Publication: 1–4.

Tripp, Gabriel. 2018. "A Mine Blast Sent Him to Jail. Miners May Send Him to Congress. *The New York Times*, February 26, A1.

Trump v. Hawaii, 2018. 585 U.S.

Turkel, Gerald. 1996. *Law and Society: Critical Approaches*. Boston: Allyn and Bacon.

U. S. Constitution. Amendment I; Amendment V.

U.S. Chamber of Commerce, Institute for Legal Reform. Faces of Lawsuit Abuse. 2017. "Most Ridiculous Lawsuits of 2017." http://www.instituteforlegalreform.com/ December 20.

Unger, Roberto Mangabeira. 1976. *Law in Modern Society: Toward a Criticism of Social Theory*. New York: The Free Press.

United States Census Bureau. 2017, July 1. "Quick Facts." Suitland-Silver Hill, MD. https://www.census.gov/quickfacts/fact/table/US/PST045217.

United States Citizenship and Immigration Services. "Citizenship Through Naturalization." Washington, DC. https://www.uscis.gov/us-citizenship/citizenship-through-naturalization.

United States Congressional Documents and Debates, 1774–1875. "A Century of Lawmaking for a New Nation." Washington, DC: Library of Congress. https://memory.loc.gov/ammem/amlaw/.

United States Courts. n.d. "Fact of Case Summary—Korematsu v. U.S." https://www.uscourts.gov/educational-resources/educational-activities/facts-and-case-summary-korematsu-v-ushttps://www.uscourts.gov/educational-resources/educational-activities/facts-and-case-summary-korematsu-v-us

Vago, Steven. 2012. *Law and Society,* 10th ed. Boston: Prentice Hall.

Vault. 2019. Vault Law 100. http://www.vault.com/company-rankings/law/vault-law-100/?sRankID=2.

Vile, M. J. C. [1967] 1998. *Constitutionalism and the Separation of Powers,* 2nd ed. Indianapolis, IN: Liberty Fund, Inc. Retrieved September 23, 2017, from Online Library of Liberty, http://oll.libertyfund.org/titles/vile-constitutionalism-and-the-separation-of-powers.

Walsh, Anthony and Craig Hemmens. 2016. *Law, Justice, and Society: A Sociolegal Introduction,* 4th ed. New York: Oxford University Press.

Walshe, Sadhbh. 2013. "America's 'Litigious Society' is a Myth." *The Guardian,* October 24. https://www.theguardian.com/commentisfree/2013/oct/24/america-litigious-society-myth.

Ward, Stephanie Francis. 2018. "The 'Trump Bump' for Law School Applicants Is Real and Significant, Survey Says." *ABA Journal,* February 22. http://www.abajournal.com/news/article/the_trump_bump_for_law_school_applicants_is_real_and_significant_survey_say.

Warner, Ralph. 2016. *Everybody's Guide to Small Claims Courts,* 16th ed. Berkeley: NOLO Publisher.

Weber, Max. [1905] 1978. *Economy and Society: An Outline of Interpretive Sociology,* Vol. 2. Berkeley: University of California Press.

Weber, Max. [1922] 1958. "Bureaucracy." pp. 196–239 in *From Max Weber: Essays in Sociology,* edited and translated by Hans Gerth, and C. Wright Mills. New York: Oxford University Press.

Weber, Max. [1947] 1964. *The Theory of Social and Economic Organization,* Edited with an Introduction by Talcott Parson. New York: The Free Press, MacMillan Publishing Co., Inc.

Weber, Max. [1905] 1978. *Economy and Society: An Outline of Interpretive Sociology,* Vol. 2, edited by G. Roth and C. Wittich. Berkeley: University of California Press.

Wells, Ida B. and Jacqueline Jones Royster, eds. 2016. *Southern Horrors and Other Writings: The Anti-Lynching Campaign of Ida B. Wells, 1892–1900,* 2nd ed. Boston: Bedford/St. Martin's Press.

Wells-Barnett, Ida B. 1895. *The Red Record: Tabulated Statistics and Alleged Causes of Lynching in the United States of America. Free Access through Project Gutenberg*, EBook #14977.

Welter, Barbara. 1966. "The Cult of True Womanhood: 1820–1860." *American Quarterly* 18:151–174.

Williams, Wendy. 1981. "Firing Women to Protect the Fetus: The Reconciliation of Fetal Protection with Equal Opportunity Goals Under Title VII." *Georgetown Law Journal* 69:641–704.

Winkler, Adam. 2018. "'Corporations Are People' Is Built on an Incredible 19th-Century Lie." *The Atlantic*, Business Archive. March 5.

Wright, Danaya C. 2012. "Theorizing History: Separate Spheres, the Public/Private Binary and a New Analytic for Family Law History." University of Florida Law Scholarship Repository. ANZLH E-Journal, Refereed Paper No 2, (44), http://scholarship.law.ufl.edu/facultypub/651.

Yates, Jeff, Belinda Creel Davis, and Henry R. Glick. 2001. "The Politics of Torts: Explaining Litigation Rates in the American States." *State Politics & Policy Quarterly* 1:127–143.

Zaretsky, Staci. 2018a. "In Historic Move, ABA Revokes Abysmal Law School's Accreditation." Above the Law, June 11. https://abovethelaw.com/2018/06/in-historic-move-aba-revokes-abysmal-law-schools-accreditation/.

Zaretsky, Staci. 2018b. "Women Are Flocking to Law Schools Thanks to Donald Trump." Above the Law, May 4. https://abovethelaw.com/2018/05/women-are-flocking-to-law-school-thanks-to-donald-trump/.

Zraick, Karen. 2018. "Lawyers Say They Face Persistent Racial and Gender Bias at Work. *The New York Times*, September 5, B5.

Index